FIFTY YEARS OF INDIAN AGRICULTURE

VOLUME – 2 : DETERMINANTS OF PRODUCTION

Vol. 1 : Production and Self-sufficiency
Vol. 2 : Determinants of Production

About the Editors

Prof. Ali Mohammad is a distinguished author and teacher. An M.A. and Ph.D. from Aligarh Muslim University. His field of specialization is Agricultural Geography, Food Security and Nutritional Problems in rural India. He worked as a Senior Research Fellow in Jawaharlal Nehru University, as an Associate Professor at the Centre of West Asian Studies, Aligarh Muslim University, Aligarh, Associate Professor in Egerton University, Kenya, Professor in Asmara University East Africa, Eritea, and at present Professor in the Department of Geography, Aligarh Muslim University, Aligarh, Dr. Ali Mohammad has in his credit numerous research papers and more than one dozen books on Agriculture, Food Security and Nutritional Deficiency.

Prof. Abdul Munir, Senior Reader, Department of Geography, Aligarh Muslim University, Aligarh, U.P.

Dr. Shamsul Haque Siddiqui, Senior Reader, Department of Geography, Aligarh Muslim University, Aligarh, U.P.

FIFTY YEARS OF INDIAN AGRICULTURE

VOLUME – 2

DETERMINANTS OF PRODUCTION

Edited by

ALI MOHAMMAD
ABDUL MUNIR
SHAMSUL HAQUE SIDDIQUI

CONCEPT PUBLISHING COMPANY, NEW DELHI-110059

Cataloging in Publication Data—DK
Courtesy: D.K. Agencies (P) Ltd. <docinfo@dkagencies.com>

Fifty years of Indian agriculture / edited by Ali Mohammad, Abdul Munir, Hifzur Rehman.
2 v. cm.
Contributed articles.
Vol. 2 has editors: Ali Mohammad, Abdul Munir, Shamsul Haque Siddiqui.
Includes bibliographical references.
Includes indexes.
ISBN 8180693600

1. Agriculture—India—History. 2. Agricultural productivity—India—History. 3. Agriculture and state—India—History. I. Mohammad, Ali. II. Munir, Abdul. III. Rehman, Hifzur.

DDC 338.109 54 22

ISBN : 81-8069-360-0 (Set)
ISBN : 81-8069-361-9 (Vol. I)
ISBN : 81-8069-362-7 (Vol. II)

First Published 2007

Published and Printed by
Ashok Kumar Mittal
Concept Publishing Company
A/15-16, Commercial Block, Mohan Garden
New Delhi-110059 (INDIA)
Phone : 25351460, 25351794
Fax : 091-11-25357103
Email : publishing@conceptpub.com

PREFACE

The idea to complete a book on the performance of Indian agriculture after independence was originated with the discussion by Sompalji (Member Planning Commission) at Nagpur in the National Association of Geographers of India (NAGI) Conference and was decided that such a critical issue and a proper evaluation is possible only through organizing a conference at national level in an interdisciplinary manner. The much cherished aim to develop the agriculture was either fulfilled or remained incomplete was discussed in the conference within various agreement and disagreement. The issue of food self-sufficiency, being the main thrust while the food security as a dependent factor not only on food self-sufficiency, but various issues such as distributional factor at regional level was discussed. Environmental factors were also discussed at great length because during the conference period it was argued that environment was more or less favourable with the period 1989 till 2006 but fluctuation in food grain production was recorded very high in many years. It was also pointed out that during the inception of green revolutionary period wheat belt was highly encouraged while rice region was neglected inspite of that our two-third population is rice eater. A critical evaluation was highly appreciated that irrigation which is a crucial factor in agriculture was neglected as its increase was only 19 to 43 percent after independence till 50 years, while the fertilizer use, mechanization etc. was encouraged in an abnormal manner as compared to irrigation.

Some political aspects were also discussed in the context of the agricultural development after the division of the country. The focus was on rice and wheat production area. Our best land of wheat production and rice region both went to Pakistan as well as the two major dynamic community, i.e., Punjabi and Bengali largely remained with Pakistan which affected the production aspect of the country to such an extent that it was not easy to come out with the production gap created. Various other major issues were discussed in a highly interesting manner.

Among various issues of agricultural development after independence, British period was mentioned in relation to the land involved in food grain production and amount of land involved in commercial crops. The result of the argument was appreciated that instead of devoting 30 percent land in commercial only 10 percent should be given for this purpose. Additional land was responsible for the increase in production. But the argument took the turn that till now only 20 percent land was increased but production increased from 50 million tonnes to 210 million tonnes, the responsibility for such a high increase is thrown on the increase in per hectare productivity, therefore, only one option is left that productivity factors should be discussed and involved for further increase in production. Still the productivity per hectare of Indian agriculture is just half to the developed countries, therefore, this aspect i.e., productivity response factors should be identified at great length. A very optimistic picture emerged that such an agriculturally giant country can keep upper hand in food politics at least in Indian Ocean Countries.

Need is great to acknowledge the help received from various quarters in the preparation of this work. Mention must be made of the Department of Geography as a full cooperation of all the faculty members both teaching and non-teaching; of Mr. Sompalji ex-Minister of Agriculture and Member Planning Commission of India who thoroughly discussed the problem and especially appreciated the idea to evaluate the performance of Indian agriculture after independence; of Dr. K.V. Sundaram who inspired to hold such a conference and gave the direction being as a geographer and planner also was involved in various governments in planning; of Dr. M. Moni, Deputy Director General of Technology and Communication. There is a long list to be mentioned to acknowledge the people of various walks of life but we are especially thankful to all the authors of articles published in these two volumes.

Editors

CONTENTS

INTRODUCTION

Indian Agriculture govern the fortunes of national economy as it contributes about 40 per cent of gross domestic products and employing about two-third of the country's labour force. It is a well-established fact that rapid agricultural growth holds the key to the solution of the endemic socio-economic problems and elevation of rural poverty confronting the country. The much-vaunted trickle down effect of industrial sector has not materialized. Therefore, agriculture will remain as a major source of sustainable livelihood for the two-third of the total population. The Green Revolution has solved the food problem of the country and helped to keep the growth rate of food production ahead of the population growth rate of the country but has created the regional imbalances in agricultural development which is against the basic spirit of the planning objectives, i.e., to remove the regional imbalances and bring the social justice.

It was a challenge to the planners because a depressing picture. How far the objectives achieved after fifty years of independence on a very poor base has been taken into account in this conference. During the British period over 80 per cent of the sown area was under cultivation of foodgrain crops and yet the total output of foodgrains was insufficient for the needs of the country. The large part of the farming was of subsistence nature and average size of holdings was small and uneconomic. About 25 per cent of the total sown area received irrigation and the rest 75 per cent had to depend on rainfall for raising any crop, which created a situation of high level of fluctuations causing food insecurity. The incentives for greater efforts on the part of the farmer for increased production or for the landowner to make investments in permanent improvements of land were practically non-existent. During the end of the British period the peasantry was mired in poverty and heavy indebtedness. These were little institutional credit available and borrowing that was mainly for consumption purposes had to be from the village moneylenders and the urban traders to whom the farmer would pledge to next year's produce. The number of landless labours had been increasing for the last several decades and today it is reached to the level of 17 per cent. Apart from unemployment for more than six months in a year, the wage rate paid to the farm labours during the days of employment were low but after 50 years of independence the situation has taken a bit positive turn, i.e., unemployment period is reduced and wage rate has been changed because of the increased rate of irrigation in many pockets of India as well as development in transportation system which has increased the efficiency in movement of labours to the regions of high productivity area. During the end of the British period scientific agriculture was yet to make its appearance in the country. No doubt the adoption and diffusion of HYV and pesticides as well as irrigation and fertilizer intake the move towards Green Revolution has changed the total scenario in achieving the food self-sufficiency till the end of the century. No doubt lapses are there as there was a great emphasis to develop the wheat belt as compared to the rice belt and pulses production remained stagnant. During the end of the British period lift irrigation and ploughing were based on drought animals but today in larger part of the area it is done with the help of tractors, pumping sets and tubewells. An interesting picture has emerged, i.e., small landholders are hiring these facilities from the large size farmers to plough the land and irrigate the crops. It will not be non-serious to mention that the situation has taken just opposite to the long prevailing system, i.e., small and marginal farmers were being hired to plough, irrigate and harvest the crop but now large size of landholders are being hired for these activities. What are the positive and negative impact of such a system needs further investigation. It is also being observed that big international companies are acquiring the land for agro-based industrial set-up. After an intensive survey of large number of villages, spreading from Punjab to West Bengal (Indo-Gangetic plain), it is observed that scientific agriculture has been adopted in all the regions in different locations in the Indo-Gangetic plain with variations in scale out of 10 locations of the region (Indo-Gangetic) the situation twenty-five years before was negligible in terms of the scientific agriculture except of three location, i.e., Etah, Aligarh, Meerut, Rohtak, Karnal and Patiala-Ludhiana. After 1985 no doubt tube-well irrigation has spread in well-identified locations with great success such as in Eastern U.P. and North Bihar plain. These regions were far behind the level of self-sufficiency but today these were one of the poorest food regions of the country is producing more than 18 per cent in surplus. Farmers may turn their policies to change the cropping pattern replacing with high remunerative value crops. An individual decision may lead the cropping pattern in a wrong direction.

The historical shortcoming either have been removed or still prevailing is a matter of discussion. It is removed either it has taken a wrong direction or helped the farmer in a sustainable manner.

On the whole British period provided a very poor base to achieve the required level of food self-sufficiency because of the overemphasis on non-commercial crops by 30 per cent of gross cultivated area. After independence till 2001 it is reduce upto 10 per cent only and to achieve the self-sufficiency 90 per cent is being devoted to foodgrain crops. After 1965 emphasis was given on two major crops, i.e., Wheat and Rice occupying about 67 per cent of the gross cultivated area. These two crops are characterized as the highest productivity crops and till 1985 the performance is now characterized as self-sufficient in foodgrains production. With the increase of irrigation, fertilizers and HYV, the best pulses growing area was converted under wheat or rice crops. The most required protein rich pulses crops remained stagnant both in terms of area and total production with an insignificant variation from 10.7 million hectare to 12.6 million hectare after independence. With the increase of population per head availability declined from 64 grams to 24 grams per day. The prices of pulses increased very high in the ratio of prices of cereals, and importation became a big liability on the nation. During 1960s it was being considered as a poor man's diet now it is the rich man's diet as compared to the substitutes available such as potato and vegetables.

To what extent these above mentioned shortcomings were removed within the fifty years of independence and national need was fulfilled were discussed during the period of the conference. Basically a set of articles were presented on the total achievements of the fifty years and large number of articles were presented on the existing level of achievements and the results obtained can be related with past situation.

After independence we started the agricultural development planning with the following objectives:

(i) Increase in foodgrain production and protective foods to improve the food security situation through the basic food items and improve the pulses situation because of its value as a protective food.

(ii) To improve the situation of regional imbalances in agriculture performance with the major consideration of social justice.

(iii) Stimulating production of raw materials for industry and exports.

(iv) Securing remunerative prices for the producer and fare wages to agricultural labour.

(v) Ensuring fare distribution of the food produced as it is one of the major components of food security. The situation till now is very critical. Firstly, the storing performance is so poor that trucks used to wait for more than one week to unload the foodgrains and it is stored at various places in the half constructed buildings without roof.[1] Similarly the distribution of foodgrains at critical period of time the region effected by some natural disasters remain untouched with food distribution. A major problem is already existing and likely to take a serious turn in future, i.e., distribution of food production among the most disadvantageous and deprived segment of population. They are identified as population below the poverty line such as urban-slum dwellers with poor purchasing power, landless agricultural labourers, small-marginal farmers etc. The system of the distribution of foodgrains is needed to be improved also among all the sections of population either rural or urban. Any judicious exercise is needed in fixing the sale prices as well as the scale and size of production is to be decided with the increase and change of rural and urban population and change in income. All these is needed to decide the quality and quantity of production in order to check the disbalanced production effecting the fluctuations in prices. A very serious attempt is still needed for the benefit of both producers and consumers.

(vi) Increase in area under foodgrain, non-foodgrain and fodder is needed in a situation of largest share of small and marginal farmers to the total number of landholdings as well as increasing landlessness. It will provide the landownership among these segments of population which will check the unplanned rural out-migration to the big and industrial cities. The attempt during the period of 'fifty years' is going on by establishing the landuse board in various states but it is most unsuccessful in the hilly, mountainous and semi-desert regions. The reclamation of culturable wastelands and its distribution even without reclaiming the land is under plan but not very laudable, though a large share of land is available under this category of land, i.e., about 124 million hectare land is under net cultivated area and 64 million hectare under culturable wasteland in the country. Intensification of cultivated area is still needed as its scope and possibilities is about 300 per cent but today it is only 141

1. A survey result of storage of foodgrains between Aligarh to Moradabad Road on 15th June 2001.

per cent. The direction of landuse pattern needs special attention, i.e., land capacity analysis is required and share of land under different uses should be scientifically and economically decided. Therefore an intensive analysis of land cover and landuse change at micro level is needed. Similarly the diversification of cropping pattern needs special attention differently among large size and small size landholders with remunerative value of crops. The practice and policy of large-scale foodgrain production is being rejected by some of the regions after achieving the food self-sufficiency because of the low remunerative value as compared to some of the cash and commercial crops. The best example so far available is derived from the most recent agricultural data from seven districts of Western Uttar Pradesh mostly along the border of Haryana where about 70 per cent of the cultivated area is devoted to non-foodgrain crops. It shows that the model presented by the Punjab and Haryana is now no more applicable and useful to the farmers. Only one option is left with the existing system of foodgrain production, i.e., the country is surrounded by some of the chronic food deficit regions with Geographical proximity such as West Asian and Indian ocean coastal African countries. If India compete with the quality in the international foodgrain market it will help in minimizing the deficit trade balance especially with the Middle Eastern countries. However, distribution is one of the best indicators to promote quality, quantity and type of production.

(vii) An assured base of water supply for irrigation will remain a crucial factor in a country like India where about 80 per cent of the cultivated area is depend on natural rainfall while only 20 per cent is free from enviromental influence. The level of irrigation could not increase to a desirable extent because of the low priority as compare to the fertilizer, HYV etc. the increase after fifty years is recorded only from 19 per cent to 47 per cent while during early 1970s Water Commission emphasized that if all the cultivated area is irrigated the nation can produce 450 million metric tonnes of foodgrains. In some of the pockets the identification of the means of irrigation boosted the production after 1980 such as spread of tubewells.

Still the desired level of irrigation is not achieved which needs a special emphasis at regional level to remove the high level of fluctuations in foodgrain production which is still considered as a major threat to food security system. The unequal distribution of irrigation rate is affecting the spread of improved variety of seeds and needed fertilizer intake. The situation is still in the same ratio as it was in the beginning of the Green Revolution.

With the beginning of Green Revolution in 1967-68, there was a dramatic change in the situation. The revolution caused a qualitative change in the food and agriculture situation. The Pearson report described the change as 'one of the authentic marvels of our time'.

In the fourth plan growth with social justice policy was adopted to help the vulnerable section of backward areas. Beside attainment of self-sufficiency in foodgrains, the plan envisaged building-up of a sizeable buffer stock of foodgrains and stoppage of concessional imports of foodgrains.

The fifth plan, while adhering the basic policies of the fourth plan, made some modifications in the programmes for agriculture with a view of increasing their efficiency. It was proposed to cover more food crops under HYV. New programme was to cover not only irrigated agriculture but also dry farming areas in a large scale. A new programme was chalked out particularly for oil seeds and pulses, which were in serious short supply. Drought prone areas to tackle in a systematic way during the plan period. Subsequently in sixth to eighth plans the objective of planning remained more or less the same except of the emphasis on 'growth with social justice'.

The experience upto eighth five year plan seems to be encouraging at cereal front but the situation of pulses is still very poor and availability per head is declining causing heavy imports; on the whole the nation has achieved the food self-sufficiency but the contribution of pulses has gone down just to half after independence. The foodgrains growth from the last many years is recorded more than the population growth but on a very poor base of availability. Still the foodgrains production fluctuation is a serious problem to be tackled causing food insecurity among the small farmers and disadvantageous rural classes.

However, the following are the basic issues to be raised and to be solved :

1. Growth with social justice.
2. Control over the foodgrain fluctuation situation.
3. Scarcity in plenty—the chief characteristic of water resources on irrigation front should be tackled.
4. Regional inequality in agricultural development.
5. Population and food availability should be the basic criteria to identify the agricultural backward areas.
6. After achieving the national goal of food self-sufficiency, a new direction of agricultural development in relation to international

perspective should be the objective as the country is surrounded by the chronic food deficit countries and regions.

7. A diversified cropping pattern is needed and a thorough research and survey is needed at micro-level to introduce the high value crops among the disadvantageous group of small and marginal farmers. Only an integrated approach is needed to prepare a sound plan for this segment of population, which can provide sustainable livelihood in the villages in order to minimize the unplanned movement of population to many of unattractive locations.

The proceeding of the conference is divided into two volumes, i.e., Production and Self-Sufficiency and Determinants of Production.

Swaminathan in his article of Indian agriculture has pin-pointed that the prevention of famines and achieving self-sufficiency in foodgrain has been the outstanding feature of Indian agriculture after independence. Political will and action being the factor responsible for the transformation. Thus, on the threshold of new century and millennium, India is poised to become the flagship of a global movement for an evergreen revolution on the farms rooted in the principles of ecology, economies, social and gender equity, energy conservation and employment generation.

Sundaram in his article of the small farmer development strategies for the next millennium, attempted to synthesize the various operational ways adopted by government in the developing countries of Asia to encourage small farmers' development. During the course of the discussion, the relevance of as well as the inadequacies in the various strategies adopted by government has been critically commented upon. The author points out to certain corrective measures as well as lessons and provide some direction for change. This sufficient indication on the analysis shows that the small farmers have not received the just and equitable share of development benefits from the normal development strategies.

Husain in his study of Green Revolution in India and the performance of major cereal crops has found that the adoption of HYV of major cereal crops like wheat and rice has been considered a significant achievement after the Green Revolution. These varieties of seeds have revolutionized the agricultural landscape of India by enhancing area, production and yield of wheat and rice significantly. The author has emphasized that there are inter and intra-regional variations in the productivity of wheat and rice which is a cause of great concern of the Indian agriculture.

Arora and Mangal in their article of Fifty Years of Vegetable Research in India revealed that in past three decades India has made a quantum jump in vegetable production, securing second position in the world. Vegetable research in India gained momentum after first-half of the century to acquire the present status having moderate infrastructure facilities and research priorities for vegetables in Indian institutions. However, authors pointed out that the amount of vegetable production is much less than our requirement. Thus, the strategy and guidelines may be used for bridging the existing gap between production and requirement.

Tapeshwar Singh in his study of Green Revolution, food security and agricultural sustainability in India revealed that the achievements of the Green Revolution in the context of natural food security and agro-ecological problems play an important role. Sustainability aspects of the current policies and practices of agricultural development is also examined in the present study. Efficient management of natural resources and environment-friendly farm technology may play a pivotal role in crop production and sustainable agricultural development.

Siddiqui in his paper, dimension of agricultural land resource and population pressure in Deoria district of U.P. pointed out that the increasing pressure of human resource on land resources are creating problems in agro-based societies. The author has pointed out that, if these lands are utilized at maximum level the pressure of human resources on land may be minimized. Further, if multi-cropping system is encouraged and current fallow land are brought under cultivation the pressure on land resources and security of food may be reduced.

Asad and Sami in his study of hydrological environment and water resource evolution of an alluvial aquifer in the central Ganga plain found out that the rapid agricultural growth, rising standards of living and changing social structure have in recent years put severe stress on water resources. Because of its stable quality, groundwater has long been reliable source of water for domestic, agricultural and industrial users. Authors have drawn conclusion after investigation that study area has large potential of good quality groundwater.

Ahmad and Rahman in their study of techno-institutional and socio-economic determinants and their correlation with the adoption of agricultural innovations in Upper Ganga-Yamuna Doab, revealed that with the inception of Green Revolution, different forms of agricultural innovations have been introduced in India, which has radically transformed the methods and techniques used in agricultural practices. The variations are among farmers to the adoption of these new methods and techniques due to existing diverse physico-cultural and socio-economic conditions in ecological setting of the region. Study further reveals that all the factors considered in the discussion have positive correlation with the adoption of agricultural innovations.

Khursheed and Jeelani in the hydro-geo-chemical investigation of major springs of Kashmir Valley found that the discharge of the spring responds directly to the melting of snow in the upper reaches. Rock water interaction of the springs has a direct control over the quality of water. Author, classified twenty samples in two classes, i.e. cold (sixteen) and hot (four) springs. Analytical parameters show that the spring water in Anantnag, Kashmir is potable and can be used for irrigation and other purposes.

R. K. Sharma in his article population growth and agricultural change in India since independence discussed that despite the population growth, there is sustainable increase in food production, which has increased significantly after independence. The compound increase in cropping area, irrigation facilities and use of multiple cropping and HYV. Author emphasized that in order to reduce dependency on agriculture, Government should create employment opportunities in the rural areas by developing agro-based industries in rural areas.

Sharma and Tripathi have made the study of assessment of the potential and demand of water resources of Tons basin and found out that the use of water is not limited to drinking, domestic and irrigation purposes, but has multiplied. Contrary to the expanding demand, its supply is limited and can be depleted or made unusable by excessive utilization, inadequate conservation, misutilization, pollution or careless management. Multifaceted approach would be necessary to ensure a balance in the water system. Technical means can also minimize the damage caused by floods, which is a major natural hazard.

Nikhil and Mobin have analyzed the management of irrigation efficiency in Damodar river basin. They observed that the basic problem facing the agriculturists and engineers is how to use the water efficiently so that maximum profit can be obtained. Irrigation efficiency according to them is the percentage of delivered irrigation water that is stored in the soil and available for consumption and use by crops. The proper water management is not simple, especially, for the farmers of developing countries due to lack of modern technology.

Iqbal in his study of scientific approach through local adages in Indian agriculture analyzed that agriculture plays significant role in the economy of India. The Indian peasants have good knowledge of weather and may forecast it. They have also through scientific knowledge of timely irrigation, weeding of crops, application of manures and fertilizers, methods of harvesting etc. although the majority of the peasant population is not literate but they achieved the scientific knowledge for good agriculture harvest through their long practical experience which is really commendable.

Ahmad and Kausar have studied the trend and level of diffusion of irrigation and its impact on the adoption of agricultural innovations in Upper Ganga-Yamuna Doab. They concluded that irrigation is not only essential for the sustenance of agriculture but also its assured and timely supply is prerequisite for diversifying agriculture and to enhance resource efficiency of related inputs. The adoption of certain agricultural innovations like chemical fertilizers, HYV, plant protection chemicals etc, is solely depends upon assured and timely availability of water. Analysis also revealed that new package programmes have a profound influence to bring more and more area under irrigation.

Gill and Yadav in their article, consequences of groundwater depletion in a semi-arid tract of Haryana, attempted to analyze the consequences of depletion of groundwater in Dochana village of Haryana. The village witnessed rapid increase in area under tubewell irrigation during 1975-85 which, in turn, led to depletion of its groundwater resources. Consequently, most of the tubewells had gone dry in the village by early 1990s. The study focuses on the socio-economic impact of the rise and fall in the tubewell irrigated area in this semi-arid tract of Haryana.

Bagchi has discussed the locating data gaps in planning strategies for micro-level development of difficult rained areas of eastern India with particular focus on soil and water resources management. He has elaborated that the participatory resource mapping being supplemented with computer aided tools like GIS can come to our aid not only to identify resource endowment but also to prioritize development steps.

Ahmad and Ghazala in their article of the study of regional imbalances of agricultural productivity have pointed out that in terms of social justice the imbalances in level of agriculture productivity should be minimized to attain an over all self sufficiency at spatial level and not only at national level and a strategy for planning and development should be evolved.

Ala Eldin *et al.*, in their study of assessment of seepage losses from canal in Ganga Kali sub-basin, have analyzed that the irrigated agricultural area in the central Ganga-Plain is dependent mainly on the groundwater resources for sustained growth and prosperity. However, declining water levels and increase in demand for more groundwater exploitation threatened the future development of agriculture that is solely dependent on groundwater. The groundwater balance in study shows that half of the seepage losses from the canals leaves the basin as groundwater effluence to Ganga, Chioyya and Nim rivers.

Surendra in his paper, regional dimensions of agricultural growth potentials, incorporated a normative production function for the analysis of identifying and regionalizing growth potential phenomena for preparing regional investment strategy area development. It is concluded that the lowland areas of main rivers have higher intensity and magnitude of production potentials than the central part of the study area.

Rangi and Sidhu have analyzed the problems and prospects of agriculture in Punjab and pointed out that, the number of factors have made possible the progress in farm sector in Punjab. These include the introduction of HYV, assured price policy and supporting infrastructure for supply of different inputs and dissemination of technical knowledge. To enhance income of the farmers of state, subsidiary enterprises may be encouraged by the policy makers and administrators.

Shafiqullah in his study of pattern of agriculture employment in Uttar Pradesh found that Uttar Pradesh is predominantly agriculture economy, having population pressure on agriculture and reflects the lack of development in other sectors. Study further revealed that agricultural employment is inversely proportional to urbanization, industrialization, vital process, literacy rate and workers in other sectors.

Yasir and Mahfooz in their study of the development of floriculture in India found that floriculture has become a potential money spinner for the developing country like ours. Authors concluded that India has immense potential of floriculture to exploit it commercially in the domestic market as well as for export.

Irfan in his article of principles of pest control of agro-ecosystem pointed out that the ultimate objective of the integrated pest control system is to produce the optimum crop yield of high quality at minimum cost taking into consideration the ecological and sociological constraints in that particular agro-ecosystem and the long-term preservation of the environment.

Yasir and Jamshed have discussed the crisis, constraints and causes in pulses production in Uttar Pradesh since independence. The low productivity of pulses in various parts of the state and country as well are due to non-availability of high yielding disease resistant varieties, cultivation on marginal and sub-marginal lands under deficit moisture, fertility and poor pest management.

Mansoor and Ameenul in their article quality of water for irrigation of Garra River, have emphasized on the suitability of water for irrigation. On the basis of analysis of water quality parameters, authors concluded that quality of water has greater importance than quantity of water.

Mansoor and Mujtaba examined the inter-state pulses situation in India. They analyzed the variation in availability of pulses per capita per day at state level. Study revealed the declining trend of availability of pulses since 1970s. They emphasized the need for enhancing area under pulses production, besides having more attention to formulate the suitable programmes and policies from planners and researchers.

Mansoor, Yasir and Mujtaba in their article foodgrains availability in Indo-Gangetic plain made an elaborate study of foodgrains availability in this physiographic division of India taking it as a whole. Although Indo-Gangetic plain is self-sufficient in foodgrains production but in terms of per capita availability at micro level they are not self-sufficient. They emphasized that there is a need to re-evaluate and re-organize the plan and policies at priority basis to eradicate the imbalances in per capita availability of foodgrains.

LIST OF THE CONTRIBUTORS

A.A. Pujari, U.G.C. Fellow, Department of Geography, Shivaji University, Kolhapur (Maharashtra)

A.K. Chhaukar, Reader, Department of Geography, N.R.E.C. College, Khurja (U.P.)

Abdurraheem, Lecturer, Department of Museology, Aligarh Muslim University, Aligarh (U.P.)

Ameenul Islam, (Research Scholar), Department of Geography, Aligarh Muslim University, Aligarh (U.P.)

Anisur Rehman, (Research Scholar), Department of Geography, Aligarh Muslim University, Aligarh (U.P.)

Anuradha Pathania, Research Scholar, Department of Geography, Delhi School of Economics, Delhi University, Delhi

Asad Umar, (Research Scholar), Department of Geology, Aligarh Muslim University, Aligarh (U.P.)

Ateeque Ahmad, Reader, Department of Geography, Aligarh Muslim University, Aligarh (U.P.)

C.T. Pawar, U.G.C. Fellow, Department of Geography, Shivaji University, Kolhapur (Maharashtra)

D.K. Bagchi, Agricultural Science Unit, Indian Statistical Institute, Calcutta

D.K. Tripathi, Department of Geography, Dr. H.S. Gaur University, Sagar (M.P.)

F.A. Siddiqui, Reader, Department of Geography, Aligarh Muslim University, Aligarh (U.P.)

Fazlur Rehman, Department of Geography, Aligarh Muslim University, Aligarh (U.P.)

H.N. Mishra, Department of Geography, Allahabad University, Allahabad (U.P.)

J.K. Sandoola, Department of Horticulture, C.C.S. Haryana Agricultural University, Hissar (Haryana)

J.L. Mangal, Department of Horticulture, C.C.S. Haryana Agricultural University, Hissar (Haryana)

Kumar Nihkil, Scientist, Environmental Management Group, Central Mining Institute, Dhanbad (Bihar)

M. Sami Ahmad, Department of Geology, Aligarh Muslim University, Aligarh (U.P.)

M.I. Siddiqui, Department of Geography, Rohail Khand University, Bareilly (U.P.)

M.S. Gill, Department of Geography, Punjabi University, Patiala (Punjab)

Mansoor Ali, (Research Scholar), Department of Geography, Aligarh Muslim University, Aligarh (U.P.)

Miss Ananya Taraphder, (Research Scholar), Department of Geography Burdwan University, Burdwan (W.B.)

Mobin Ahmad, Scientist, Environmental Management Group, Central Mining Institute, Dhanbad (Bihar)

Mohammad Irfan, Department of Museology, Aligarh Muslim University, Aligarh (U.P.)

N.K. De, (Research Scholar), Department of Geography, Burdwan University, Burdwan (W.B.)

Noor Mohammad, Head, Department of Geography, Delhi School of Economics, Delhi University, Delhi

R.N. Yadav, Lecturer, J.V.M.G.R.R. College, Charkhi Dadri (Haryana)

Rajnish Kumar, ICSSR Fellow, GBP Social Science Institute, Jhusi, Allahabad (U.P.)

S. Lal, Department of Horticulture, C.C.S. Haryana Agricultural University, Hissar (Haryana)

S.K. Sharma, Department of Geography, Dr. H.S. Gaur University, Sagar (M.P.)

Saleem Siddiqui, Department of Horticulture, C.C.S. Haryana Agricultural University, Hissar (Haryana)

Shafiqullah, Department of Geography, Aligarh Muslim University, Aligarh (U.P.)

Shamsul Haque Siddiqui, Reader, Department of Geography, Aligarh Muslim University, Aligarh (U.P.)

Soumendu Chatterjee, (Research Scholar), Department of Geography Burdwan University, Burdwan (W.B.)

Tapeshwar Singh, Department of Geography, M.M.H (CCS University), Ghaziabad (U.P.)

Yogesh Kumar Mittal, Department of Geography, J.V.M.G.R. College, Charkhi Dadri (Haryana)

1

GREEN REVOLUTION, FOOD SECURITY AND AGRICULTURAL SUSTAINABILITY IN INDIA

The Conflicts and Solutions

TAPESHWAR SINGH

Introduction

In 1970, not long ago, the American botanist Norman Borlaug was honoured with the Nobel Peace Prize for having set in motion a worldwide agricultural revolution, later to be known as "Green Revolution". Based on genetic improvement of particularly productive plants, his innovation increased the yields of wheat, rice and maize two-three times in a very short period of time. Borlaug's so called 'miracle wheat' doubled and tripled the yields in a very short period. Similar increases were soon achieved with maize, and at International Rice Research Institute (IRRI) in Philippines with rice (Glaeser, 1987). The success stories of the new developed strains and Green Revolution appear limitless. In our country these strains were introduced in mid-sixties and within one and a half decades India became self-sufficient in foodgrain production. The foodgrain production significantly increased from 50.82 million tonnes in 1950-51 to 129.59 million tonnes in 1980-81 and further to 200.1 million tonnes in 1998-99. Impressive improvement in food production would not have been achieved without this technology, the scientific breakthrough that provided high-yielding varieties (HYV) of rice, wheat and maize. However, later on, it turns environmentally unfriendly. In fact, tremendous increase in food production has resulted from select crops (rice and wheat) and that too in some select regions.

An Overview

Before the mid-sixties increase in foodgrain output in the country was attributed mostly to the growth of the cultivated area and the extension of irrigation. Since then, the new farming system symbolized by HYV seeds, use of agrochemical, and mechanization had the powerful impact on the food sector of the country. New technology supported by appropriate services and public policies have helped to prove doomsday predictions wrong and have led to the agricultural revolution (the Green Revolution) becoming one of the most significant of the scientific and socially meaningful revolutions of this century (Swaminathan, 1999). The production of wheat nearly tripled between 1961 and 1980. During 1998-99 wheat production in India exceeded 70 million tonnes i.e. a ten-fold increase in about 50 years. However, in the late 1970's and early 1980s a number of studies raised concerns about a possible deceleration in the growth of foodgrains production indicating a decline in the momentum of the Green Revolution and possible exhaustion of the potential of available technology (Alagh & Sharma, 1980; Desai and Namboodiri, 1983). Dantwala (1978) found that the HYV technology brought about a significant improvement in the productivity of cereal crops, but its overall effect on foodgrain production, especially when evaluated in per capita terms, was not significant. In case of pulses a number of earlier studies have shown a sluggish and erratic growth in the production (Moorti, *et al.,* 1991; Bhatia, 1991). Per capita net availability of foodgrain has marginally increased from 394.9 grams per capita per day in 1951 to 484.1 in 1998. Though, in case of gram and pulses the situation is quite disappointing. The per capita availability of gram and pulses has significantly decreased from 22.5 and 60.7 to 13.7 and 33.2 respectively over the same period (Table 1.1). Thus, mere increase in the quantum of foodgrain production does not matter very much. The focus has to be on per capita availability of foodgrain and the overall improvement in the purchasing capacity of the people. Despite being self-sufficient in food production nearly one-fifth of the country's population is chronically malnourished. We have to pay much attention to this fact, if food security has to be secured in real sense.

Turns Environment-Unfriendly

In recent years, it has been felt that Green Revolution technology, though very successful in achieving spectacular results in foodgrains production during the past decades, it has unleashed many agro-ecological problems. It has badly damaged the natural resource base. The technology adopted for bringing about revolutionary increase in crop production is, however, not resource-neutral. In contrast it appears to be resource-intensive and ecologically unsustainable. In pursuit of achieving higher and higher production, farmers put heavy stress on agricultural resource base, consequently degrading the agroecosystem through putting heavy doses of agrochemicals while ignoring the long-term hazardous effects on soil health-nutrients. As a result, agricultural productivity has reached a plateau in some parts of the country. For instance, intensification of farming in Punjab has created serious imbalances in agroecosystem—the problems of groundwater depletion, soil degradation and desertification, and alarming appearance of pests, disease and weeds. Hence, the risk of sustainability of agriculture is growing.

The food production growth is set to suffer from the falling return to investments and inputs. The problems is further intensified as the 'Green Revolution' has run its course or exhausted its potential especially in the agriculturally most advanced areas. North-western India, parts of Andhra Pradesh and Tamil Nadu show a clear trends of yields and outputs falling despite significant additions of inputs. Diminishing return to input increases can be widespread in near future. The diffusion of Green Revolution technology has also slowed down.

Table 1.1: Per Capita Net Availability of Foodgrain in India

(grams per day)

Sl. No.	*Year*	*Rice*	*Wheat*	*Other Cereal*	*Cereals*	*Gram*	*Pulses*	*Food-grains*
1.	1951	158.9	65.7	109.6	334.2	22.5	60.7	394.9
2.	1961	201.1	79.1	119.5	399.7	32.2	69.0	468.7
3.	1971	192.6	103.6	121.4	417.6	20.0	51.2	468.8
4.	1981	197.8	129.6	89.9	417.3	13.4	37.5	454.8
5.	1991	221.7	166.8	80.0	468.5	13.4	41.6	510.1
6.	1996	212.1	178.1	62.7	452.9	11.5	32.9	485.8
7.	1997P	221.1	178.1	74.5	473.7	12.9	38.4	512.1
8.	1998P	216.4	168.2	63.3	450.9	13.7	33.2	484.1
9.	1999P							

Source: Agricultural Statistics at a Glance, 1999, p. 88.
P — Provisional.

However, the potential future flux of problem emanating from the technology is still not well understood. Less emphasis is placed on the view that natural resources are finite and non-renewable and there are limits to growth. We might run out of material capacity of the ecosystem sustenance than was so before the onset of Green Revolution. The fear of decelerating carrying capacity of the country's agroecosystem should be taken care of seriously. This fear is not unfounded because depleting resources are further compounded with decline in quality. Garbrecht (1993) observed that "tap the groundwater potential only up to and never beyond limits of natural replenishment and as a consequence, do not imbalance the hydrological equilibrium of the region". In other words, we can harness nature but cannot overtax it. Lester Brown and Hal Kane (1994) have predicted that the current rate of population growth and environmental degradation coupled with an improvement in consumption capacity of the poor, India will have to import annually over 40 million tonnes of foodgrains by the year 2030. India for instance, with nearly 1000 million people is faced with challenge of stagnation and decline in grain production in some regions. Thus, the most serious challenges in agricultural sectors appear to be the following:

(i) How to further increase and diversify production using modern inputs.
(ii) How to reduce disparities between various social groups and regions as well as crops which have already emerged due to failure of these technologies in unfavourable biophysical environment.
(iii) How to overcome various agroecological problems unleashed by these technologies achieving the desired rate of agricultural growth without damaging the natural resource base and lessening its long-term potential.
(iv) To ascertain the socio-economic conditions governing the introduction of ecologically oriented agricultural production and to evaluate their benefits for the society.
(v) To assess the ability of the present system to further absorb its spillover effects and retain an ecosystem which is sustainable for crop production with the aims of providing food security to every citizen.

However, there has been at least now a growing realisation of some degree of ineffectiveness and degrading potential of such technologies. In this chapter an attempt has been made to critically evaluate the achievements of the Green Revolution technologies. It is also tried to highlight some of the problems emanating from it and suggesting its revitalization as well as alternative methods of production for sustainable agricultural development and food security.

Cropping Pattern Changes

India has derived enormous net benefits from the adoption of the technology. There is no doubt that the diffusion and adoption of these technologies enhanced substantially the productive capabilities of the agricultural base of the country as a whole and was responsible for the large gains in food output. It was very effective in immensely increasing the yields of main crops and ensuring food production to keep pace with the rapidly growing population. India's population has shot up from 361.1 million in 1951 to 846.3 in 1991. Now it has crossed the 1000 million mark and in 2050 it is expected to stand at 1,529 million. The growth in crop production so far may be ascribed to three factors: increase in arable land, cropping intensity and higher yield per acre. In pre-Green Revolution period expansion of arable area has been the main source of agricultural growth. But, starting around mid-sixties high yields have mainly contributed to food output growth. However, this tempo could not be maintained during 1980's and onward and the trend became quite erratic (Table 1.2). The growth rate of area under foodgrains during 1950-1996 has been just 0.45 per cent whereas yields have been increased at a growth rate of 1.74 per cent (Table 1.3). The cropping intensity has increased from 111.07 in 1950-51 to 145.7 in 1994-95. If we look at the

Table 1.2: Production of Foodgrains in India

(*Million Tonnes*)

Sl. No.	*Years*	*Rice*	*Wheat*	*Pulses*	*Coarse Cereals*	*Nine Oilseeds*	*Total Food-grains*
1.	1950-51	20.58	6.46	8.41	15.38	5.16	50.80
2.	1960-61	34.58	11.00	12.70	23.74	6.98	82.02
3.	1970-71	42.22	23.83	11.80	30.53	9.63	108.42
4.	1980-81	53.63	36.31	10.63	29.02	9.37	129.59
5.	1990-91	74.29	55.14	14.30	32.70	18.61	176.39
6.	1994-95	81.81	65.77	14.30	30.40	21.34	191.50
7.	1995-96	76.98	62.10	12.31	29.03	22.11	185.05
8.	1996-97	81.74	69.35	17.24	34.10	24.38	199.44
9.	1997-98	82.30	65.91	13.03	31.16	22.02	192.43
10.	1998-99	-	-	-	-	-	200.10

Source: *Agricultural Statistics at a Glance*, 1999.

Table 1.3: All India Compound Growth Rates of Area, Production and Yield of Principal Crops

(Base: T.E. 1981-82=100 per cent per annum)

Crops	*1949-50 to 1995-96*			*1949 to 1964-65*			*1967-68 to 1995-96*		
	A	*P*	*Y*	*A*	*P*	*Y*	*A*	*P*	*Y*
Rice	0.79	2.68	1.88	1.21	2.50	2.25	0.64	2.90	2.33
Wheat	2.28	5.56	3.21	2.69	3.98	1.27	1.55	4.72	3.11
Coarse Cereals	0.52	2.91	2.02	1.25	3.21	1.77	0.03	2.91	2.42
Total Pulses	0.20	0.53	0.41	1.72	1.41	-0.18	0.21	0.93	0.72
Total Foodgrains	0.45	2.52	1.74	1.35	2.82	1.36	0.06	2.67	2.24
Total Oilseeds	1.20	2.69	1.09	2.67	3.20	0.30	1.33	3.53	1.68
Non-Foodgrains	1.24	2.94	1.35	2.44	3.74	0.89	1.36	3.29	1.74
All Crops	0.64	2.67	1.58	1.58	3.15	1.21	0.38	2.89	2.00

Source: Directorate of Economics and Statistics, Ministry of Agriculture, Government of India, 1997, *Agricultural Statistics at a Glance*, p. 131.

A— Growth rates of area. P— Growth rates of production. Y— Growth rates of yields.

area allocation among the broad groups, the share of area under total cereals, total pulses and total foodgrains has shown certain degree of decline. Coarse cereals–*Jowar, ragi* and *bajra* have lost much of their shares, perhaps to wheat and oilseeds (Table 1.4). Thus, it is evident that diffusion process in these crops has not made much headway and quantum increase in yields is also not encouraging. Further diffusion will largely depend on eco-friendly technologies of irrigation and biogenetic knowledge in farm practices and policies.

Table 1.4: Broad Cropping Pattern in India According to Land-use Statistics

(Percentage to Total Cropped Area)

Sl. No.	*Crops*	*50-51*	*60-61*	*70-71*	*80-81*	*90-91*	*92-93*	*93-94*	*94-95*
1.	Rice	23.6	23.3	22.6	23.3	23.0	22.6	22.88	22.84
2.	Wheat	7.6	8.5	11.0	12.8	13.0	13.3	13.51	13.74
3.	Jowar	11.8	12.01	10.2	9.5	7.7	7.1	6.94	6.23
4.	Bajra	7.4	7.5	8.0	6.8	5.7	5.8	5.22	5.49
5.	Maize	2.4	2.9	3.5	3.5	3.2	3.3	3.27	3.26
6.	Total Cereals	61.1	60.2	61.4	60.8	55.6	54.8	5.35	54.01
7.	Total Pulses	15.6	15.5	14.0	13.2	13.5	12.7	12.55	12.91
8.	Total Foodgrains	76.7	75.7	75.4	73.9	69.5	67.5	66.90	66.91
9.	Total Oilseed	8.3	8.3	8.9	9.1	13.5	14.4	15.29	14.44

Source: Agricultural Statistics at a Glance, 1998.

Green Revolution Turns Unsound

The slowdown trend in foodgrain production has already started to emerge. The rate of growth of output of foodgrains has slowed down to 1.7 per cent per annum during the first seven years of the current decade (1990-91 to 1996-97) whereas population continues to grow at around 2 per cent (*Economic Survey*, 1997). The production of pulses in the country has been stagnating at around 8 to 14 million tonnes for the last 40 years. The per capita availability of pulses has come down from 69 grams in 1961 to about 33.2 grams in 1998. In fact, stagnation in the output of pulses has pulled down the overall foodgrain output growth. The nineties also witnessed the rate of growth of rice falling to 1.52 per cent, and more and more area being shared by commercial crops that might have caused foodgrains growth rate lagging behind population growth rate: Experts admit that the productivity in the fertile soils has reached the plateau. In Punjab the yield is up to 46 quintal a hectare in Ludhiana district against the national average of 25 quintal and area under wheat has declined since it is no longer profitable to grow the crop. Farmers are switching over the cash crops. Area under wheat has declined from peak of 33.35 lakh hectares to 32.8 in 1995-96. However, decline in area is not steady.

Weeds, pests, and diseases of crops have developed resistance to chemicals. Any decline in area under wheat in Punjab which accounts for 22 per cent of the country's wheat production and provides 70 per cent of the central wheat pool, will adversely affect the country's food security. As a consequence, growth rates of both the crops will further decline as the growth rates of both area and yield have declining trends. Further, compound growth rate of area and production of coarse cereals is also declining (Table 1.5).

Moreover, efforts need to be focussed on increasing the production growth rates of the crops which have not been benefited by the technology. These crops (coarse cereals, pulses, and oilseeds) are generally grown in climatically fragile area, and are adapted to some degree to the prevailing environmental conditions. Research on these crops has made significant breakthrough and has already produced technical options on this vast fragile ecological zone constituting about 65 per cent of the area. Still these crops suffer high degree of risks in events of weather aberrations. This risk factor has made the diffusion of new technological option more difficult. So their widespread application requires special policy measures. It needs appropriate policies to induce

Table 1.5: Compound Growth Rates of Area and Production of Coarse Cereals

(Base 1981-82=100% per annum)

Crops	*1967-68 to 1995-96**		*1967-68 to 1980-81*		*1980-81 to 1995-96**	
	A	*P*	*A*	*P*	*A*	*P*
Jowar	-1.2	0.64	-1.15	2.04	-2.48	-0.70
Bajra	-0.87	0.68	-1.15	-0.38	-1.15	1.15
Maize	0.20	1.66	0.01	0.02	0.19	2.43
Ragi	-0.84	0.96	0.91	3.38	-2.23	-0.07
Small Millets	-3.65	-3.00	-1.18	-0.81	-5.44	-4.36
Barley	-4.97	-2.59	-3.88	-2.72	-4.92	-1.89
Coarse Cereals	-1.30	0.57	-1.30	0.67	-1.96	0.39
Total Cereals	0.03	2.91	0.37	2.61	-0.34	2.95
Grams	-0.68	-0.08	-0.55	-1.02	-0.51	0.61

Source: Agricultural Statistics at a Glance, 1997, p. 132.
A—Area. P—Production. *Provisional.

expansion of area under these crops. As area, yield and production of some of these crops such as *jowar, ragi* and *gram*, for example, are declining, the significant increase in production growth rates will be contingent on these factors. In fact, very high potential of agricultural production as well as overall economic growth lies in the optimum development of such environmentally fragile areas. There still remains a vast scope for increasing foodgrain production by improving present yield level in green revolution areas as the overall yields in India are still much lower than many other countries of the world. At the same time, for achieving equitable growth our country should pay adequate attention on research to improving the traditional foodgrain crops which are not only location specific but more nutritious and environmentally sustainable.

In fact, this approach may meet the ever growing food needs of the country in the years to come. In late eighties degradation of agroecology as a result of haphazard and imbalanced application of the modern technology came to surface and sustainability of this strategy was questioned. Pierre Spitz (1987) examines some of India's food systems and discovers that the "Green Revolution" in India was mainly a 'wheat revolution' patterned after the agricultural models of the industrialised countries. He questions the very appropriateness of this model for India. He makes a plea for alternative technologies which could ensure a less uneven development between crops, regions and social groups-reducing disparities between them as well as between seasonal income, employment and year-to-year production. R.N. Roy (1987) felt that India's water scarcity and soil erosion problems stem from intensive cropping using unsuitable imported technology, and from the country's socio-politico-economic reality which has mortgaged long-term sustainability and development for short-term profit involving exploitation of the masses who work on the land. In the present form this technology seems to have lost its momentum in sustaining India's food production.

Limit to Growth

In the country, several physical constraints have emerged. In many respects we have reached the "limit of growth". Many experts have begun to question the very possibility of "unlimited growth". Thus, the very comprehensive agricultural development plans have to be initiated under situations of limited resources and established environmental qualities. They must be related to region's carrying capacity. In the classical wildlife biologist's term "carrying capacity is the ability of an ecosystem to support a given number of consumers and remain healthy and productive". The explosive population growth exerted on the limited physical space which has given rise to numerous environmental stresses. As a result of excessively utilising and depleting the agroecosystem, its sustainability is threatened. For instance, per capita availability of land in the country is declining. Per capita availability of land would shrink from 0.50 ha in 1981 to 0.33 ha in 2000 and to 0.19 ha in the year 2035 (Bali, 1988). The land-use trends reveal that the area under non-agricultural uses is increasing and net area sown is declining. Though, the net irrigated area has substantially increased from 22.85 Mha in 1950-51 to about 53.00 Mha in 1994-95, i.e. 37.2 per cent of the net area sown (142.82 Mha in 1994-95). It is estimated that even after achieving the full irrigation potential, nearly 50 per cent of the total cultivated area will remain rainfed. Overall, the availability of renewable fresh water resources per capita in India fell from around 6000 cubic metres per year in 1947 to about 2300 cubic metres in 1997. It is estimated that by 2017 India will be 'water stressed' – per capita water availability will be as low as 1600 cubic metres (TERI, 1997). The spread of "Green Revolution" technology has been accompanied by a phenomenal increase in private shallow tubewells. These increased from about a thousand in 1947 to 3.6 million in 1968-69 and to

Table 1.6: Per Capita Availability of Land in India

(in hectares)

Year	*Total*	*Cultivable Land*
1951	0.89	0.48
1981	0.50	0.20
1993	0.37	0.16
2000	0.33	0.14
2035	0.19	0.088

Source: Bali (1995).

6.0 million in 1997. There is a wide gap in irrigation potential created and utilised over the plan periods. While 100 per cent of the potential created was utilised before 1951, it came down to 80 per cent in 1993-94. More disturbing feature has been the high level of waste. It is estimated that 45 per cent of irrigation potential was wasted by seepage through unlined field channels and another 15 per cent was wasted due to over-application. Agriculture scientists and environment experts find in its use include: degradation of agricultural lands, decline in soil nutrients, desertification, humus, decline in moisture retaining and infiltration capacities, nitrate leaching, eutrophication, pollution of soil and water, decline in crop resistance to pest and disease, loss of biodiversity, alarming increase in weeds and decline in their response to weedicides, cadmium, and at large, the generation of greenhouse gases which ultimately intensifies the global warming phenomenon and climate change deem to affect agriculture in different ways. Intensification of farming has further resulted in the pollution of groundwater in many parts of the country. As per NEERI reports about 70 per cent of the groundwater is polluted. In many parts of the country extraction of groundwater has been extensive. For example, in 1998, Directorate of Ground Water Development, Uttar Pradesh, has declared 111 blocks out of 819 blocks as *dark* where groundwater is already exploited to the extent of 85 per cent and above. One hundred and ninety eight blocks are declared *grey* which have utilised between 65 to 85 and 510 as *white* where groundwater is exploited below 65 per cent. Lowering of groundwater table is another problem. Most of the areas have groundwater level below 15 metres from the surface. NEERI (National Environment Engineering Research Institute, Nagpur) reported that groundwater level in much of the country is steadily sinking. The fall in little over a decade has been two to four metres in many districts. Depletion of groundwater, if not replenished by recharge, will result in permanent lowering of groundwater table causing a wide range of environmental and socio-economic problems. Over extraction, however is emerging as a severe environmental crisis in the vast areas of the country. The majority of the tubewells have been rendered infructuous. Lowering of groundwater table has caused saline-water intrusion in coastal areas. Declining watertable has also resulted in increased energy consumption and more investment on operative cost of tubewells. Thus, rapid expansion of groundwater exploitation under the aegis of Green Revolution has already put extreme stresses on static resources and ecological equilibrium. Further, inefficient use of water resources (irrigation) has intensified the process of land degradation: soil erosion, waterlogging, alkalinity, acidification and salinization etc. It is estimated that an area of 174.2 million hectares is potentially exposed to various degradation forces like water (153.2 Mha) and wind erosion (15.0 Mha), about 40.0 Mha is subjected to floods and 22.0 Mha is not reclaimable for agricultural uses. An area of about 25.0 Mha is affected by acidity having *p*H value below 5.5 and 33.7 Mha is degraded because of specific problems like waterlogging (8.5 Mha), sodicity (3.6 Mha), shifting cultivation (5.0 Mha) ravine and gullies (40.0 Mha) and 2.37 Mha to riverine and torrent lands (Singh, 1998). The Indian agriculture is running with a net negative balance of plant nutrient @ 8-10 million tonnes a year. In addition more than 8,000 million tonnes of top-soil is eroded every year. Thus, our main agricultural systems are trapped and we will have to develop ecotechnology, which is oriented towards fulfilling the basic needs of everyone, promoting self-reliance in agriculture, and striving for environment compatibility. Appropriate biotechnology is another important area of interest which can create new opportunities to meet the environmental conservation, abatement of agricultural pollution and sustainability of the agricultural production. The physical and biological production environment and genetic potential for increase in productivity, and the socio-economic circumstances in which our farmer operate can be enriched through various other methods—organic farming, integrated soil nutrient management, integrated pest management, exploitation of farmer's traditional knowledge and practices, soil-water conservation, soil management and protection, and conservation of bio-diversities etc. Hence, sustainability of the agroecosystem should be more dominant objective of agricultural development planning in the future than in the past. The immediate need, therefore, is to mobilise greater national efforts in formulating comprehensive and balance resource use and production policies for strengthening the system sustainability. This calls for greater resolve to ensure synergism among productivity, profitability and sustainability of the major cropping systems. Since sustainable agricultural development cannot subsist on a degrading and depleting agroecosystem, it will be imperative to strengthen research for their conservation and improvement. However, natural resources should not be seen in isolation for sustaining the production in future, as development of eco-friendly and resource-use-efficient agro-technologies will have to remain on priority agenda. In years to come our goal would be "to develop eco-friendly technologies for attaining the production goals while ensuring sustainable use of natural resources" (Singh, 1998). However, it is disappointing to note that our research institutions are languishing under financial strain. For example, our country spends only US$ 3 per capita per year on research and development (R&D) whereas Japan and United States spend US$ 600 per capita per annum.

Concluding Remarks

- India has achieved tremendous success on food front through the package of Green Revolution technologies in short time. But it is area and crop specific and has unleashed many agro-ecological problems.
- The complex and basic problems of food security, poverty, equity and sustainability of resource base continue to be serious cause of concern.
- The biotic and abiotic stresses on the resource base are increasing which requires to enlarge the carrying capacity of the system to meet the demands of growing population.
- A hunger free India will be possible if we pay concurrent attention to improving food availability through ecologically sustainable methods of production and revitalizing the earlier tradition of cultivating a wide range of food crops.
- Farming will have to be knowledge-intensive, using information from remote sensing, Geographical Information System (GIS), Global Positioning System (GPS) and information and computer techniques.
- With necessary caution to prevent unforeseen problems associated with Biotechnology the adoption of this technology will play an important role in strengthening food security in twenty-first century.
- The cropping pattern in the country has undergone a sea-change. The productivity of major crop has stagnated and even declined in certain areas.

— The gene revolution, the ecotechnology revolution and the communication revolution have to be included as the main components of the national agricultural policy for sustainable development of agriculture in future.
— Soil, water, biodiversity and climate-basic natural resources for agricultural growth and development, are subjected to various forms of deteriorating influences and indiscriminate exploitation.
— For achieving the short-term goal of food production over exploitation and reckless use of resources have threatened the future sustainability of the agroecosystem itself.
— In 1990's population growth has outpaced the food output growth.
— In fact, the complex and intrinsic relationship between environment and agricultural development have received insufficient attention.
— Improvement of environmental health for the goal of achieving sustainable agricultural development.
— The potential ability of the system to meet future food need must be measured against constraints being imposed by limited resources, mounting degradation and unfavourable policies since these factors will hamper the future growth and development.
— Instead of agrochemical-intensive agricultural policy, it should be based on bio-intensive cropping system.
— A second Green Revolution is needed for environmentally fragile areas and people. But this should not repeat the first revolution—it needs to aim both at increasing yield and at preserving and developing the environmental base.
— Finally, our agricultural policy should be ecologically sound, economically viable and socially sustainable for different agro-climatic systems keeping in view the needs of the present as well as the future generation.

References

Alagh, Y.K., and P.S. Sharma (1980), Growth of crop production: 1960-61 to 1978-79 is Decelerating? *Indian Journal of Agricultural Economics*, Vol. 35, No. 2, pp. 104-118.

Alexandratos, N. (ed.) (1980), *World Agriculture Towards 2000*. New York University Press, New York. *Soil and Water Conservation,* Vol. 39, Nos. 3-4 pp. 99-111.

Bali, J.S. (1995), Strategies for Soil and Water Conservation Under Empowered Panchayats. *Journal of Soil and Water Conservation*, Vol. 39, Nos. 3-4, pp. 99-111.

Bernard Coventry (1910), Has the fertility of land in India decreased? *The Agricultural Journal of India*, Vol. V, Part IV, Oct. 1910.

Bhalla, G.S. & Y.K. Alagh (1997) *Performance of Indian Agriculture: A District-wise Study*. Sterling Publisher, New Delhi.

Bhatia, M.S. (1991), Economic constraints in increasing pulses production. *Agricultural Situation in India*, Vol. 46, No. 5, pp. 276-284.

Brown, Lester R. and Hal Kane (1994), Full House: *Reassessing the Earth's Population Carrying Capacity*. Worldwatch Institute, New York.

Bumb, Balul, and Carlos A. Baanante (1996), IFPRI (International Food Policy Research Institute). The Role of Fertilizer in Sustaining Food Security and Protecting the Environment to 2020. *Food Agriculture and the Environment Discussion* Paper 17. Washington, D.C.

Dantwala, M.L. (1978), Future of institutional reform and technological change in Indian Agricultural Development. *Economic and Political Weekly*, Special Number, August 1978, pp. 1299-1306.

Desai, Gunwant M. and N.V. Namboodiri (1983), The deceleration Hypothesis and yield-increasing input in Indian Agriculture. *I.J.A. Eco.*, Vol. 38, No. 4, pp. 497-508.

Directorate of Economics & Statistics, Ministry of Agriculture, Government of India. *Agricultural Statistics at a Glance* (1997).

Directorate of Economics & Statistics, Government of India, *Agricultural Statistics at a Glance* (1998).

Directorate of Economics & Statistics, Government of India, *Economic Survey* (1997-98).

Garbretch, Gunter (1983), Ancient Water works—lessons from History. *Impact of Science and Society*. UNESCO, No.1, p. 10.

Giacomo De Sabata, (1995), The False Myth of Unlimited Economic Growth: A Fundamental Fault. *Environmental Conservation*, Vol. 22, No. 3, pp. 199-200.

Glaeser, Berhard (ed.) (1984), *Ecodevelopment: Concepts, Projects in Strategies*. Oxford: Pergamon.

Glaeser, Berhard (ed.) (1987), *The Green Revolution Revisited*. Allen and Unwin, London.

Howard, Sir Albert (1940), *An Agricultural Testament*. Present Impression is published by the Other India Press, Goa.

Joshi, P.K. and D. Jha (1990), Environment of Eternalities in Surface Irrigation Systems in India. In *Environmental Aspects of Agricultural Development*, IFPRI, Washington, D.C.

Moore, R. and Jan Ryan (ed.) (1995), *Sustainable Development: Policy and Practice*. New Age International (Publisher), New Delhi.

Moorti, T.V., K.D. Sharma, and D.R. Thakur (1991), Trends in the Production of Pulses and Oilseeds in Himachal Pradesh. *Agricultural Situation in India*, Vol. 46, No. 5, pp. 303-308.

Pierce, John T. (1990), *The Food Resource*, Longman Scientific and Technical, New York.

Roy, R.N. (1987), Trees: Appropriate Tools for Soil and Water Management in Bernhard Glaeser (ed). The *Green Revolution Revisited*, Allen and Unwin, London, pp. 56-57.

Sekhon, M.K. and Manjeet Kaur (1996), Green Revolution in Punjab: Other side of the Coinn Asii, Vol. LII, No. 11, *Agricultural Situation in India.*

Shah, Deepak, (1997), Foodgrain Production in India: A Drive Towards Self Sufficiency. *Artha Vijnana*, Vol. XXXIC, No. 2, pp. 219-239.

Sharma, T.C. and O. Coutinho (1998), *Green Revolution Gap.* Rawat, Jaipur.

Singh, G.B. (1998), Natural Resources Management for Sustainable Agriculture in 21st Century. *Indian Farming.* Vol. 44, No. 5, pp. 7-12.

Singh, Tapeshwar (1978), *Drought Prone Areas in India.* People's Publishing House (PPH), New Delhi.

Singh, Tapeshwar (1995), *Drought Disaster and Agricultural Development in India*, PPH, New Delhi.

Singh, Tapeshwar (1996), Ecological Farming: Main Ingredients. *IASSI Quarterly*, Vol. 15, No. 3, New Delhi, pp. 129-135.

Singh, Tapeshwar, (1997) Ecological Farming System and Prospects. In Jagdish Singh (ed.). *Sustainable Land-use* Board, Government of Uttar Pradesh, pp. 112-29.

Singh, Tapeshwar, (1997) Ecofarming: Beyond Green Revolution. *Critique Quarterly*, Vol. 1, No. 2-3, pp. 53-76.

Spitz, Pierre (1987), The Green Revolution Re-examined in India. In B. Glaeser (ed.). *The Green Revolution Revisited.* Allen & Unwin, London, pp. 56-57.

Swaminathan, M.S. (1991), Towards Sustainable Agriculture. *Update Agriculture*, July 1991.

Swaminathan, M.S. (1999), Science in Response to Basic Human Needs. *Current Science*, Vol. 77, No. 3, pp. 341-353.

Sud, Surinder (1997), Crop Productivity and Sustainability. *Yojana*, Feb. 1997 pp. 5 & 8.

Tandan, H.L.S. (1995), Fertilizer and Integrated Nutrients Recommendations for Balance and Efficiency. *Fertilizer Development and Consultation Organization* (FDCO), New Delhi, p. 4.

TERI (1997), *Looking Back to Think Ahead.* Green India 2047, p. 2.

Vandana, Shiva (1989), *The Violence of the Green Revolution.* Research Foundation for Science and Ecology (RFSE), Dehradun.

2

DIMENSIONS OF AGRICULTURAL LAND RESOURCE AND POPULATION PRESSURE

A Case Study of Deoria District in U.P.

FARASAT ALI SIDDIQUI

Resources as substances or properties satisfy human needs and whether they satisfy human needs or not depends largely on the numbers and characteristics of the population in the area concerned (Clarke, 1973). Although one cannot make any clear cut generalizations about the effects of population growth upon economic development (Easterlin, 1967). But increasing numbers have stimulated development such as the intensification in agricultural systems in tropical Africa (Boserup, 1965; Gleave and White, 1968). Resources also tend to grow with the aims, talents and efforts of people, with their economic and cultural attainments, and with their capacity to exploit them.

Population pressure is a loosely defined term. Population pressure is the product of population number and the efficiency of the production system (Munir and Siddiqui, 1983). It generally refers to 'the imbalance between human numbers and their needs; and between physical and human resources of the area' (Clarke, 1970). It is a 'long term process of deteriorating physical and human conditions occurring at many scales as a result excess numbers of human and/or animals in relation to the ability of the land to support them' (Bernard, 1977). This view of population pressure leads to the concept of 'optimum population density'. Some scholars have implied the concept of 'critical population density' or 'carrying capacity' (Allan, 1949). Carrying capacity of an area is an estimate of the number of people that an area will support in perpetuity under a given system of land usage, without deterioration of land resource. But there is little land left for the expansion of cultivation in all of the regions with a high ratio of population to resources, including both technology source and technology deficient areas (Ackerman, 1967). The highest quality agriculture lands adapted to most productive farming is now in use. Nevertheless, important extensions of the cultivated land are still possible and are badly needed because of steadily growing population in many developing countries like India.

The increasing pressure of human resource on broadly speaking, inextensible land resources are creating problem in agricultural based societies. There are few lands which are not being used for cultivation. If these lands are utilised at maximum level the pressure of human resources on land may be minimised. But the nature of utilisable land is quite different. There are lands like barren land which are saline and alkali, and kans-infested; they cannot be used easily for cultivation because of quite expensive land reclamation. On the other hands current fallows and culturable land can be easily reclaimed and brought under proper cultivation.

In the light of these points this chapter aims to study trends of land and human resource in Deoria district of Uttar Pradesh, corroborate block-wise distribution of cultivable land and population pressure, and explain proposed population pressure on agricultural land resource.

Deoria is one of the eastern districts of U.P. It lies between 26° and 28° N latitudes, and 83° and 85° E longitudes. It is a district of 3538 villages, comprised 93 per cent of population. It covers an area of 544 km^2 and has a population of 6.00 million (1991). The density of population is 776 persons per km^2. It occupies 1.9 per cent areas, and 3.2 per cent population of the State. It comprises four tehsils of Padrauna, Hata, Deoria Sadar and Salempur. The district is comprised of twenty-nine block developments (Fig. 2.1) The total land under cultivation is accounted for 0.44 million hectares. Fifty-one per cent of the area is under multiple cropping. Among the cereals wheat occupies the highest hectarage (2,36,582 ha) followed by rice (2,36,081 ha).

Trends of Land and Human Resources

There had been fluctuations in cultivable land resource since 1961-62. It was recorded to be the highest (27,093 ha in 1961-62), it declined to 14,738 ha in a quinquennial year i.e., 1966-67 (Table 2.1). In 1971-72 it was observed to be an increase of about 21.4 per cent over five years, it again rose to 19.1 per cent (31,217 ha) in 1976-77. It declined to 23

Fig. 2.1: Deoria District—Administrative Division 1991

per cent (24,475 ha) in 1981-82 and about 27 per cent (2,380 ha) in 1986-87. Since a slight, increase of 2 per cent in cultivable land was registered during 1986-87 to 1991-92. It may be inferred that there had been a notable increase in fallow land even a maximum use of chemical fertilizers but the keeping of fallow land was alarmingly causing to maintain soil fertility.

Table 2.1: Trends of Cultivable Land and Agricultural Population in Deoria District (1961-62 to 1991-92)

Year	*Cultivable Land (in ha)*	*Agricultural Population (in million)*
1961-62	27,093	0.88
1966-67	14,738	0.82
1971-72	17,787	0.75
1976-77	31,217	0.80
1981-82	24,475	0.84
1986-87	23,806	0.91
1991-92	25,301	1.01

In case of agricultural employment fluctuations had been observed since 1961 caused by general population growth and change in the definition of workers. Population growth during 1961-71 added to increase agricultural employment in the district but it was registered to be declined due to the declaration of workers of 1961 as non-workers in 1971. But since 1971 a continuous increase in agricultural employment was found, it was 0.75 million in 1976-77 and it rose to 0.80 million in 1981-82 with the absolute addition of 0.05 million. In 1981-82 the addition was meagre (0.04 million). Since this year the figure tended to increase continuously as it rose to 0.91 million in 1986-87 with the addition of 0.07 million and 1.01 in 1991-92 with the addition of 0.10 million.

It may be noted that quinquennial variations in cultivable land were wide and in agricultural employment relatively narrow. The other point to be noted here was that the gradient of trend line of cultivable land during thirty years (1961-91) was gentler than that of agricultural employment as shown in Fig. 2.2.

Distribution of Cultivable Land

The distribution of cultivable land is attempted under two main points. One is concerned with the simple percentage of cultivable land to total area for cultivation. Second refers to index of specialization. The latter is a technique of location quotient which is applied to identify land resource regions in the district. It provides an index of 'Surplus or Deficit' percentage of cultivation in each block with reference to district average as the norm. The L.Q. of the blocks of Deoria district each of which compares the ratio of the block's share of cultivable land to its share of all the cultivable lands with the similar ratio for all the cultivable lands, with the similar ratio for all the blocks combined. It is a ratio of ratios.

Cultivable Land in Deoria District, U.P. 1960-61 to 1991-92

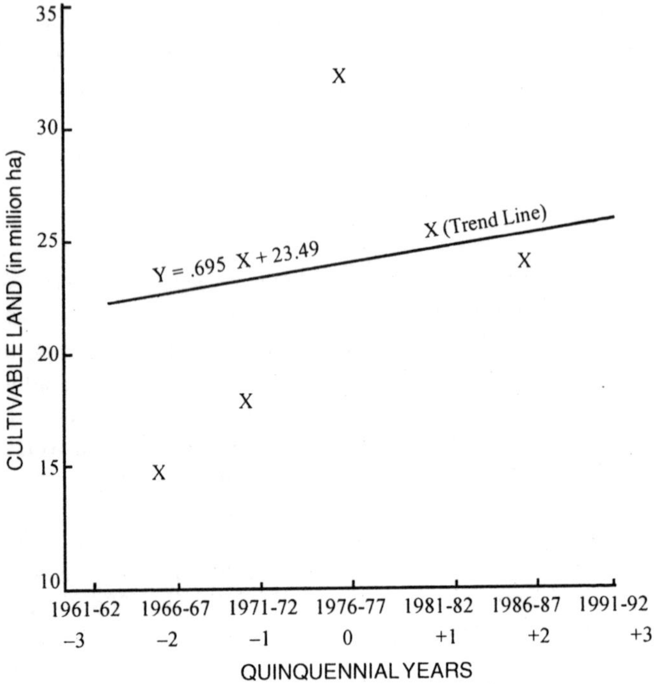

Agricultural Workers in Deoria District, U.P. 1961-91

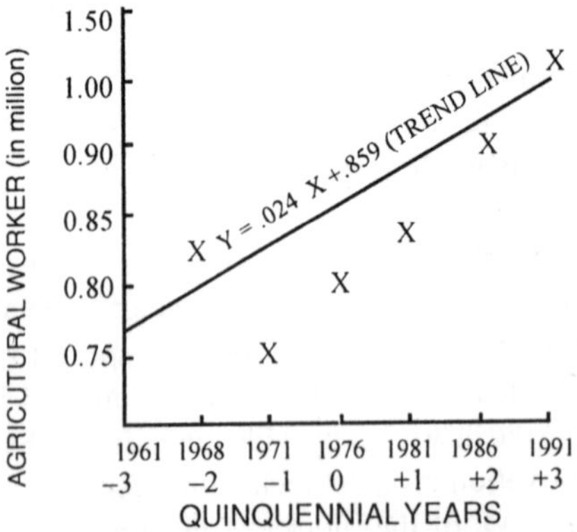

Fig. 2.2: Cultivable Land 1960-61 to 1991-92 and Agricultural Workders 1961-91 in Deoria District, U.P.

The operational equation used for the derivation of this index is read as

$$LQd = Ob * MB/OB * Mb$$

Where LQd is index of specialization for cultivable land in block b. Ob is the cultivable land in block b, MB is the total land for cultivation M in all blocks B, OB is the cultivable land in blocks B and Mb is the total land for cultivation M in a block b.

Table 2.2: Block-wise Distribution of Agricultural Land and Population Pressure in Deoria District, 1991-92

Sl. No.	*Block*	*Arith-metical Density*	*Cultivable land*		*Population Pressure*	
			in percent	*by L.Q.*	*Actual*	*Proposed*
1.	Captainganj	792	3.49	0.71	264	253
2.	Khadda	459	8.41	1.70	223	199
3.	Nebua Naurangia	646	2.32	0.47	224	219
4.	Motichak	813	4.92	0.99	271	255
5.	Romkola	828	1.78	0.36	228	223
6.	Sukrauli	858	3.64	0.74	273	261
7.	Hata	857	4.44	0.99	247	235
8.	Kasia	929	4.25	0.86	258	245
9.	Tamkuhi	864	2.77	0.56	246	238
10.	Dudhai	758	5.47	1.06	256	239
11.	Padrauna	824	2.32	0.47	261	254
12.	Fazilnagar	792	4.14	0.84	252	240
13.	Bishunpura	712	3.21	0.65	241	232
14.	Seorahi	688	6.10	1.21	260	244
15.	Gauri Bazaar	893	4.92	0.99	247	234
16.	Deoria	889	9.55	1.93	227	208
17.	Desai Deoria	846	8.21	1.66	239	219
18.	Patherdewa	809	6.06	1.22	227	211
19.	Baitalpur	812	8.75	1.77	261	236
20.	Rampur Karkhana	860	10.19	2.06	239	210
21.	Rudrapur	663	4.90	0.99	173	191
22.	Bankata	856	4.83	0.98	219	207
23.	Barhaj	706	3.74	0.76	182	172
24.	Bhagalpur	709	4.53	0.92	181	171
25.	Bhatni	832	9.63	1.95	210	187
26.	Bhatpar Rani	895	3.45	0.70	218	209
27.	Bhaluani	585	3.69	0.75	174	167
28.	Lar	893	3.36	0.68	188	179
29.	Salempur	959	8.84	1.79	208	167
	Deoria District	776	4.95	1.00	236	**222**

Source: Statistical Bulletin of Agriculture, U.P. (1961-91), Lucknow.
Statistical Bulletin (1991-93), Deoria.
Statistical Diary, U.P. (1979-91), Lucknow.

In inter-block or inter-regional comparisons if a block or a region obtains an index exceeding 1.00 it is considered as having 'more than its share', whereas if it obtains a quotient of less than 1.00 (the quotient can never be less than zero) it is taken as having 'less than its share'. These two categories are also termed as 'over-represented' and 'under-represented' respectively.

Percentage of cultivable land to total area for cultivation is more unevenly distributed in the district during 1991-92. Among blocks the percentage of cultivable land ranges from 1.0 to 11.0 with a minimum of 1.78 per cent in Ramkola and a maximum of 10.19 per cent in Rampur Karkhana giving an average of 4.95 per cent for the district. Table 2.2 shows that about twenty blocks out of twenty nine record cultivable land below district level which explains sharper variations found at the higher side of the slab. The graded distribution depicts that a distinct region of very high percentage of cultivable land (8 and over) is found in south-central part of the district (Fig. 2.3). It is composed of six blocks of Desai, Deoria (8.21), Baitalpur (8.75), Rampur Karkhana (10.19), Deoria (9.55), Bhatni (9.63) and Salempur (8.84). Khadda block of the same slab lies in the extreme north. This region is surrounded by the blocks of 4 to 6 per cent cultivable lands which form almost a dominant continuous belt. In the immediate north of this zone a belt of relatively very low percentage of cultivable land (below 4 per cent) is observed. This zone comprises five blocks, namely Nebua Naurangia, Bishnupura, Ramkola, Padrauna and Tamkuhi. Bhatpar Rani block (3.45 percent) of the same slab lies in the extreme south-eastern part. It may be noted that the central blocks of the district depict the highest share of cultivable land. It tends to decline northward and southward but the rate of decline is found to be relatively sharp to the south. The serpentine structure of perennial river—Little Gandak and the seasonal streams, namely, Khanua, Doranchi, Kurna, etc. cover relatively large areas of the central blocks of the district.

With few exceptions almost the same patterns of distribution of cultivable land by L.Q. are observed as have been depicted in Fig. 2.3 of the block-wise percentage distribution of cultivable land. Fig. 2.4 shows that high over-represented blocks are located in the southern half where they constitute a prominent region comprised of Salempur, Bhatni, Bhaluani, Deoria, Baitalpur and Rampur Karkhana. This high value of L.Q. is mainly shared by perennial river and some seasonal streams. The three blocks of over representation (1.00 – 1.49 L.Q.) are found in the eastern part of the district where they do not form an identifiable zone. Relatively high proportion of share of cultivable land in these blocks is caused by Jharhi and Khanua Nala.

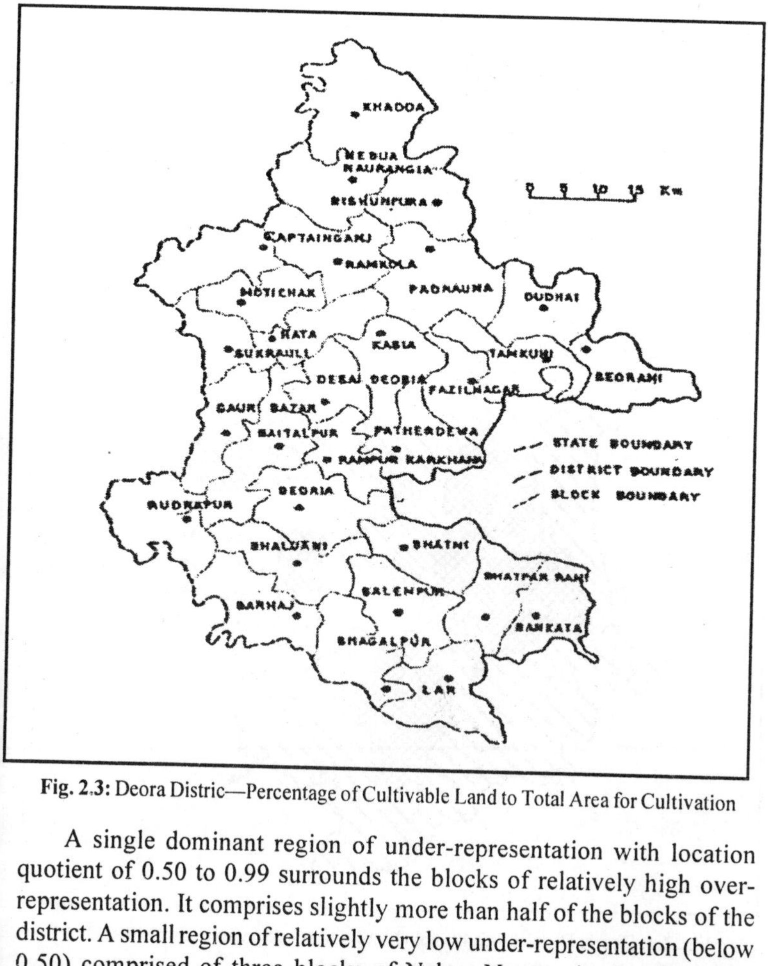

Fig. 2.3: Deora Distric—Percentage of Cultivable Land to Total Area for Cultivation

A single dominant region of under-representation with location quotient of 0.50 to 0.99 surrounds the blocks of relatively high over-representation. It comprises slightly more than half of the blocks of the district. A small region of relatively very low under-representation (below 0.50) comprised of three blocks of Nebua Naurangia, Ramkola and Padrauna, lies in the northern part which belongs to tarai belt of the district. In this region modern technological inputs, normal climatic conditions and maximum area under sugarcane cultivation has aided to maximize the use of land throughout the year. These lands are not even kept vacant to maintain soil fertility.

Population Pressure

The term 'population pressure' although widely used in the literature is difficult to define and is prone to subjective interpretation. It is here

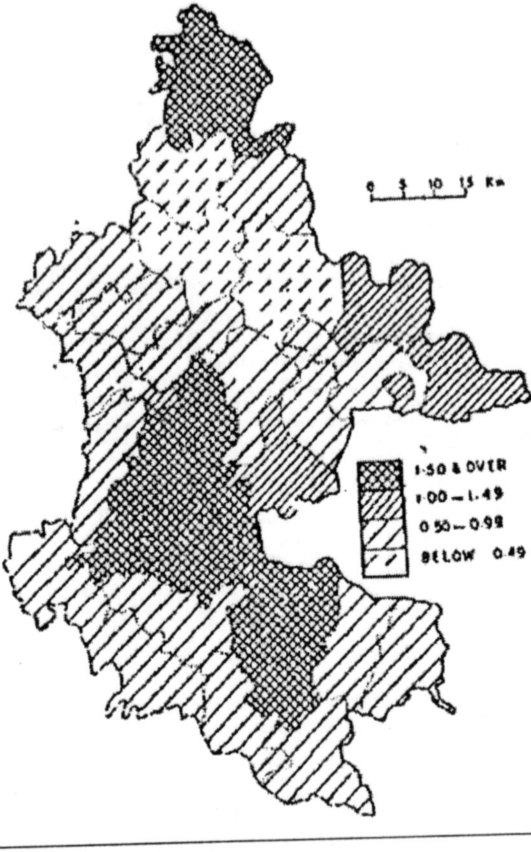

Fig. 2.4: Deoria District—Cultivable Land (Index of Specialization) 1991-92

defined as a situation where population growth, usually in combination with other related influences, make it difficult for some or all, of the population in area to maintain their need. Poverty becomes more widespread, food shortage more frequent and in some circumstances the environmental resources of the area may be damaged and a cycle of degradation established.

In the present analysis the block-wise distribution of population pressure i.e., the number of agricultural workers per 100 hectares of net sown area in 1991-92 varies from 173 in Rudrapur to 273 in Sukrauli block whereas the district average accounts for 236. Since the range of variations in the micro level study is considerably large, the pattern of regional distribution of the population pressure in the district may be projected systematically by grouping the blocks into four grades of below 200, 200-225, 225-250 and 250 and over. The principal feature revealed by this graded distribution is that in about two-thirds of the blocks the population pressure is above 225. This indicates the sharper and striking variations are confined to the blocks which are at higher side of the scale. Fig. 2.5 depicts that the blocks under the first grade of 250 and over form two distinct zones in central part. They are separated vertically by second grade blocks of population pressure. As many as one-third of the blocks falls under the grade of 225-250. With the exception of Tamkuhi and Gauri-Bazaar, all the blocks of this slab form a narrow belt stretched from Bishunpura in north to Deoria in south. Two small

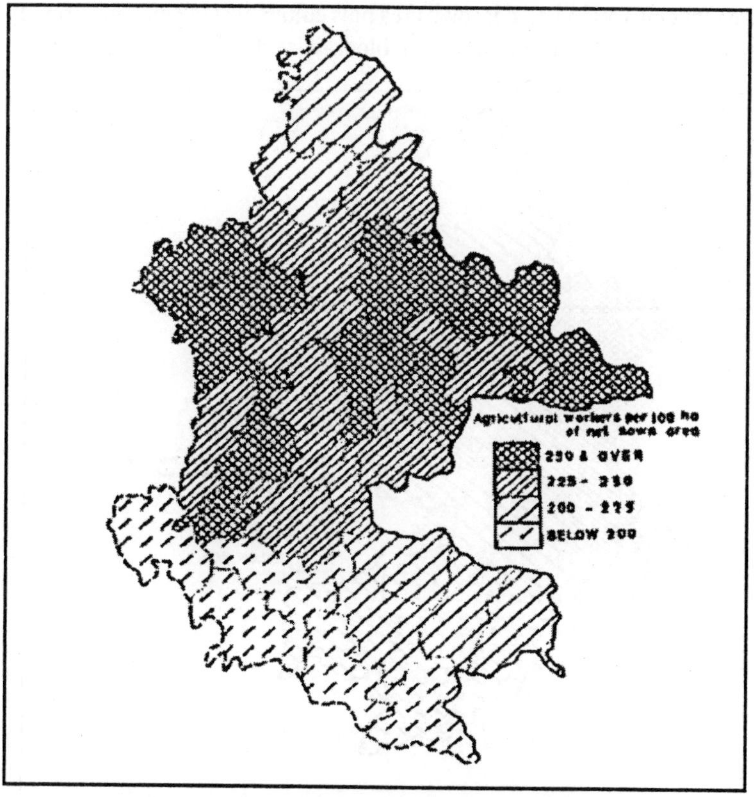

Fig 2.5: Deoria District—Population Pressure 1991-92

zones of 200-225 population pressure are notable in the district: one comprised of four blocks of Salempur, Bhatni, Bhatpar Rani and Bankata lies in the extreme south-eastern part, and the second zone, though less prominent is formed by only two blocks of northern part. They against their population pressure are Nebua Naurangia (224) and Khadda (223). Fig. 2.5 shows that five blocks of relatively very low population pressure of below 200 delimit a notable zone in the southern part. These blocks against their population pressure are Rudrapur (173), Bhaluani (174), Bhagalpur (181), Barhaj (182) and Lar (188).

Proposed Population Pressure

The ratio between the number of agricultural population and the proposed area for cultivation i.e., net sown area plus cultivable land may be termed proposed population pressure. The block-wise distribution of this ratio

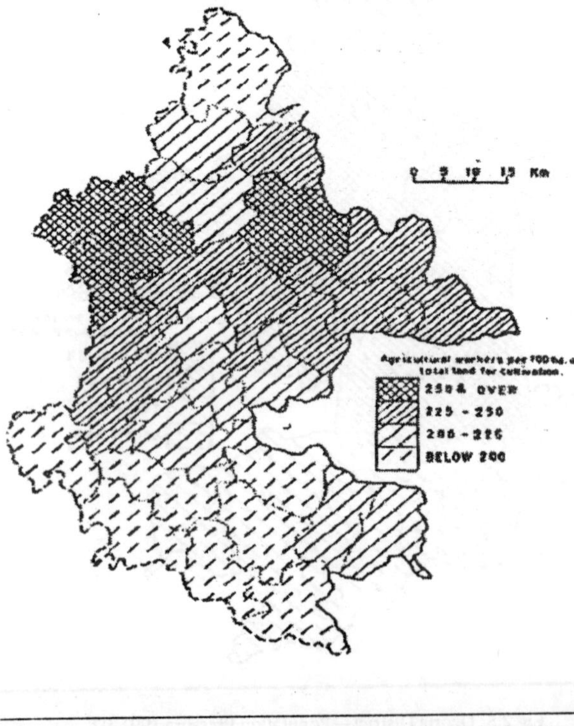

Fig. 2.6: Deoria District—Proposed Population Pressure 1991-92

for the year 1991-92 corroborates that proposed population pressure for the district as a whole is about 14 points less than that of the actual pressure. The areas of relatively high percentage of cultivable land may get their ratio minimised if the full use of cultivable land is encouraged.

There are however notable regional variations. The exact population pressure of relatively very high slab of 250 and over shares one-third of the blocks but the proposed population pressure under the slab is spread over only four blocks of Padrauna, Captainganj, Motichak and Sukrauli (Fig. 2.6). About one-third blocks are confined to very low slab of below 200 population pressure and the majority of them form a prominent region in southern part of the district. The majority of the blocks of relatively very high population pressure (250 and over) have been incorporated to the grade of high proposed population pressure (225-250) and spread over northern half of the district. Some of the blocks lie under the same grade of 200-225 but they were previously reported at the higher side, now they are registered to be at the lower side of the grade. They are Bankata (207), Bhatpar Rani (209) and Nebua Naurangia (219). But the remaining five blocks of this slab are drawn from the previously high population pressure slab of 225-250. They are Desai Deoria (219), Rampur Karkhana (210), Patherdewa (211), Deoria (208) and Ramkola (223).

Conclusion

There is a continuous fluctuation in cultivable land resources since 1961-62. A deviation of about 2000 ha of cultivable land is observed during 1961-62 to 1991-92. The fluctuation in agricultural employment during the same period was caused by population growth and change in the definition of workers. The latter aided to decline in agricultural employment during 1961-71. The continuous quinquennial increase in employment was observed since 1971. It may be pointed out that the gradient of change in cultivable land was gentler than that of agricultural employment.

The distribution of cultivable land among the blocks during 1991-92 shows sharp variation at the higher side of the scale. The areas drained by seasonal streams and the perennial river Gandak have relatively high proportion of share of cultivable land. The northern belt i.e., tarai records maximum use of land under sugarcane cultivation due to normal climatic condition and modern technological input. Population pressure discussed in this chapter depicts that the sharper and striking variations are confined to the blocks which lie at the higher side of the scale. Moderate level of pressure is observed in almost central part.

The proposed population pressure for the district as a whole is about 14 points less than that of the actual population pressure. The areas having high proportion of cultivable land may get their population pressure minimised if full use of cultivable land is initiated and moreover, double and triple cropping system is encouraged. It may be inferred that if cultivable and current fallow lands are brought under cultivation the growing population may be fed easily without any extra inputs except irrigation at least upto the first quadrant of twenty-first century.

References

Ackerman (1967), Population, Natural Resources and Technology, *The Annals of the American Academy of Political & Social Sciences*, No. 369, pp. 84-97.

Allan, W.A. (1949), Studies in African Land Usage in Northern Rhodesia, *Rhodes-Livingston Papers*, No. 15, London: Oxford.

Bernard, F.E. (1977), Population Pressure: A Preliminary Assessment with Special Reference to Kenya, *East African Geographical Review*, No. 15, pp. 43-68.

Boserup, E. (1965), *The Conditions of Agricultural Growth*, London: Faber.

Clarke, C.G. (1970), An Over-crowded Metropolis: Kingston, Jamaica, in *Geography and a Crowding World*, Edited by Wilbur Zelinsky *et al.*, New York: Oxford University Press.

Clarke, J.I. (1973), Population Pressure on Resources: The Problem of Evaluation, in *Resources and Population*, Edited by B. Benjamin *et al.*, London, Academic Press.

District Census Handbook (1981), *Deoria: Primary Census.*

Easterlin, R.A. (1967), Effects of Population Growth on the Economic Development of Developing Countries, *The Annals of the American Academy of Political and Social Science*, No. 369, pp. 98-106.

Gleave, M.B. and White, H.P. (1968), Population Density and Agricultural System in West Africa, in *Environment and Land-use in Africa*, Edited by M.F. Thomas an1 G.W. Whitlington, London: Methuess.

Munir A. and Siddiqui, F.A. (1983), Population Pressure and Agricultural Product vity in Gonda District, *The Geographer*, Vol. 30, No. 1, pp. 94-99.

3

HYDROGEOLOGICAL ENVIRONMENT AND WATER RESOURCE EVALUATION OF AN ALLUVIAL AQUIFER IN THE CENTRAL GANGA PLAIN

ASAD UMAR & M. SAMI AHMAD

Introduction

The Ganga alluvial plain is a densely populated region and is one of the largest groundwater repositories of the world. But rising population, rapid urbanization, unsustainable agricultural practices and growth of industries have put greater stress on groundwater resources. For sustainable water development understanding of hydrogeological framework and a refined quantitative evaluation of groundwater resources at micro level should be the focus of future studies.

This will provide an understanding of the aquifer system and their lateral and vertical extensions, which will contribute to the effective water management. This chapter is an attempt in this direction. The study area, Sidhpura block lies between the latitude 27°33′ to 27° 45′N and longitude 78°47′ to 79°0′ E and falls in the survey of India topo sheet No. 54 I/14 (Fig. 3.1).

Physiographically, from east to west Etah district is divisible into three distinct units; the low valley of the Ganga, the Central upland and the low valley of Kali. Sidhpura block forms a part of Central upland and low valley of Kali and is spread over an area of 260 km^2. General slope of the block is due south-east. River Kali drains through the southern margin of the study area.

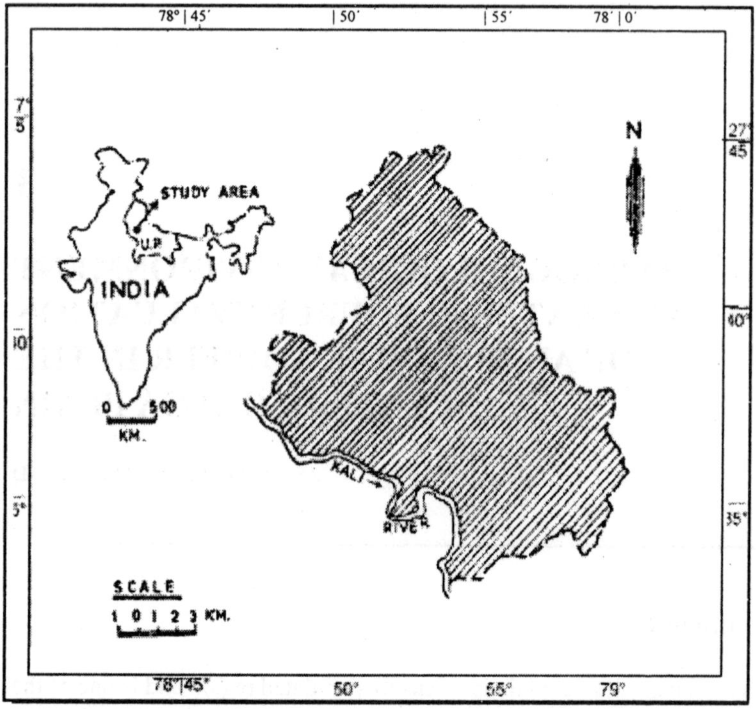

Fig. 3.1: Location Map of the Study Area

Hydrography

The climate of the area is a humid sub-tropical type. It is divided into three seasons: the cold, the hot and the monsoon season. The cold season extends from November to February. January is the coldest month with temperature below 10°C. During the summer season May is the hottest month with temperature up to 42°C. This is followed by the monsoon season. Heavy rainfall occurs during July, August and September. Usually 70-80 per cent of the total annual rainfall occurs during this period. The average annual rainfall in the area is 700 mm. For the greater part of the year, high temperature conditions prevail over the plain and a large amount of water is lost through evapotranspiration.

Regional Setting

The Ganga plain is an active foreland basin formed as a result of the continent-continent collision of the Indian plate with the Asian plate.

Due to this collision, the northern margin of the Indian plate with its sedimentary cover was sliced, piled up and raised forming the Himalayan mountains. Rivers originating from the Himalayas and the Peninsula deposit their sediment load in the world's largest alluvial tract, which is known as Indo-Gangetic Alluvial tract. Its central part is drained by the Ganga River system and is known as the Ganga plain (I.B. Singh, 1996). The Sidhpura block is a part of the Central Ganga plain and is situated of the left bank of the river Kali.

Geologically, the Bundelkhand granite forms the basement complex which is unconformably overlain by the Bijawar, Upper Bhander shale of Upper Proterozoie age and in turn is farther overlain by the quaternary alluvium. The quaternary alluvium consists of alternate beds of the sand and clay with occasional intercalation of calcareous concretion. The basement topography comprises alternate ridges and depression.

Hydrogeological Framework

The evolution of the aquifer in the fluvial system is dependent upon the hydrodynamics of the flow regime, geology and topography of the area leading to the terrigenous clastic depositional system. In the area of study coarser clastics in the alluvial sequences form the major repository of groundwater.

Aquifer Geometry

By aquifer geometry means length, width, thickness and its vertical and lateral extents (Walton, 1970). Based on the lithological logs of the bore holes drilled by State government, a fence diagram has been constructed (Fig. 3.2), which reveals the presence of one to two tier aquifer system down to a depth of 130 m b.g.1. and their lateral and vertical extents. Generally the aquifer occurs in alternation with the clay beds which at places pinches out giving thereby a single aquifer system down to 130 m depth. These aquifers are divided in two categories.

Top Aquifer

The top aquifer in the area occurs just below top clay layer and extends down to a depth of 50 m b.g.1. comprising mainly fine to medium

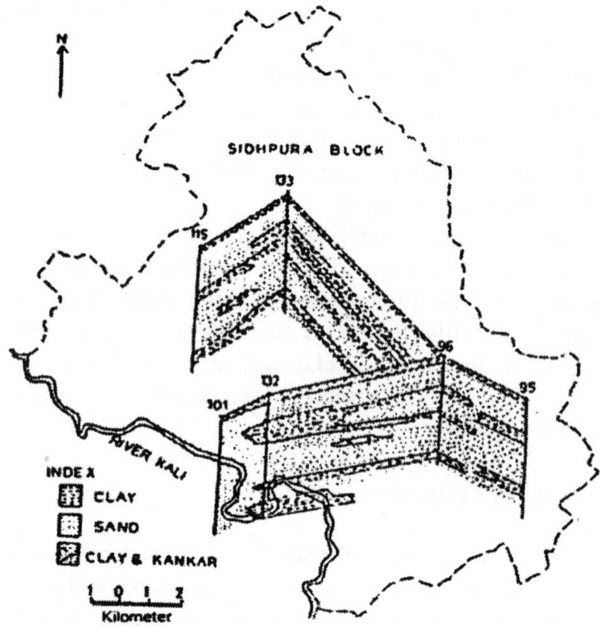

Fig. 3.2: Fence Diagram showing Aquifer Disposition in the Study Area

sand. Groundwater in this aquifer zone occurs under phreatic condition. But due to excessive withdrawal of groundwater they are moderately strained.

The groundwater development through shallow tubewells has been done in a very big way much higher than the quantum of the average annual recharge leading to the declining water level. The rapid fall in water level is clearly indicated by the hydrograph of the key observation wells at Sidhpura and Bakawali. The rate of declining water level is observed as 0.204 m/year at Sidhpura and 0.134 m/year at Bakawali. [Fig. 3.3 (a) and (b)].

Deep Aquifers

Aquifer groups occurring below 50 m b.g.1. depth comprising fine through medium to coarse sand mixed with gravels are considered as deep aquifer. The ground water development of these aquifers in the block have been done through deep tubewells, where the discharge ranges from 32 to 52 l.p.s. respectively, with economic drawdown.

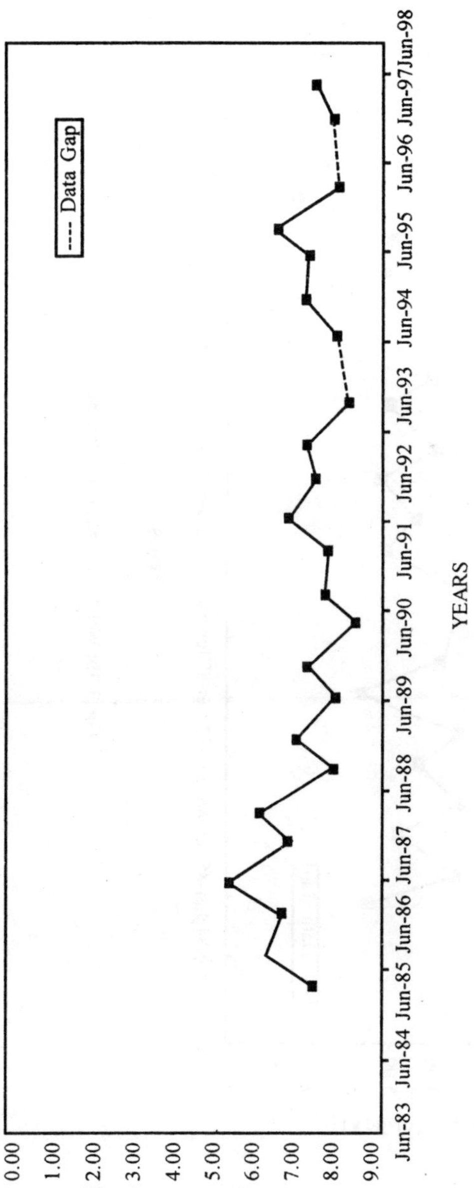

Fig. 3.3a: Well Hydrograph of Bakawali

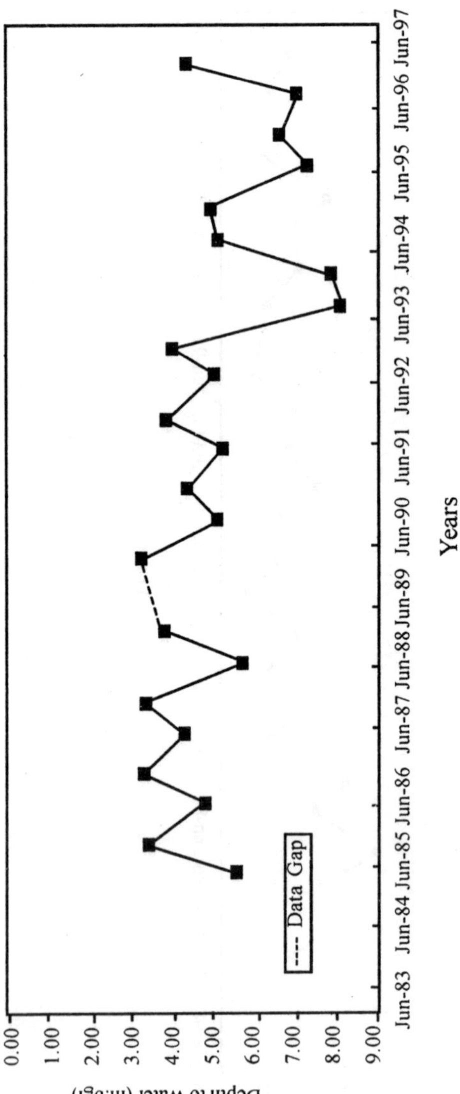

Fig. 3.3b: Well Hydrograph of Sidhpura

The hydraulic properties of the aquifer is determined by analyzing pumping test data where the value of transmissivity (*T*) is 2178 m^2/day, storativity (*S*) is 1.12×10^{-5} and hydraulic conductivity (*K*) is 121 m/day. These properties and aquifer geometry determine the response of water level in an aquifer to pumpage. The above values show that the deeper aquifer behave as a confined aquifer.

Groundwater Regime

Depth to Water Level

The water level in a well indicates the elevation at which atmospheric pressure equals the hydrostatic pressure in the aquifer (Todd, 1980). The pre-monsoon depth to water level ranges between 2.50 m to 6.75 m b.g.1. The maximum depth to water level was recorded at Bakawali and minimum at village Basai. The post-monsoon depth to water level ranges between 1.85 to 5.10 m b.g.1. In post-monsoon the maximum area is covered by 2-4 m zone.

Measuring the fluctuations of water levels is a key element in any study of groundwater resources (Freeze and Cherry, 1979). The seasonal water level fluctuation ranges between 0.95 to 1.75 m. The magnitude of the fluctuation is governed by the water bearing properties of the material in the zone of water level fluctuation (Karanth, 1997).

Movement of Groundwater

Fig. 3.4 shows the pre-monsoon watertable contour map of the block where the altitude of watertable ranges between 164 m in northwest to 154 m in the southeast, which shows that the regional groundwater flow is due southeast. However, the local flow of groundwater is towards the Kali River, which indicates that the river Kali is an effluent stream. The hydraulic gradient in the area ranges between 3.33 m/km to 0.29 m/km. The former value shows steep gradient while the latter shows a flat gradient in the area of study. A single groundwater mound is observed along the lower Ganga canal, which is formed due to excessive seepage into shallow aquifer from the canal, which passes through the northern margin of the study area.

Groundwater Resource Potential

The basic objective of groundwater resource evaluation is to estimate the total quantity of groundwater resource available and their future

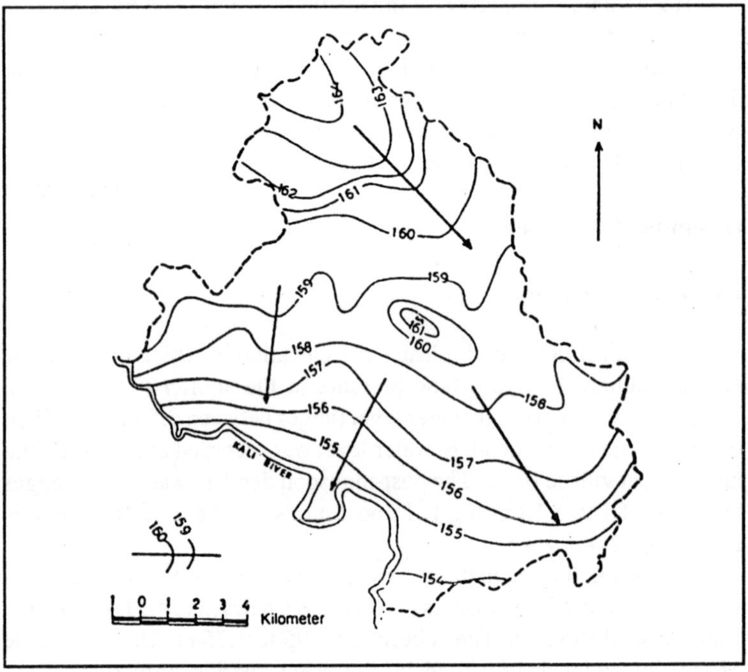

Fig 3.4: Depth to Water Table Coutour Map

supply potential to predict conflict between supply and demand and to provide a scientific database for rational water resources utilisation (Earth Summit, 1992). The groundwater resource estimation in the study area has been done by water level fluctuation and specific yield method.

Annual Recharge

Monsoon recharge (ham) = (Geographical area × Sp. Yield × W.T. fluctuation) + Gross Kharif Draft – (Monsoon canal seepage + Monsoon recharge from surface water irrigation + Monsoon recharge from ground-water irrigation)

$$\times \frac{\text{(Normal monsoon rainfall)}}{\text{(Average monsoon rainfall)}}$$

+ Monsoon recharge from surface water irrigation

I. Monsoon Recharge

Geographical area	(ha)	=	26000
Pre-monsoon water level	(mbgl)	=	5.29
Post-monsoon water level	(mbgl)	=	4.24
Water level fluctuation	(m)	=	1.05
Specific yield	(%)	=	15%
IMD normal yearly rainfall	(mm)	=	716.8
IMD normal monsoon rainfall	(mm)	=	647.90
IMD normal non-monsoon rainfall	(mm)	=	43.50
Average monsoon rainfall	(mm)	=	667.17
Gross Kharif Draft	(ham)	=	1055.30

$$[(26000 \times 0.15 \times 1.05) + 1055.30 - (95.36 + 769.18 + 316.59)]$$

$$\times \frac{647.90}{667.17} + 95.36 + 769.18 = 4869.15 \text{ ham.}$$

II. Non-monsoon Rainfall Recharge

Infiltration factor	25%
Non-monsoon rainfall recharge	331.48 ham.

Recharge from Surface Sources

1. *Recharge from Canal*

Applied seepage factor	=	15 ham/day/10^6 sqm
Non-monsoon recharge	=	317.84 ham
Monsoon recharge	=	95.36 ham
Total yearly recharge	=	413.20 ham

2. *Recharge from Irrigation Return Flow*

Applied seepage factor	=	30%
Non-monsoon recharge	=	998.52 ham
Monsoon	=	769.18 ham

3. *Recharge from Tanks*

Applied seepage factor	=	55 cm/year

Total recharge = 8.40 ham.

Potential recharge from shallow watertable area = 1728.8 ham.

Total annual recharge available = monsoon recharge + Non-monsoon recharge.

= 4869.15 + 331.48 + 317.48 + 998.5 + 8.40 + 1728.8

= 8253. 86 ham

Net annual recharge = 85% of total annual recharge

= 7015.78 ham. or 70.16 MCM

Groundwater Draft

1. *Dugwells with PS*

Nos.	=	2666
Unit Draft per year (ham)	=	1.4
Monsoon Draft (ham)	=	933.10
Non-monsoon Draft (ham)	=	2799.30
Gross Yearly Draft (ham)	=	3732.40

2. *Shallow tubewells*

Nos.	=	124
Unit Draft per year (ham)	=	2.2
Monsoon Draft (ham)	=	68.20
Non-monsoon Draft (ham)	=	204.60
Gross Yearly Draft (ham)	=	272.80

3. *Deep tubewells*

Nos.	=	12
Unit Draft per year (ham)	=	18
Monsoon Draft (ham)	=	54.00
Non-monsoon Draft (ham)	=	162.00
Gross Yearly Draft (ham)	=	216.20
Total Gross Yearly Draft	=	**4221.2 ham**
Net Annual Draft	=	70% of Gross annual draft
	=	2954.84 ham. or 29.55 MCM

Groundwater Balance (ham)

= Net annual recharge available for development – net annual draft.

= 7015.78 – 2954.84 = 4060.94 or 40.61 MCM

Stage of Groundwater Development (%)

$$= \frac{\text{Net annual draft}}{\text{Net annual recharge}} \times 100$$

$$= 7015.78/2954.84 = 42.11\%$$

The study shows that only 43% of the groundwater resources of the block have been utilized so far. And as per NABARD's norm the area falls under the white category having ample scope for large-scale groundwater development through shallow and deep tubewells.

Conclusion

The study shows that a refined quantitative evaluation of groundwater resource potential is possible only through micro level groundwater studies, encompassing the homogeneities and inhomogeneities in the aquifer system.

It is observed that large scale groundwater development in the block through shallow farmers tubewells with complete disregard to proper well spacing, has given a declining trend of watertable as evident from the observation wells at Bakawali and Sidhpura. Therefore restrictions should be imposed for further development of groundwater through shallow tubewells. The utilizable groundwater resource potential of the block is estimated as 39.94 MCM. Given this amount of recharge available and also the size and hydraulic properties of the aquifer, prospects for the development of high capacity deep tubewells with proper well spacing in the study area appears favourable.

Acknowledgements

The authors acknowledge the help and co-operation of Prof. S.M. Zainuddin, Chairman, Department of Geology, AMU, Aligarh.

References

Earth Summit (1992), Agenda 21, Programme of Action for Sustainable Development. The United Nations Conference on Environment & Development, Rio-de-Janeiro, Brazil, pp. 174-75.

Freeze, R.A.; Cherry, A. (1979), Groundwater, Published by Prentice-Hall Inc., Englewood Cliffs, p. 604.

Karanth, K.R. (1997), *Groundwater Assessment Development and Management*, Tata McGraw Hill Publishing Company Limited, New Delhi, p. 720.

Khanna, S.P. (1992), Hydrogeology of Central Ganga Plain, Uttar Pradesh, In: *Gangetic Plain: Terra Incognita*, (Ed. Singh, I.B.) pp. 23-27.

Singh, I.B. (1996), Geological Evolution of Ganga Plain – An over view. *Jour., of Palaeontological Society of India*. Vol. 41, pp. 99-137.

Todd, D.K., (1980), *Groundwater Hydrology*, New York, John Wiley & Sons, p. 336

Walton, W.C. (1970), *Groundwater Resources Evaluation*, McGraw-Hill Series in *Water Resources and Environmental Engineering* McGraw-Hill Book Company, New York, p. 664.

4

POPULATION GROWTH AND AGRICULTURAL CHANGE IN INDIA SINCE INDEPENDENCE

RAVENDRA KUMAR SHARMA

Introduction

Indian population grew from 361 million in 1951 to 846 million in 1991 and it is still increasing at the rate 1.8 per cent annually (NSS, 1998). India comprises approximately 16 per cent of the World's total population and has only 2.4 per cent of the World's land area. Besides growth in population, increases in purchasing power associated with economic growth enhance not only the demand of foodgrains, but also the demand of other agriculture products. Despite the population growth, there is a sustainable increase in food production, which has increased from 51 million tonnes in 1950-51 to 198.96 million tonnes in 1996-97 (*Economic Survey* 1997-98). The net per capita availability of foodgrains per day increased from around 395 grams in year 1951 to 510 grams in year 1996. It is compound result of increase in cropping area, irrigation facilities, and use of multiple cropping and high yield variety seeds. Today, country is self-sufficient in food production.

While production has increased, the increase in the population and improvement in the consumption expenditure, following improving per capita income, resulting in the higher demand of foodgrains and other agriculture production. On the basis of trends in the consumption and income, Ninth Plan estimate that the total foodgrain requirement will be 220.5 million tonnes in 2001-02. This will mean an annual agricultural growth of 6.5 percent. But looking in the past performance in the growth rate of foodgrains it seems to be impossible. As the land, a vital resource of agriculture production has almost reached the maximum limit that can be ploughed under cultivation (*The Hindu Agriculture Survey*, 1995).

The availability of required food is not only single problem of rapidly growing population. The rapid population growth has several influences on the economy and society; i.e. employment is another problem. As in the developing world major proportion of the population derive means of their livelihood from the primary sector (especially agriculture). Even highly developed countries (e.g. USA, UK, Germany and Japan etc.), before industrial revolution, were also dependent on the agriculture up to the extent of 80 to 90 per cent of their population, but today hardly 10 per cent population of these countries is engaged in agriculture. In India, even after fifty years of independence position is quite different as 65 per cent of the work force is engaged in agriculture, and it contributes about 30 per cent of national income.

It is clear that rapidly increasing population has resulted in the increased labour force, on the other hand non-agricultural sector is not producing the required number of jobs. Therefore the population pressure and the continuous fragmentation of the land has resulted in diminishing size of average land holding which is not suitable (economically and practically) for application of improved agricultural implements and recent technologies. The average size of land holding has reduced from 1.71 hectares in 1960-61 to 0.74 hectare in 1991-92 (NSS, 1992). The increased number of small, marginal and landless workers has resulted in reduced capacity of the investment which adversely affects the productivity in long run.

Population and agriculture are highly correlated. On the one hand population remains as an important input, of the agricultural production, in the form of labourer, cultivator and innovator. On the other hand the larger size of population have a negative impact as it reduces the capacity of investment and size of land for cultivation. The forward and backward linkage of the agriculture to rest of the economy helps in improving the quality of the life. So it is interesting to examine trends in population and agriculture as well linkages over the years.

Review of Literature

The relationship between agriculture and population is not new; perhaps it is as old as a man himself is.

Malthus, in his pioneer work on the insufficient land supply and food production recognised the implication of a growing population on the use of the available resources. Recently Bongats (1996) said that a large increase in agriculture output would be needed to satisfy increased population growth and improvement in diets in the developing World. Food demand will be greatest in the high population density countries like India and China, Indonesia, Pakistan. In his study Greenspan (1994) has found that urban growth has moved on to farmland and farmer have been pushed on to more marginal lands or have become landless. In 1994, Ganguli has tried to study the consequence of population growth. He found that increased population pressure lead to deforestation, soil erosion, and decline in the agriculture production, he suggest that crop choice is determined by the climate, monsoon and population pressures. In his study in Bangladesh, Choudhary (1976) found a negative and highly statistical significant relationship between density and per capita rice production and suggested that higher productivity per worker found in low-density districts.

According to Prof. V.K.R.V. Rao (1974), India requires a minimum growth rate of 4 per cent in foodgrains and 6 per cent in the non-foodgrains during the reset of this century to meet the basic requirement of the economy for food and agricultural raw materials. In his district level analysis Mitra (1978) found that the high productive districts in India have high density and their productivity is much higher than average productivity for country. In same type of study in Madhya Pradesh, Jain (1996) found that the average size of holding is very small in high density districts and the productivity of these districts is low as compared to the low-density districts. He suggests that the decline in the net sown area per person since 1961 must be offset with population control. In his case study of Ahmednagar district (Maharashtra), Vaidya (1996) found that growth of net cropped area is much less than population growth in most of the talukas. The population pressure on the land was particularly acted in the more irrigated area. According to Bhalla and Singh (1997) the productivity levels of agriculture workers has remained quite low in India because of low yield and as a result of excessive population pressure on land.

In his study Mishra (1996), said that high population density and rapid population growth during the post-Independence periods, together with major changes in mortality and industrialization, are responsible for the significant changes in land-use, cropping intensity, irrigation intensity, and fertilizer intensity in India.

Need for the Study

The literature suggested that Population and Agriculture are highly inter-related. A lot of studies have proved this relationship, but all these available studies had either devoted to food supply or population density. Thus there is a need of a study which can explore the new dimensions of this relationship i.e. change in holding pattern, employment elasticity etc. adequately.

Objectives of Study

The main objectives of this study are given below:

1. To examine the trends in the population size, growth, and its distribution in rural and urban area.
2. To examine the trends in agriculture production, productivity, area under cultivation, distribution of land holdings and elasticity of labour absorption in agriculture sector.
3. To examine the relationship between agriculture productivity (yield) and its inputs i.e. irrigation, HYVs, agriculture workers, and fertilizer consumption, etc.

Sources of Data

1. Data related to area, production and yield of agriculture output are collected from various issues of 'Area and Production of Principle Crops in India' and CMIE reports.
2. Data on agriculture inputs like fertilizer and power consumption, tractors and oil engines and wholesale price index for agricultural products are collected from CMIE reports.
3. Data on gross capital formation in agriculture and GDP in agriculture sector are taken from CMIE reports and National Accounts Statistics.
4. Data on rainfall is obtained from various issues of Statistical Abstract of India.
5. Time series data for total population, agricultural population and economic active agricultural population are collected from various issues of Food and Agricultural Organization (FAG).
6. Population data for census years is collected from corresponding Census publications.

Methodology

In order to examine the above objectives the following techniques have been employed in the present study.

Trend Analysis

Trends in both agriculture and population computed in tabular form. Annual growth rate for population and agriculture production, area and yield has been computed by exponential method.

The Elasticity of Labour Absorption

Elasticity of Labour Absorption is computed by log linear equation of the form

$$\log_e(EAAP/H) + \log_e(c) + \log_e(VO/H)$$

where VO = Agriculture output (in Rs.)
H = Net sown area (in hectares)
EAAP = Economic Active Agriculture Population
C = Constant

Correlation and Agriculture Production Function

We have taken the help of factor analysis to select the appropriate variables for present study, and we chose a set of seven variables out of 26 variables selected from literature. These are fertilizer consumption (kg./per hectare), area under the high yield varieties (in million hectares), average rainfall (in millimetres)[1], percentage of irrigated land, number of tractors per lakh hectares, percentage of agriculture population in total population, and percentage of economically active agriculture population in total agriculture population[2]. Yield has taken as a dependent variable for present study, as most of the scholars had suggested to take yield as dependent variable in their respective studies, (Dandekar, 1980; Rao, 1980; Sharma & Gandhi, 1990).

Production Function

Using time series data (1950-51 to 1992-93) in an attempt to assess the relationship between inputs and outputs carried out production function analysis. This was done on an input-output basis without bringing the prices in analysis. Input prices are expected to reflect the input use. Finally the percentage of agriculture population in total population was also dropped, since this accentuated the multi-collinearity and it was not found very useful also, especially when percentage of economic active agriculture population was already included as one variable.

There are three forms of Agriculture Production Function (APF), which are generally used (i.e. linear, Cobb-Douglas, and transcendental forms). Linear form is simplest but it is based on the crude assumption of constant marginal productivity. Cobb-Douglas form is also based on the crude assumption of constant elasticity, while transcendental form provide comparatively better result, as it can accommodate increasing, decreasing and classical production forms. But it doubles the number of parameters to be estimated i.e. reduce the degree of freedom. So for the sake of simplicity and assuming that APF follows a linear shape, linear form of APF has selected for the analysis.

Analysis and Discussion

Demographic Profile of India since Independence

Indis has the second largest population in the world, and it is still increasing at the rate 1.8 per cent annually. A few characteristic of it can be studied under the following headings.

Changes in Population Size, Distribution, Growth Rate, and Sex Ratio in India

Table 4.1 shows population size at the corresponding census years since India's independence. The total population of India has increased from 361.1 million in 1951 to 846.3 million in 1991, i.e., with a percentage increment of 134.4 percent. Whereas the rural population increased from 298.7 million in 1951 to 628.7 million in 1991, i.e., an increment of 110.5 percentage. The corresponding figures for urban population were 62.4 million in 1951 to 217.6 million in 1991 i.e., an increment of 248.7 percent. It is observed that the urban population has increased on a higher rate than the rural population. One of the possible reasons for the drastic increment in urban areas may be migration of rural population to urban areas. In the year 1951, only 17.3 per cent of total population were living in urban areas. In successive years it increased to 18 per cent and 19.9 per cent in 1961 and 1971 respectively. But after 1971 the urban population increased rapidly and in 1981 share of urban population increased to 23.3 per cent of the total population. The latest 1991 census reveals that 25.7 per cent of total population are living in urban areas which is compound result of increase in rural-urban migration and natural increment of population. It clearly indicates increase in the demand of urban land.

The growth rates of total population have always shows increasing trends, except in last decade (1981-91), when it declined to 2.11 per cent annually. During 1951 to 1971 population grew at an annual rate of 0.83 percent, while in last two decades it grew on an average rate of 2.09 per cent annually. But growth rate of rural population has started declining from census year 1971.

From Table 4.1 it is clear that the population density has gone up from 117 in 1951 to 274 persons per sq. km. in 1991 and it is continuously increasing since independence. In the year 1961, 25 persons were added per square kilometre and the density was increased to 142. Similarly the increase in number of persons per square kilometre for the years 1971, 1981 and 1991 are 35, 39 and 51 respectively. Population density has increased more than two times during time period 1951-1991.

Table 4.1: Population Size, Sex Ratio and Density in India

Year	*Population (in million)*			*Sex Ratio (per '000 male)*	*Density (Person/ sq.km.)*	*Annual Exp. Growth Rate (in percent)*		
	Total	*Rural*	*Urban*			*Total*	*Rural*	*Urban*
1951	361.1	298.7 (82.7)	62.4 (17.3)	946	117	—	—	—
1961	439.2	360.3 (82.0	78.9 (18.0)	941	142	1.96	1.87	2.35
1971	548.2	439.1 (80.1)	109.1 (19.9)	930	177	2.22	1.98	3.24
1981	685.2	525.7 (76.7)	159.5 (23.3)	934	216	2.23	1.8	3.8
1991*	846.3	628.7 (74.3)	217.6 (25.7)	927	274	2.11	1.79	3.11

*Including the population of Jammu and Kashmir, projecting by Standing Committee of Experts on population projection.
Source: Census (corresponding years).

The most serious concern to the country is the sex ratio defined as the number of females per 1000 males. Over the census years the sex ratio has always found adverse to the females. Sex ratio has been declining since 1951, except in during 1981, where it has slightly increased from 930 in 1971 to 934 in 1981. But again it reduced to 927 females for thousand males in 1991. One possible reasons of the decline in the sex ratio in 1991 would be the more under count of females in 1991 (*see* Srinivasan, 1996 p. 81).

Some Demographic Key Indicators

Table 4.2 shows the CBR, CDR, TFR, IMR and Life Expectancy for time period 1951-91. The crude birth rate has declined from 39.9 birth per thousand population in 1951 to 29.3 in 1991. At the same time crude death rate has also declined from 27.4 to 9.8 death per thousand population and over the period CDR has declined on a higher rate as compared to CBR. The maximum reduction in CBR, CDR has taken place during last decade (1981-91). The TFR has also declined from about 6 children per woman to 3.8 children per woman in 1991. Infant Mortality Rate (IMR, death of children, who do not celebrate their first birthday), per thousand have steadily declined to 80 in 1991 from 148 to 1951. Life expectancy at birth has significantly improved from 32.1 years to about 60 years during the same period.

Table 4.2: Key Demographic Indicator for India (1951-91)

Year	*C.B.R.*	*C.D.R.*	*T.F.R.*	*I.M.R.*	*Life Expectancy at Birth*
1951	39.9	27.4	5.96	148	32.1
1961	41.7	22.8	5.87	139	41.3
1971	41.1	18.9	5.94	129	45.6
1981	37.2	15.0	5.13	110	50.5
1991	29.3	9.8	3.8	80	58.9*

Sources: Srinivasan K. (1996).
**Economic Survey,* 1995-96.

Agriculture Production

Agriculture production has increased over the period significantly and it has been increasing continuously since the Green Revolution. It is product of change in cropping pattern, use of new technologies, fertilizer consumption land reforms etc. The changes can be studied under these headings.

Changes in the Cropping Pattern in India

In Table 4.3, three-year average is used to study the variation in the area under the cultivation of the different crops. Total gross sown area has increased from 1200.9 lakh hectares in 1949-52 to 1717.9 lakh hectares in 1990-93. If we observed the distribution of area under the different crops at different time periods, we find significant changes. In 1949-52, 81.5 per cent of total gross area was used to cultivate only food crops, which reduced to 77.7 per cent and 72.6 per cent in 1962-65 and 1990-93 respectively. The percentage share of area under non-food crops has increased from 18.5 per cent in 1949-52 to 27.4 per cent in 1990-93. Within the foodgrain crops the percentage share of the area in rice, *jowar*, *bajra* and pulses has declined from 1949-52 to 1990-93. While during the same period the percentage share of wheat has increased. Within the non-foodgrain crops the percentage share of area under all non-foodgrain crops has increased except in case of fibres, where it declined from 5.7 per cent in 1949-52 to 5 per cent of all area under the production of non-foodgrain crops in 1990-93. The percentage share of area under the plantation crop in total gross area under non-foodgrain crops has remained almost constant since independence. Area under the spice crops has increased about twice during this period.

Changes in Growth Rates of Sown Area, Production and Yield

The annual growth rate of area, production, and yield has shown in Table 4.4. To study the trends in the growth rates, it is always better to divide the time period in at least to two categories pre-Green Revolution period (1949-50 to 1965-66) and post-Green Revolution period (since 1966-67). For the present analysis the second categories (post-Green Revolution period) has been taken up to 1994-95. Before the Green Revolution area under the all crops has increased by a rate of 1.28 per cent annually where it was 2.56 per cent and 0.94 per cent for the non-foodgrains and foodgrains respectively. But in post-Green Revolution period the growth rate of area under the cultivation has declined for all crops. But the rate of non-foodgrain crops was remaining higher as compared to the food crops. If we divide the post-Green Revolution period in two periods (1966-67 to 1985-86 and 1986-87 to 1994-95), then we find that growth rate of area was negative for foodgrain crops in period 1986-87 to 1994-95. This shows that the diversification of the area from foodgrain crops to non-foodgrain crops and the rates of

Table 4.3: Cropping Pattern in India (1949-92)

Crops	*Gross Area (Lakh hect.)**			*Percentage Share in Total Gross Cropped Area**		
	1949-50 to 1951-52	*1962-63 to 1964-65*	*1990-91 to 1992-93*	*1949-50 to 1951-52*	*1962-63 to 1964-65*	*1990-91 to 1992-93*
Foodgrains	978.5	1177.9	1247.6	81.5	77.7	72.6
Rice	303.9	359.9	423.2	25.3	23.7	24.6
Wheat	96.6	135.0	239.5	8.0	8.9	13.9
Jowar	156.8	182.8	132.7	13.1	12.1	7.7
Bajra	92.7	113.0	103.6	7.7	7.5	6.0
Pulses	193.4	241.1	236.5	16.1	15.9	13.8
Non-foodgrains	222.3	337.7	470.3	18.5	22.2	27.4
Oilseed	114.2	169.7	267.2	9.5	11.2	15.6
Fibres	67.9	95.5	86.7	5.7	6.3	5.0
Plantation	4.7	6.1	10.3	0.4	0.4	0.6
Spices	7.6	13.6	20.0	0.6	0.9	1.2
Veg. & Fruits	7.7	12.0	23.6	0.6	0.8	1.4
Miscel. Crops	20.4	40.8	62.4	1.7	2.7	3.6
All Crops	1200.9	1515.7	1717.9	100.0	100.0	100.0

*Three-year average.
Source: C.M.I.E, Basics Statistics All India, August 1994, Mumbai.

Table 4.4: Annual Compound Growth Rates of Foodgrains and Non-Foodgrains

Periods	*Foodgrains*			*Non-Foodgrains*			*All Crops*		
	A	*P*	*Y*	*A*	*P*	*Y*	*A*	*P*	*Y*
1949-50 to 1965-66	0.940	1.022	0.062	2.563	2.756	-0.414	1.280	1.666	-0.034
1966-67 to 1985-86	0.551	3.796	2.812	1.052	2.831	1.761	0.688	3.431	2.419
1986-87 to 1994-95	-0.366	3.614	3.457	2.034	5.961	3.438	0.231	4.510	3.217
1966-67 to 1994-95	0.247	3.406	2.716	1.200	3.596	2.251	0.490	3.478	2.469
1949-50 to 1994-95	0.493	2.483	1.710	1.631	3.138	1.194	0.757	2.727	1.529

Note: A = Area. P = Production. Y = Yield.
Source: Government of India, *Area and Production of Principle Crops in India* 1994-95, New Delhi.

diversification have increased in the second period. The growth rate for production for all crops has increased from 1.67 per cent in pre-Green Revolution period to 3.48 per cent in the post-Green Revolution period.

The growth rate of production of non-foodgrain crops was higher in both the periods. But the growth rate of production for foodgrain crops was much higher in the period 1966-67 to 1985-86. It might be because in starting the Green Revolution was mainly concentrated to foodgrain crops. In the period 1986-87 to 1994-95 the growth rate of production for non-foodgrain crops was 5.96 per cent annually, which was much higher than the growth rate of production of foodgrain crops in the same period. There might be two possible reasons for this increment in the growth rate, one was increased in the area under the cultivation of non-foodgrain crops and another was use of high yield varieties in the production of non-foodgrain crops in this period.

Growth rate of the yield (productivity per hectare) has also shown the significant changes in pre- and post-Green Revolution period. Growth rate of yield was negative in pre-Green Revolution period for the productivity of all crops and non-foodgrain crops, but the growth rate of yield of foodgrain crops was almost (0.062 per cent annually) zero. In post-Green Revolution period the productivity of both foodgrain and non-foodgrain crops has increased. But in the period 1966-67 to 1985-86 the yield of the foodgrain crops has increased rapidly as compared to the increment in the yield of non-foodgrain crops. It might be because of the use of new seed in the production of foodgrain crops during the same period. In time period 1986-87 to 1994-95 the growth rate of yield for foodgrain crops remain higher as compared to non-foodgrain crops, but the improvement in rate was higher in case of non-foodgrain crops where it improved from 1.761 per cent annually in period 1966-67 to 1985-86, to 3.438 per cent annually in period 1986-87 to 1994-95, it might be because of increment in irrigation facility, fertilizer consumption, introduction of new seeds, and improvement in the prices of non-foodgrain crops.

Consequence of Population Pressure on Agriculture

The effect of population can be measured by different ways. Some scholar have been suggesting that the effect of the population can be measured in terms of land-man ratio, worker productivity and by cropping intensity, [Mishra (1996), Ganguli (1994), Bhalla (1997)].

Here, we have tried to examine the changes in cropping intensity, land-man ratio and agriculture workers' productivity. Table 4.5 shows the cropping intensity, production, and productivity of land and agriculture workers. Net sown area has increased from 118.75 million hectares in 1950-51 to 142.25 million hectares in 1990-91. During this period cropping intensity has increased from 111.06 per cent to 142.25 per cent which indicated that in 1950-51 only 11.06 per cent land has been used by more than one time, while in 1990-91, 30 per cent of the land has used more than once. Percentages increment of irrigated shows the increment in the irrigation facilities. In 1950-51 only 17.55 per cent of net sown area was irrigated, while in year 1990-91, 33.59 per cent of net sown area was irrigated. During the same period the irrigation intensity has also increased from 108.2 per cent to 130.75 percent. It indicated the more use of irrigated land for cropping. The value of agriculture production (at the price level of 1980-81) has increased from Rs. 2,37,410 million in 1950-51 to Rs. 6,56,530 million in 1990-91. It has increased by the rate of 2.576 per cent annually. The number of agriculture worker has also increased from 101.43 million in 1950-51 to 191.33 million in 1990-91. The number of agriculture workers shown a little decline in the 1970-71; it might be because of change in the definition of agriculture workers in 1971 census. The productivity of land and agriculture workers has increasing trends. But the productivity of land has increased on a higher rate in comparision to the productivity of agriculture worker. The net sown area has increased by a slower rate in comparision to the number of agriculture workers. So the land per worker has been reduced from 1.17 hectares in 1950-51 to 0.74 hectare in 1990-91. In the year 1970-71, some increment has been observed; it was because of decline in the numbers of the agriculture workers in the 1971 census. This reduction in agriculture workers was either due to diversification of agriculture worker to non-agriculture sector or may due to change in the definition of agriculture workers.

Changes in the Distribution of the Operational Holding

Table 4.6 shows real picture of the operational holdings in India. A size of operational holding less than a minimum optimum size, decrease the efficiency of investment and increased the wastage of the land (Dutta & Sundharam 1995). From Table 4.6 we can easily found that more and more holding are coming in the marginal category over the periods. In the year 1960-61, 39.10 per cent of the holding came under marginal category which have only 22.6 per cent of the total operational area and have an average size of 0.46 hectare. The large category has only 4.50 per cent of total operational holdings and has 29.0 per cent of the total operational area which has an average size of the 16.98 hectares, which is about 37 times more than the average size of

Table 4.5: Productivity of Land and Worker in India

Year	*Net Sown Area (NSA)*	*Crops Intensity*	*Production*	*Irrigated Area*		*Value of Ag. Sector (at 1980-81 price)*	*Agriculture Worker*	*Productivity of Worker (at 1980-81 price)*	*Productivity of Land (at 1980-81 price)*	*Land-Man Ratio*
				Net	*Per. of NSA*					
	(mil. hec)	*(%)*	*(mil. ton)*	*(mil. hec)*	*(%)*	*(mil. Rs.)*	*(mil.)*	*(Rs.)*	*(Rs.)*	*(H/W)*
1950-51	118.75	111.06	158.24	20.85	17.55	237410	101.43	2340.63	1999.24	1.171
1960-61	133.20	114.69	222.64	24.66	18.51	319950	136.18	2349.46	2402.03	0.978
1970-71	138.77	116.93	277.97	30.2	21.76	402140	129.96	3094.34	2897.89	1.068
1980-81	140.00	123.31	330.39	38.72	27.28	466490	156.74	2976.20	3332.07	0.893
1990-91	142.25	130.69	480.22	47.78	33.59	656530	191.33	3431.40	4615.33	0.743

Annual Compounded Growth Rate (in %)

Periods	*Net Sown Area*	*Crops Intensity*	*Production*	*Irrigated area*		*Value of Ag. Sector (at 1980-81 price)*	*Agriculture Worker**	*Productivity of Worker*	*Productivity of Land*	*Land-Man Ratio*
				Net	*Per. of NSA*					
	(mil. hec)	*(%)*	*(mil. ton)*	*(mil. hec)*	*(%)*	*(mil. Rs.)*	*(mil.)*	*(Rs.)*	*(Rs.)*	*(H/W)*
A	1.155	0.322	3.473	1.692	0.534	3.029	2.990	0.038	1.852	-1.782
B	0.411	0.194	2.244	2.047	1.631	2.313	-0.466	2.792	1.894	0.881
C	0.088	0.533	1.743	2.516	2.287	1.495	1.891	-0.388	1.406	-1.770
D	0.160	0.583	3.811	2.125	2.103	3.476	2.014	1.433	3.312	-1.818
E	0.452	0.408	2.814	2.095	1.636	2.576	1.889	0.961	2.114	-1.129

*Agriculture Worker for 1951, 1961, 1971 are taken from Mishra S.N. (1996).

Note: A = 1960-61 over 1950-51; B = 1970-71 over 1960-61; C = 1980-81 over 1970-71; D = 1990-91 over 1980-81; E = 1990-91 over 1950-51

Sources: Government of India, *Statistical Abstract India* 1992, C.S.O. New Delhi.
Government of India, *Agricultural Statistics at a Glance* 1994, Ministry of Agriculture, New Delhi.
Government of India, *Population Census of India*, for corresponding years, New Delhi.

marginal category. In the 1970-71 total number of the holding has increased to 57.07 million, but the area of all the operational holdings has reduced to 125.68 million hectares and it further reduced to 118.57 million hectares in the year 1980-81. The numbers of holding has increased to 71.04 million, and the average size has reduced to 1.67 hectares in 1980-81. The area under the total operational holdings has reduced because of the ceiling plan of the Government. It could be observed from the table that numbers and area of large size holdings has been decreasing with a rapid rate as compared to the other categories. In 1991-92 the total area of operational holdings has increased to 125.10 hectares because of redistribution of the ceiling land[3], and the change in the definition of operation holding by NSSO. In the 1980-81 about 56 per cent of the total holdings belonged to the marginal categories, which had only 11.5 per cent of the area of total holdings. The growth rate of area and numbers of holdings was negative for semi-medium, medium, and large categories which shows that more and more holdings transferred into the marginal and small size categories. In the 1991-92 about 62.8 per cent of total holdings belonged to marginal category, and had only 15.6 per cent of the area of total area of operational holdings. The average size of this category reduced to the level of 0.33 hectare. While the number and area of large category has reduced to 1.30 million and 15.2 million hectares respectively. The average size of large category was 15.58 hectares, which is about 47 times of average size of the marginal holdings in 1991-92. The average size of Indian holdings reduced to 1.34 hectares, which is smaller than the average size of holdings of the small size category.

Elasticity of Labour Absorption in Agriculture (1950-51 to 1990-91)

One of the main reasons of decline in the size of holding is the very slow diversification of labour force from agriculture to non-agriculture sector. Labour absorption in agriculture (employment elasticity) is mostly affected by value by productivity of land and economic active people and it is also affected by other factors like social and legal rules of holdings, extent of mechanization, cropping intensity, crop composition and other technological changes in the production process (Bhalla & Singh 1997). Table 4.7 shows the elasticity of absorption in agriculture. These figures show that the employment elasticity has always remained

Table 4.6: Change in Land Holdings in India (1960-61 to 1990-91).

Sizes		*1960-61*		*1970-71*		*1980-81*		*1991-92*	
		X	*Y*	*X*	*Y*	*X*	*Y*	*X*	*Y*
Marginal (< 1 hec)	A	39.10	6.90	45.70	9.20	56.00	11.50	62.80	15.60
	B	19.85	9.21	26.10	11.56	39.78	13.64	58.69	19.52
	C	-na-	-na-	2.78	2.30	4.30	1.67	3.60	3.31
	D	-na-	0.46	-na-	0.44	-na-	0.34	-na-	0.33
Small (1.01–2 hec)	A	22.60	12.30	22.40	14.70	19.30	16.60	17.80	18.70
	B	11.47	16.42	12.78	18.48	13.71	19.68	16.63	23.39
	C	-na-	-na-	1.09	1.19	0.70	0.63	1.77	1.58
	D	-na-	1.43	-na-	1.45	-na-	1.44	-na-	1.41
Semi-medium (2.01 – 4 hec)	A	19.80	20.60	17.70	22.60	14.20	23.60	12.00	24.10
	B	10.06	27.50	10.10	28.41	10.09	27.98	11.21	30.15
	C	-na-	-na-	0.04	0.33	-0.01	-0.15	0.96	0.68
	D	-na-	2.73	-na-	2.81	-na-	2.77	-na-	2.69
Medium (4.01 – 10 hec)	A	14.00	31.20	11.10	30.50	8.60	30.10	6.10	26.40
	B	7.11	41.64	6.33	38.33	6.11	35.69	5.70	33.30
	C	-na-	-na-	-1.16	-0.82	-0.35	-0.71	-0.63	-0.63
	D	-na-	5.86	-na-	6.06	-na-	5.84	-na-	5.84
Large (10 + hec)	A	4.50	29.00	3.10	23.00	1.90	18.20	1.30	15.20
	B	2.28	38.71	1.76	28.91	1.35	21.58	1.22	19.01
	C	-na-	-na-	-2.56	-2.88	-2.62	-2.88	-0.92	-1.15
	D	-na-	16.98	-na-	16.43	-na-	15.99	-na-	15.58
Total	A	100.00	100.00	100.00	100.00	100.00	100.00	100.00	100.00
	B	50.77	133.48	57.07	125.68	71.04	118.57	93.45	125.10
	C	-na-	-na-	1.18	-0.60	2.21	-0.58	2.52	0.49
	D	-na-	2.63	-na-	2.20	-na-	1.67	-na-	1.34

Source: Computed from N.S.S. report 1997.

Note: X = Number of operational holdings (in million). Y = Area of operational holdings (in million hec.). A = %Total Nos. and area of total operational holdings, B = Absolute number/ area under operational holdings, C = Annual compound growth rate (%), D = Averege size of holding.

inelastic in agriculture since independence. It declined in the period 1960-61 to 1970-71 and 1970-71 to 1980-81 may be because during these periods the growth rate of the increase in the net sown area, value of agriculture-sector, productivity of land was comparatively lower than other periods. In the time period 1980-81 to 1990-91 the elasticity has improved to 0.9115, because of the higher growth rate of net sown area, cropping intensity, value of agriculture sector, productivity of land, in the above period (see Table 4.5).

Table 4.7: Elasticity of Labour Absorption in Agricultre in India (1950-51 to 1990-91)
$\log_e$ (EAAP/H) = $\log_e C + \log_e$(VO/H).

Periods	*Intercept*	*S.E. (β)*	*Reg.coff*	*adj R^2*
1950-51 to 1960-61	-22.44	.466689	0.8994(***)	0.78
1960-61 to 1970-71	-3.71	.301122	0.4731(ns)	0.33
1970-71 to 1980-81	-3.11	.165432	0.6421(*)	0.34
1980-81 to 1990-91	-4.70	.092454	0.9116(***)	0.81
1950-51 to 1990-91	-8.52	.092175	0.8829(***)	0.77

Note: Significance level
*** = 0.01%, = 1%, * = 5%, ns = no sign.

Correlation between Selected Variables (Zero Order and Partial)

The zero order correlation of the selective variable are given in Table 4.8 which shows that percentage of agricultural population in total population have a negative and significant correlation with all the other variables. Percentages of irrigated land have a positive and significant correlation with yield. Percentages of economically active agricultural population to total agricultural population have a positive and significant correlation with yield. Rainfall is not significantly correlated with any other variable. The magnitude of correlation coefficients between percentages of economically active agricultural population to total agricultural population and yield was smaller than coefficient between agricultural population in total population and yield. The fertilizer consumption, number of tractors, and high yielding variety seeds have also a positive and significant correlation with yield.

To find a real association between the variables and partial correlation technique has been applied. In Table 4.9 partial correlation of each input variable with yield has shown (the keeping influence of other variables as constant). The association of yield with rainfall, fertilizer, area under high yield varieties, and economically active agricultural population, shows a positive and significant relationship. While the correlation between yield and the number of tractors, yield and percentage of agricultural population in total population shows a positive but insignificant correlation. The correlation between yield and percentage of irrigated land shows an unexpected negative but insignificant correlation.

Agricultural Production Function

The results of Agricultural Production Function (APF) have been given in Table 4.10, which shows that except the number of tractors, all the

Table 4.8: Result of Zero Order Correlation Matrix

	V8	*V12*	*V13*	*V14*	*V21*	*V22*	*V24*	*V20*
V8	1	0.1251	0.0946	0.1351	0.0886	0.2064	-0.2118	0.2179
V12		1	0.9136@	0.9674@	0.9818@	0.5151@	-0.8902@	0.9744@
V13			1	0.9272@	0.9887@	0.4938@	-0.8879@	0.9517@
V14				1	0.9517@	0.4727@	-0.8902@	0.9527@
V21					1	0.5582@	-0.8916@	0.9617@
V22						1	-0.4722@	0.5870@
V24							1	–0.8806@
V20								1

Note: Lavel of significance
@ = 0.01%.

Table 4.9: Result of Partial Correlation Matrix

Variables	*Correlation Coefficients*	*Controlled Variables*
V20, V8	0.3062*	V12 V13 V14 V21 V22 V24
V20, V12	0.4096**	V8 V13 V14 V21 V22 V24
V20, V13	0.4280**	V8 V12 V14 V21 V22 V24
V20, V14	0.1754ns	V8 V12 V13 V21 V22 V24
V20, V21	-0.2746ns	V8 V12 V13 V14 V22 V24
V20, V22	0.5309***	V8 V12 V13 V14 V21 V24
V20, V24	0.0930ns	V8 V12 V13 V14 V21 V22

Note: Level of significance * = 5%, ** = 1%, *** = 0.1%, ns = not significant.
V8 = Rainfall (in millimetres), V12 = Fertilizer consumption (kg/h).
V13 = Area under the HYVs (million hect.), V14 = No. of tractors per lakh hect.
V21 = Percentage of irrigated land, V22 = % of Eco Active Agri. population in total agricultural population, V24 = % of Ag. population in total agricultural population, V20 = Yield (tonne per hect.).

other variables plays a significant role in yield determination. The sign of beta value shows the direction for all the variables as expected except in case of percentage of irrigated land. The possible reasons for this unexpected result could be (a) Heterogeneity in irrigation facilities in our country, (b) it may be due to the inner-relationship of the other input variables, (c) it may be due to the poor quality of the data for this variable, or (d) in our case we have assumed the APF follows a linear form but in many cases it may follow any other form like Cobb-Douglas or Transdental forms. In such cases the direction of β (beta) values may differ. This set of inputs explains 96.75 per cent of total variation in the yield. The value of static F shows a significant result. Durbin-Watson static (d-statistics) also shows there is no auto-correlation in the data.

Table 4.10: Result of Agriculture Production Function
[(Dependent Variable = V20 (Yield)]

Variables	*Variables Name*	*SE(β)*	*Reg. Coeff. β (beta)*	*Coeff.*
V8	Rainfall	0.003863	0.063218*	adj.R^2 = 0.9675
V12	Fertilizer	0.218786	0.698949**	
V13	HYVs	0.205046	0.705711**	F=148.51***
V14	Tractors	0.012414	0.228015ns	
V21	% Irrigated land	1.15979	-0.740286*	d = 2.187
V22	% Eco. Act agri. Population	0.189005	0.17096***	
	Constant	19.3605	83.30431***	

Note: Significance level * = 5%, ** = 1%, *** = 0.1%, ns = not significant.

Summary and Conclusion

Indian population has increased from 361.1 million in 1951 to 846.3 million in 1991 and it is increasing at a growth rate of slightly lower than 2 per cent annually, and the share of rural population has started declining. Since the independence the sex ratio remain unfavourable to women. The growth rate of the population has declined significantly, but it is still much higher. Population density has increased about two times since the independence.

Agricultural cropping pattern shows a diversification of land under the cultivation from foodgrains to non-foodgrain crops. Among the foodgrain crops share of land under the wheat cultivation has increased significantly. The annual compound growth rate of production and yield has increased rapidly in post-Green Revolution in comparison to the pre-Green Revolution period. While the growth rate of the area under cultivation has declined over the period. Cropping intensity has increased from 111.06 per cent in 1951 to 135.69 per cent in 1991. Area under irrigation has also increased from 17.55 per cent of net sown area in 1951 to 33.59 per cent in 1991. The productivity of worker has increased only 1.5 times during this period, while the productivity of land has increased about 2.3 times during the same period. The land per worker has reduced from 1.71 hectares in 1951 to 0.743 hectares in 1991. The increase in the agricultural population is responsible for fragmentation of the land. The numbers of operation holding has increased from 50.71 million in 1960-61 to 93.45 million in 1991-92. The number of marginal holdings has increased rapidly, in 1960-61 it was only 39.10 per cent of total holdings while in 1991, 62.8 per cent of the total holdings belonged to this category. The elasticity of labour absorption in India always remains inelastic. During the period 1980-81 to 1991 it shows a significant increase and becomes close to the unity. The Agricultural Production Function shows that economically active agricultural population plays a significant role in production, but the total agricultural population (economically active plus their dependants) does not play any significant role. Now it is necessary to take some steps to reduce the fragmentation of the holdings. To stop the fragmentation Government can put a minimum limit of the holdings under its ceiling plans or it can make some improvement in the heritage laws. To reduce the dependency on the agriculture, Government should create employment opportunity in the rural areas, by developing new agriculture based industries in rural areas.

Notes

1. Data on rainfall in the simple average of the rainfall figures collected on 35 places, all over India.
2. According to FAG production report (1992) agriculture population include all those persons who depend for their livelihood on agriculture. This comprises all those persons actively engaged in agriculture and their non-working dependants. Economically active agriculture population is defined as, all those economically active persons engaged principally in agriculture and its allied activities.
3. Dutta & Sundharam (1995), 'till 1970 only about 55 per cent of the surplus land was redistribution, while in 1980 and 1992 redistribution increased to 73 per cent and 80 per cent respectively.

References

Bhalla G.S. and Singh Gurmal (1997), "Recent Development in Indian Agriculture: A State level analysis", *Economic and Political Weekly*, March 29.

Bongarts J. (1996), "Population Pressure and the Food Supply System in the Developing World", *New York Population Council*, New York.

Choudhary R.H. (1976), "Demographic Changes and Food Production in Bangladesh", *Population and Development Review*, 1976.

Dandekar V.M. (1980), "Introduction", *Indian Journal of Agriculture Economics*, Vol. XXXV No. 2, April-June.

Dutta R. & Sundharam K.P.M. (1995), *Indian Economy*, Sultan Chand & Company Ltd., New Delhi.

Ganguli B. (1994), *Trends of Agriculture and Population in Ganga Valley: A Study in the Agriculture Economics*, compiled by Indian Council of Social Science Research, New Delhi.

Greenspan A. (1994), "Apocalypse when? Population and Food Supply in South Asia", *Asia-Pacific Population and Policy*, Dec. 1994.

Jain C.K. (1996), "Growth of Population and Agriculture Changes in Madhya Pradesh", in Tripathi & Tiwari (eds.), *Population Growth and Development in India*, New Delhi.

Mishra, S.N. (1996), "Capital Formation and Accumulation in Indian Agriculture since Independence", *Indian Journal of Agriculture Economics*, Vol. 51, No. 1 & 2, Jan.-Jun.

Mishra V.C. (1996), "Population Growth and Agriculture Intensification in Post-independence India", (Unpublished) Presented at the Annual Meeting of the Population Association of America, New Orleans, May 9-11.

Rao V.K.R.V. (1974), "New Challenge before Agriculture" (Dr. Panse Memorial Lecture) 25-28 April, (Mimeographed).

Rao V.M. (1980), "Methodological Issues in measuring agricultural growth; Lesion of Recent Indian Researches", *Indian Journal of Agriculture Economics*, Vol. XXXV, No. 2, April-June.

Sharma J.S. & Gandhi V.P. (1990), 'Production and Consumption of Foodgrains in India: Implication of Accelerated Economic Growth and Poverty Alleviation", International Food Policy Research Institute, Research Report 81, July.

Srinivasan K. (1996), "An Overview Demographic Transition in India", in Srinivasan (eds.), *Policy and Reproductive Health*, New Delhi.

Vaidya B.C. (1996), "Population Growth and Agriculture Land in the Semi- Arid Region: A Case Study of the Ahmadnagar district (Maharashtra)", in Tripathi & Tiwari (eds.) *Population Growth and Development in India*, New Delhi.

5

WATER RESOURCES OF THE TONS BASIN

Assessment of the Potential and Demand

S.K. SHARMA & D.K. TRIPATHI

Water is essential for the existence of the biotic world and is required nearly for all activities of man. At present the use of water is not only limited to drinking, domestic and irrigation purposes but has multiplied and it functions as a source of power, an industrial ingredient, a media of transport, a waste remover and purifying agent as well as recreational asset. Contrary to the expanding demand, its supply is limited and can be depleted or made unusable by excessive utilization, inadequate conservation, misutilization, pollution or careless management. Distribution of water resource is also uneven. Under such situation it is urgently needed to assess the potential as well as need for water resources and their spatial distribution. This chapter attempts to present the assessment of possible availability and present requirements of water in a densely populated agricultural region, facing water crisis, of eastern Madhya Pradesh, known as the Tons Basin. It is one of the sub-basins of the Ganga drainage basin.

Assessment of Water Potential

The primary source of water supply on the earth is precipitation. Much of it is lost as evaporation; a good deal of it goes as run-off and is called as 'surface water'; and a small amount penetrates into ground and is known as 'ground water'. The surface water is feasible through rivers, streams, tanks and reservoirs. The rainfall regimes, geological structure, terrain and soils determine its feasibility and local supply. Survey of its potentials and possibility of utilization of water resource has been carried out by the Irrigation Department, Government of Madhya Pradesh. Information collected through these surveys has been used to assess the water resource of the basin.

Surface Water Resource

All water reaching the stream is potentially available as surface water supply. It is also available in other waterbodies. The quantity of water flowing through rivers can be estimated by the discharge data. Alternatively, water balance concept has been proposed (UNESCO, 1978). By this method, mean annual water balance of a river basin can be stated as: run-off = precipitation – evapotranspiran. But the run-off of the Tons basin has been estimated on the basis of stream flow. There are five gauge discharge sites within this basin; two of them are on the Tons River itself. These are Madhogarh in Satna and at Purwa in Rewa district. Gauge and discharge data at Purwa site on Tons are available for years from 1960 to 1977, from which run-off series at Tons barrage have been worked out. These data have been used for estimating the surface water resource of the entire basin.

Catchment area above the Tons barrage is 4509 sq. km. and average annual flow at 75 per cent dependable yield is 844.927 million cubic metres (29.838 TMC). Applying this 75 per cent dependable yield factor, yield for the complete basin has been worked out. On average, yield per square kilometre works to be 0.18739 million cubic metres. Total area of the basin is 11974 sq. km. Thus total yield of surface water for the basin works out to be 2243.81 million cubic metres (79.23 TMC). It is worthmentioning that about 632 sq. km. of the Tons basin is out of Rewa-Satna districts. Total estimated run-off of this area is 118.83 Mcum. On the other hand, about 2475 sq. km. of these districts is in sub-basins of the Ken, Baghin, Paisuni and Son rivers. Total of water drained by these rivers at 75 per cent dependability basis if 578 Mcum. Thus, aggregate surface water potential of Rewa and Satna districts arrives at (2243.81 – 118.43 + 578) = 2703.38 Mcum; while that of the Tons basin it is 2243.81 Mcum.

On the basis of average yield of run-off at the barrage site on the Tons River, water potential of each block of its basin can be estimated, though it may not be very accurate because of the spatial variation in rainfall. However, it can be taken as the basis for the water resource development planning. Estimates for each block is presented in

Table 5.1. It ranges from 70.87 Mcum in Naigarhi block of Rewa district to 295.38 Mcum in Majhgawan block of Satna district. Only two blocks, viz. Naigarhi and Mauganj have lower potential than 100 Mcum each. Contrary to it, seven blocks have surface water potential more than 150 Mcum each. They are Majhgawan, Maihar, Hanumana, Rampur, Nagod, Sirmaur and Unchehara. Most of them are in the central high plain area.

Table 5.1 Tons Basin: Block-wise Estimated Run-off of Surface Water (in Mcum)

Blocks	*Area (Sq. km.)*	*Estimated Flow*	*Percent*
Rewa	690.14	129.33	5.0
Raipur	635.52	119.09	4.6
Sirmaur	879.00	164.72	6.4
Gangeo	589.64	110.49	4.3
Teonthar	797.14	149.38	5.8
Jewa	787.34	147.54	5.8
Naigarhi	378.18	70.87	2.8
Mauganj	525.2	98.42	3.8
Hanumana	957.92	179.5	7.0
Rampur	912.38	170.97	6.7
Maihar	1135.24	212.73	8.3
Amarpatan	653.3	122.42	4.8
Ramnagar	600.67	112.56	4.4
Nagod	920.25	172.45	6.7
Unchehara	882.12	165.3	6.4
Majhgawan	1576.26	295.38	11.5
Sohawal	758.15	142.07	5.5

Groundwater Potentials

Groundwater potential is another source of water. Its occurrence depends on the climatic conditions, character of soils, vegetative cover, and land-use and, after all, geological structure of the area. The precipitation that fall upon land surface is the main source of groundwater recharge. As soon as precipitation falls over the land surface, a portion of it is utilized in vegetative growth and other biotic uses; some part of it soaked in the sub-surface through the cracks and joints in the rocks, and maximum portion goes as surface run-off and contributes directly to surface water. Some portion of the soaked water is retained as suspended particles, making only moist zone and part of it goes to join ground-water reservoirs. The groundwater available in the area occurs in both unconfined and semi-confined conditions. The dug wells are tapping water from watertable conditions, whereas the dug-*cum*-borewells and tubewells are tapping water from semi-confined conditions. It is observed that confining conditions are generally met with at an approximate depth between 25 and 35 metres below the land surface.

Groundwater resources are the quantities of water that can be withdrawn from groundwater storage. They are quite varied in nature. The available resource can be computed by adopting different techniques; three of them are popular. They are: (i) calculation of groundwater resource from geological structure and water level fluctuation data, (ii) computation of groundwater resource by groundwater flow techniques, and (iii) calculation of water resource from geological and climatological data. The groundwater survey units of the State has adopted the first technique for evaluation of the groundwater resource. It is based on various parameters, information about them are estimated, collected, compiled and evaluated in the course of field survey.

First important parameter is the hydraulic constant of the aquifers, which is determined with the help of aquifer geometry of the different lithological units. Second variable used in this method is the water level fluctuation which is worked out from the data of water levels in the wells in different seasons. The specific yield of the aquifer materials, the third parameter of the equation, is determined by conducting laboratory studies for sedimentary formations and by conducting aquifer performance tests in the field in specific hard rock areas. Thus the total quantity of groundwater available in the area of the investigation is computed by using the formula:

$$Q = A \times RGL \times Sp.Yd.$$

where Q = Total quantity of groundwater potential,
A = Area of investigation,
RGL = Rise in groundwater level, and
$Sp.Yd.$ = Specific yield in percentage.

The above formula has slightly been modified, and groundwater recharge for monsoon and non-monsoon seasons has been estimated separately. The modified formula as used by the Groundwater Survey Unit is as follows:

Monsoon recharge = [Area × specific yield × watertable fluctuation + gross kharif draft – (monsoon canal seepage + monsoon recharge from groundwater irrigation)] × (normal monsoon rainfall % average rainfall) + (monsoon canal seepage + monsoon recharge from surface water irrigation).

The method employed in the estimation of groundwater resources can be explained by taking data of different parameters of Nagod block of Satna district. Total area of the block is 97,600 hectares, out of which 23,700 hectares are hilly and highly dissected, and therefore, this area has been treated as unsuitable for groundwater recharge. Thus only 73,900 hectares have been taken into account for calculating total recharge. First of all monsoon recharge of groundwater is estimated with the help of above modified formula. Information about the parameters used in the formula for Nagod block are as noted below:

1.	Geographical area (in hectares)	73,900
2.	Average depth (m) of water level b.g.1 (May/June)	7.95
3.	Average depth (m) of watertable b.g.1 (November)	3.65
4.	Watertable fluctuation (m)	4.30
5.	IMD Normal monsoon rainfall (mm)	969.70
6.	IMD Normal non-monsoon rainfall (mm)	127.30
7.	Average monsoon rainfall (mm) during 1986-92	1094.65
8.	Average non-monsoon rainfall (mm) during 1986-92	44.19
9.	Gross kharif draft (ha.m)	255
10.	Specific yield (in per cent)	3
11.	Monsoon seepage from canals (ha. m)	4
12.	Recharge due to monsoon surface water irrigation (ha. m)	14
13.	Monsoon recharge from groundwater irrigation (ha. m)	77

I. *Total monsoon recharge* (ha. m) would be:
[73900 × 0.03 × 4.30 + 255 – (4+14+77)] × (969.7% + 1094.65) + (4 + 14) = 8602 ha. m.

This estimate of monsoon recharge is compared with the possible recharge calculated with the help of rainfall data. It is called 'ad hoc norm' method. Recharge in monsoon season by this method is calculated as follows:

Geographical area (ha) × IMD Normal monsoon rainfall (mm) × Recharge factor.

In the present case it is 73,900 × 969.70 × 0.1/1000 = 7166.08 hectometres. Net monsoon recharge due to rainfall arrives at [8602–4 (recharge from canals) –14 (recharge from surface water irrigation) = 8584 hectometres]. Thus the difference between these two estimates arrives at 8584–7166=1418, which is 19.79 per cent of the recharge calculated employing 'ad hoc norms' method. It is accepted that if this variation is more than 20 per cent, the watertable fluctuation approach may not be accepted.

II. *Non-monsoon* recharge is calculated using following formula:
Geographical area × average rainfall (mm) × infiltration factor/1000.
73900 × 44.19 × 0.1/1000 = 326.56 = 327 hectometres.
Recharge from canals 119 ha. m.
Recharge from surface water irrigation 200 ha. m.
Recharge from tanks 162 ha. m.

III. *Total Annual Recharge* = Monsoon recharge + Non-monsoon recharge + Recharge from canals + Recharge from surface water irrigation + Recharge from tanks + 30% of tubewell recharge.
Thus it arrives at 8602 + 327 + 119 + 200 + 102 + 0 = 9350 hectometres.
Only 85 per cent of the total annual recharge are supposed to be available for development purposes. Thus, in Nagod block (9350 × 0.85) 7948 hectare metres groundwater is available for development.

Spatial Distribution of Groundwater Resources

Using the above method, annual recharge of water for each block of the basin has been calculated and presented in Table 5.2.

It is evident from Table 5.2 that the distribution of ground water potential is uneven in this region. It ranges from only 3806 hectometres in Gangeo block of Rewa district to 12611 ha.m in Hanumana block of the same district. It is lower than 5000 ha.m in four blocks, viz., Rewa, Raipur, Gangeo and Amarpatan. On the other hand, net recharge is more than 7000 ha.m in eight blocks, highest being 12611 ha.m in Hanumana block. Other blocks with large potential are Teonthar, Jewa, Rampur, Maihar, Nagod, Majhgawan and Sohawal. Each of them has more than 6.0 per cent of net groundwater resource of the basin.

Block-wise Gross Water Resources

Summation of surface run-off and net recharge of groundwater presents the holistic picture of potential water resource of each block. For this

Table 5.2 Tons Basin: Block-wise Assessment of Groundwater Potential (in hectometre ha.m)

Blocks	*Total Annual Recharge*	*85% of Recharge*	*% of Net Recharge*	*Net Draft (1992)*	*Net Balance Available*	*% of Net Recharge*
Rewa	5600	4760	4.1	1940	2820	59.2
Raipur	5822	4949	4.3	2140	2809	56.8
Sirmaur	7559	6425	5.5	1190	5235	81.5
Gangeo	4478	3806	3.3	772	3034	79.7
Teonthar	8312	7065	6.1	1764	5301	75.0
Jewa	8521	7243	6.2	206	7037	97.2
Naigarhi	7450	6333	5.4	996	5337	84.3
Mauganj	7910	6724	5.8	888	5836	86.8
Hanumana	14837	12611	10.8	710	11901	94.4
Rampur	9134	7764	6.7	1665	6099	78.6
Maihar	9978	8481	7.3	1471	7010	82.7
Amarpatan	5442	4626	4.0	986	3640	78.7
Ramnagar	6266	5326	4.6	914	4412	82.8
Nagod	9355	7952	6.3	1781	6171	77.6
Unchehara	6513	5536	4.8	1258	4278	77.3
Majhgawan	11409	9358	8.0	897	8461	90.4
Sohawal	8733	7423	6.4	1997	5426	73.1
Rewa Distt.	70489	59916	51.5	10606	49310	82.3
Satna Distt.	66430	56466	48.5	10969	45497	80.6
Basin	137919	116382	100.0	21575	91807	81.5

Source: Reports of the Divisional Groundwater Survey Units, Rewa.

purpose, net recharge of groundwater has been converted from hectometre to cubic metre. One hectare metre means one metre depth of water over one hectare (100 × 100) of land. Thus it is equivalent to 10,000 cubic metres. Thus, 100 hectare metres are equal to 1 million cubic metres. Total water potential of the blocks of this basin is presented in Table 5.3.

Assessment of the Demand of Water

Water is demanded for multiple uses and purposes. These uses and their resulting effects are interwoven regionally and nationally. The uses that make most demand upon water supply and water-related services vary with the degree of development. Consequently, developed countries and regions have a long list of the uses of water while it is comparatively smaller in developing region. However, certain needs are universal, such as for drinking purpose for man and animals and other domestic purposes. Besides them, water use for irrigation and manufacturing purposes is increasing phenomenally. Among them, irrigation is confined

Table 5.3: Tons Basin: Block-wise Potential of Water Resources
(*Million cubic metres*)

Block	*Surface Water (75% Dependability)*	*Ground water (85% Dependability)*	*Total Water Resource*	*% of Basin*
Rewa	129.33	47.6	176.93	4.6
Raipur	119.09	49.49	168.58	4.4
Sirmaur	164.72	64.25	228.97	5.9
Gangeo	110.49	38.06	148.55	3.8
Teonthar	149.38	70.65	223.03	5.7
Jewa	147.54	72.43	219.97	5.7
Naigarhi	70.87	63.33	134.20	3.5
Mauganj	98.42	67.24	165.66	4.3
Hanumana	179.5	126.11	305.61	7.9
Rampur	170.97	77.64	248.61	6.4
Maihar	212.73	84.91	297.54	7.7
Amarpatan	122.42	46.26	168.68	4.4
Ramnagar	112.56	53.26	165.82	4.3
Nagod	172.4	79.52	251.97	6.5
Unchehara	165.30	55.36	220.66	5.7
Majhagawn	295.38	93.58	388.96	10.1
Sohawal	142.07	74.23	216.30	5.6
Total	2703.38	1163.82	3867.2	100.0

to certain environment while industrial need is confined mostly to urbanised areas, where water is used for cooling, processing and for waste disposal purposes. Hydropower generation and recreational uses are getting significance in our country also. In this comparatively less developed area of the country, statistical information do not permit the computation of need of water for above purposes. However, requirements of water for major and existing necessities are assessed here.

Requirement for Drinking and Domestic Purposes

Requirement for drinking and domestic purposes depends on physical as well as socio-economic level of development. However, World Health Organization has estimated this need at 200 litres per capita per day in perspective of western countries. It would be very high in Indian context. It is estimated that 200 litres would be sufficient for one person per day living in towns and only 70 litres per person for people living in villages not using flush latrines. Taking these averages, requirements of drinking and domestic purposes have been estimated on the basis of rural and urban population of 1991. Total rural population of this basin is 2494.4 thousand persons and urban population is 526 thousand persons. Thus, total requirements of rural people per annum arrives at 1317.0 million cubic metres and for urban people it is 793.18 million cubic metres.

There is wide variation in this requirement which is the consequence of the size of rural and urban population. Rural necessity ranges from 55.725 Mcum. in Naigarhi block to 107.095 Mcum. in Maihar block of Satna district (Table 5.4). It is simply the reflection of the number of the people living in these blocks. Rural population of Maihar block is 202.8 thousand in 1991, while it is lowest i.e., 105.5 thousand in Naigarhi block of Rewa. Smaller number of population in Naigarhi block is due to smaller size of the block. Density of rural population is (291 rural persons per sq. km.) is highest in this block in the region. Contrary to it, larger population size in Maihar block is due to its larger areal size. Consequently, rural density (180) is quite low. Requirement of water for domestic uses in rural areas is more than 75.0 Mcum. in Majhagawan, Rampur, Nagod, Maihar, Sirmaur, Gangeo, Teonthar, Jewa, Hanumana, Rewa and Raipur blocks.

Table 5.4: Tons Basin: Requirement of Water for Domestic and Drinking Purposes, 1991

Block	*Population ('000) Persons*		*Requirements (Mcum)*		
	Rural	*Urban*	*Rural*	*Urban*	*Total*
Rewa	168.0	137.4	88.729	207.226	295.955
Raipur	165.0	10.8	87.094	16.259	103.353
Sirmaur	178.1	24.8	94.057	37.335	131.392
Gangeo	149.9	9.3	79.154	14.034	93.188
Toenthar	145.3	18.7	76.700	28.199	140.899
Jewa	143.7	—	75.853	—	75.853
Naigarhi	105.5	7.3	55.725	10.936	66.661
Mauganj	109.9	17.3	58.035	26.016	84.051
Hanumana	152.7	11.3	80.642	17.109	97.751
Rampur	162.6	43.3	85.862	65.236	151.098
Maihar	202.8	26.2	107.095	39.533	146.628
Amarpatan	133.2	15.0	70.325	22.665	92.990
Ramnagar	116.5	—	61.505	—	61.505
Nagod	143.4	14.4	75.741	21.769	97.510
Unchehara	111.9	14.8	59.092	22.253	81.345
Majhgawan	170.0	11.2	89.733	16.874	106.607
Sohawal	135.8	164.3	71.688	247.723	319.415
Basin	2494.4	526.0	1317.039	793.176	2110.215

Source: Census of India, 1991, Madhya Pradesh: General Population Tables.

There are still two blocks without any town even in 1991. They are Jewa of Rewa and Ramnagar block of Satna district. Largest city in the basin is Satna urban agglomeration, population of which is 160.5 thousand. Therefore, water requirement of urban population of only this block arrives at 242.03 Mcum. It does not include the industrial requirements of water. It is proper to mention that such large industrial establishments as cement factory, cable, textile, etc. are located in this urban agglomeration. Next to Satna is Rewa with 1,28,981 persons, requiring more than 194.50 million cubic metres per annum. Other towns are smaller in size and none of them require more than 20 Mcum per annum.

Water Required for Irrigation

With the modernization of agricultural technology, irrigation has become imperative. In fact, the 'Green Revolution' was started in areas where reliable sources of irrigation existed. It is necessary not only for raising output but also for stabilising the cropping pattern. Total net sown area is 734.0 thousand hectares in the basin 1994-95 and less than one-fourth of it (23.8%) is irrigated, while average for the State is 30.0 percent. It means water resource of the region must be used for this purpose. The irrigation department of Madhya Pradesh has taken the delta of 1.0 m per sq. km. of area for estimation of water requirement for irrigation in this basin area. Taking this delta total and block-wise requirements of irrigation water can be estimated. It is proposed to estimate this requirement for only half of the net sown area in the first instance. This estimate is presented in Table 5.5. For the entire Basin this requirement arrives at 3670.39 million cubic metres.

Water requirement for irrigation depends on several factors such as the characteristics of soil, season of cultivation, nature of crops and even the method of the cropping. But all these factors could not be taken into account at present because of lack of most of these information, and therefore, the present one is the rough estimation of the requirement. Among blocks, Rampur has largest net sown area, 57.7 thousand hectares, requiring more than 288.56 million cubic metres of water for irrigating just half of it. Nagod block of Satna is at second place, requiring 263.40 Mcum of water. There are eleven blocks out of seventeen, placing their irrational requirements above 200 million cubic metres (Mcum). Other four blocks require between 150 to 200 Mcum per annum and only two need less than this amount. The fact that this is primarily a *rabi* cropped area which increases the requirement. Rainfall is very scanty and evapotranspiration is much higher than this amount, creating deficit of moisture. Therefore, this deficit must be compensated by irrigation.

Table 5.5: Tons Basin: Block-wise Requirements of Water for Irrigation and Livestock

(Million cubic metres)

Block	*Net Sown Area*	*Water Required to Irrigate 50%*	*No. of Livestocks*	*Water Required*	*Total Requirement*
Rewa	44020	220.10	122683	42.49	262.59
Raipur	40989	204.94	118148	44.56	249.50
Sirmaur	52097	260.48	146171	55.12	315.60
Gangeo	42677	213.38	115422	43.53	256.91
Toenthar	49238	246.19	145289	54.79	300.98
Jewa	34502	172.51	138631	52.28	224.79
Naigarhi	28193	140.96	82386	31.07	172.03
Mauganj	31636	158.18	96444	36.37	194.55
Hanumana	46065	230.32	139463	52.59	282.91
Rampur	57712	288.56	158279	59.69	348.25
Maihar	51849	259.24	259030	97.69	356.93
Amarpatan	39411	197.05	116484	43.93	240.98
Ramnagar	27744	138.72	100625	37.95	176.67
Nagod	52681	163.40	148559	56.03	319.43
Unchehara	31968	159.84	110471	41.66	201.50
Majhgawan	48434	242.17	189715	71.55	313.72
Sohawal	51434	257.17	128697	48.53	305.70
Basin	734078	3670.39	2306497	869.92	4540.31

Domestication of animal is integral part of farming in this basin. Total livestock population was 2306.5 thousand in 1990-91. It is presumed that, on average, 50 litres of water is required by one animal. It works 18250 litres of water per annum per animal. It is equivalent to 377.16 cubic metres. Thus total requirement of water for animals arrives at 869.92 million cubic metres. It varies from 31.1 million cubic metres in Naigarhi block to 97.69 Mcum in Maihar block. Thus, total requirements for agricultural purposes arrives at 4540.31 million cubic metres per annum.

Industrial Requirements

Industries require water for several purposes, such as for cooling, for industrial processes and moreover, for the disposal of affluents of the factory. It is because of these facts supply of water is assured before establishing the industrial plants and industrial activities are not hampered by the scarcity of water. But there are several problems hindering the estimation of industrial requirements of water. Firstly distribution of industries, by nature, is localised phenomenon. Secondly, requirements vary with the size and nature of manufacturing. Therefore, requirement per industrial unit cannot be generalised and estimated. However, at present about 20.0 million cubic metres of water are utilised by the industrial plants located within this basin. Looking to the prospects of future industrial development, another 25.0 Mcum of water is proposed to be made available in future. In nutshell, there would not be problem of water supply to the industrial units to be located in this basin even in future. This requirement cannot be distributed among blocks.

Total Estimated Requirements

The requirement of water for different purposes can be aggregated as follows (Table 5.6) for presenting the holistic picture for the basin.

Table 5.6: Tons Basin: Total Water Requirements

Purpose	*Requirement (in Mcum)*	*Remarks*
Drinking and domestic	2110.215	For 1991
Rural	1317.039	"
Urban	793.176	"
Irrigation	3670.390	1994-95
Livestock	869.918	1990-91
Industrial	45.000	1995
Gross demand	6695.523	—

Demand-Supply Relationship

The real problem not only in this basin but throughout the world is how best to reconcile the increasing use of a fixed supply with the needs and constraints of the society in a way that will maintain a stable environment. On the regional level total demand is estimated at 6695.523 Mcum on a conservative scale while total potential supply is estimated at 3867.20 Mcum. Thus even if total potential of water resources is put to use, which is not feasible, the stipulated demand will not be met. Only half (57.8%) of the demand can be met with the regional potential of water resources. Under this situation two actions are needed simultaneously, one flow of water from other basins and complete regulation of available resources. It is pertinent to mention that there is proposal to provide sufficient amount of water to this basin from the Bansagar project under construction across the Sen river just south of this region. But regulation and proper management of the available water resource is yet to be planned.

Spatial Pattern of Relationship between Demand and Supply

On basin level, there is gap of about 2828.322 million cubic metres of water which is nearly half (42.2%) of the regional demand which remains unfulfilled. Further, requirements will increase in future with the increasing population and raising the standard of living, expanding and modernization of agriculture and increasing industrialization. It will engrave the situation. Relationship between supply, utilisation and demand is estimated and presented in Table 5.7.

Table 5.7: Tons Basin: Block-wise Accounting of Potential and Demands of Water
(in *Million cubic metres*)

Block	*Net Potential*	*Total Demand*	*Net Balance*	*Availability as % of Demands*
Rewa	176.93	558.55	381.62	31.7
Raipur	168.58	352.85	184.27	47.8
Sirmaur	228.97	446.99	218.02	51.2
Gangeo	148.55	350.10	201.55	42.4
Toenthar	220.03	405.88	185.85	54.2
Jewa	219.97	300.64	80.67	73.2
Naigarhi	134.20	238.69	104.49	56.2
Mauganj	165.66	278.60	112.94	59.5
Hanumana	305.61	380.67	75.06	80.3
Rampur	248.61	499.35	250.74	47.8
Maihar	297.54	503.56	206.02	59.1
Amarpatan	168.68	333.97	165.29	50.5
Ramnagar	165.82	238.18	72.36	69.6
Nagod	251.97	416.94	164.97	60.4
Unchehara	220.66	282.85	62.19	78.0
Majhgawan	388.96	420.33	31.37	92.5
Sohawal	216.30	625.12	408.82	34.6
Basin	3867.20	6695.52*	2828.32*	57.8

*Including industrial requirement.

It is evident from Table 5.7 that there would be scarcity of water in each and every block of the region if stipulated socio-economic development is achieved. Intensity of scarcity varies widely. All potential water resources are capable of meeting only one-third of the demand in Rewa and Satna (Sohawal) blocks. In fact, these two blocks support Rewa and Satna cities respectively. Because of this fact their demand for domestic and drinking purposes is very high. Other three blocks, viz., Gangeo, Raipur and Rampur also be able to fulfil less than half of their demand if the total potential is harnessed. Thus these five blocks are bound to face acute scarcity of water in near future. Contrary to them, only three blocks, i.e., Majhagawan (92.5%), Hanumana (80.3%) and Unchehara (78.0%) have water potentials sufficient to meet more than three-fourths of their estimated demand. Other blocks fall between these two extremes.

In absolute terms, deficit ranges from 31.37 Mcum in Majhagawan block to 408.82 Mcum in Sohawal block, both in Satna district. There are five blocks (Jewa, Hanumana, Ramnagar, Unchehara and Majhagawan) with deficit less than 100.0 Mcum each. These are sparsely populated and comparatively low developed blocks of the region. In six blocks (Raipur, Teonthar, Naigarhi, Mauganj, Amarpatan and Nagod) deficit ranges from 100 to 200 Mcum each. On the other side, deficit is between 200 to 300 Mcum in four blocks–Sirmaur, Gangeo, Rampur and Maihar and more than 300 Mcum in two blocks–Rewa and Satna (Sohawal). These are densely populated, urbanised blocks, and are also developed agriculturally. Thus the matter of anxiety for planners in this region is the scarcity of water resources.

Status of Development of Water Resources

Man has been utilising water for different purposes since time immemorial. But there is no account of the tradition uses of water. Even, no data is available of water used for remunerative uses. It is to be estimated. On the experience gained during fieldwork, it is presumed that, on average, per capita consumption of water for drinking, domestic and animal purposes is not more than 30 litres per day in rural areas. Taking this average total consumption of ruralites of water has been estimated for each block utilising rural population in 1991. Similarly, water consumption in urban areas is estimated presuming per capita daily consumption of 50 litres. Total non-tradition uses of water thus estimated is 2607.02 Mcum.

Similarly, water used for irrigation is estimated assuming that 1.0 cm water is required to irrigate one square metre of area. This data has been accepted by the irrigation department of the State. Net irrigated area was 1,74,565 hectares in 1994-95. Thus total water used for irrigating this much area would be 1745.65 Mcum. Out of this irrigated area, only 34,158 hectares were irrigated by governmental sources. Thus less than one-fifth of the irrigation water is regulated by the government agencies. It proves that water is a public resource but its utilization is in private hands. Therefore, proper utilization of this precious resource has to be regulated and people have to be taught ways and methods of its optimum utilization. By now, more than two-thirds (67.41%) of the net water potentials have been used. However, there is still vast potentiality of increasing use of water.

Spatial Variation in Utilization

Present amount of water utilized in each block has also been estimated in the manner described earlier. Like water potential, pattern of utilization also varies spatially. It is presented in Table 5.8.

Table 5.8: Tons Basin: Block-wise Utilisation of Water Resource for Different Purposes

(Million cubic metres)

Block	*Total Potential*	*Irrigation*	*Human Use*		*Total Use*	*Use as % of Potential*
			Rural	*Urban*		
Rewa	176.93	166.33	38.00	77.70	283.00	159.95
Raipur	168.58	44.53	37.32	6.11	87.96	52.17
Sirmaur	228.97	136.33	40.29	14.02	190.64	83.25
Gangeo	148.55	64.23	33.91	5.26	103.40	69.60
Toenthar	220.03	158.64	32.87	10.57	202.08	91.84
Jewa	219.97	90.71	32.50	—	123.21	56.01
Naigarhi	134.20	28.12	23.86	4.13	56.11	41.81
Mauganj	165.66	54.61	24.86	9.76	80.25	48.44
Hanumana	205.61	77.87	34.54	6.39	118.80	38.87
Rampur	248.61	206.66	36.78	24.49	267.93	107.77
Maihar	297.54	119.74	45.87	14.82	180.43	60.64
Amarpatan	168.68	103.76	30.13	8.48	142.37	84.40
Ramnagar	165.82	28.40	26.35	—	54.75	33.01
Nagod	251.97	122.48	32.44	8.14	163.06	64.71
Unchehara	220.66	112.64	25.31	8.37	146.32	66.31
Majhgawan	388.96	93.90	38.45	6.33	138.68	35.65
Sohawal	216.30	144.41	30.72	92.9	268.03	123.91
Basin	3867.20	1745.65	564.23	297.45	26207.02	67.41

It is evident from Table 5.8 that Rewa block has utilised more than one and half times of its water potential. Such high consumption is because of two factors. One is the location of Rewa city and the other is the development of irrigation. Similar situation is of Sohawal block supporting Satna urban agglomeration. Rampur block of Satna also has crossed the limit of potentiality. Along with them, three other blocks—Amarpatan (84.4%), Sirmaur (83.3%) and Teonthar (91.84%) have used more than three-fourths of their potential water resources. Other six blocks (Raipur, Gangeo, Jewa, Maihar, Nagod and Unchehara) have utilization to total potential is less than 50 per cent in five blocks. Ramnagar block of Satna district is at bottom with 33.0 per cent, followed by Majhgawan (35.7%) and Hanumana block (38.9%). These are comparatively undulating blocks with sparse population and low developed agriculture, which result in low utilization of water. Naigarhi and Mauganj blocks also belong to this class. Thus, less developed blocks have high possibility of expansion of irrigation for raising agricultural productivity.

Planning for Water Resource Management

It is evident from the preceding analysis that the central issue in the water resource management is to match the supply and demand imbalance through structural facilities of storage, conveyance, processing and their operations. Groundwater and surface water are in hydraulic continuity and hence are components of the same system. Development and conservation should therefore involve the conjunctive uses of surface and groundwater resources. Further, their allocation for different uses should be based on the principles of ecology and should aim at optimization of social benefits rather than individual gains. It is particularly significant because water is a 'common property resource' and its benefits should reach to all members of the society.

In fact, objectives of development planning are economic progress, social development and inter-regional balance with least deterioration in the environmental conditions. These objectives are achieved by varied means such as intensification of agriculture, establishment of industries, promotions of tourism, growth of cities, modernization of rural areas and so on. These economic activities use water and then, after use, discharge it as waste. Traditionally water is regarded as a god-gift and people hardly give any thought either to the quantity used or to the quality of their discharge. But by now it has been proved that water is most potent element of the environment and changes in its quantity and quality severely affects the conditions of other elements. Experience has long showed that needs always exceeded available resources. Therefore collective actions are essential to ensure a balance in the water system.

Multifaceted approach would be necessary to ensure stability in water resources. Such as technical means can be applied to increase resource, for purification of discharges and reduction of water damage. Water resource can be increased by regularization over a period of time, intra-basin and inter-basin transfer of resources, conjunctive use of surface and groundwater, recycling of water after first use and by reducing demand for water. Technical means can also minimise the damage caused by floods which is a major natural hazard.

6

MANAGEMENT OF IRRIGATION EFFICIENCY IN DAMODAR RIVER BASIN

KUMAR NIKHIL & MOBIN AHMAD

Introduction

Agriculture has been the main user of water resource on earth, and it has also been identified as a major source of wastage of the resource. Owing to the rapid growth of population and the development of other sectors besides agriculture in most of the countries, water is becoming a scarce resource and more costly to develop. Most of the water needed for agriculture is irrigation water, and it is a foregone conclusion that irrigation is vital for agricultural production. The basic problem facing agriculturists and engineers is how to use the water efficiently so that maximum profit can be obtained.

In the developed countries, although the competition for water among various sectors is more serious, but the problem of efficient water use is far less acute than in the developing countries. Because in the developing countries, the percentage of population involve in agriculture is very high, and so the average farm holding is small which in turn impedes the application of some modern irrigation techniques. However, this does not imply that high efficiency cannot be attained under the prevailing condition, but it does mean that the task is more difficult.

In this chapter, the definitions of various efficiency terms are defined and their implication with respect to irrigation management are discussed. A case study is also presented in order to illustrate some of the practical problems encountered.

Irrigation Efficiencies

The process of irrigation is to bring water from the source through distribution system down to the farm and apply the water to the soil. The distribution system can be divided into main, sub-main, lateral, sub-lateral and tertiary, also the system can be either of open ditches or pipes. For the application part, there are a number of methods such as surface, sub-surface, sprinkler and trickler method, of irrigation. There are losses of water associate at various stages of the irrigation process, some can be avoided or controlled, while the others are unavoidable. The key to efficient water use is to minimise the losses that most of the water diverted from the source can be beneficially utilised by crops.

Efficiency is a measure of effectiveness or performance and irrigation efficiencies are measures of effectiveness of different stages in irrigation process. The determination or evaluation of efficiencies are very useful and necessary for the improvement of irrigation system or project. By knowing the efficiency or effectiveness of the various stages, problems or causes of ineffectiveness can be identified and corrective measures can be taken in order to improve the system. In this chapter, various efficiency terms will be discussed.

Irrigation Efficiency

It is defined as the percentage of, delivered irrigation water that is stored in the soil and available for consumptive use by crops. When the delivered water is measured as farm gate, it is called *farm irrigation efficiency*, when measured at the field it is called *field irrigation efficiency*. This term indicates how well a set goal is being reached, and the goal can be defined according to the objective of the project.

Conveyance Efficiency

It is defined as the ratio of water received at inlet to a block of fields to that released at the project head-works. Conveyance efficiency can be divided for main canal, lateral and sub-lateral. Several factors affecting conveyance efficiency, namely; size of the irrigated acreage, method of water delivery, areas under different crops, canal lining and the technical and managerial facilities of water control. This term tells how much water is lost in the conveyance system.

Based on a literature study, average conveyance efficiency of surface irrigation with respect to method of water delivery and irrigated area are summarised in Table 6.1.

Table 6.1: Average, Conveyance Efficiency

Irrigation Method	*Method of Water Delivery*	*Irrigated Area (ha)*	*Efficiency %*
Basin for rice cultivation	Continuous supply with no substantial change in flow	—	90
Surface irrigation (Basin, Border and Furrow)	Rotation supply based predetermined schedule with effective management	3000-5000	88
	Rotational supply based on predetermined schedule with less effective management	<1,000->10,000	70
	Rotational supply based on advance request	<1,000->10,000	65

Farm Ditch Efficiency

It is defined as ratio of water received at the field inlet to that received at the inlet of block of fields. Farm ditch efficiency is affected primarily by the method and control of operation, soil types, length of the farm ditch and size of the irrigation block.

Based on a literature study, average farm ditch efficiency under various conditions are summarised in Table 6.2.

Table 6.2: Average Farm Ditch Efficiency

Irrigation Method	*Method of Delivery*	*Soil Type and Ditch Condition*	*Block Size (ha)*	*Efficiency %*
Basin for	Continuous	Unlined: Clay to heavy cla lined	up to 3	90
	Rotation or Intermittent	Unlined: Clay to heavy cla lined	<20	80
			>20	90
Surface Irrigation	Rotation or Intermittent	Unlined: Silt clay	<20	60-70
		lined	>20	80
	Rotation or Intermittent	Unlined: Sand, loam	<20	55
		lined	>20	65

It is defined as the percentage of, delivered irrigation water that is stored in the soil and available for consumptive use by crops. When the delivered water is measured at farm gate, it is called '*farm irrigation efficiency*'; when measured at the field, it is called '*field irrigation efficiency*', and when measured at the point of diversion, it is called '*project efficiency*'. This term indicates how well a set goal is being reached, and the goal can be defined according to the objective of the project.

Distribution efficiency which can be defined as the percentage of water released at the head-work that is received at the field inlet. A summary of study conducted by ICID on water distribution study can be shown in Table 6.3.

Table 6.3: Average Distribution Efficiency of Rotational Supply Under Optimum Conditions

Adequate organisation and communication	65%
Sufficient organisation and communication	55%
Insufficient organisation and communication	40%
Poor organisation and communication	33%

Conveyance losses can be further divided into two components, one is fixed losses i.e. seepage, percolation and evaporation, the other is operational losses i.e. lack of or malfunction of control devices, untimely opening and closing of gates etc.

Water Application Efficiency

It is defined as the ratio of the minimum depth of water stored in the root zone to the average depth of water applied.

This term merely shows the fraction of the applied water that are stored within the root zone and potentially accessible for crop use, but with the absolute minimum value, it may be exaggerately low. Instead of the minimum depth, it was suggested to use the average of the lowest quarter. This efficiency is dependent on irrigation method, soil type, crop and water availability.

Based on a literature study; average application efficiency of various irrigation method can be summarised in Table 6.4.

Potential Water Application Efficiency

It is defined as the ratio of the minimum depth infiltrated just equalling soil moisture deficiency to the average depth of water applied. This

Table 6.4: Average Application Efficiency

Irrigation Method	*Method of Delivery*	*Soil Type*	*Depth of Application (mm)*	*Efficiency %*
Basin	Continuous	Clay Heavy clay	> 60	40~10
Furrow	Intermittent	Light soil	~ 60	60
Border	Intermittent	Light soil	260	60
Basin	Intermittent	All soil	> 60	60
Sprinkler	Intermittent	Sand, loam	< 60	70

term gives a measure of irrigation system performance attainable when applying a full irrigation.

Distribution Uniformity

It is defined as the ratio of minimum depth infiltrated to the average depth infiltrated. This term gives an indication of the uniformity of infiltration throughout the field, and is useful as an indicator of the magnitude of the distribution problems. For surface irrigation, in order to get a high distribution uniformity, the field has to be properly levelled or graded.

Overall or Project Efficiency

The project efficiency is determined by considering the various stages of water conveyance and application, or it is the product of all efficiencies starting from the diversion head-work up to the water stored in the root zone depth. Some average farm, conveyance and project efficiencies are shown in Table 6.5.

Case Study

The Damodar River Basin (DRB) is a sub-basin and part of Ganges River System spreading over an area of about 23,173 sq. km. in the State of Bihar and West Bengal. The geographical boundary of the basin lies between 22°15' to 24°30'N latitude and 84°30' to 88°15'E longitude (Fig. 6.1). The basin extends over six districts of Bihar State viz., Palamau, Hazaribagh, Giridih, Dhanbad, Santhal Paragana and Ranchi and five districts of West Bengal viz., Purulia, Bankura, Burdwan, Hooghly and Howrah.

Table 6.5: Average Farm, Conveyance and Project Efficiencies with respect to Method of Delivery

Method	*Efficiency in percent*		
	Farm	*Conveyance*	*Project*
Continuous block supply with small changes discharge for paddy fields	27	90	25
Rotational supply based on pre-determined schedule	41	70	29
Rotational supply based on advance request by farmer	53	53	28
Supply on demand, supply by pipe lines system under pressure, sprinkler irrigation	70	73	51

*Farm efficiency is the product of the application and farm ditch efficiency.

Study Area

The Damodar River Basin (DRB) is a sub-basin and part of Ganga River System spreading over an area of about 23,173 sq. km. in the State of Bihar and West Bengal. The geographical boundary of the basin lies between 22°15' to 24°30'N latitude and 84°30' to 88°15'E longitude (Fig. 6.2). The basin extends over six districts of Bihar State viz., Palamau, Hazaribagh, Giridih, Dhanbad, Santhal Paragana and Ranchi and five districts of West Bengal viz., Purulia, Bankura, Burdwan, Hooghly and Howrah. The distinctive feature of the basin is that around three-fourth of its area (slightly more than 72% i.e., 1.76 million ha. of the total area); which represents the upper catchment, falls in Bihar, while the low lying flood plains (about 28% i.e., 0.68 million ha.) entirely lie in West Bengal.

Damodar River and its tributaries viz. Barakar, Jamunia, Bokaro, Konar, Gowai, Bhairasi, Usri, Tilaiya, serves as the main source of surface water, besides two natural lakes, namely Topchanchi and Nalkari of the region. Damodar is the rainfed river and was proverbially known as river of sorrow because of the frequent incurrence of floods. After the construction of dams, five large water resources, namely Tenughat, Konar, Tillaiya, Panchet and Maithon, the flood problem of the region has been mitigated and the reservoirs now serve as the main surface water resources of the region.

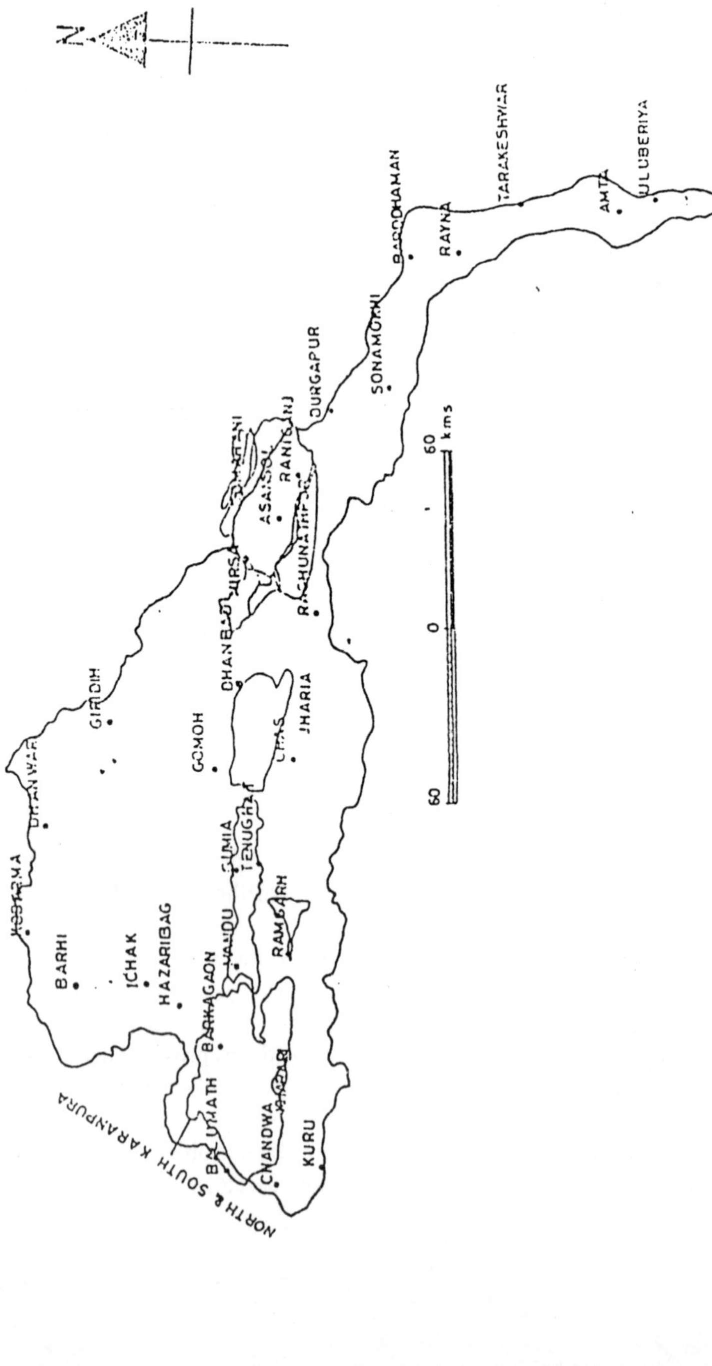

Fig. 6.1: Study Area

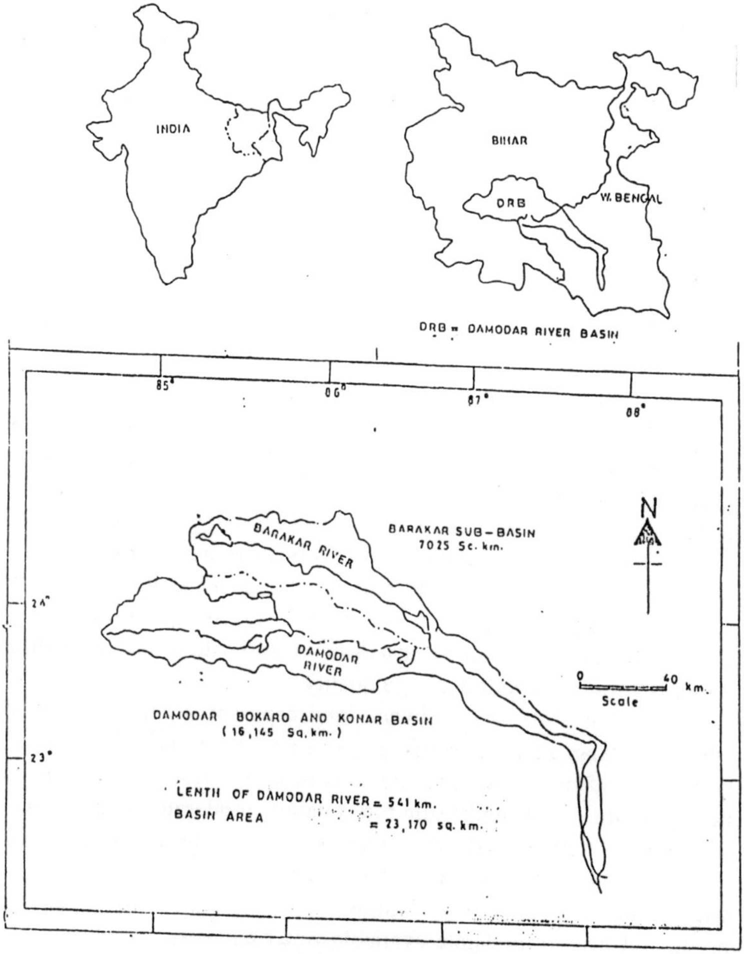

Fig. 6.2: Damodar River Basin

Climate

The project area is located in the warm sub-tropical zone and its climate is influenced by Bay of Bengal monsoon. Rainfall is irregular; about 85 per cent of total annual rainfall occurs in the rainy season (June to September) and the remaining 15 per cent in the winter season (October to December). In summer season average maximum temperature of 43°C and minimum of 30°C. Winter having average maximum temperature of 25°C and minimum of 10°C. Sometimes temperature goes below 4°C. Annual rainfall over the basin varies from 765 to 1607 mm with an average of 1200 mm. The evaporation is maximum during summer (21 mm) and minimum in monsoon (2.5 mm) with humidity 70 per cent.

Soils

The whole part of Damodar River Basin is mainly divided into three major soil types. One is soils of granites gneiss landslope spread over district Giridih, Dhanbad, Hazaribagh, Palamau, Lohardanga and Santhal Parganas. Among this soil type four sub soil-type were identified which soils of hilly terrain covering major portion of the area is under the forests with rock outcrops having moderate to steep slopes, severe rooting depth, allow erosion at places and stonimen at places. Second is soil is undulating plateau covering area is partly under cultivation for paddy, millets and soil seeds, having shallow root depth, stonimen, acidity with low to medium available water holding capacity. Third is soils of undulating plain and upland covering the area partly under thin to moderate dense forests and partly being cultivated for rice with moderate acidity, erosion prone. Fourth and last is soils of valley covering cultivated paddy area with wheat as second crop with irrigation facilities in rabi season with poor drainage quality.

Second is soils of Gondwana landscape spreading over part of Dhanbad, Palamau and Hazaribagh. Among this soil type four sub-soil types were identified which were soils of hilly terrain covering major portion of the area is under thin forest having moderate to steep slopes, severe erosion, shallow depth and low available water capacity. Second is soils of undulating plateau covering under forest and paddy cultivation with undulating topography, shallow depth, moderate to severe erosion prone and low to moderate available water capacity. Third is soil of undulating plain covering area under the cultivation of paddy and jawar with undulating topography and moderate to severe erosion. Fourth is soil of river valley covering the area of paddy cultivation having poor drainage and moderate erosion.

Third main division is of soils of Damodar landscape spread over Hazaribagh district only. They are divided into three sub-group of soils. First is soil of hilly terrain covering thin forest area with moderate to steep slopes, severe erosion, stonimen, low available water capacity and acidic. Second sub-type is soil of undulating plain covering paddy, millets and maize growing area with undulating topography and imperfect drainages. Third and last sub-type is soils of undulating upland with valley covering area partly under degraded forest and area partly cultivated for paddy and wheat with having undulating topography and poor drainage.

Irrigation

The water stored in the reservoirs and dry weather flows are utilised to meet the committed requirement for various purposes like *rabi* irrigation. The quantum of water available over committed requirement is utilised for basin irrigation. Irrigation is an important sector in which water resources of Damodar river basin are extensively being utilised. Around 1454.2 MCM of water are being utilised for 3,26,600 ha of *kharif* crop whereas 597.2 MCM for 66,200 ha of *rabi* and Boro irrigation mostly for West Bengal state. Out of total 4048 Mm^3 surface water availability only 2850 Mm^3 is utilised for irrigation (1990) which is 70.37 per cent of the total utilisation. Out of total groundwater reserves of Damodar river basin 2844.54 Mm^3 year it is only 2417.85 Mm^3 per year is used for irrigation.

Results

Main canal efficiency—Construction of Durgapur barrage was constructed at Damodar river for irrigation utilization.

Flow measurements were taken at two points, one near the head regulator and another at 4.6 kilometres down stream, and based on the loss rate obtained, the main canal conveyance efficiency was determined. For the length of about 11 kilometres, the conveyance efficiency was estimated as 80 per cent.

Lateral conveyance efficiency—Cut throat flumes were used for measuring flow in the laterals. The conveyance efficiencies on a lined and an unlined laterals were found to be 53 per cent and 59 per cent respectively. The lower efficiency of the lined lateral was mainly due to operational losses, whereas most of the losses of the unlined lateral was due to seepage and percolation losses.

Farm ditch efficiency—Short sections along an unlined tertiary were selected at random for the determination of farm ditch efficiency and flow measurement were done with the use of cut throat flumes. The values obtained ranges from 50 to 70 per cent with an average of 63 per cent.

Application efficiency—Field measurements were carried out on 32 field plots spreading across three laterals and cultivated with three crops; namely Mustard, Maize and Cucumber. The mean values obtained ranges from 40 per cent to 80 per cent, and it was found that higher efficiency is closely related to deeper root zone depth. The average value for the study area was taken as 51 per cent.

Project efficiency—The product of the conveyance, farm ditch and application efficiencies represent the project efficiency. In this study, the project efficiency in only 14 per cent which is very low. The immediate questions are why it is low and how it can be improved; and they will be discussed in the next section.

Seepage and Percolation—Seepage and percolation losses of low land paddies were estimated by subtracting the estimated consumptive use from the total water use which was determined by using the water subsidence method. An average value of 3.3 mm per day was estimated as seepage and percolation losses at the study area.

Discussion

The conclusion of the study should be qualified in recognition of difficulties in carrying out the field observation. As all the 7 data collected from the field are subjected to certain degree of inaccuracy with respect to the proper selection and installation of instrument, measurement, record keeping and finally human errors. Nevertheless the general conclusions will present the picture of the performance of the project and the associate problems.

The main conclusions are:

(i) The overall project efficiency is very low, which is due to both operation and management of the project. In all categories of efficiencies of the project, they are below average. Hence, improvement in operation and management are necessary.

(ii) No significant difference between conveyance efficiencies of lined and unlined lateral was observed. Although the seepage losses as determined in the study for unlined canal is higher than lined canal as expected, but the difference is not significant. This is due to cracks and breakage in the canal lining. For this particular project, field engineers are faced with the problem of breakage and sliding of canal lining due to *high* groundwater table which results in high backwater pressure on the canal lining. There is also problem with flow regulation due to inadequate flow control devices and negligence of the operators.

(iii) The existing regulating structures were not properly maintained, in addition, at all laterals and territories inlets no flow measuring devices were provided. So proper allocation of water for the entire project cannot be accomplished.

(iv) Canal and ditch systems were not properly maintained, weed and silt were not cleaned prior to irrigation season. This is due to lack of manpower and lack of participation on the part of the farmers.

(v) The farmers and the project field personnel still do not have good understanding of basic irrigation and water management concepts. Training programmes and extension service are required in order to attain higher project efficiency.

Conclusion

Irrigation can be divided into two components each dependent on the other for attaining satisfactory results. The first is the harnessing and distribution of water which involves mostly engineering expertise, including geology, hydrology, hydraulics, design and construction.

The second is the utilization and management of the distributed water which requires a sound knowledge of engineering as well as basic irrigation concepts, farm irrigation system design and operation, drainage and on farm water management. The co-ordination of these two components and integration of the other disciplines in both components are necessary to insure a successful irrigation scheme.

On-farm water management requires good knowledge of basic irrigation concepts, or in simple term it requires good answers to the following three questions, When to apply water?, How much water to be applied? and How to apply the water? On-farm water management phase is usually arbitrarily taken as from the farm ditch inlet to the root zone of crops. Though the path of flow is relatively short, but proper water management is not simple especially for the farmers of the developing countries. The basic information concerning soil and crop are required, and they have to be measured as well. At the present stage, farmers in the region (Asia and Near East) still do not have the resource, experience and skill to handle this problem, and will take time and effort to transfer some of the basic concepts to them. In addition, the zone men and water tenders also need training in this respect, besides they are also overloaded in the sense that they are usually given too large an area to do a satisfactory job. The modern technology cannot do much yet until pre-development programmes such as training programmes and extension service were implemented, and only then can one expect significant improvement in water utilization.

Some of the major causes of low water utilisation efficiencies can be summed up as follows:

- (i) Lack of appropriate farm irrigation distribution facilities such as ditches, regulatory structures, gates and measuring devices. This in turn hinders the control of flow and usually results in wastage of water.
- (ii) Lack of proper land preparation which results in uneven water distribution.
- (iii) Conveyance and distribution canals are often not lined probably due to high initial cost, consequently seepage loss is very considerable and can cause salinity problem in some areas.
- (iv) Lack of information on soil moisture content and crop water requirement at different stages of growth which leads to untimely irrigation.
- (v) Lack of experience in drawing up agricultural development programmes with adequate provision for water management and control at the farm level.
- (iv) The transfer of knowledge on water management and irrigated agriculture to farmers is lacking. There is also the tendency to oversimplify the problem of scientific water management.

References

Merriam, J., Ke. Ller, J. and Alfaro, J. (1973), *Irrigation System Evaluation and Improvement*, Utah State University, U.S.A.

Ullah, Enayet (1979), Irrigation Efficiency Evaluation of Lam Pao Project, Unpublished, M. Eng. Thesis, Asian Institute of Technology, Bangkok.

Yjangsadipoera, M. (1979), A Review of Irrigation Efficiency, Unpublished, M. Eng. Thesis, Asian Institute of Technology, Bangkok.

7

CONSEQUENCES OF GROUNDWATER DEPLETION IN A SEMI-ARID TRACT OF HARYANA

M.S. GILL & R.N. YADAV

Introduction

Availability of water for drinking and irrigation purposes is of crucial importance for the human geography of an area (Rao, 1975, p.1). Its role is all the more important in semi-arid and arid regions where even a little decline in the availability of water, whether from underground aquifers or from other sources, including precipitation, is enough to upset not only the fragile balance in human-land relations but also various threads of socio-economic contours of the affected area (Dabi and Anderson, 1999, p. 120).

Irrigation plays a catalytic role in agricultural development of an area. This is particularly the case in arid/semi-arid areas marked by annual/seasonal deficit of moisture. Apart from paucity of rain water in absolute terms, such areas also suffer from higher variability of precipitation from year to year. In such a context, there are two options for agriculture development: (i) to evolve suitable dry-farming techniques and introduce high-yielding varieties of drought-resistance crops; and (ii) to make provision for irrigation suited to the climatic and edaphic setting of the tract. However, in view of the very slow pace of recharge of groundwater in semi-arid/arid areas, the irrigation methods also need to be designed accordingly.

Following the success of the Green Revolution in Punjab and Haryana in the late 1960s and early 1970s, the practice of irrigated farming, based on flood irrigation, was also extended to the semi-arid tracts in southwest Haryana. With the objective of enhancing their agricultural incomes, the farmers in such tracts adopted tubewell irrigation to a considerable extent. Mahendragarh District was one such area where tubewell irrigation has made rapid strides since mid-1970s.

The Study Village

The study is based on field work as well as secondary data relating to Dochana village in Mahendragarh District of Haryana (Fig. 7.1). The village is located on the State's border with Rajasthan some 14 kilometres to the west of Narnaul town. As per the 1991 census, the village had a total area of 304.72 hectares of which 80.22 per cent was under cultivation. The village was characterised by notable proportion of 'area not available for cultivation' (16.59 per cent) as well as 'cultivable wasteland' (3.19 per cent).

According to the census enumeration in 1991, Dochana village's population stood at 1680 of which 22.26 per cent were Scheduled Castes. Its rural literacy rate was 39.82 per cent only (males: 53.71 per cent and females: 25.18 per cent) as against the District and State average of 40.09 per cent (male: 52.19 per cent and female: 26.09 per cent) and 44.71 per cent (male 60.70 per cent, and female 27.16 per cent) respectively. About 55 per cent of the workers were engaged in agriculture, while about 20 per cent were recorded in 'other services'. Besides 'trade and commerce', 'transport, storage and communications' and 'construction' were other important industrial categories claiming 6.31 per cent, 5.30 per cent, and 5.05 per cent of the workers in the village. Significantly, the proportion of female workers to total female population was reported to be very low, i.e., 1.22 per cent as compared to the high figure of 44.78 per cent in case of males.

Irrigation in the Study Village

Before the advent of tubewell irrigation in the village in mid-1970s, *charsa* was the main method for irrigation. Under this method water was drawn from the wells using a large leather bag tied to a long rope. As this method was labour intensive, time-consuming and quite inefficient, only a small proportion of the village's cultivated area was irrigated before the period of tubewell irrigation. However, with the coming of cheap hydroelectricity to the village in 1975 as well as the

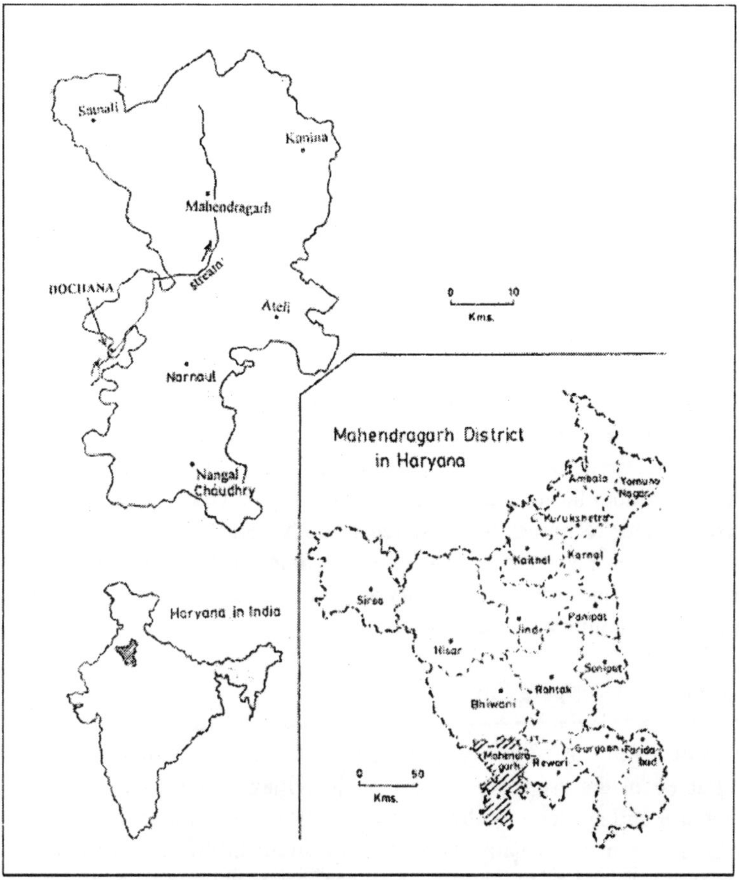

diffusion of high yielding varieties of crops in the wake of the Green Revolution in other parts of Haryana in early 1970s, people opted to go for tubewell irrigation in a big way. The first tubewell was installed in 1975; the number of tubewells increased rapidly and it had gone upto about 80 in early 1980s. As a result the proportion of irrigated area also went up from about 6 per cent in 1974-75 to about 75 per cent at the peak period of irrigation in mid-1980s.

It deserves mention here that despite installation of several tubewells in the village during 1975-80, the groundwater table had also registered perceptible rise. It was due mainly to the damming of Dohan stream by the Haryana Government in 1978. The rise in watertable further encouraged installation of more tubewells in the village.

Subsequently, however, the groundwater dwindled rapidly due chiefly to: (i) damming of the Dohan stream by Rajasthan Government in 1980-81 at a distance of about 25 kilometres upstream of Dochana village resulting in sharp decline in the rate of groundwater recharge in the study area; and (ii) continual draft of groundwater by a large number of tubewells installed in the village since 1975.

The problem of depletion of groundwater came to be felt perceptibly by the early 1980s in terms of decreasing water pressure in the tubewells. Gradually, the tubewells started running out of water after working a few hours at a stretch. The groundwater table receded further and further down, and by the end of the 1980s the tubewells began to go out of operation. Consequently, the village came to be characterised by acute water scarcity. Even, drinking water had to be fetched from another village, named Shimla, located at a distance of about 3 kilometres in Rajasthan territory. The cost of installing deep tubewells was so high that individual farmers could not afford doing it. Thus, the depletion of groundwater resources had resulted in both water supply problems as well as water management problems (A1-Saleh, 1992, p. 220). By 1992 most of the tubewells had gone dry and the village came in for bad days, both in economic and social terms.

Impact on Cropping Pattern

The changing availability of irrigation water was expectedly well reflected in the cropping pattern of the village. The main impact of increase and subsequent decline in irrigation was on the *rabi* crops as winter season is virtually without any rainfall in the area. In the pre-irrigation period gram was the main crop followed by *sarson* and barley in terms of acreage. With the coming of tubewell irrigation in the mid-1970s, area under wheat registered rapid increase making it soon the first ranking *rabi* crop in the village. The gain in wheat acreage was at the expense of gram which, consequently, declined to second position among the *rabi* crops. However, with the depletion of groundwater, wheat slided down to lower rank. Similarly, the share of fallow land has also gone up quite high again. In other words, the cropping pattern has returned almost to the same as was there in the early 1970s.

A further notable change has been effected in *rabi* cropping pattern since the depletion of groundwater by tubewell irrigation. *Sarson*, a cash crop, has now acquired the top rank among *rabi* crops. This crop requires less of moisture as well as labour than that needed for wheat which was at the first rank during the thick of irrigation period. The change in emphasis from barely to *sarson* in the *rabi* season is closely related to the decline in animal population since mid-1970s. As against the pre-1975 period, the village now has a much smaller number of animals, and, thus, there is a considerably reduced requirement for fodder as compared to that in the earlier period. Consequently, *sarson* cultivation gets preference over barley which, to a large extent, was grown for fodder earlier. The increase in *sarson* acreage after the depletion of groundwater has also adversely affected the area under *bajra* in the *kharif* season. As after the *bajra* crop the soil is not left with adequate moisture for proper growth of *sarson*, farmers prefer to forgo the former to get the latter crop.

However, the extension of irrigation in the village did not make perceptible difference in the cropping pattern of *kharif* season. There was no change in the relative ranking of the top three *kharif* crops, i.e., *bajra*, *guar* and *jowar* notwithstanding the fact that the acreage under *bajra* and *guar* has gradually come down between 1974-75 and 1995-96.

Impact on Livestock

As mentioned earlier, the village faced acute water scarcity for 3-4 years even for drinking purposes. When drinking water for humans and animals had to be fetched from the adjoining village at a distance of 3 kilometres in Rajasthan, it had naturally become difficult to support as large a cattle population as in the previous years. Consequently, the number of animals, which had gone up considerably during the heyday of tubewell irrigation, have come down in recent years (Table 7.1). The decline in the number draught animals like bullocks, camels and donkeys was understandable in view of the rise in the number of tractors, but the village witnessed fall in all categories of livestock including the milch cattle. This reflects that the worsening agricultural conditions in the wake of depletion of groundwater resources in the village have also made an adverse impact on cattle population.

Change in Tree Cover

The period of tubewell irrigation also witnessed large scale felling of trees in the village due mainly to: (i) Tractorization, which came in the wake of the extension of tubewell irrigation, worked to stop growth of

Table 7.1: Livestock in Dochana Village, 1971-1996

Year	*Cows*	*Buffaloes*	*Bullocks (pairs)*	*Camels*	*Donkeys*	*Goats*	*Sheep*	*Total*
1971	130	205	70	72	69	80	60	756
1981	100	299	26	60	42	105	135	793
1986	67	283	14	42	32	85	120	657
1996	20	250	2	30	15	75	50	444

Source: Office of the Director, Animal Husbandry, Narnaul.

new seedlings through greater frequency of deep ploughing in the fields. Besides, the farmers had also cut down many trees which hindered unobstructed and easy mobility of tractors in the fields; (ii) Land consolidation in the late 1960s had also made its own contribution in the removal of trees in the fields. Each household had cut down many of the trees on their land which was likely to be allotted to someone else; (iii) The decline in the number of goats and sheep and increasing restriction on the grazing in the fields further added to the problem of declining number of *jand* trees as the *jand* seeds do not germinate if these have not passed through the digestive system of these animals.

Social Consequences

General thrift and limited consumption was a hallmark of the people in village before the commencement of tubewell irrigation. Even tea taking was quite uncommon in the village during that period, and people generally happened to taste it when on a visit to Narnaul or some other town. Such an attitude of pervasive thrift was well in tune with that found in areas marked by profoundly subsistence economy.

However, consequent upon extension of tubewell irrigation, the village experienced quick rise in its prosperity after 1975. A major share of sharply enhanced agricultural income was spent on building *pucca* houses. Many families also invested considerable part of their incomes on buying tractors, trolleys and other machinery used for various agricultural operations. Besides, the period also witnessed notable rise in the number of bicycles and scooters.

Another conspicuous consequence of rapid rise in agricultural incomes in the wake of tubewell irrigation in the village was considerable increase in the expenditure on dowry and substantial spurt in the consumption of liquor. Significantly, the expenditure on dowry and liquor has remained virtually as high as that during the peak period of agricultural incomes even after the depletion of groundwater and the consequent erosion of agricultural prosperity in the village.

When Dochana village was stricken by acute water scarcity during 1991-94, even drinking water had to be fetched from a nearby village Shimla, located in Jhunjhunu District of Rajasthan. The water was either brought on head, or on animal backs and camel carts. During that period, the villagers even had to go without bath for days together. It is notable that most of the task of water fetching had to be performed by females. It shows that any erosion of resources, including drinking water, impacts more adversely on weaker segments of society. The problem of fetching drinking water from another village was solved when the government installed a deep tubewell in the village itself for this purpose. The situation became further favourable in this regard following good rains in 1995 owing to which considerable water got stored up behind Dohan check dam near the village which led to perceptible rise in watertable. Consequently, a few tubewells in the village are now able to work for 4-5 hours each day. However, if there is no repetition of good rains to fill the Dohan channel storage, the decline of groundwater table may again put the tubewells out of operation.

With the decline in agricultural incomes in the villages in the 1990s, Dochana village suffered decline in its social position in the area. Among others, one manifestation of its declined social status was that the people from the surrounding villages were not forthcoming to make matrimonial ties in the village. The people did not want to marry their daughters in the village where even drinking water had to be fetched from another village at a distance of about 3 kilometres. Similarly, outside villagers were also not interested in getting brides from Dochana village as not much dowry would be available in the context of obtaining poverty among the village population at large. As a result, very few marriages took place here during the period of acute water shortage i.e. 1991-1994. The people preferred to postpone the marriages in the hope of better days to come. Similarly, there was little addition to *pucca* houses during this period.

Summing Up

Introduction of tubewell irrigation to semi-arid areas results in notable changes in cropping pattern in favour of cash crops. However, when the groundwater resources get depleted, the cropping pattern reverts more or less to the earlier position.

There occurs a rapid rise and then equally rapid fall in agricultural income with the increase and decrease in area under irrigation. Expectedly, the village also undergoes corresponding enhancement and decline in its social status in the area. Similarly, the paucity of drinking water, resulting from depletion of groundwater resources by tubewell irrigation, further adds to the strain as well as drudgery of female work. Decline in cattle population and even that of trees is another outcome of this situation.

It follows from the study that it is not prudent to apply the method of flood irrigation in semi-arid/arid areas as it is wasteful of scarce groundwater resources. To pursue such a course amounts to deliberate undermining of the sustainability of the area as it ultimately exhausts the very foundation of life, i.e., water (Nagaraj *et al.*, 1999, p. 94). Drip irrigation seems to be the best suited in such environments. Besides, water-prudent crops should be grown instead of water-expensive ones. In other words, cropping pattern needs to be carefully designed as per the specificities of local areas. Wholesale imitation of cropping pattern of sub-humid/humid tracts is not in tune with sustainability of semi-arid/arid areas. Thus, the problem of groundwater decline in such areas is "both a management and a water shortage problem" (Al-Saleh, 1992, p. 222).

In brief, any sustainable development in agriculture could only be achieved in a meaningful manner if it is done after taking into account the socio-economic, cultural and ecological pulse of the area. Any blind duplication of the experience of other areas may do more harm than good to both the land and the people. Besides, water management need to be accorded a top priority in such areas.

References

Al-Saleh, Mohammed Abdullah (1992) "Declining Groundwater Level of the Minjur Aquifer, Tebrak area, Saudi Arabia", *The Geographical Journal*, Vol. 158, No. 2, pp. 215-222.

Dabi Daniel Davou and Anderson, William P. (1999) "Water Use for Commodity Production in Katarko Village, Northern Nigeria", *Applied Geography*, Vol. 19, No. 2, pp. 105-122.

Nagaraj, N. *et al.* (1999) "Ground Water Institutions in US and India: Sustainable and Equitable Resource Use", *Economic and Political Review*, Vol. 34, No. 26, June 26-July 2, pp. A93-A104.

Rao, K.L. (1975) *India's Water Wealth*, New Delhi, Orient Longman Ltd.

8

LOCATING DATA GAPS IN PLANNING STRATEGIES FOR MICROLEVEL DEVELOPMENT OF DIFFICULT RAINFED AREAS OF EASTERN INDIA

Focus on Soil and Water Resource Management

D.K. BAGCHI

Introduction

After critical evaluation of India's performance since independence, Amartya Sen in an interview to '*Frontline*' reporter (August, 1997) suggested that our greatest achievement is to continue with our democratic set-up while greatest failure is to address the burning issue of social inequality. This situation needs serious introspection about the existing utilization status of different sectors alongwith respective potentials so that future planning programmes can address 'Sustainability' which in turn covers productivity, stability, equitability and rational resource use. India being predominantly dependent on agriculture, now contributes about 33 per cent of GDP while absorbing nearly 66 per cent of total labour force. So planners must pay attention to this sector to achieve food security and reduce poverty.

A few criteria of agricultural growth and pattern of changes as also its social and environmental implications are well established and recently documented in various publications (Rao, 1994; Bhalla and Singh, 1997; Mishra, 1997) and numerous statistical handbooks and tables prepared by central and State agencies. These primarily point out (i) very low productivity of rainfed crops/systems, (ii) regional imbalances in production scenario where eastern and central States are far behind although eastern India, specially West Bengal since 80s are showing upward trend in production, (iii) nearly 85 per cent of poor households are operating on 36 per cent of cultivated area with very small holdings of approximately 0.4 to 1 hectare, and (iv) difficult areas are mostly subjected to degradation with unsustainable land and water resource base.

If we concentrate on eastern India having larger rainfed area with major concentration of small and marginal farmers, we are in conformity with Bhalla and Singh (1997) that eastern region ought to receive highest priority in plan investment for several reasons. Firstly the expenditure involved in capital-output ratio is low because of heavy rainfall and water availability at surface depths. Secondly, for various reasons the eastern had a much lower level of investment compared to other regions. Finally the pay-off of agricultural development is high in this region since characterised by heavy population pressure. An increase of agricultural productivity in vast areas of small farm holdings will trigger the process of rapid growth in other sectors and tend to reduce rural poverty.

However, as has been explained by Chambers and Ghildyal (1985) poor rainfed farmers in difficult areas mostly operate on CDR, i.e., Complex-diversified-riskprone system. This eventually makes it obligatory for the planners to be equipped with technologies satisfying ideal production conditions to address firstly the above mentioned system characteristics. Next step is to examine whether these are suited to optimally stable productivity with sustainable use of resources base covering both natural and human resources. To be specific, goal of agricultural development in these areas should be to (i) increase system productivity without degrading resource base, (ii) augment employment generation, and (iii) address equity.

With 73rd Constitutional amendment for stressing on decentralised planning through Panchayat systems, it becomes essential for the planners to have reliable information at microlevel to know the present status and thus take effective steps for closing the gaps between actual and potential of system productivity. This pre supposes that we must have good data base regarding extent and nature of complexity and diversity as also the decision-making process of mainly the poor farmers in selecting appropriate technologies.

This chapter would attempt to argue whether we have sufficient informations or data base to reasonably hypothesise the objective situations in small farm holdings alongwith associated ecological and socio-economic environments. Next our efforts will be to prioritise few of the major elements affecting productivity and to find out whether specific informations and data base generated at microlevel will satisfy the need of appraisal of the situation better for future plan. While generalising the issues in the following sections, this chapter will try to strengthen the arguments picked up from the studies conducted by the author and his associates in rainfed plateau areas of South Bihar and West Bengal (Maiti & Bagchi, 1993; Bagchi *et al.,* 1995; Bagchi *et al.,* 1997; Bagchi, 1997).

Why Informations and in which Areas?

Real challenge in rainfed systems, specially in sub-humid regions of eastern India is to quantify uncertainty based on informations which provided a practical solution to decision-making. Uncertainty arises a practical solution to decision-making and intuitively speaking, the more informations we have the less is uncertainty and consequently the less is the loss in decision-making. The new paradigm of logical equation as put forward by C.R. Rao (1989).

[Uncertain Knowledge] + [Amount of uncertainty in it] = [Certain Knowledge]

Studies in Rainfed Areas

Interestingly as A. Gupta (1990) has pointed out that the Ph.D. dissertations of Agricultural and allied sciences in India devoted to rainfed crops and systems only are about 15 per cent of the total although on area coverage this is 92 million hectares compared to 48 million hectares of irrigated sector. In rainfed systems, technologies to augment productivity are plenty with huge amount of published materials and reports. Mostly the yield reductions as Widwaski & O'Toole (1991) pointed out in rice production system are at actual farmers' plots from on-farm trials. Constraints located are adverse weather and soil as also agro-ecological and socio-economic parameters influencing poor farmers' decision-making process. This consequently suggests that good data base on weather-soil-crop relations and then integrating these parameters with microlevel ecology and socio-economic indicators. Simultaneous efforts need to be taken up to analyse the events forcing the farmers to adopt diversified livelihood opportunities. In all these spheres at microlevel, data requirement is both of quantitative and qualitative nature necessitating inputs from different disciplines. While data supply from individual discipline is reasonably well, integrated data to apprise us about the whole scenario is mostly absent. We would try to explain a few documented during our studies at eastern plateau.

Water Resource Data

Our experience in rainfed eastern plateau covering 46, 16 and 19 per cent of geographical areas of Bihar, West Bengal and Orissa respectively show that even with reasonably good amount of annual rainfall ranging between 1300-1400 mm, main resource constraint seems to be the water (Sen *et al.,* 1985). Rainfall mainly distributed over 4 monsoon months amount to 85 to 90 per cent of the total. However, undulated top sequences leading to scarcity of moisture at upland while excess of it in low land pose constraints for double cropping in follow up months of monsoon. Again our long-term rainfall data analysis supports the hypothesis that even in monsoon months, frequent dry spells just after monsoon onset and during September-October coincides often with seedling establishment and reproductive stages respectively of main crop paddy causing drastic yield reduction (Bagchi *et al.,* 1995). However, few data exists to show firstly about the pattern of rainfall distribution over different microlevel regions and next the time series data of crops and varieties giving somewhat stable and optimum yields under fluctuating rainfall in farmers' fields. Again although plenty of water harvesting techniques have been advocated, very few ideal models could be located to assist the planners in developing ecologically suited ones acceptable to the targeted users.

Resource Management

This at least theoretically emphasises conceptualization and management at grassroot levels of land, water and bio resources including human (Parikh, 1991). Here technologies related to soil water conservation and eco-friendly technological adoption to produce food-fodder-fuel are aimed at. With 73rd Constitutional amendment on decentralised planning, we expect that participation from supposedly targetted beneficiaries will flourish and thus productivity and equity criteria will be addressed.

However, initial status report of available resources and their utilization pattern are mostly absent. Thus plans and execution of the same are taken in haste and somewhat arbitrarily with less than enthusiastic participation from the beneficiaries. Mukherjee & Bandopadhyay (1991) while reviewing the Panchayat activities in West Bengal stressed on initial participatory resource mapping programmes. Recent district-wise resource mapping initiated by L.U.S.S.P. (I.C.A.R.) can be better strengthened at lower levels if it is taken up as suggested and implemented by Bharatiya Gyan Vigyan Samiti (Sinha and Verma, 1991). This enables us to identify the status and priority activities through channelising local human resources and thus data generated can be of real asset for future planning. Uniqueness of resource mapping is that it encompasses topography, hydrology, land characteristics, resource use and cropping system on village/plot basis using local farmers' knowledge and participation. Thus it can well be used for future planning at microlevel.

Technology Transfer

'Lab' to 'Land' programmes being recently modified into 'Lab' to 'Land' to 'Lab' have raised some interesting issues requiring examination of quantitative and qualitative data. Here also we do lack a good data base. In eastern plateau technologies for erosion check like afforestation, water harvesting, plantations and ecologically suited crops and cropping systems have failed to generate any fruitful results. Our observations regarding non-participation of supposed beneficiaries may be due to the fact that they do not find any short-term gains out of these activities. In soil and water conservation long-term goal of achieving good resource base and biomass and thus improving economy gets thwarted by non-participation phenomenon where these measures do not specifically fulfil short-term needs of subsistent and poor farmers.

Perception and Decision-Making

Farmer's perception about the development programmes and their subsequent decision-making processes are types of data where very few studies have been taken up. Our project (Maiti & Bagchi) on this aspect in Bihar plateau suggests that here studies should encompass both quantitative and qualitative parameters where poor farmer's major concern is to satisfy subsistence need first.

Again in relation to spread of HYV/improved technologies, rather dismal performance in south Bihar may, in our opinion be due to their risk perception for which informations are rather scanty. Thus they are attached to traditional technologies giving them somewhat stable optimum productivity whereas modern ones are regarded to give maximum but unstable yields caused through erratic rainfall. Here our data base with regards to varieties/fertilizers and other inputs mostly report about yield although extent of annual variation in production caused due to uncertain rain, soil management, pest and diseases etc. in farmers' fields are mostly unknown. As discussed earlier complex situation in rainfed systems often compel the farmers to diversified cropping and farming systems as contingent plans. In Bihar plateau although some contingent measures have been advocated (Mohsin, 1990) there are very few informations about the effectiveness of the suggested ones and consequent acceptability by the farmers so that future planning can be based on these findings.

We have noted significant deviations in farmers' practices from the suggested technology packages for different crops but very few data could be assessed on the rate of productivity increase/decrease and also resources status of water and land due to these changes. These seem to be essential because farmers have their own perception or compulsion in modifying the packages to suit their social and economic conditions. Thus part adaptations and results achieved thereof may suggest the planners to go for pragmatic plans suited to ecological and socio-economic needs. Here again comes the question of diversified cropping/farming system. Our studies in Bihar plateau have shown that crops of poor and subsistent farmers specifically coarse cereals, pulses and small millets have been given little attention to evolve improved genotypes. Thus traditional crops and varieties suited to eroded upland are gradually faded away although some could have contributed enormously to our genepool for outstanding drought/pest resistant characteristics.

Farming System Research (FSR)

The process of FSR is not strictly a sequential series of events but there are a number of definable phases: *Appraisal* – when the current production system in an area are described and analysed and a resource audit farm hh. is made; *Experimentation* – during which potential improvements to existing production systems are developed; *Evaluation* – when promising technologies are tested in farmers' fields and demonstrated to local farmers and finally *Extension* – to the target group of farmers. The whole process is obviously dynamic in nature and there are strong feedback elements between the phases (Hildebrand, 1990).

Integrated Approach

In rainfed systems, poor and marginal farmers having small farm sizes are forced to adopt diversified farming system activities specially to earn subsistent living through acquiring mainly the three 'F' components i.e., food, fodder and fuel. This necessarily suggests that microlevel planning programmes should be holistic in nature to produce and maintain not only sufficient food but also enough fodder for livestock and good amount of forest or other energy sources to supply fuels. With this in mind, our plans for the future is to make effective integration of activities of different department/agencies working in respect to small farm development as also livelihood security of farmers and agricultural labourers dependent on it. Our data related to this aspect has been mostly worked out by economists/statisticians on one hand and natural scientists on the other working on appropriate technologies to augment productivity. But informations are sadly lacking about small farmers' risk perception phenomenon which is highly correlated with ecological, economical, agronomical and social variables. As variability is highly correlated with return, small farmers' risks in uncertain rainfed degraded environments becomes crucial and thus holistic approach to integrate variables and correlate this with productivity, stability and equitability phenomena demands maximum stress. In this area our data base probably is the weakest and when found, mostly is not comprehensively examined.

Planning Approach and Data Base

Balanced development includes proper characterization of the zones/ sub-zones delineated on the basis of broad agroclimatic divisions, presently numbering 15. Then, as suggested by (Singh & Singh, 1991), these are characterised by 20 indicators.

These include resource related variables such as sown area, forest area, land available for cultivation (on per capita basis), soil index, mean and CV of rainfall, share of problem soil, percentage irrigation of sown area, groundwater balance per unit sown area and its available soil moisture. Some socio-economic variables like literacy, population density, share of male and female in total workers, share of unemployed as also marginal workers in population are to be considered. Besides these three performance variables are yield of crops, cropping system and productivity of land and two input variables like financial credits and yield affecting inputs.

With the study of correlations while grouping different regions, a pattern of resource endowment and development could be assessed this way (Basu & Rajagopalan, 1990).

Conclusion

At the microlevel, however, participatory resource mapping being supplemented with computer aided tools like GIS can come to our aid not only to identify resource endowment but also to prioritise development steps. Here data feedback needs expansion to some qualitative indicators where technologies and systems for yield stability and ecological sustainability alongwith increasing employment opportunities and livelihood diversified incomes could be identified for experimenting at microlevel. Invariably this requires multidisciplinary approach through involving scientists/academicians/planners and most importantly the supposed and targeted beneficiaries. Constitutional amendments for decentralized planning may offer future scope for data generation in this way and make subsequent plan to increase productivity and secured livelihood through reducing poverty.

References

Bagchi, D.K., Banik, P. and Sasmal T. (1995), *Selection of appropriate technologies for upland rainfed rice growing on the Bihar plateau.* In: Fragile Lives in Fragile Ecosystems, Proceedings of International Rice Research Conference (ed.) R.A. Zeigler, Philippines, 127-134.

Bagchi, D.K., Banik P. and Sasmal, T. (1997), *Changes in rice production systems in West Bengal and rainfed plateau areas: Challenges for the future*. Paper presented at the workshop on 'Economic Aspects of Changes in Rice Production Systems in Eastern India' held in New Delhi, 2-4 April, 1997.

Bagchi, D.K. (1997), *Changing modes of agriculture and rural resource use with particular focus on small farm in few rainfed areas on eastern plateau.* Paper presented to the Annual Conference of the Development Studies Association, held on 11-13 September, 1997, at University of East Anglia, Norwich, U.K.

Bhalla, G.S. and Singh, Gurmail (1997), Recent Development in Indian Agriculture–A State Level Analysis. *Economic and Political Weekly*, XXXIII, 13, A2-18.

Chambers, R. and Ghildyal, B.P. (1985), Agricultural Research for resource poor farmers: The farmer first and last model. *Agricultural Administration*. 20, 1.

Gupta Anil (1990), Documenting Farmers' Innovations or how do people survive through innovations in risky regions. Technical Discussion Paper from IIM, Ahmedabad.

Hildebrand, P.E. (1990), Farming system research extension. In: Jones, J.G.W. and Street, P.R. (ed.) *System Theory Applied to Agriculture and Food Chain*, Elsevier, U.K., 131-143.

Maiti, A.K. and Bagchi, D.K. (1993), Perception, Performance and Potential of Development in Usri Watershed Area of Bihar Plateau Region: An Ecosystemic Approach, Report submitted to ICSSR, New Delhi, India.

Mishra, S.N. (1997), Agricultural liberalisation and development strategy in Ninth Plan. *Economic and Political Weekly*, XXXIII, 13, A 19-31.

Mohsin, M.A. (1990), Prospect of increasing productivity through rainfed farming system. Paper presented in the seminar entitled "Problems and Prospects of Agricultural Development in Tribal Areas of Bihar", BAU, Ranchi.

Mukherji, N. and Bandopadhyay, D. (1993), New Horizons for West Bengal, A Report for the Government of West Bengal.

Parikh, K.S. (1991), Towards a National Resource Accounting System. Discussion Paper No. 45. Indira Gandhi Institute of Development Research.

Rao, C.R. (1989), Taming of Uncertainty. Paper read out at 24th Convocation as Chief Guest in I.S.I. Calcutta.

Rao, Hanumanth, C.H. (1994), *Agricultural Growth, Rural Poverty and Environmental Degradation in India*, Oxford University Press.

Sen, A. (1997), *Frontline*, August, 1997.

Sen, S.R., Mukherjee, S.K., Pradhan, H.S.P., Rammurthy, K. and Singh, H. (1984), *Agricultural Productivity in Eastern India*. (Vol. I & II) Report submitted to Reserve Bank of India.

Singh, R.K. and Singh, D.N. (1993), An agroclimatic approach to agricultural development in India. In: F.W.T. Pening de Vries *et al.* (eds.) *System Approaches for Agricultural Development*, Kluwer Academic Publishers, The Netherlands, 11-125.

Sinha, S. and Verma, Ajoy (1995), *A Hand Book of Land Literacy: Participatory Resource Mapping Programme for Self-reliant Panchayats*. Bhartiya Gyan Vigyan Samiti, New Delhi.

Sinha, S. and Ghosh, Arun (1997), Literacy Campaign, Land Literacy and Watershed Development. *Economic & Political Weekly*, XXXIII 281-288.

Widwaski, D.A. and O'Toole, J.C. (1990), Prioritising the Rice Biotechnology Research Agenda for Eastern India. The Report submitted to Rockfeller Foundation, New Delhi.

9

PATTERN OF AGRICULTURAL EMPLOYMENT IN UTTAR PRADESH

SHAFIQULLAH

Agriculture is undoubtedly one of the most important economic activities of man. It provides not only the food to the teeming billions of world, numbers of industrials material but also a dominant form of employment. Agriculture being the function of physical, socio-institutional and techno-economic factors which is dynamic in nature, keeping on changing with the basic objective of increase production and generation of foodgrain surplus. Due to the variation in physical and socio-economic conditions, these changes in agriculture and its employment not uniform all over the country either spatially or temporally. Uttar Pradesh has vast changes, unequal distribution of population and natural resources, diversified nature of technological innovation, unequal opportunities to gain and utilize resource base have been responsible for the variation in agricultural employment.

Although, Uttar Pradesh is predominantly agricultural economy involving about 73 per cent (67 per cent India 1991) of the total working population, it has languishing for a long period of time. This indicates a heavy population pressure on agriculture and reflects the lack of development in other sectors (secondary and tertiary). Despite several attempt through various plans have failed as they were not properly channelised to create employment outside the agriculture and this pressure of population on agriculture has gradually increased creating conditions of widespread disguised unemployment.

In the light of above notion the basic objective of this work is to describe the trends of agricultural employment since 1961. The study further attempts to explain the spatial pattern of agricultural employment rate 1991 and also analyse the causal relationship between agricultural employment and independent variables.

Data Source and Methodology

The study is based on secondary source of data obtained from Census of India Publication, New Delhi and State Planning Institute, Lucknow, U.P., on district level for the year 1961 to 1991. Districts have been selected as the unit of the study. Although there are 63 districts have been taken. Twenty-six variables[1] were considered for the present analysis with respect to employment determinants. For analysing the data, correlation matrix has been used to assess the relationship.

Study Area

Uttar Pradesh is located in the central north of India and shares the international boundaries with Nepal and Tibet in the north. It extending over 23°52' to 31°28'N latitude and 77°04' to 84°38'E longitude. It is the most populous State of India with a population count of 139.1 million during 1991 census. It inhabits 16.4 per cent of the population in about 10.7 per cent of the land area of the country. The population density (per. sq. km.) for the year 1991 is found to be 473 compared to 273 for India. Within the State, the pressure of population on land varies highest density being in the eastern and western districts and the lowest in the hilly districts. It is predominantly an agricultural State with about 80 per cent of its population living in rural areas (compared to 74 per cent for all India). Agriculture is the single largest sector of its economy, employing about 72 per cent of its labour force. Industrially it is one of the most backward States in India. The per capita income, lack of adequate health facilities and level of living of its people is quite low. The State is divided into 63 administrative districts and five quite different geographical regions—Hills, western, Bundelkhand, central and eastern regions. These regions are different not only in their socio-cultural profiles but show very different demographic profiles as well. With the above background and demographic profiles, this chapter evaluates the pattern of agricultural employment in Uttar Pradesh.

Trends of Agricultural Employment since 1961

Though Uttar Pradesh has been seen to be a predominantly an agricultural State having dominant form of employment. Table 9.1 and Fig. 9.1 shows the trend during four periods 1961, 1971, 1981 and 1991 compared with the trend in India.

Table 9.1: Trends of Agricultural Employment in Uttar Pradesh and India (1961-1991)

Year	*Uttar Pradesh*			*India*		
	Total	*Rural*	*Urban*	*Total*	*Rural*	*Urban*
1961	75.2	83	6.3	69.6	79.4	10.1
1971	77.4	87	9.7	69.1	82.6	11.2
1981	74.4	86.3	15.3	66.7	81.2	11.4
1991	71.9	84.5	9.7	64.9	80.3	11.7

Source: Census of India, 1961-1991.

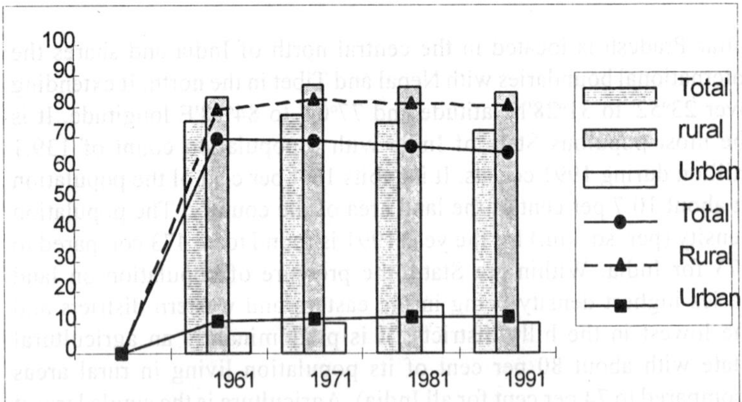

Fig. 9.1: Trends of Agricultural Employmennt in U.P. and India, 1961-91.

It reveals that the agricultural employment in Uttar Pradesh had increased to almost eight per cent during 30 years periods. The agricultural employment in 1961 was 75.2 per cent in Uttar Pradesh, whereas it was slightly lower and accounted for 69.5 per cent in India. But in 1971 State slightly rises 2.2 per cent point, caused by the Green Revolution in sixties and its impact on employment which in turn improve the economic condition of the rural people. During the two decades 1971 to 1981 the agricultural employment rate fell sharply both in the State and country. The figures for different censuses are not comparable because the definition of agricultural employment has been modified from time-to-time and heavy industries had received high priority under the strategy have planned development.

The trend of rural agricultural employment rate has, by and large, been the same as those noted above in respect of general rate. Fig. 9.1 shows that the rural agricultural employment in Uttar Pradesh as well as India have been fluctuating over the decades. The trend of urban agricultural employment rate is different from that of general and rural population. In 1961 it was 6.3 per cent in the State and below the national average (10.1 per cent). In 1971 both (State and country) witnessed an increase in the rate as accounted for 9.7 and 11.2 per cent respectively. This increase continued in 1981. This is significantly due to a substantial part of their rural population of 1971 being treated as urban in 1981 with the adjustment having been made on this account while working out the growth rate of workers.

Spatial Variation of Agricultural Employment Rate (1991)

This is evident from Table 9.2 that about 72 per cent main workers are agricultural employment. It is dominant both at the State and districts level. The agricultural employment rate is marked with notable variation in its distribution among the States. It varies from 89.61 per cent (Nainital) to 16.65 per cent (Kanpur Nagar) with the State average of 71.9 per cent. The entire range of variation may be grouped into five grades of below 70, 70 to 75, 75 to 80, 80 to 85, and 85 and above.

It may be seen (Fig. 9.2) that the districts having very low agricultural employment rate (below 70 per cent) is mainly confined in the north-western part of the State. On the other hand the district which fall under very high percentage (85 and above) is situated along foot hill of Himalayas and composed of Nainital, Kheri, Bahraich, Gonda, Basti, and Maharajganj districts and form a continuous region in the State. Fig. 9.2 shows that the high percentage districts (80 to 85) composed of central-southern districts, which form a prominent region. No less significant is the third grade of medium agricultural employment (75 to 80 per cent). This grade includes about twenty five per cent districts of the State which de-limit two dominant regions. One lies in the eastern part and the other in the central southern part. The other small region of the same grade is found in the Himalayan zone. The districts of low percentage (70 to 75 per cent) agricultural employment are scatteredly

Table 9.2: District-wise Distribution of Agricultural Employment in U.P. (1991)

Sl. No.	*District*	*Total*	*Rural*	*Urban*
1.	Uttar Kashi	78.87	82.37	14.59
2.	Chamoli	73.90	79.12	17.75
3.	Tehri Garhwal	78.93	83.37	4.97
4.	Dehra Dun	31.93	56.92	3.11
5.	Garhwal	64.19	72.85	3.03
6.	Pithoragarh	74.23	78.02	9.26
7.	Almora	77.42	81.78	3.73
8.	Nainital	89.61	77.32	15.32
9.	Bijnore	66.07	78.73	25.00
10.	Moradabad	67.37	86.96	15.86
11.	Rampur	72.59	89.67	21.20
12.	Saharanpur	54.53	79.20	13.27
13.	Haridwar	54.84	75.11	6.03
14.	Muzaffarnagar	67.93	78.84	29.89
15.	Meerut	54.02	63.98	17.24
16.	Ghaziabad	38.71	66.37	7.57
17.	Bulandsahar	66.64	79.23	21.56
18.	Aligarh	54.05	80.18	11.77
19.	Mathura	64.24	78.54	14.47
20.	Agra	47.25	74.84	5.49
21.	Firozabad	58.75	77.33	5.03
22.	Etah	79.07	87.73	24.60
23.	Mainpuri	79.61	87.60	20.79
24.	Badaun	84.91	93.05	40.45
25.	Bareily	69.52	78.23	19.94
26.	Pilibhit	79.17	90.51	24.09
27.	Shahjahanpur	77.91	92.33	19.01
28.	Kheri	87.34	93.18	30.47
29.	Sitapur	83.18	91.45	20.88
30.	Hardoi	84.27	91.37	32.55
31.	Unnao	82.08	88.74	29.68
32.	Lucknow	38.26	82.51	6.49
33.	Raibareli	80.95	86.20	18.88
34.	Farrukhabad	75.86	87.68	22.39
35.	Etawah	76.34	86.23	18.52
36.	Kanpur Dehat	82.93	85.67	33.81
37.	Kanpur Nagar	16.55	77.01	3.37
38.	Jalaun	78.15	90.53	26.02
39.	Jhansi	62.13	86.01	16.39
40.	Lalitpur	80.96	88.81	19.91
41.	Hamirpur	81.66	88.94	39.04
42.	Banda	85.74	91.83	31.38
43.	Fatehpur	81.13	85.86	28.08
44.	Pratapgarh	82.89	85.68	26.24
45.	Allahabad	71.20	81.21	9.25
46.	Bahraich	87.83	92.32	21.92

TABLE 9.2:*Contd.*

Sl. No.	*District*	*Total*	*Rural*	*Urban*
47.	Gonda	87.97	92.24	18.20
48.	Barabanki	83.53	88.23	28.30
49.	Faizabad	79.14	87.02	13.07
50.	Sultanpur	84.19	87.06	12.80
51.	Siddharthnagar	80.73	92.52	30.37
52.	Maharajganj	88.96	91.24	32.35
53.	Basti	85.48	89.12	23.51
54.	Gorakhpur	71.07	82.66	13.75
55.	Deoria	82.61	86.36	28.42
56.	Mau	68.29	78.16	8.99
57.	Azamgarh	79.70	84.50	14.67
58.	Jaunpur	76.39	80.79	12.42
59.	Ballia	79.07	83.35	35.18
60.	Ghazipur	79.08	83.31	16.68
61.	Varanasi	50.98	67.11	4.38
62.	Mirzapur	66.26	73.65	9.93
63.	Sonbhadra	76.99	84.98	4.22
	U.P.	72.15	84.47	9.73

Source: Census of India, 1991.

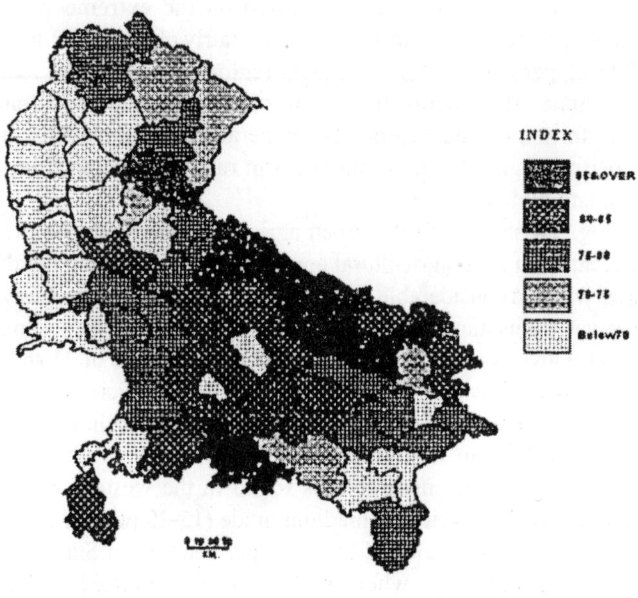

Fig. 9.2: Uttar Pradesh: Agricultual Employment (Total) 1991

distributed and do not form a single identifiable region. The regional pattern is characterised by a gradual increase in agricultural employment rate from west to east.

Rural/Urban Distribution

The agricultural employment rate of the rural and the urban population is considerably different. The average rate of agricultural employment in rural areas is substantially higher than the urban areas. It is about 84.50 per cent against 9.70 per cent of urban areas. But the range of agricultural employment of rural and urban areas is also different. It runs from 93.05 to 56.92 per cent, whereas in urban areas from 40.45 per cent to 3.73 per cent of agricultural employment. The regional distribution of agricultural employment in rural population may be broken into five grades of below 75, 75 to 80, 80 to 85, 85 to 90 and 90 and above.

Fig. 9.3 shows that a continuous zone of very high grade (90 and over) of agricultural employment are found in the north, eastern, south central and western part of the State. On the contrary, the very low grade (below 70 per cent) and low grade (75 to 80 per cent) of agricultural employment are mainly concentrated on the extreme western and Himalayan zone. The districts which are fairly close to the State average (80 to 85 per cent) form a dominant region in the extreme eastern part of the State. The other districts of this grade are scattered in nature and fail to form a distinct region. The general pattern shows that there is a decrease in agricultural employment in rural population from north to south and almost east to west.

Fig. 9.4 shows that the urban agricultural employment rate is quite different from rural agricultural employment rate. Among the districts it varies within a considerable range of 40.45 to 3.73 per cent. Conveniently these variations may be grouped into five grades. The largest number of districts (seventeen) falling under the very high grade of 25 and over are chiefly concentrated in the south-central districts which form a dominant region. The other small but distinct region observed in the extreme eastern part includes the districts of Ballia, Deoria, Maharajganj and Sidharthnagar. One small zone is found in the western part, which is separated by the districts of medium grade (15-20 per cent).

Two distinct regions of 20 to 25 per cent are in State. One lies in the north-eastern part, whereas the other is identified in the western part. The districts, which occupy about twenty per cent of the State

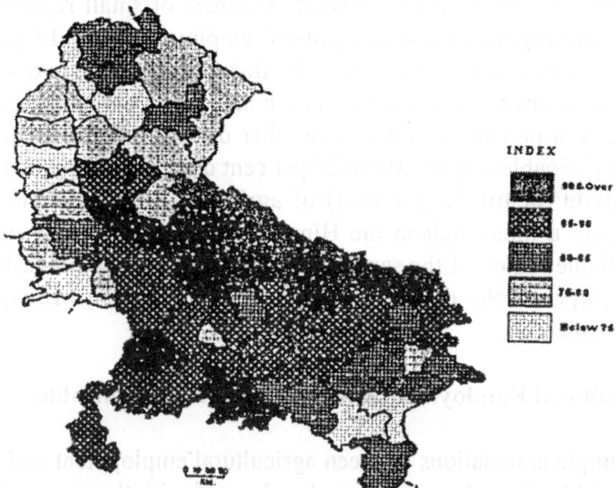

Fig 9.3: Uttar Pradesh Agricultural Employment (Rural) 1991

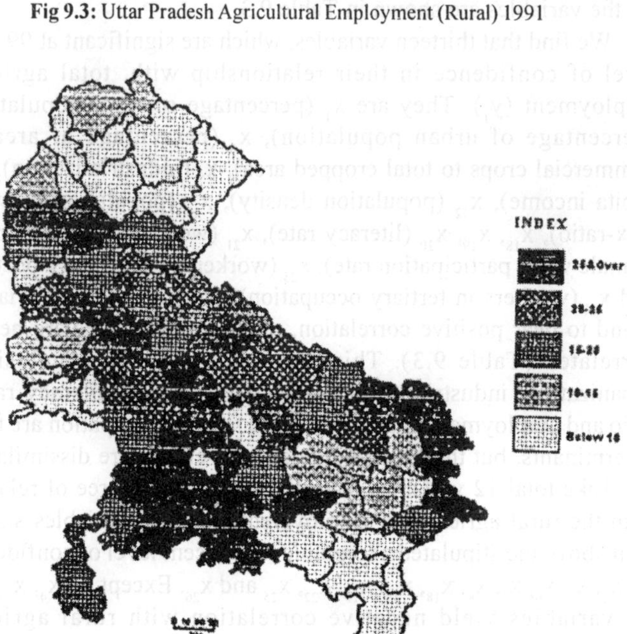

Fig 9.4: Uttar Pradesh Agricultural Employment (Urban) 1991

under the 15-20 per cent, constitute numbers of small regions in the State. The region of low agricultural employment (10-15 per cent) includes about thirteen per cent of the districts constitute two small but distinct regions in the State. One lies in the eastern part and the other in the western part of the State. The other districts of this grade fail to form a definable region. About 25 per cent districts occupy by the very low grade (below 75 per cent) of agricultural employment, which constitute a linear belt in the Himalayan zone. The other small but identifiable region of the same grade is found in the south-eastern part and comprises the districts of Allahabad, Varanasi, Mirzapur and Sonbhadra.

Agricultural Employment and the Independent Variables

The simple associations between agricultural employment and each of the variables have been computed and tested with the assumption that linear relationship existed in all the cases (total, rural, urban). The results for the variables are shown in Table 9.3.

We find that thirteen variables, which are significant at 99 per cent level of confidence in their relationship with, total agricultural employment (y_1). They are x_1 (percentage of rural population), x_2 (percentage of urban population), x_6 (percentage of area under commercial crops to total cropped area), x_7 (industrialization), x_8 (per capita income), x_{12} (population density), x_{13} (population growth), x_{14} (sex-ratio), x_{18}, x_{19}, x_{20} (literacy rate), x_{21} (work participation rate), x_{23} (female work participation rate), x_{25} (workers in secondary occupation) and x_{26} (workers in tertiary occupation). Only x_1 and x_{21} variables are found to bear positive correlation, remaining variables are negatively correlated (Table 9.3). This discussion leads to conclusion that urbanization, industrialization, population density, literacy rate, sex-ratio and employment in secondary and tertiary occupation are the chief determinants, but their magnitude of their effects are dissimilar.

Like total 12 variables recorded significant degree of relationship with the rural agricultural employment (y_2). The variables significant well above the stipulated acceptable 99 per cent level of confidence are: x_1, x_2, x_3, x_6, x_7, x_8, x_{18}, x_{19}, x_{20}, x_{22}, x_{25} and x_{26}. Except x_1, x_4, x_{18}, x_{19} and x_{22} variables yield negative correlation with rural agricultural employment (y_2).

Significant association of urban agricultural employment (y_3) with independent variables reveals that eleven variables of x_1, x_2, x_7, x_{14}, x_{15},

Table 9.3: Result of Correlation between Agricultural Employment (Total, Rural, Urban) and other Selected Variables in Uttar Pradesh, 1991

Variables	*Definition*	*Total (y_1)*	*Rural (y_2)*	*Urban (y_3)*
x_1	Percentage of Rural Population	0.899*	0.495*	0.337*
x_2	Percentage of Urban Population	-0.896*	-0.437*	-0.391*
x_3	Migration Rate	-0.237*	-0.404*	-0.195
x_4	Percentage of Net Area Sown to the Total Reporting Area	-0.003	0.207**	0.243*
x_5	Intensity of Cropping	-0.023	-0.197	-0.239*
x_6	Percentage of Area Under Commercial Crop to Total Cropped Area	-0.323*	-0.285*	-0.115
x_7	Industrialization	-0.682*	-0.478*	-0.374*
x_8	Per Capita Income	-0.280*	-0.368*	-0.069
x_9	School/Student Ratio	-0.002	0.026	-0.042
x_{10}	Teacher/Student Ratio	-0.083	0.055	-0.012
x_{11}	Percentage of SC and ST to Total Population	0.098	0.065	-0.012
x_{12}	Population Density	-0.544*	-0.166	-0.210**
x_{13}	Percentage of Population Growth	-0.408*	-0.001	-0.246**
x_{14}	Sex Ratio	0.219**	-0.173	0.270*
x_{15}	Dependency Ratio	0.190	0.102	0.498*
x_{16}	Birth Rate	-0.083	0.112	-0.276*
x_{17}	Death Rate	-0.147	0.112	0.008
x_{18}	Literacy Rate	-0.624*	0.622*	-0.320*
x_{19}	Male Literacy Rate	-0.452*	0.591*	-0.432*
x_{20}	Female Literacy Rate	-0.716*	-0.596*	-0.568*
x_{21}	Work Participation Rate	0.291*	0.068	-0.113
x_{22}	Male Work Participation Rate	0.126	0.418*	0.070
x_{23}	Female Work Participation Rate	0.201	-0.130	-0.242**
x_{24}	Percentage of Workers in Primary Occupation	—	—	—
x_{25}	Percentage of Workers in Secondary Occupation	-0.864*	-0.788*	-0.615*
x_{26}	Percentage of Workers in Tertiary Occupation	-0.922*	-0.849*	-0.280*

*Significant at 1 per cent level = 0.265; ** Significant at 1 per cent level = 0.200.

x_{16}, x_{18}, x_{19}, x_{20}, x_{25} and x_{26} are found to be well above the adopted level of confidence, x_1, x_{14} and x_{15} out of eleven have positive relationship. Remaining nine variables have negative relationship. On the other hand five variables are significant at 95 per cent level of confidence. Out of these, only one variable (x_4) has positive relationship and the remaining four x_5, x_{12}, x_{13} and x_{23} have negative correlation with urban agricultural employment (y_3).

It may be noted that urbanization, industrialization, birth rate, literacy rate and workers in secondary and tertiary occupation mainly cause the regional variation in agricultural employment of urban population.

Conclusion

The study presents some notable characteristics in the regional distribution of agricultural employment. It is marked by high rate in the majority of the north-eastern, central and southern districts. It is inversely proportional to urbanization, industrialization, vital processes, literacy rate and workers in secondary and tertiary occupation. In case of rural population with few exceptions, it is similar to the total population. The agricultural employment in urban areas is appreciably high in the majority. Western, central and southern districts, which are relatively more developed than the eastern and Himalayan zone. This pattern is inversely and significant by proportional to urbanization, industrialization, birth rate, literacy rate and workers in secondary and tertiary occupation.

References

Agrawal, A.N. (1980), *Indian Agriculture*, Vikas Publishing House, New Delhi.

Bhalla, G.S. and Alagh, Y.K. (1979), *Performance of Indian Agriculture*, Sterling Publishing House, New Delhi.

Bhattacharya, B.B. and Mitra, A. (1989), Industry Agriculture Growth Rates: Widening Disparity-An Explanation, *Economic and Political Weekly*, August 26.

Census of India (1991), General Population Table, U.P. Series 25, Part II-A, New Delhi.

District-wise Development Indicators of Uttar Pradesh (1991), Planning Institute, Lucknow.

Gosal, G.S. and Gopal K. (1984), Regional Disparities in Levels of Socio-economic Development in Punjab, *Kurukshetra*.

Gulati, S.C. (1977), Dimensions of Inter-district Disparities, *Indian Journal of Regional Science*, Vol. 9, No. 2.

Mishra and Puri (1991), *Indian Economy*, Himalayan Publishing House, New Delhi.

Planning Commission (1990), Employment: Past Trends and Prospects for 1990s: What Do the Date Tell Us?, *Economic and Political Weekly*, April 13.

Singh H. (1989), *Regional Development and Disparities in India*, Criterion Publication, New Delhi.

Srivastava S.L. (1983), Regional Disparities in Agricultural Development in M.P., *Indian Journal of Regional Science*, Vol. 15, No. 2.

10

PRINCIPLES OF INTEGRATED PEST CONTROL AND AGROECOSYSTEM

MOHAMMAD IRFAN

Integrated pest control is a broad ecological approach to pest control utilizing a variety of control technologies compatibly in a single pest management system. In integrated pest control, stress is placed on the importance of realistic economic injury levels which are used to determine the need for control actions. At the same time, all possible is done to protect and preserve naturally occurring biotic mortality agents such as parasites, predators and pathogens. When artificial controls are needed, for example, chemical pesticide applications, they are employed in as selective manner as possible and only when their use is economically and ecologically justified. The ultimate objective of the integrated pest control system is to produce the optimum crop yield of high quality at minimum cost, taking into consideration the ecological and sociological constraints in that particular agroecosystem and the long-term preservation of the environment.

In the broadest spectrum, it considers all the key pests in an agroecosystem; namely, insects, pathogens, weeds and nematodes. In its most restricted form, integrated control may apply to a single major pest. However, its major importance is the application of the philosophy and ecological principles inherent in the concept.

Identify the Pests (Diseases, Insects, Weeds, etc.) to be managed in the Crop Production System or Agroecosystem

(a) An organism should not be called a pest until it is proven to be a pest. A particular species may be a pest in some situations and not in other or at certain times and not in others.

(b) Identification of pest status should be coupled with the establishment of economic injury thresholds.
Pests interact with one another and this interaction may compound or offset their effects on the crop plant. We should not assume their effects are additive.

(c) *Categories of pest status*

1. *Key pests* are serious, perennially occurring persistent species that require control measures to be taken regularly because in the absence of control they frequently occur at above economic injury thresholds. Usually there are only a very few key pests (sometimes only one or two) in any agroecosystem. The key pest are the focal point of the pest management systems.
2. *Part time pests*, these occasional or secondary pests are relatively minor pests that rise to economically damaging levels only at certain times or in certain places. These occasional pests are especially susceptible to an integrated pest control approach aimed at preventing these occasional outbreaks. Prediction technology is especially useful for these pests.
3. *Potential pests* cause no significant damage under the conditions currently prevailing in the agroecosystems. In attempts to manage key pests or occasional pests, care must be taken not to alter the conditions of the agroecosystem so that then potential pests erupt as severe pests.
4. *Migrant pests* are non-residents of the agroecosystems that enter periodically and which may cause severe economic damage, e.g. migratory locusts and armyworms. The ecological approach to the control of such pests is still valid but must be applied in the perspective of a very large geographic area.
5. Many other phytophagous forms may be present in the agroecosystem but are considered to be non-pests.

Define the Management Unit (Agroecosystem)

(a) The limits of the agroecosystem are determined principally by the characteristics of the local cropping system and the characteristics of the pests (particularly their patterns of movements or vagility). The limits may circumscribe, for example, a tree, or an orchard, or a valley, or other large ecological unit.

(b) The definition of the management unit is another way of approaching the definition of the target pest population (Rabb, 1978).

(c) To define the limits of an agroecosystem properly requires an intimate knowledge of the interrelationships and mobility of the key pests in the agroecosystem.

Develop the Pest Management Strategy

(a) The fundamental strategy of pest management is the coordinated use of multiple tactics in a single integrated system with the goal to hold pest numbers and damage to tolerable levels. It is a containment strategy rather than an eradication strategy.

(b) The fundamental tactics of integrated pest control are:
1. Utilization of indigenous natural control.
2. Management through cultural practices.
3. Use of inherent plant resistance and tolerance.
4. Selective use of chemical pesticides.

Now these tactics utilized will depend on the specific agroecosystem and the nature of its key pests.

(c) Any pest control procedure must only be applied when economically and ecologically justified.

(d) How does agroecosystem diversity relate to pest management strategy? It depends on the kind, or quality of diversity. This aspect of diversity must be understood in developing agroecosystem management strategy.

(e) Pest Management Strategy can aim at;
1. Reducing level of original pest infestation or inoculum in the agroecosystem.
2. Modifying the rate at which the pest increase in the agroecosystem.
3. Reducing the influx of pest invaders into the agroecosystem.
4. Some combination of the above three. The exact combination will depend on the characteristics of the pest and the agroecosystem.

Establish Economic Injury Thresholds

(a) The economic injury threshold is that pest population level or level of pest intensity that produces an incremental reduction in crop value greater than the cost of implementing a pest management action.

(b) Often the economic injury thresholds are varied according to either phenological time or physiological state of the crop plants.

(c) To establish an economic injury threshold something must be known of the following:

1. Methods of measuring plant response to pest injury or impact.
2. Methods of measuring directly or indirectly the pest abundance or intensity, i.e. sampling.
3. The crop loss from the anticipated level of pest intensity in terms of quantity and quality of the crop and its economic value.
4. A cost/benefit analysis of the proposed pest management action.

(d) Economic treatment threshold is a level at which action must be taken to prevent economic damage. It is a somewhat lower level of pest intensity than the economic injury level. At the economic treatment threshold, if a decision to take a pest management action is made, time is still sufficient, before the economic injury threshold will be reached, to permit the control actions to be carried out and for them to have their anticipated impact on the pest.

To establish an economic treatment threshold requires some knowledge of:

1. Future patterns of pest intensity.
2. Factors influencing the economic injury threshold.
3. Pest damage potential in the specific crop situation.

(e) Not all pest control actions are based on direct response to levels of pest intensity. For example:

Preventative or prophyllactic action which may be taken far in advance of the presence of the pest. They are (i) aimed at lowering the mean level of the pest, (ii) altering the pest population distribution, or (iii) altering the basic structure of the crop system.

But many other must be taken duri g the course of the growing season to response to seasonal deve pment of pests in crop, or to the presence or absence of key elements in the management system, or changes in levels of pests.

The in-season response is usually a temporary, suppressive action, e.g. a cultural practices or application of a pesticide.

(f) The goal of an integrated pest control system is to manage and manipulate the agroecosystem so that the incidence of the pests always remains below the economic injury threshold.

Develop Reliable Monitoring and Predictive Techniques

(a) Develop a sufficient understanding of the crop production system and associated agroecosystem to forecast with both short and long-term predictions potential problem so that it is possible to undertake the necessary measures to prevent these events from occurring.

(b) The development of a sound predictive technique may be based on one or a combination of the following:

1. An understanding of the crop phenology and related pest correlatives.
2. An understanding of pest phenology.
3. Monitoring of pest incidence.
4. Monitoring of weather conditions.

11

QUALITY OF WATER FOR IRRIGATION

A Case Study of Garra River (Tributary of Subaranrekha)

MANSOOR ALI & AMEENUL ISLAM

Introduction

Self-sufficiency in agricultural production was the basic objective of Indian agriculture after independence. The country has achieved a commendable success in this direction. It was because of the use of modern agricultural techniques and various inputs such as high yielding variety seeds, chemical fertilizers and increased irrigation facility. Irrigation has become an essential part and parcel of modern farming system. More and more area under irrigation was brought but in terms of assured irrigation we are still lagging behind on international standard. There is only about 20 per cent of agricultural area under assured irrigation in India and rest of agricultural land lies under the category of unassured water supply system. The faulty irrigation system has been noted which has created a major problem such as salinity, siltation and water logging. Consequently it has turned the productive land into decreased productive one. Therefore proper utilization of land resources and water resources needs a systematic planning and an appropriate system. A remunerative return in agricultural sector is granted only by assured irrigation system supported by the other factors. The assured irrigation is not only concerned to the ample supply of irrigation water to the fields. It has several aspects also. It depends upon the demand of irrigation water in an area, availability of irrigation water and its supply, as well as on quantity and quality of irrigation water and lastly regions suitable for various techniques of irrigation may be considered on priority basis. As the common practice is faulty such as flood irrigation and overuse of water in most of the areas appropriate irrigation facilities are available. Therefore quality and quantity of water must be judiciously judged and used. Even changing pattern of crop, land-use can be changed if needed and chemical analysis of water may be suggested at regional level.

In recent years it has been considerably recognised that quality of water has greater importance than the quantity. If proper attention will not be given to the quality of water alongwith appropriate planning and with its judicious use it will certainly lead towards the disastrous end. Irrigation system should be operated with adequate knowledge of quality of water and of various methods and techniques for applying it properly. The types of salt contents, alkalinity and basicity, salinity, electrical conductivity and hardness are few important factors for determination of irrigation suitability. The carbonates, bicarbonates, calcium, magnesium, phosphorus and nitrogen contents are also some very important factors. Without the knowledge of geo-chemistry of irrigation water and its management with soils, a sound agricultural planning is doubtful. Water quality analysis for various uses includes the investigation of the physical, chemical and bacteriological characteristics of water. In this study the main emphasis has been given on determination of the quality of water for irrigation purposes of few selected samples of Garra river. It also includes a comparison of the accepted standards with that of the selected water samples. However the accuracy and method of water quality analysis is related to a certain extent to the experimental procedures and on its numerical calculations.

Study Region

Garra river is a small tributary of Subaranrekha river joining it on its right bank further eastward to Jadugora, a uranium mines town. It drains in Chhotanagpur plateau region encompassing an area of about 725 sq. km. The water samples have been collected in the first week of June of the year of 1999 from seven selected spots. Those are Bazargoratola, Potka, Dabanki, Hesalbil, Sahada, Sankarda and Murgaghutu near Narva mines. All the above mentioned sites are located on the bank of Garra river except Hesalbil and Sahada. There two spots are situated on the bank of Chandi Nala and Dudh Naidi respectively. The Garra Catchment is selected for this study because of two reasons. Firstly it drains through and rugged topographical region and secondly its water is the only source of irrigation available in this region. All the above mentioned spots are situated between an elevation of 100 mts to 200 mts above mean sea level. This particular band of elevation covers an area of about 72 per cent to total catchment area. The population residing in this belt is about more than 90 per cent of the total population and it also shares 71 per cent of the agricultural land to the total agricultural area available in this region. As we know the quality of water depends upon geological structure geo-chemical characteristics of the earth as well as on environmental conditions. So, a brief account about the geology of the region and its soil characteristics has been incorporated here for a better understanding.

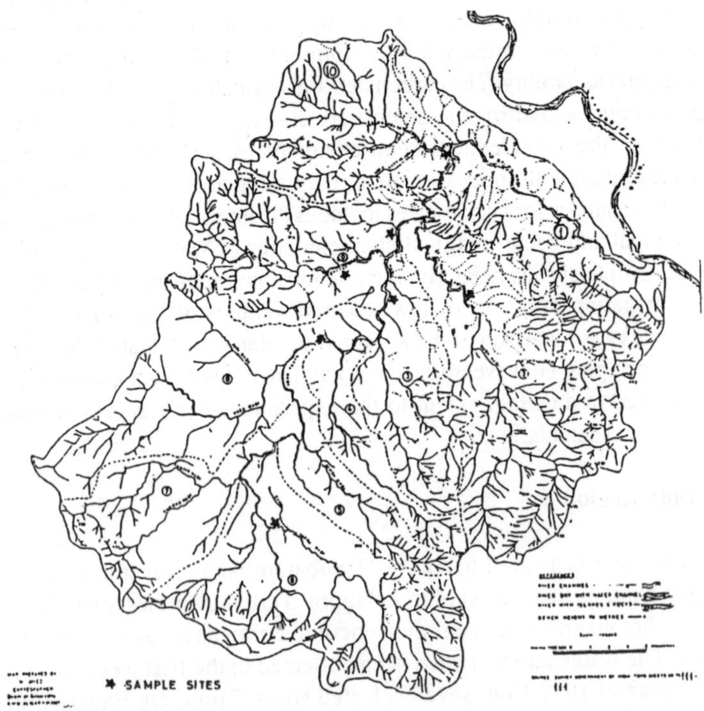

Fig. 11.1: Garra River Catchment (Tributary of Subaranrekha) Singhbhum (East) South Bihar

Geological structure of the study region reveals that the rocks are of archaean periods consisting of sub-metamorphic series. They occur in a group of metamorphosed rocks like conglomerates, sandstones, limestones, shales and are infested with banded-haematite-quartzite at few places. The granites with some sills of basic compositions are also found in collaboration with carbonaceous phyllites and gondites etc. at some places. The soils are generally considered to be rich in lime and aluminium. The upland soils are usually red brown, brownish-red, reddish-yellow or brownish-yellow in colour. The lowland soils are dark grey or greyish brown in colour and clayey in texture. The soils are poor and have low contents of nitrogen, phosphate, calcium and magnesium. The carbonate content is either absent or very low.

Experimental Procedure

The electrical conductivity of water samples is measured by conductivity bridge (CM 185, Elico India), *p*H was measured by using a *p*H meter (LI-120, Elico India), carbonates, bicarbonates and chlorides are analysed, by titrimetric methods using standard sulphuric acid and silver nitrate solutions respective. Calcium and magnesium are determined by titrimetrically with the help of standard disodium salt of ethylene diamine tetraacetic acid (EDTA) as titrant and ammonium perpurate and erichrome black T (EBT) as indicator. Phosphorus is determined by calorimetric methods with the help of spectronic 20D, Milton Ray spectrophotometer. Determination of nitrogen has been achieved titrimetrically using standard sulphuric acid after distilling the ammonia in boric acid. Demineralised water was used throughout the experiment. Every reading was checked at least by duplicate run.

Analysis of Water Quality Parameter and Discussion

Electrical Conductivity

The amount of total soluble salts in any sample is generally expressed in terms of electrical conductivity (EC). The most common unit of EC being followed is dsm^{-1} (decisiemen per metre) which is equal to the older unit of millimhos per centimetre. The electrical conductivity of Garra river water varies from 0.82×10^3 dsm^{-1} (820 millimhos/cm) to 2.12×103 dsm^{-1} (2120 millimhos/cm). The lowest value of EC was observed in water of Sahada (S#5) and the highest value was recorded in Potka's (sample 2) water. The water drawn from Sankarda has next highest value of EC after Potka i.e. 1.98×10^3 dsm^{-1} (1980 millimhos/cm), followed by Murgaghutu with a value of 1.95×10^3 dsm^{-1} (1950 millimhos/cm) of

EC. The water drawn from Bazargoratola, Dabanki and Hesalbil have a value of EC's as 1.83×10^3 dsm^{-1}, 1.5×10^3 dsm^{-1} and 1.28×10^3 dsm^{-1} respectively (Table 11.1). The value of electrical conductivity is high in water which traverses through a sandy clay soil and is low in the areas of gravelly clay soils. It is because of ample quantity of salts which is available in sandy clay soils than the gravely clay soils.

Table 11.1

	Water Quality Parameters	*I* *Bazar-goratola*	*II* *Potka*	*III* *Dabanki*	*IV* *Hesalbil*	*V* *Sahada*	*VI* *Sank-arda*	*VII* *Murga-ghutu*
1.	Electrical conductivity dsm^{-1} (umhos)	1.83×10^3 1.83	2.12×10^3 2.12	1.5×10^3 1.5	1.28×10^3 1.28	0.82×10^3 0.82	1.98×10^3 1.98	1.95×10^3 1.95
2.	*p*H	8.04	8.31	7.81	7.31	7.52	7.92	7.79
3.	Carbonate (CO_3^{2-})*	0.00	0.00	0.00	0.00	0.00	0.00	0.00
4.	Bicarbonate (HCO_3^{2-})*	176.90	183.00	140.30	122.0	128.10	152.50	164.70
5.	Chloride (Cl^-) *	57.69	53.25	48.81	53.25	48.81	66.56	48.81
6.	Calcium (Ca^{2+})*	16.03	21.24	12.83	11.22	6.01	18.84	15.23
7.	Magnesium (Mg^{2+})*	8.26	6.32	6.80	3.64	4.37	6.32	5.83
8.	(Mg^{2+}) + (Ca^{2+})*	24.29	27.56	19.63	14.86	10.38	25.16	21.06
9.	Phosphate – Phosphorus (PO_4^{-3}) *	0.02 Neg	0.02 Neg	0.28	0.60	0.28	0.36	0.12
10.	Ammonia-nitrogen (NH_3-N)*	0.28	0.84	1.40	2.24	1.96	0.56	1.40
11.	Nitrate-nitrogen (NO_3-N)*	10.36	01.96	06.72	18.20	11.20	13.44	06.44

*Unit in mg/lit.

*p*H: The term *p*H was derived from the French word "Pouvoir Hydrogen" means hydrogen power. *p*H is the negative logarithm of hydrogen ion concentration. It is expressed as $pH = -\log_{10}{}^{(H+)}$. The scale of *p*H unit extends from 0 to 14. For *p*H below 7 the hydrogen ion (H^+) concentration exceeds, the hydroxyl ion (OH^+) and the range is acidic in nature when OH concentration is more than H^+, *p*H lies between 7 to 14, and the range is alkaline. *p*H 7 is generally treated as neutral point where both the H^+ and OH^- are equal to each other.

In this study *p*H of sample waters varies from 7.31 to 8.31 (Table 11.1). The maximum value of *p*H 8.31 was recorded in water collected from Garra river near Potka bridge. The lowest value was observed at Hesalbil (S#4) with *p*H 7.31. The next highest value of *p*H was registered at Bazargoratola (S#1) i.e. 8.04 followed by Sankarda (S#6) with a *p*H value of 7.92, while *p*H of water samples collected from Dabanki, Murgaghutu and Sahada are 7.81, 7.79 and 7.52 respectively. From the above analysis we can make a conclusion that all the water samples which are collected from Garra river are basic in nature. Strong basic character of water inhibit micro-organismic growth which are unfavourable for plants health and for their growth. The study reveals that *p*H increases in the areas where sandy clay soil are dominant.

Carbonates and Bicarbonates

The carbonates and bicarbonates are the important constituents of anion group of chemicals. The carbonate and bicarbonate content in surface water are associated with weathered crystalline rocks of magnesium and calcium. The analysis of water samples in this study shows that carbonate (CO_3^{2-}) content in surface water is absent but bicarbonate (HCO_3^-) is present in considerable proportion. It has been expressed in milligram per litre. The value of bicarbonate content varies from 122 mg/lit of 183.00 mg/lit. The maximum value was recorded it Potka (S#2) equals to 183 mg/lit of water and the minimum value i.e. 122 mg/lit was found in water sample 4 drawn from Hesalbil. The next highest value of bicarbonate content was observed in water of Bazargoratola which is equal to 176.9 mg/lit followed by water drawn from Murgaghutu, Sankarda, Dabanki and Sahada with a value of 164.7 mg/lit, 152.5 mg/lit, 140.3 mg/lit and 128.1 mg/lit of water respectively (Table 11.1). The sum of the carbonate (CO_3^{2-}) and bicarbonates (HCO_3^-) ions constitutes the total alkalinity of the water as temporary hardness and raises its *p*H to more than 7.5. This alkalinity also causes corrosion. In Garra catchment calcium and magnesium oxides are in abundance and reacts with carbonate and bicarbonates ions which seldom creates a problem of alkalinity.

Chloride (Cl) is an important content of anion group of chemicals. The concentration of chloride generally increases with the increase in electrical conductivity of irrigation water. In this particular case study the chloride content in water samples ranges from 48.81 mg/lit to 66.56 mg/lit. The highest value i.e. 66.56 mg/lit of chloride content is found in water sample 6, that is of Sankarda followed by samples 1, 2 and 4 with value of 57.69 mg/lit, and 53.25 mg/lit in case of the last two samples, i.e. Potka and Hesalbil. The lowest value of chloride content was found is water drawn from Dabanki, Sahada and Murgaghutu, i.e. 48.81 mg/lit in each case.

Calcium (Ca^{2+}) and Magnesium (Mg^{2+}) are the major cations present in irrigation water. The total sum of Ca^{2+} and Mg^{2+} cations denotes the hardness of the water. The highest calcium (Ca^{2+}) cation content was found in sample 2 and the lowest in sample 5 of waters drawn from Potka and Sahada, with a value equal to 21.24 mg/lit and 6.01 mg/lit respectively. In case of magnesium (Mg^{2+}) cation content all the water samples are poor. In general magnesium content varies in between 3.64 mg/lit to 8.26 mg/lit of water in sample 4 and 1, which have been drawn from Hesalbil and Bazargoratola. Probably it is due to the chemical composition of the soils through which the river is traversing. The soils are sandy clay loom sandy clay with dark reddish brown to yellowish or dark yellowish brown in colour due to the high content iron of draw and aluminium. But at few places it is gravelly loamy sand to gravelly clay in texture with yellowish red to dark grayish brown in colour.

In case of total hardness (Sum of $Ca^{2+}{}_2$ + Mg^{2+} cations) of the water samples, it varies from 27.50 mg/lit at Potka to 10.30 mg/lit at Sahada.

Table 11.2

Water Samples No.	*Hardness*
1	24.29 mg/lit
2	27.56 mg/lit
3	19.63 mg/lit
4	14.86 mg/lit
5	10.38 mg/lit
6	25.16 mg/lit
7	21.06 mg/lit

The water drawn from Sankarda and Bazargoratola has a hardness of 25.16 mg/lit and 24.29 mg/lit followed by sample 7 collected from Murgaghutu near Narva mines is equal to 21.06 mg/lit of water.

Phosphate-phosphorus (Po_4^{3-}) is very much important for plant growth. It has also an effect on the size of grains. Phosphate-phosphorus content of surface water in all samples collected from the Garra catchment is too much low. In some water samples it is near to negligible i.e. 0.02 mg/lit. The highest content of Po_4^{3-} has been registered in water collected from Hesalbil which is equal to 0.60 mg/lit (Table 11.1). This clearly shows that surface water of Garra river catchment is deficient in phosphate phosphorus content.

Ammonia Nitrogen (NH_3-N) and Nitrate-Nitrogen are important source of nutrients for plant growth. It effects on crop production and as well as yield of the crops. The NH_3-N value ranges from 0.28 mg/lit in sample 1 to the maximum of value of 2.24 mg/lit in sample 5, which have been collected from Bazargoratola and Hesalbil respectively. The ammonia-nitrogen content in water drawn from Sankarda is 1.96 mg/lit but in case of Dabanki and Murgaghutu it is 1.40 mg/lit of water.

The status of nitrate-nitrogen (NO_3-N) content in all the samples of water is better than the NH_3-N. The NO_3-N content ranges from 1.96 mg/lit of water is Potka which is the lowest to 18.20 mg/lit of water collected from Hesalbil. The next highest value of NO_3-N was recorded in water from Sankarda followed by Sahada which is equal to 13.44 mg/lit and 11.20 mg/lit respectively. The water collected from Bazargoratola has NO_3-N content about 10.36 mg/lit. The presence of K^+ and NO_3 ions in appreciable amount in irrigation water has been found to partially counteract the adverse effect of salinity and sodocity on plant growth. In drinking water nitrate content higher than 10 mg/lit (ppm) of nitrate-nitrogen may cause illness called methaemoglobinacmia or the so called blue baby syndrome in infants.

Conclusion and Suggestion

The suitability of water for irrigation purposes will be done by comparing the calculated value to the accepted standard value of water. In present study it will be achieved by the help of electrical conductivity (EC), Hardness, RSC and Mg/Ca. ratio. The analysis of *p*H determination shows that all sample waters are basic in nature.

According to USSL classification the irrigation water be classified on their electrical conductivity (EC) ranges in natural water from 100-250 millimhos/cm. The categories formed on this basis are below:

Low	=	100-250	millimhos/cm
Medium	=	250-750	"
High	=	750-2250	"
Very High	=	2250 and above	"

From Table 11.1 it is quite clear that electrical conductivity of water samples ranges from 820 to 2120 millimhos/cm. Following the above classification, all water samples drawn from Garra catchment lie in the high group of EC i.e. their use for irrigational purposes is doubtful. It is partially suitable. In terms of EC, water needs special treatment by applying some particular chemicals and fertilizer to lower down the EC, which will make the water suitable for irrigation.

The total salts content in water is treated as hardness. The degree of hardness in water is commonly classified following Sawyer & McCarty as follow:

Softwater	=	0-75 mg/lit
Moderate	=	75-150 mg/lit
Hard	=	150-300 mg/lit
Very hard	=	300 and above

Table 11.2 indicates that all water samples collected from different location in Garra catchment lie under the category of softwater. So, on this basis we can consider that Garra river water is very much excellent for irrigation purposes.

Residual Sodium Carbonate (RSC). This index is important for carbonate and bicarbonate rich irrigation waters. It indicates their tendency to precipitate Ca^{2+} as $CaCO_3$. RSC is calculated as under.

RSC (me/lit) = $(CO_3^{2-} + HCO_3^{-}) - (Ca^{2+} + Mg^{2+})$. The concentration of both cations and anions are in me/lit. Sodocity hazards in terms of RSC is categorised as under (Richards 1954).

Safe	=	RSC<1.25
Moderate	=	RSC 1.25 – 2.5
Unsafe	=	RSC > 2.5

The residual sodium carbonate of the sample water are calculated using the above formula. They are as follows in me/lit be made that surface water of Garra river catchment is highly suitable for irrigation.

On the basis of standard adopted from environmental Hygiene committee report 1949 the lower and upper limit of bicarbonate-carbonate content and chloride content are categorised as follows:

	Lower limit	*Higher limit*
Bicarbonate-carbonate	200	500
Chloride	100	300

In Case of Bicarbonate-Carbonate

Safe	=	< 200
Moderately safe	=	200-500
Unsafe	=	> 500

In Case of Chloride

Safe	=	< 100
Moderately	=	100-300
Unsafe	=	> 300

On the basis of above categorisation we can make a conclusion from Table 11.1 that in terms of bicarbonate-carbonate and chloride the surface water of Garra catchment is very much safe and suitable for irrigation.

Finally a conclusion can be drawn from above analysis and discussion considering the accepted standards and their comparison with the calculated values that Garra river water is quite safe and suitable for irrigation with a minor discrepancies at few places. This minor unsuitability can be or should be treated through some suitable techniques using some chemicals and fertilizers directly to the agricultural fields to make the water suitable for irrigation purposes.

Water Sample No.	*RSC (Residual Sodium Carbonate)*
1	2.61
2	2.605
3	2.00
4	1.78
5	1.93
6	2.135
7	2.39

Considering the RSC, the water drawn from Bazargoratola and Potka is unsafe for irrigation. But rest of water samples collected from Dabanki, Hesalbil, Sahada, Sankarda and Murgaghutu are moderately safe to safe for irrigation purposes.

Magnesium Calcium Ratio (Mg/Ca ratio). It has now been established that calcium and magnesium do not behave equally in soil system and magnesium deteriorates soil structure particularly when water are sodium – dominated and highly saline. High level of Mg usually promotes higher development of exchangeable sodium in irrigated soils. Based on ratio of Mg to Ca water are categorised as below:

Safe	=	Mg/Ca ratio	< 1.5
Moderate	=	"	1.5 – 3.0
Unsafe	=	"	> 3.0

The Mg/Ca ratio of sample waters are as follow:

Water Sample No.	*Mg/Ca ratio*
1	0.515
2	0.306
3	0.530
4	0.324
5	0.727
6	0.335
7	0.383

In view of the above classification all the sample waters lie in the category of safe for irrigation.

Acknowledgement

The authors are highly thankful to Prof. Ali Mohammad for his valuable guidance, suggestions and constant encouragement.

References

D. Van Nostrand, Princeton, New Jersey, p. 2095.

Elampooranam, T. and P.H. Anand (1991), Quality of Irrigation waters in Kaveri Delta, South India. *The Indian Geographical Journal*, Vol. 66, No. 2, pp. 98-105.

Kumaraswamy, K. and N. Sivagnanam (1988), Surface Water Quality aspects of Viper Basin South India. *The Indian Geographical Journal*, Vol. 63, No. 2, pp. 79-89.

Mohring, J.R. (1972), *J. Chem. Edu.*, 49, 1, p. 15

Mukherjee, P.K. (1990), *A Text Book of Geology*. The World Press Pvt. Ltd. Calcutta, pp. 316-318.

Rajan, S. and Jaypaul, Azariah (1989), A Survey on the Quality of Drinking Water of Madras City and Public Health Implications, *The Indian Geographical Journal*, Chennnai, Vol. 64, No. 1, pp. 72-79.

Raychaudhuri, S.P. (1963), *Soils of India*, Indian Council of Agricultural Research, New Delhi, pp. 65-89.

Rao, S.V.R. (1995), Water Quality of Bandal River in Maldeota Phospharite Mining Area, Uttar Pradesh. *The Indian Geographical Journal*, Vol. 70, No. 2, pp. 118-121.

Scott, W.W. (1939), *Standard Methods of Chemical Analysis*, 5th edition.

Singh, R.L. (1971), *India: A Regional Geography*, National Geographical Society of India, Varanasi, pp. 649-675.

Trivedi, R.K. and P.K. Goel (1984), *Chemical and Biological Methods of Water Pollution Studies*, Environment Publications, Karnal, Chapter – 2, p. 74.

Wadia, D.N. (1952), *Geology of India*, Macmillan pp. 105-110.

Yadav, B.R. and M.S. Khera (1993), *An Analysis of Irrigation Water, Methods of Analysis of Soil, Plants, Water & Fertiliser*, edited by H.L.S. Tandon, F.D. & C. Organisation, New Delhi, p. 100.

12

MANAGEMENT OF WATER RESOURCES FOR AGRICULTURE IN BURDWAN, WEST BENGAL

N.K. DE & MISS ANANYA TARAPHDER

Introduction

In India proper planning and management of water resources is crucial for the development of agriculture to meet the needs of the growing population. Not only the primary, but the secondary and tertiary sectors of economy, also require water. It may be mentioned that the available water sources in India are unevenly distributed, both in space and time—resulting in floods and droughts.

Burdwan district is developed both industrially (Western half) and agriculturally (Eastern half). To cope with the industrial development, the demand for water has increased further. Accordingly the water (surface and sub-surface) is being used in an indiscriminate fashion. If it is allowed to continue, the district is bound to face shortage of water in the near future, keeping these aspects in mind a laudable attempt has been made in this chapter to assess and conserve the water resources of the district. After evaluating the ecological constraints an integrated plan for management of water resources has been put forward to meet the ever increasing demand of water in the area under consideration. It may be pointed out that agriculture in the district is mainly concentrated in the east, which is drained by multiple channels of the lower Ajay, Damodar and Bhagirathi rivers. As this chapter deals with agriculture, emphasis has been given on the eastern half of Burdwan district mainly.

Study Area

The district of Burdwan lies between 22°56'N and 23°53'N latitude and 85°48'E and 88°25' longitude. The district has an area of 7028 sq. km. Physically it can broadly be divided into three parts. The western part having higher relief shows a barren look. The eastern part with highly fertile soil presents almost a level surface. In between lies the rolling upland, which gradually merges with the monotonously flat plain in the east. The economy of the district mainly depends on both agriculture and industry.

Methodology

The methodology followed in this chapter can be divided into three phases. Pre-field—consists of collection of secondary data and information from journals, reports, available literatures (both published and unpublished); Field—includes collection of primary data from some selected areas, which have been subsequently verified also with the secondary information, already collected; Post-field—includes arranging, processing, tabulating and analysis of the data and finally presenting them in pictorial forms (maps and diagrams).

The quantitative analysis of the finalised data includes—

1. Calculation of Arithmetic Mean of the individual variables collected from each block in the district.
2. Calculation of Composite Index (*Ci*)—

   Composite index (*Ci*) = $\frac{X_1}{\overline{X}_1} + \frac{X_2}{\overline{X}_2} + \ldots + \frac{X_n}{\overline{X}_n}$

   where $\overline{X}_1, \overline{X}_2, \ldots \overline{X}_n$ are means of $\overline{X}_1, \overline{X}_2, \ldots \overline{X}_n$ variables.
3. The parametric data are analysed by —
   (a) Product moment correlation between cropping intensity and groundwater potential (also between cropping intensity and total surface water area) as under—

$$\left.\begin{aligned} Y-\overline{y} &= r\frac{d_x}{d_y}(X-\overline{x}) \\ X-\overline{x} &= r\frac{d_y}{d_x}(Y-\overline{y}) \end{aligned}\right\} \text{where } r \text{ (correlation coefficient)}$$

$$\frac{\Sigma xy}{N d_x d_y}$$

(b) Rank correlation coefficient (R) = $1 - \frac{6\sum d^2}{N(N^2-1)}$

Factors affecting Agriculture in Burdwan

Both physical and cultural factors have profound influence on agriculture in the district.

As stated earlier the district of Burdwan can be divided in three regions—The Western Upland Terrain/Plateau Fringe Area, the Central Rolling Plain and the Eastern Flat Plain. Relief is maximum in the west. The Central rolling plain has an uneven character with less variation in relief. The Eastern monotonous flood plain region is drained by rivers—Bhagirathi, Ajay and Damodar. The general slope is from west to east. Climate is in general, hot humid (monsoon) type. Rainfall is high in the east (152 cm), which decreases towards west (below 132 cm). West has a stony and skeletal soil. Soil is clay loam to sandy loam in the east. In between, the central part is covered by red and lateritic soil. In the district, vegetation character changes with land character—western part covered by grasses and shrubs, the middle portion once under forest but presently barren and eastern part mainly under crop culture.

As regards the cultural parameters, agriculture in the district has a positive relationship between educational and agricultural development. Literacy percentage, distribution of population and their character, female work participation, age-sex structure, settlement pattern – all are favourable for agricultural development in the eastern part of the district.

Water Resources of Burdwan

Burdwan is blessed by a number of rivers like—Damodar, Bhagirathi, Bhalluka, Khari, Behula etc. Agriculture has flourished due to favourable agro-climatic conditions. But Damodar with its devastating floods almost in every alternative year had a negative impact on the economy. Even before and just after independence agriculture of the district was mainly dependent on natural sources of water and accordingly agriculture was basically rainfed (Table 12.1).

Damodar Valley Corporation (DVC) was the first human imprint to regulate the natural flow of River Damodar. With the advent of Green

Table 12.1: Availability of Water from Natural Sources and Land Situation

Name of the Blocks	*Nature of land (in '000 Hec.)*		*Rainfall (in cm)*	*Total Water Area (in Hec.)*	*River Discharge (Annual Average) P.S. wise*	*Ground Water Yield (lit/sec.)*
	Flood Prone	*Drought Prone*				
Burdwan	0.600	-	152.40	936.51	482.2899	38
Galsi-I	0.800	-	134.62	774.05	219.6671	20
Galsi-II	0.100	-	132.08	1277.09	-	18
Bhatar	0.950	-	127.00	2376.13	3697.3080	25
Ausgram-I	3.100	1.000	121.92	1625.30	-	22
Ausgram-II	0.650	2.600	134.62	700.15	-	25
Memari-I	0.080	-	152.40	1500.35	-	40
Memari-II	1.725	-	144.78	996.35	-	38
Jamalpur	0.404	-	149.86	1218.21	-	39
Khandaghosh	1.090	-	142.24	1535.67	-	26
Raina-I	2.890	-	147.32	900.21	-	36
Raina-II	2.400	-	149.86	720.28	-	30
Faridpur	-	5.000	134.62	880.44	-	02
Kanksa	0.200	7.000	109.22	1094.00	-	08
Andal	-	4.500	132.08	718.67	-	02
Hirapur	-	3.050	142.24	169.64	-	02
Raniganj	-	0.800	132.08	291.60	-	04
Jamuria-I	-	3.500	142.24	360.19	-	02
Jamuria-II	-	3.400	142.24	250.10	-	03
Salanpur	-	3.500	152.40	290.79	-	01
Barabani	-	6.500	147.32	597.34	-	05
Kalna-I	1.500	-	147.32	950.50	-	36
Kalna-II	0.400	-	149.86	754.25	-	39
Purbasthalli-I	3.400	-	144.78	600.34	21720.9770	40
Purbasthalli-II	1.800	-	149.86	601.30	-	38
Monteswar	1.000	-	142.24	774.10	-	35
Katwa-I	1.200	-	134.62	300.00	758.1894	38
Katwa-II	1.600	-	142.24	395.02	-	39
Ketugram-I	1.600	-	127.00	600.30	-	39
Ketugram-II	2.000	-	121.92	659.00	-	40
Mongolkote	2.070	-	132.08	2466.65	-	29

Source: Surface Water Investigation Department, Burdwan.

Revolution, transformation of agriculture took place not only in the use of water by taking recourse to irrigation but also in the other aspects of advanced agricultural technology. Both surface and sub-surface water sources are accordingly tapped for the agricultural development in the district. They are as follows (Table 12.2).

(a) *Major Irrigation*

Surface water sources (Canal and Others):

Table 12.2: Evaluation of Irrigation Sources

Name of the Blocks	Cropping Intensity	Net Area Under Irrigation	Major Irrigation Sources			Minor Irrigation Sources					Rating Value of Minor Irri. Sources	Total Rating Values of Irrigation
			No. of Canals	No. of Tanks	Rating Value of Major Irri. Sources	No. of DTW	No. of MDTW	No. of LDTW	No. of STW	No. of RLI		
(1)	(2)	(3)	(4)	(5)	(6)	(7)	(8)	(9)	(10)	(11)	(12)	(13)
Burdwan	206	58,915	1	896	1896	13	01	—	2391	08	2486	4382
Galsi-I	190	23,800	—	2028	2028	04	—	—	641	—	657	2685
Galsi-II	185	39,525	1	1198	2198	56	—	—	1780	—	2004	4202
Bhatar	172	50,993	1	—	1000	02	—	—	1820	13	1893	2893
Ausgram-I	165	22,410	1	2783	3783	—	—	—	923	—	923	4706
Ausgram-II	125	12,266	1	153	1153	07	—	—	750	09	823	1976
Memari-I	219	30,670	1	1200	2200	05	02	06	1461	01	1504	3704
Memari-II	200	30,035	1	1439	2439	18	02	06	2234	08	2364	4803
Jamalpur	225	47,265	1	1250	2250	21	—	06	2740	12	2896	5146
Khandoghosh	147	28,105	1	850	1850	25	—	—	1537	02	1647	3497
Raina-I	159	36,400	1	415	1415	33	—	06	1327	03	1486	2901
Raina-II	155	30,264	1	520	1520	19	—	—	1618	07	1729	3249
Faridpur	101	2,510	1	—	1000	01	—	—	16	04	40	1040
Kanksa	135	14,493	1	103	1103	06	—	—	—	20	124	1227
Andal	115	625	—	230	230	—	—	—	15	02	25	255
Hirapur	115	1,000	—	37	37	—	—	—	—	—	—	37
Raniganj	117	700	—	103	103	—	—	—	02	02	12	115

TABLE 12.2: *(Contd....)*

(1)	*(2)*	*(3)*	*(4)*	*(5)*	*(6)*	*(7)*	*(8)*	*(9)*	*(10)*	*(11)*	*(12)*	*(13)*
Jamuria-I	115	670	—	685	685	—	—	—	—	—	—	685
Jamuria-II	114	360	—	10	10	—	—	—	02	—	02	12
Salanpur	109	320	—	520	520	—	—	—	—	—	—	520
Barabani	115	530	—	520	520	—	—	—	—	02	10	530
Kalna-I	190	26465	1	2207	3207	43	02	18	1791	33	2170	5377
Kalna-II	199	27721	1	63	1063	34	02	06	1541	07	1730	2793
Purbasthali-I	185	22975	—	93	93	56	01	06	1442	51	1936	2029
Purbasthali-II	199	27015	—	400	400	57	02	—	2548	22	2892	4292
Monteswar	147	38730	1	1000	2000	40	—	—	2214	20	2474	4474
Katwa-I	178	20670	1	765	1765	18	06	—	1580	04	1690	3455
Katwa-II	186	20220	1	184	1184	25	01	—	1162	13	1330	2514
Ketugram-I	156	27140	1	700	1700	08	—	—	1391	03	1438	3138
Ketugram-II	150	18700	1	652	1652	18	01	—	1723	33	1963	3615
Mongolkote	156	37419	1	1502	2502	06	—	42	1817	05	1950	4452

Source: Lead Bank Report.

N.B. *Rating Values*

1 Canal	= 1000	1 Low deep tubewell (LDTW)	= 2
1 Deep tubewell (DTW)	= 4	1 Shallow tubewell (STW)	= 1
1 Medium deep tubewell (MDTW)	= 3	1 River Life Irrigation System (RLI)	= 5

(i) Canal—Canal irrigation network is well knitted in the eastern half of the district.
(ii) Tank, pond and other local (spot) sources of surface water are also profoundly used.

(b) *Minor Irrigation*
Underground water sources are given below:

i) D.T.W. – Deep Tube Well
ii) M.D.T.W. – Medium Deep Tube Well
iii) S.T.W. – Shallow Tube Well
iv) R.L.I. – River Lift Irrigation Method

Now-a-days, in Burdwan mostly underground water is being used for irrigation purposes. The intensity of agriculture is high in those blocks, where underground water is used at random.

Water vis-à-vis Agriculture

Agriculture is dependent on physical as well as climatic conditions of an area. But the most important of all of them is water. Based on water availability (rainfall, total water area, river discharge, groundwater yield) the district can be divided into three categories high, medium and low (Table 12.1, Map 12.1).

Category-I (High)

The area approximately bounded by the rivers—Ajay, Damodar and Bhagirathi, has the most favourable condition for water supply and accordingly is most suitable for agricultural development. It covers Ketugram I and II, Mongalkote, Katwa I (Part), Monteswar, Purbasthali I (South), Kalna I and II, Memari I and II (East), Jamalpur, Raina I and II (West), Khandoghosh, Burdwan (South), Bhatar (North) blocks mainly confining to the eastern part of the district.

Category-II (Medium)

Availability of surface water is not that much favourable for agriculture in this section as compared to Category I. Whatever agricultural activity is to be found here, depends on groundwater (yield rate 10-25 litres/

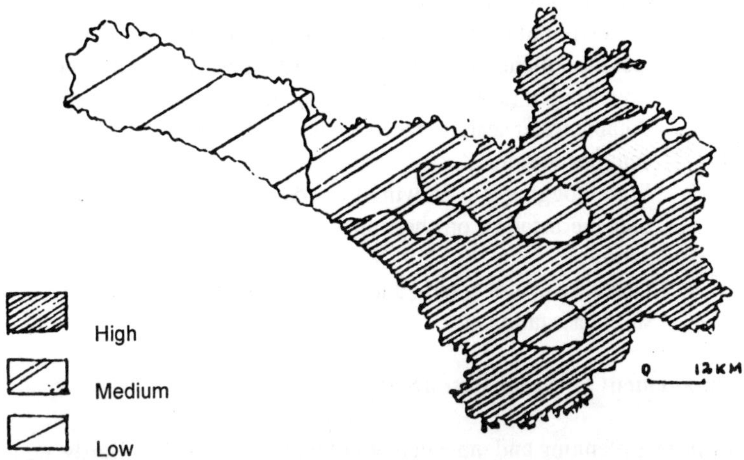

Map 12.1: Availability of Water—Burdwan District

sec.) and rainfall (160 cm). Blocks included in this category are Burdwan and Bhatar (Part), Memari I and II (Part), Kanksa, Ausgram I and II (Part).

Category-III (Low)

Surface discharge of water is negligible in this section due to construction of dams on Damodar and Ajay in their upper reaches. Groundwater yield (1-5 litres/sec.) and rainfall are not significant for agriculture. The extreme western part of the district is within this category and it comprises the blocks of Durgapur, Faridpur, Andal, Raniganj, Jamuria I and II, Hirapur, Barabani, Salanpur, Kulti, etc.

Problems faced by Agriculture with special reference to Water

Use of surface and sub-surface water in agriculture has given good results in terms of crop production as has already been discussed. But some problems associated with new package programme i.e. HYV seeds, pesticides, insecticides, weedicides alongwith irrigation water are now cropping up in the district under consideration. The major problems accordingly faced by the farmers are as follows:

1. Wastage of water (both surface and sub-surface), excess water overflows the farmland.
2. Water pollution (excess water from agricultural field carries residues of chemical fertilizers, pesticides, weedicides, etc.)
3. Lowering of ground watertable due to excess of overlifting.
4. Potable water scarcity faced by the inhabitants especially during summer season.
5. Water logging and growth of weeds hampering agriculture.
6. Salt incrustation on the upper layers of soil due to capillary action.
7. Decrease in arable land due to water logging, growth of weeds, salt incrustation etc.

Management of Water Resources

For proper planning and management of water resources of Burdwan, it is of utmost importance to assess the physical as well as cultural/socio-economic resources of the district. Only through a series of analysis, one can achieve the desired development in agriculture.

Analysis

Physical Potentiality

On the basis of physical potentiality (Map 12.2, Table 12.3) the district can be divided in three major categories—high, medium and low.

Category-I (High)

Depending on rock character, water availability and other physical attributes the most favourable area (in pockets) for agriculture lies in the eastern part of the district covering the blocks of Khandoghosh, Raina I and II (West), Mongalkote, Ausgram I and II, Katwa II, Monteswar, Purbasthali I and II.

Category-II (Medium)

The moderately favourable area for agriculture in the district extends in a much wider area (East Central) covering Jamalpur, Memari I and II, Burdwan, Galsi II, Bhatar, Ausgram I and II (rest), Mongolkote (rest), Katwa I, Ketugram I and II Blocks.

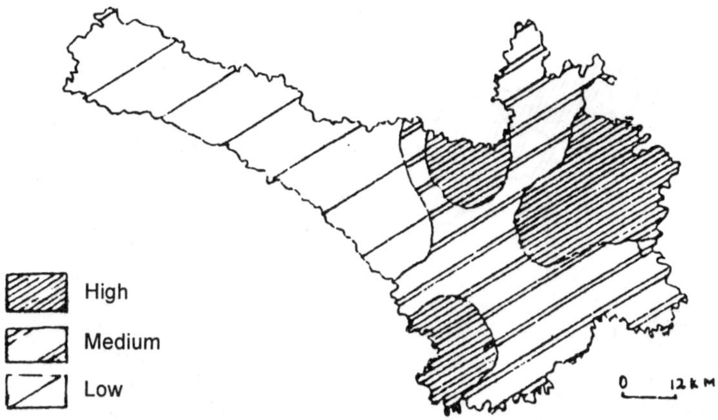

Map 12.2: Physical Potentiality—Burdwan District

Category-III (Low)

In this area agriculture is not at all favourable from the point of soil, water, climate etc. The area is dominated by mining and industrial activities. It covers Galsi I (Part), Ausgram I and II (West), Kanksa and other Western blocks of Burdwan District.

Socio-economic Potentiality

Depending on the important/major socio-economic parameters such as connectivity, availability of urban amenities, marketing, storage and educational facility, distribution of income, female work participation rate, male-female ratio etc., the district is divided into three categories—high, medium and low (Map 12.3).

Category-I (High)

On the basis of the connectivity, educational facility, higher earnings, availability of urban amenities, marketing and storage facility, female work participation, male-female ratio, the area has the highest socio-economic impact and accordingly becomes the most favourable one for agriculture. The block included in this category are Raina I and II (Part), Burdwan, Jamalpur (Part), Galsi I and II (Part), Mongolkote, Kulti, Hirapur, Jamuria I and II, Raniganj, Salanpur, Andal, Barabani, Durgapur (West), Bhatar (West).

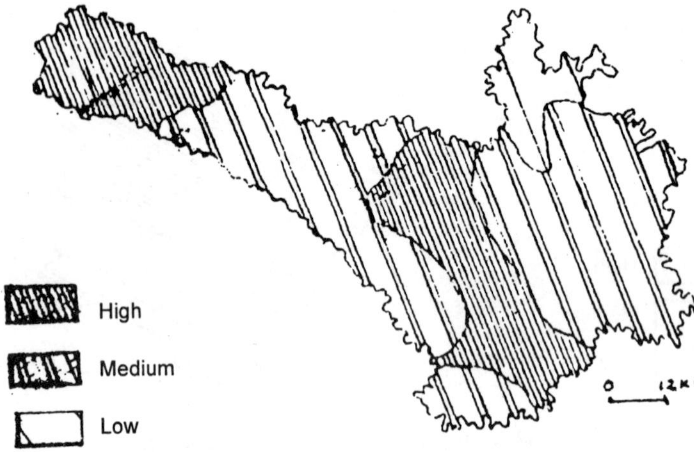

Map 12.3: Socio-Economic Impact—Burdwan District

Category-II (Medium)

Moderately favourable area lies in the central part as well as in the eastern part of the district. From the point of view of the education, marketing and storage facility including connectivity the area is far behind the category I. Blocks of this category are Purbasthali I and II, Monteswar, Kalna I and II, Memari I and II (Part), Bhatar (East), Khandaghosh, Galsi II (West), Ausgram I and II, Kanksa, Durgapur (East).

Category-III (Low)

Rural electrification as well as transport network development hinder the prosperity of the area. Blocks of this category include Ketugram I and II and Katwa I (Part).

Agricultural Development

On the basis of agricultural development, the district is divided into three categories – high, medium and low. It is done according to intensity of cropping, which is further dependent on water availability, technology adoption, marketing and storage facility and of course, physical character of the land (Map 12.4).

Table 12.3: Evaluation of Water Potential in Relation to Agriculture (by Composite Index)

Name of the Blocks	*Characteristics*	*Lithology/ Land-form*	*Soil*	*Water Potential*	*Socio-economic Potential*	*Compo-site Index Number*	*Category Identi-fied*
Burdwan I and II Galsi I and II Memari I and II Jamalpur, Kalna I and II Purbasthali I and II Katwa I and II	Relief 10 metres, Gradually raised tract from east to west. Slope 1° Groundwater Yield 25-40 litre/sec. Deep to very deep soil, medium to yellowish brown in colour. *p*H 6-7, N.P.K.>0.85% relatively moist and fertile. Educated and skilled farmer and agricultural labourer with good infrastructure.	100	100	80	65	5.209	I
Ketugram I and II Ausgram I Bhatar, Raina I and II, Monteswar, Mongolkote, Khandaghosh, Kanksa.	Relief varies between 10 and 20 metres, gently sloping surface towards east, slope 1° Groundwater yield 10-25 litre/sec. medium to deep soil, Medium to fine in texture grey brown to brown in colour. *p*H 5-6, N.P.K.—0.45% to 0.65% Moist and fertile. Dynamic farmer class, but lack of infrastructural facility.	90	90	50	75	4.560	II
Ausgram II, Faridpur, Pandabeswar, Andal, Asansol, Raniganj, Jamuria I and II, Salanpur, Barabani	Relief 35 metres to 150 metres, Peneplain with series of fault-lines (West), Rocky hillocks and low ridges (West). Slope–1° to 3° Groundwater yield 5-10 litres/sec. (East) to 1-5 litres/sec. (West). Thin soil cover, coarse to medium in texture, Dark brown to grey brown in colour, *p*H 7, N.P.K.-0.45%. People less interested in agriculture, mining and industrial activities predominant	25	60	30	35	2.231	III

N.B. *Rating Values*:

Slope : 0°–1° = 100
1°-3° = 50
3° & above = 25

Relief: 4-15 Metres = 100
15-25 Metres = 95
25-35 Metres = 90
35 Metres & above = 85

Soil: Loam = 100
Samdy Loam = 90
Clay Loam = 85
Clay = 50.

Water potential:
Groundwater Yield (litres/sec.)
40 – 25 = 80, 25 – 10 = 60, 10 – 5 = 40, 5-1 = 20
Rainfall availability: 60"-56" = 80, 56"–52" = 75
Below 52" = 70.
Surface Water Discharge

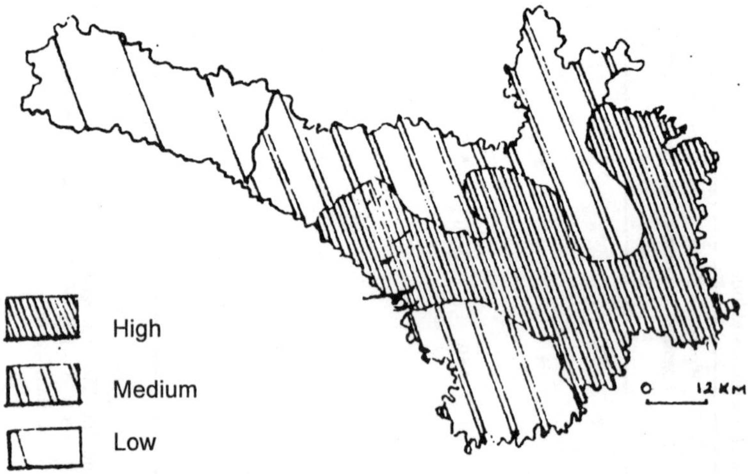

Map 12.4: Level of Agricultural Development —Cropping Intencity

Category I (High)

This category has highest cropping intensity (above 175%) comprising of Galsi II, Khandaghosh (North), Burdwan, Bhatar, Memari I and II, Jamalpur, Kalna I and II, Purbasthali I and II, Raina I and II (East), Katwa I and II blocks in the district.

Category II (Medium)

Cropping intensity is though high here, the infrastructural development is not upto the mark. Blocks included in this category are Khandaghosh, Raina I and II (West), Ketugram I and II, Monteswar, Mongalkote, Ausgram I and II, Galsi (Part), Kanksa.

Category III (Low)

Low physical potentiality as well as less water availability are hindering agricultural development in this area. Government assistance and the availability of minerals are conducive for industrial development in the area (Coal in Raniganj). Blocks belonging in this category are – Durgapur, Faridpur, Andal, Raniganj, Jamuria I and II, Barabani, Hirapur, Salanpur, Kulti.

Map 12.1 and 12.2 and Table 12.3 indicate that physical potentiality and water availability more or less coincide, though not exactly identical. It further indicates that the physical potentiality though help to some extent the development of agriculture in the east, the availability of water has much more impact on agricultural development. This has further been strengthened by correlating physical potentiality with agricultural productivity/cropping intensity (r = + 0.28, very low and positive). Whereas the correlation coefficient between groundwater potential (i.e. minor irrigation) and agricultural productivity/cropping intensity is very high and positive (r = + 0.78), indicating thereby the dependence of cropping intensity or agricultural development on minor irrigation mainly. Further correlation coefficient between cropping intensity and irrigation sources is very high and positive (r = + 0.72), which has an indication that cropping intensity in the district is depending on minor irrigation sources. Again, the correlation coefficient between major irrigation sources and net area under irrigation is (r = + 0.13) which is very low though positive. It means that major irrigation sources have a positive role to play but not a significant one.

It is already mentioned that without water even fertile soil cannot produce anything. So the development of agriculture in any region depends on water availability and water management.

Water conditions have a key position with regard to land-use strategy and planning. The landscape ecology as well as the cultural ecosystem is of utmost importance for the sustainable development of agricultural land-use. Depending on the earlier stated analysis, the following strategies may be taken up for the proper management of water resources in regard to the sustained development of agriculture in Burdwan:

(i) Instead of multipurpose irrigation projects, minor irrigation systems (especially R.L.I.) should be used.

(ii) Canal length should be restricted.

(iii) Canal beds must be cemented.

(iv) Irrigation water can be supplied to the agricultural fields through drip irrigation method.

(v) Wastage of water through irrigation can be minimised through sprinkle irrigation method.

(vi) Surface (Spot) water sources – Well, pond, tanks should be used as irrigation sources.

(vii) Series of contour-line dam construction to obstruct the natural flow of surface run-off and to increase the level of ground water table.

(viii) Watershed Area Development.

All these are to be introduced whenever possible for minimising the loss of water through percolation and other over uses.

Conclusion

The district of Burdwan is considered as the 'granary' of West Bengal. It has surplus agricultural production as compared to the needs of its people especially in terms of cereal crop/food production. It supplies foodgrains not only to the other districts of West Bengal but also to the neighbouring states. But because of the present problems arising out of the negative impact of advanced agricultural technology including indiscriminate use of water especially subsurface water, how long the fame "Burdwan, the Rice Bowl of West Bengal" will continue is a question. The Government should take immediate steps in this regard as soon as possible to keep the district's fame in tact.

References

Banerjee, B. and Lahiri, S. (1985), Impact of Urbanisation on Environment: A case study of Burdwan. *Impact of Development on Environment*, Vol. 1, Geog. Soc. of India, Calcutta, pp. 126-132.

De, N.K. and Sarkar, A.K. (1992), Alternative Strategies for Agricultural Development in India: An Ecological Perspective. Dynamics of Agricultural Development, Vol. VII, *New Dimensions in Agricultural Geography*, Concept Publishing Co., New Delhi.

Freez, R.A. and Cherry, J.A. (1979), *Ground Water*, Prentice Hall Inc., New Jersey, 1979.

Galon, R. (1964), Hydrological Research for the need of the Regional Economy. *Problems of Applied Geography*, Warsaw.

Mitra, D. (1986), *Hydrology and Ground Water Resources of Bardhman District West Bengal*, Central Ground Water Board, Eastern Region, Calcutta.

Rai, V.K. (1993), *Water Resources, Planning and Development*, Deep and Deep Publications, New Delhi.

Sarkar, A.K. and De, N.K. (1990), Agro-industries and Economic Development in Bardhman : A Study in Remote Sensing Technique, Proc., I.G.U. Sump. Role of Commercial Activities in the Econ. Dev. of Ganga Basin, Dept. of Geog., Gorakhpur University, Gorakhpur.

Thomas, H.E. (1951), *The Conservation of Ground Water*, McGraw Hill, New York.

UNESCO (1974), "World Water Balance and Water Resources of the Earth". Studies and Reports in Hydrology, No. 25, USSR Committee for the International Hydrological Decade, USSR.

United Nations (1960), "A Case Study of the Damodar Valley Corporation", Flood Control Series, No. 16, New York.

Willcocks, W. (1930), Lectures on the Ancient System of Irrigation in Bengal and Its Application to Modern Problems. University of Calcutta, Calcutta.

13

IDENTIFICATION OF CULTURABLE WASTELANDS

A Methodological Approach with Case Study

N.K. DE & SOUMENDU CHATTERJEE

Introduction

During the last few decades, the world population has increased at a rate unprecedented in the history of mankind. According to UNO the world has attained a population of 6000 million on 12th October, 1999. More than 90 million people are added to the world population in only one year. This unprecedented growth of population has created a tremendous pressure on the existing available land. In this context L.D. Stamp (1952) had also rightly remarked, "No problem confronting us is more important than that of matching the world's use of its land with its need of people". In the present world of increasing population land is an enormous asset in any consideration.

The amount of land that is suitable for food production is fixed. The man-land ratio is thus gradually decreasing. Already there is an immense food and hunger problem, particularly in the third world countries. To cope with this problem, agricultural production has been increased by using various scientific techniques. But these techniques have some direct or indirect environmental risks. Under these circumstances it is desirable to expand agriculture in the culturable wastelands. In most of the developing countries, including India, considerable stretches of land have been left fallow for which no scientific information is available. Identification of culturable wastelands from such fallow lands and their scientific utilization are the most urgent task for the present time because cultivation in the cultivable wastelands may be environmentally less hazardous and economically more suitable.

The objective of this chapter is to develop a methodology by which it is possible to collect detailed information of large areas economically and scientifically but very rapidly and subsequently to classify them on the basis of land/soil potentiality. This will ultimately help to identify the culturable wastelands. In developing the methodology, care has been taken not only for its economic feasibility but also for its universal applicability in any type of terrain and environment. In the proposed method the importance of geomorphology and its significance in integrated study has been taken into consideration. Accordingly, the methodology thus enunciated, has been tried in different case studies in different environments, in different types of terrain and in different scales of working. Only one case study (i.e., Joychandipahar hill slope in Raghunathpur, Purulia, West Bengal, India) has been cited.

Culturable Wasteland

As per the common system of land classification, culturable wasteland includes those lands, which were once cultivated but not cultivated for the last five years in succession. These wastelands are available for cultivation or abandoned after a few years for one reason or the other. These lands may be either fallow or covered with jungles and shrubs. They are not put to any use and may be existing in isolated blocks or within the cultivated holdings. Thus the connotation suggests that these lands may have potentiality to support agriculture as because they have been cultivated in the past. But now they have been abandoned because of some physical, social and/or economic problems. As per the above definition, the use of a time period of five years of non-cultivation for denoting a land as culturable wastes is probably for practical convenience but they may remain uncultivated for a long period of time. Therefore, the culturable wastes are the lands which can be cultivated and are not infertile in nature.

Need for Identification of Culturable Wastelands

Identification of culturable wastelands is very urgent to supply food the teeming population, particularly in the third world countries. As stated earlier, world population growth has become the most urgent and serious problem of the present time. The situation is more grave in the case of the developing countries (growth rates: Africa 3.0%, Latin America 2.1%, Asia 1.8%) as compared to developed ones (growth rates: North America 0.8%, Europe 0.2%). In India, though it shows a declining trend, the growth rate (1.8% per year) is still very high.

Many developing countries have achieved self-sufficiency in food production by using scientific techniques in agriculture. In India Green Revolution has made remarkable rejuvenating impact on agriculture through which India has made serious endeavours to overcome acute food shortage and has become more or less self-sufficient in food production. But it has also been estimated that with the present rate of population growth, India will have to import annually over 40 million tonnes of foodgrain by 2003 which is four times the quantity imported in 1966 i.e., before Green Revolution. Therefore, food crisis is a long persistent problem even after the various technological inventions in agricultural fields.

Different techniques have been applied to face this problem of food crisis. Vertical expansion by means of agricultural intensification and diversification (i.e. increasing agricultural productivity by introducing HYV seeds, fertilizers, supply of water, pesticides, etc.) is a very familiar method to increase production. But experience shows that excessive use of fertilizers, pesticides, irrigation have created environmental problems (like land/soil pollution, water pollution, desertification, usarification, eutrophication, biological magnification, water logging, soil erosion, soil alkalinity and salinity, disease problems, etc.). It has been estimated that, India with its current growth rate will have to produce 285 million tonnes of food crops to feed its population in 2006-2007. But it will be socially disastrous to achieve this target through standard methods of agricultural intensification. It is thus desirable to move away from the Green Revolution model towards ecologically and socially sustainable forms of agriculture.

Another important technique is expansion of agriculture in new areas (horizontal expansion). In many cases forests have been cleared for agricultural practices which have been proved to be catastrophic for the humanity and has further serious ecological problems. Again expansion of agriculture in deserts and semi-deserts through extension of irrigation facilities and other management methods have been found to be very problematic. Similarly cultivation along steep to very steep mountain slopes is also economically not viable.

On the eve of the 21st century, the greatest challenge before the scientists is to maintain food security but not at the cost of ecological imbalance and rapid exhaustion of natural resource base. Considering all these aspects, expansion of agriculture in cultivable wastelands will add a new dimension towards the sustainable solution of ever increasing food problem which is less harmful (from environmental point of view) but at the same time more economic. Therefore, identification of culturable wastelands for their subsequent scientific and economic use is the prime consideration in the present treatise.

Methodology

The land is an important resource. Easily available lands have already been used for food production by following scientific methods, as already stated. But the assessment and improvement of the culturable wastelands have not yet been tried so seriously which can be utilised for significant and necessary food supply in the developing countries including India. This objective can quickly be achieved by initial classification of land in general (e.g. goodland, badland, wasteland etc.). Wastelands can further be classified into different categories including cultivable wastelands.

In formulating the methodology, the key idea is that the form is an indicator of environment. Land can be considered as a complex system, which is governed by underlying geology, hydrological characteristics, topography, drainage, natural vegetation, soil, etc. These components are genetically and ecologically correlated to give rise to a particular land surface. The nature and type of interactions among them determine its character which vary with time and environment/process. Thus it is possible to define parcels of land or land units of various sizes which are more or less homogeneous in character. These land units of differing characteristics are naturally organised within a spatial framework to give rise to a land complex of an area.

A land complex can be scientifically classified into land units on the basis of physical parameters like rock type, hydrology, topography, soil, vegetation etc. In this respect geomorphology plays an important role as it is closely associated with the above landforming attributes. Each land unit exhibits a particular assemblage of form/forms where a particular set of landforming processes operates. Therefore, a parcel of land showing a characteristic landform pattern can be identified as a land unit. Thus geomorphology has scientific applications in the investigation, evaluation and classification of land as a resource. As such the study of landscape ecology is very much relevant for land-use planning which is concerned with the ecology of mankind as well as of plants and animals and offer a long term benefit. Such an approach to the study of land/landscape and its classification and evaluation requires a synthesis of the knowledge of the various branches of the earth science – geology, geomorphology, pedology, etc. – an integrated approach. This synthesized knowledge (integrated) is inevitable in the investigation and planning of the culturable wastelands for significant and sustainable solution to the food problem in the present context.

In the developing countries geologists, soil scientists, and others made many scientific surveys in an isolated manner for land-use development purposes. But such developmental strategies have often failed to promote overall development because the relevant experts did not give due importance to the principles of integrated study. Therefore, an integrated approach in which the results gained by one individual study is to be correlated with other types of studies. This is highly effective in identification, planning and use of culturable wastelands.

By following the above philosophy, the methodology enunciated in this chapter for identification of culturable wastelands can be summarised in the following phases (pre-field, field and post-field).

Phase I: Pre-field Method

The objective of this phase is to gain knowledge of the area under study from the existing maps, reports, literatures etc. This includes the following steps:

(i) Collection of a complete cover of topographical sheets on the desired scale, reports and other maps of the area.
(ii) Collation and interpretation of the available literature and maps thus collected.
(iii) Aerial photographs/imageries are consulted wherever available.
(iv) The base map is finalized. Roads and tracts are marked on it.
(v) A preliminary comprehension of the major land complexes is made and thus identified.
(vi) Land complexes are interpreted with the help of already available information.
(vii) Land complexes identified and demarcated with abbreviated symbols signifying geology, landforms, soil, vegetation, etc. These symbols are arbitrary and are liable to be modified on the basis of information gathered during actual fieldwork.

(viii) Subsequently traverse routes are planned and sample areas are selected.

Phase II: Field-work Method

In this type of survey, it would be better if the survey party consists of a geomorphologist, a pedologist and an ecologist who will individually collect samples, data and keep records related to their own fields of interest. At this stage the survey procedure includes the following:

(i) A reconnaissance survey of the sample site is made.
(ii) Land complex/sample site is then diagrammatically represented (not to scale) showing different land units of the land complex (sample site) alongwith their spatial relationships.
(iii) Sample areas already planned are changed and modified, if necessary, on the basis of field observations.
(iv) During traversing observations between two sample areas by different scientists of the group are coordinated.
(v) Each land unit is sampled systematically and the landform, soil and vegetation data for each unit including their relationships are recorded in a tabular form in an information sheet.
(vi) Sample area information sheets are grouped into land complexes.
(vii) A general description of each land complex is made.
(viii) Correlation of the field observations with the already collected information is made and further modifications are to be made as and when necessary.

It is to be mentioned that the geomorphologist, pedologist and the ecologist have their individual roles to play during the field survey. A geomorphologist's role is to draw slope profiles; measure amount of slope with directions; study the uniformity, variability, structure, lithology and texture of the parent materials alongwith their hydrological character, to demarcate land unit boundaries and to prepare diagrams of the land complex. The role of the ecologist is to collect information about vegetal characteristics (both natural and cultural) and also to note the nature of hazards (if any). The pedologist's role is to study soil profiles and to assess the depth and colour of soil and collect soil samples of individual land units alongwith the collection of information regarding aspect, slope, micro-relief, hydrology, vegetation, etc. The information thus collected is to be coordinated and tabulated and finally substantiated by the slope profiles already drawn. An applied geomorphologist with knowledge of geology, hydrology, morphology, soil, vegetation, etc. may serve the purpose in the present context.

Phase III: Post-field Method

This phase consists of the following steps:

(i) Land complex boundaries alongwith their associated land units are finally drawn on the basis of survey data, field experience and extrapolation to cover the untraversed tracts, if any. New land complexes are also recognised through extrapolation.
(ii) Thus land units of each land complex are environmentally evaluated and assessed in terms of potentiality for future land-use planning purposes.
(iii) In this way, land units with agricultural potentiality but presently remaining fallow can be identified as culturable wastelands.
(iv) Finally management strategies are formulated for further land-use planning.

Case Study

The above mentioned methodology has been tried in different areas of the western part of West Bengal (Bankura, Purulia, Birbhum and Western Midnapore districts, West Bengal, India). This part of West Bengal, an extension of the Chhotanagpur plateau, is agriculturally backward. Vast stretches of land are left uncultivated years after years. Monoculture is rarely practised wherever favourable agro-factors (particularly soil and water) are available. Hence, identification and reclamation of culturable land(s) will add an impetus to the further agricultural development in these districts of West Bengal, India.

It may be mentioned that the hill slopes of the western West Bengal, in particular, are mostly left abandoned as wastelands. Accordingly many case studies have been made on different hill slopes of this part of West Bengal. Out of several case studies only one case study i.e. Joychandipahar hill slope of Raghunathpur, Purulia, West Bengal has been cited in this chapter. In the present case study, although all the three phases of the methodology (cited above) have been followed systematically, only the field method has been highlighted here.

Joychandipahar is a residual hill having dry tropical monsoonal micro-climate. The entire slope stretches about two kilometres from the top – very steep crest slope, moderate middle slope and gentle foot slope, which gradually merges with the plain land. The hill slope under study bears a very rough geographical personality with underlying grinitic-gneissic rock complex. Hydrologically it is well drained. The area has characteristically very high to moderate micro-relief. Scattered grasses and thorny shrubs dotted with isolated deciduous trees are the common vegetal covers. It is covered with less fertile, very coarse to moderately coarse colluvial soil (intermixed with occasional boulders, cobbles, pebbles, etc.) which increases in depth towards the foot slope.

Abney's level was used to determine the slope variability and twenty-five soil samples (Fig. 13.1) were collected depending on the breaks of slope. The soil samples were analysed both physically and chemically. In addition, the geomorphological, hydrological, vegetational characteristics were also noted. Finally the Joychandipahar hill slope was classified into four land units (Fig. 13.1):

(a) Steep crest slope,
(b) Upper middle slope,
(c) Lower middle slope, and
(d) Foot slope.

Characteristics of each of the slope units (land units) are arranged in a tabular form and strategies suggested for future land-use practices (Table 13.1).

N.B. A three dimensional block diagram showing different land units of the land complex would have explained in more detail which has not been included here. In the absence of this a slope profile has been shown.

The above methodology can further be statistically substantiated as explained below.

Slope is an important physical parameter that can regulate the geomorphological processes, hydrological conditions, micro-environmental conditions, processes of soil formation etc. Therefore there are close relationships among slope and soil attributes. These relationships have been

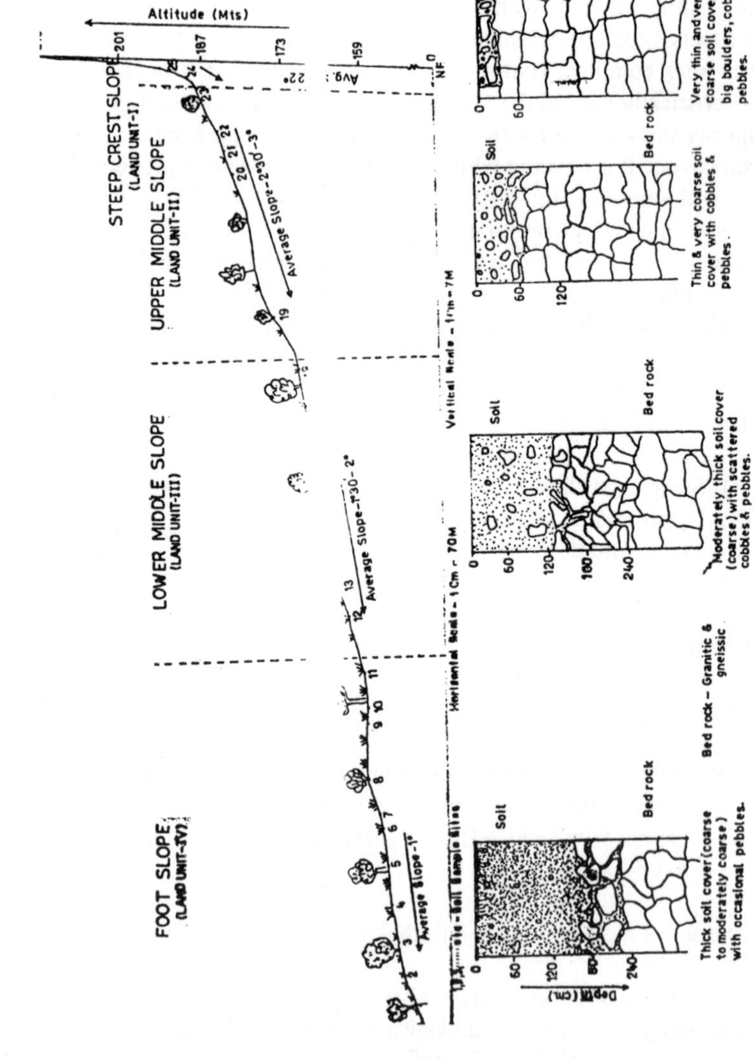

Fig. 13.1: Diagram showing different Land Units and Underlying Soil Profiles (Joychandipahar Hill Slope, Raghunathpur, Purulia, W. B.)

Table 13.1: Different Land Units of Joychandipahar Hill Slope Complex (Reghunathpur, Purulia, West Bengal) and their Characteristics

Land Unit I	*Land Unit II*	*Land Unit III*	*Land Unit IV*
Steep Crest Slope: Bed rock exposed in places; very rough and very steep strewn with big boulders, cobbles and pebbles; average slope 22°; micro-relief 6"-10"; excessive erosion; excessively drained	*Upper Middle Slope*: Extensive and steep with broad undulations, mixed with cobbles and pebbles; average slope – 2°30′-3°; micro-relief 4"-6"; excessive to moderate erosion; well drained	*Lower Middle Slope*: Very extensive, more or less steep to gentle, scattered cobbles and pebbles; average slope – 1°30′-2°; micro-relief within 4"; moderate erosion; moderate to well drained	*Foot Slope*: Very very extensive with gentle undulations occasional pebbles, average slope-1°, micro-relief less than 2", moderate to minimum erosion; moderately drained.
Almost no soil cover, very very coarse in texture % of sand – 90.86, % of silt – 4.05, % of clay–5.09, % of organic carbon–0.79, *p*H–6.4; devoid of vegetation	Thin soil cover, yellowish in colour, very coarse in texture, % of sand – 80.81, % of silt – 12.53, % of clay–6.66, % of organic carbon – 0.67%, *p*H–5.7; scattered shrubs and bushes with very thin grasses.	Medium soil cover, yellowish brown in colour, coarse texture, % of sand–69.17, % of silt–24.35, % of clay–6.47%, % of organic carbon–0.50, *p*H–5.3; thin grass cover dotted with bushes and shrubs	Moderately deep soil cover, brownish yellow in colour, coarse to moderately coarse in texture, % of sand 53.06, % of silt 34.75, % of clay 12.19, % of organic carbon-0.27, *p*H–4.8, covered with moderately deep grasses with scattered trees.
Not suitable for agriculture	May be used for plantation purposes	Relatively fertile, suitable for dry crops with conservation measures and irrigation	Comparatively fertile, can be cultivated with minimum conservation measures, suitable for monoculture.

illustrated graphically and established statistically for the above-mentioned case study (Fig. 13.2 and 13.3). Accordingly, lands (Raghunathpur hill slope in the present context) can also be evaluated and classified on the basis of slope. Greater the slope, poorer is the quality of soil/land and more is the conservation measures required (Table 13.1). As micro-level slope variations could not be plotted in the desired scale correlation between (a) altitude and soil attributes (Fig. 13.2) and (b) distance from the hill slope foot and soil attributes (Fig. 13.3) have been taken into account which are ultimately representing slope – soil attributes correlation.

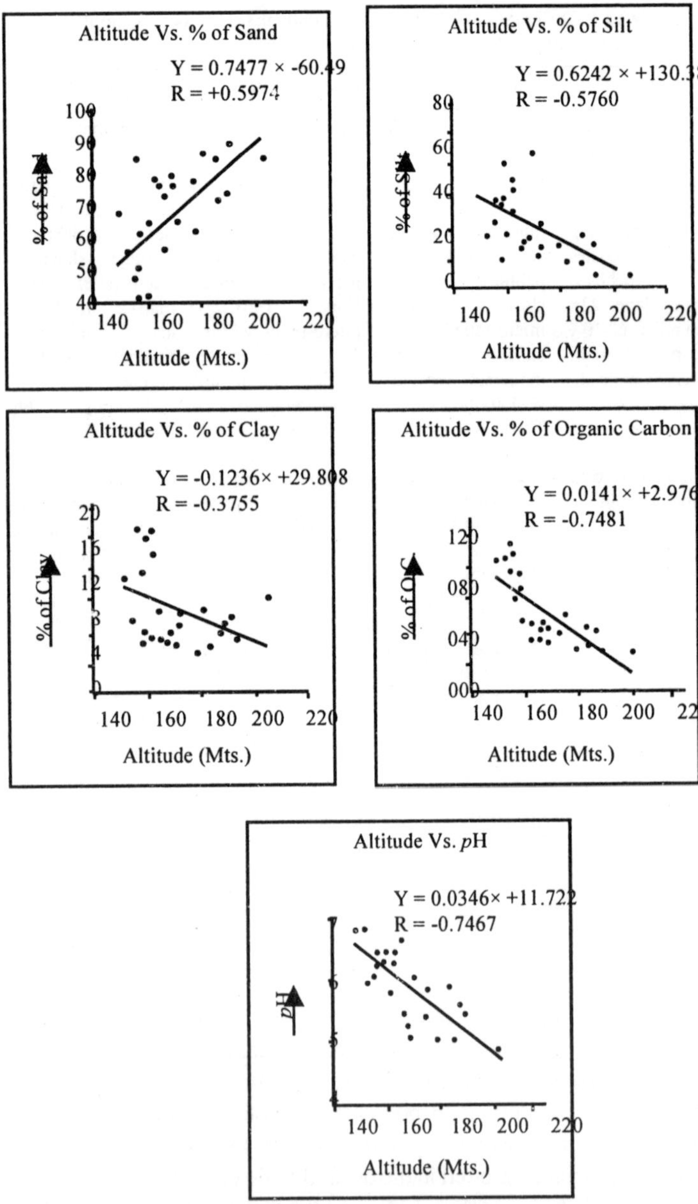

Fig. 13.2: Correlation between Altitude and Soil Attributes (Joychandipahar Hill Slope, Raghunathpur, Purulia, W.B.)

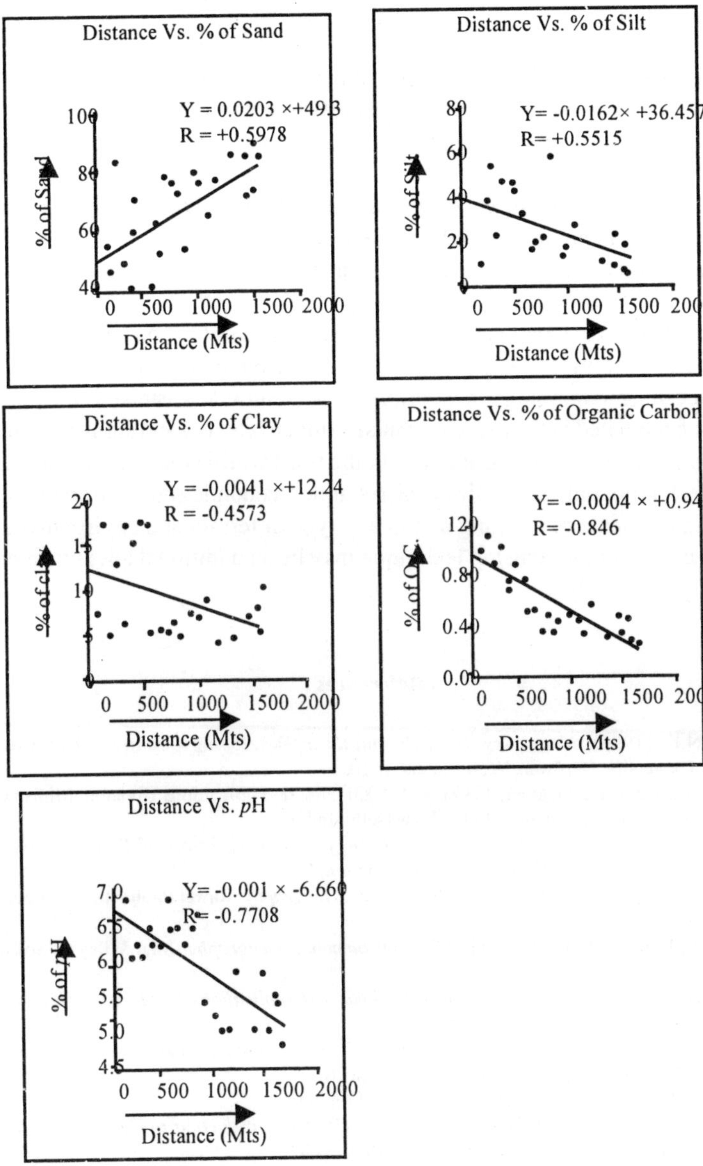

Fig. 13.3: Correlation between Distance (from Hill-Slope Foot) and Soil Attributes (Joychandipahar Hill Slope, Raghunathpur, Purulia, W.B.)

Conclusion

It has been observed that at the end of the present century India has now been able to cope with its food demand to some extent by following modern scientific methods but the overall increase in population has not yet been controlled up to the desired level even after adopting various family planning measures. As a result food shortage will be persistent in the decades to come. It should be mentioned that India is an agro-based country and its economy will depend on agriculture in the years to come also.

Under these circumstances identification and utilization of culturable wastelands to meet the growing needs of the population are inevitable. Hence, the methodology in identifying the culturable wastelands that has been enunciated in the present treatise is much relevant and significant in the present context of agriculture in the third world countries including India. It is not only scientific but also simple, economic and can be worked out in any scale of working and in any type of terrain and environment. The use of remote sensing technique may be an additional advantage in this type of study.

References

De, N.K. (1984), *Measuring Land Potentials in Developing Countries*, Burdwan University, Burdwan, West Bengal, India.

Employment News (October, 1997), Vol. XXII, No. 28, Publications Division, Ministry of I&B, Government of India, New Delhi, India.

Gerrard, John (1992), *Soil Geomorphology: An Integration of Pedology and Geomorphology*, Chapman & Hall, London, U.K.

Husain, Majid (1996), *Systematic Agricultural Geography*, Rawat Publications, Jaipur, India.

Marsh, W.M. & J.M. Grossa (1996), *Environmental Geography*, John Wiley & Sons, Canada.

Rowell, David L. (1995), *Soil Science; Methods and Applications*, Longman Group Ltd., Essex, England.

Spiegel, Murrey R. (1992), *Schaum's Outline Series of Theory and Problems of Statistics*, McGraw Hill Book Company, London, U.K.

Stamp, Dudley (1952), *Land for Tomorrow*, London

Swan, A.R.H., M. Sandilands & P. McCabe (1995), *Introduction to Geological Data Analysis*, Blackwell Science Ltd., Oxford, U.K.

White, I.D., D.N. Mottershead & S.J. Harrision (1992), *Environmental Systems – An Introductory Text* (2nd Edition), Chapman & Hall, London, U.K.

14

IMPACT OF IRRIGATION ON AGRICULTURAL PRODUCTIVITY
A Microlevel Analysis

C.T. PAWAR & A.A. PUJARI

Introduction

Irrigation is regarded as an integral part of sound infrastructure and is one of the basic ingredients of agricultural activities. It encourages farmers to adopt scientific techniques and go in for more intensive cropping thereby creating new opportunities for gainful employment. The availability of adequate irrigation facilities transforms the subsistence agricultural landscape gradually into commercial one making agrarian economy market oriented. Simultaneously, it creates healthy atmosphere to develop several agro based industries providing employment opportunities to rural masses (Pawar, 1989). In peninsular India, where agriculture is a perpetual gamble with monsoon, irrigation acts not only as a protective and stabilising factor but also a productive one. Hence it is the need of the time to assess the progress of irrigation facilities in a region, which influences the nature of agricultural development to a large extent.

Objectives

In view of the above present investigation aims to assess the growth of irrigation facilities and its impact on agricultural productivity at microlevel.

Methodology

The importance of the study lies in the fact that the entire work is based on empirical data collected through intensive fieldwork supplemented by secondary sources of data. The interview and questionnaire techniques were employed to collect the first hand information about various parameters of the theme under consideration. Stratified random sampling method is employed for the selection of case study villages. As such 12 villages are selected for intensive field work; whereas the random sampling design is adopted for the selection of the farmers. Accordingly interviews of 120 selected farmers were conducted. However, data pertaining to all the parameters of agriculture is collected for all the villages from study area as village is the areal unit for present investigation. The data so collected is processed and further represented through the tables and figures. The study is confined to the period from 1976-77 to 1998-99. The agricultural productivity is measured by the method of crop yield and concentration indices and ranking co-efficient developed by Jasbir Singh (1976).

The Study Region

Shirol taluka of Kolhapur district is selected as a study region for present investigation. It lies in the lower reaches of the Panchaganga basin, which is one of well-watered parts of Maharashtra State. The region comprises an area of 507.90 sq. km. and supports 3,05,032 persons (1991) of 52 villages. The region is benefited by four rivers, namely the Warana to the north, the Krishna to the east, the Dudhaganga to the south and the Panchaganga at the heart of the study area (Fig. 14.1). The Panchaganga basin has benefited from an unparalleled sedimentation and has developed into one of the most productive areas of the State (Dikshit, 1986). Moreover, climatically the region enjoys a moderate type of climate with very little extremes of heat and cold. The study region is located in the rain shadow zone of the Western Ghats and receives about 600 mm of rainfall. Great annual variation in precipitation are rare, but rainfall is very often, unevenly distributed during September-October. Although study area produces a variety of crops, its cropping pattern reflects the climate and increased facilities of irrigation. As such sugarcane ranks first occupying 39.38 percentage of Gross Cropped Area (G.C.A.) followed by soyabean (28.85%) as a main cash crop. Among other crops groundnuts (8.89%), pulses (8.46%), jowar (5.28%) and rice (1.47%) are important crops in the study region.

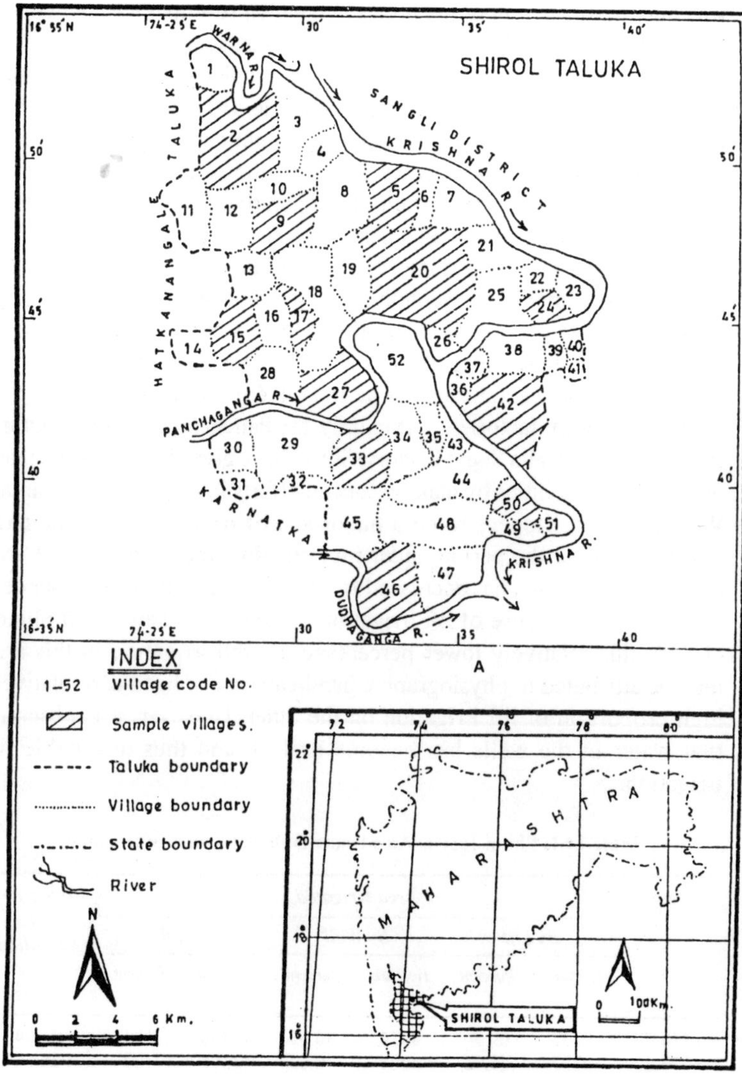

Fig. 14.1: Maharashtra: Location of Shirol Taluka in Kolhapur District

Facilities of Irrigation

Although irrigation was practised long back, its real development in study region started after independence. In 1955-56 the area under irrigation was only 6.30 per cent of net area sown which rose to 43.76 per cent in 1998-99. With the advancement of civilization, science and technology the "Budhaki System" of irrigation has been replaced by "Lift Irrigation System" in the region which enabled the farmers to irrigate large tracts of lands. The cooperative movement plays predominant role in establishing numerous lift irrigation schemes in the region. The State government also encourages the organization of cooperative lift irrigation schemes by providing financial and technical know-how.

The sources of irrigation are greatly influenced by the geological, physical and climatological conditions of a region. As such predominance of lift irrigation prevails in the region which occupies about 80.61 per cent out of total area irrigated. Its share has increased from 69.96 per cent to 80.61 per cent during the period under review (Table 14.1). The cooperative sugar factories, particularly, the Panchanganga sugar factory, Ichalkarjee and Datta Sugar Factory, Shirol have given impetus to increase the irrigation facilities by making special efforts in their command areas. Well irrigation happens to be a major source of irrigation in the past. However during the period under investigation, the proportion of area under well irrigation has decreased from 30.63 per cent to 19.39 per cent due to widespread use of lift irrigation. As stated by Pawar and Shinde (1979), this relatively lower percentage of well irrigation in this area may be attributed to physiographic handicap on one hand and relatively high proportion of lift irrigation on the other. However, it is observed that water in the wells has become brakish and thus unsuitable for irrigation.

Table 14.1: Shirol Taluka: Area Under Different Source of Irrigation

Year	*Area Irrigated*						*Intensity of Irrigation in percentage*
	By Lift		*By Well*		*Total*		
	Hectare	*Percent*	*Hectare*	*Percent*	*Hectare*	Percent	
1976-77	9332	69.96	4024	30.63	13396	100	30.64
1979-80	9332	69.96	4024	30.63	13396	100	28.66
1982-83	10160	81.67	2279	18.32	12434	100	28.37
1985-86	8491	73.89	2999	26.10	11490	100	28.48
1988-89	10062	83.43	2004	16.60	12066	100	32.45
1991-92	17705	82.28	2520	17.71	14224	100	42.29
1998-99	12710	80.61	3059	19.39	15769	100	43.76

Source: Socio-Economic Review and District Statistical Abstracts of Kolhapur District.

Areal Variation in Intensity of Irrigation

The term "intensity of irrigation" here refers to the percentage of area irrigated to net area sown. The intensity of irrigation as a whole is about 43.76 per cent in the study region which was 30.64 per cent during base year. The high and moderate intensity of irrigation (above 40% and 20 to 40%) is noted along adjacent areas of river banks (Fig. 14.2B). This region is well ended with ample supply of water from four major rivers. This can be well attributed to the availability of water in the river course of Krishna and Panchanganga and an attempt made by the industrious and innovative farmers to utilize such water by overcoming environmental limitation. Low intensity of irrigation (below 20%) is noted in few villages i.e., Jaysingpur, Tamadalge and Ghosarwad. These villages are situated away from the river banks and have rugged topography. During the period under investigation area under irrigation has increased from 13,396 hectares to 15,769 hectares (Table 14.1).

Agricultural Productivity

The level of agricultural productivity, as a concept, means the degree to which the economic, cultural, technical and organizational variables (i.e. the man-made frame) are able to exploit the abiotic resources of the area for agricultural production (Singh, 1979). Although agricultural productivity seems to be a relative term and cannot be uniformly applied everywhere, such studies provide a rational base for further orientation in agricultural planning. In view of the above, it is proposed to examine as to how irrigation affects the productivity of the crops in the study area; for the important goal of irrigation, in association with the other inputs, is to raise per hectare yield in particular to overall productivity in general.

The study of agricultural productivity has been attempted by many scholars, by devising and improving different techniques. Stamp (1953) determined the agricultural productivity on global scale by selecting a number of countries and some major crops. The areal units were graded in ranking order according to their output per unit area and ranking co-efficient was derived. Shafi (1960) applied his technique in determining the agricultural efficiency in Uttar Pradesh. Buck (1937) and many others measured the agricultural productivity in terms of grain equivalents per head of population. Whereas Hussain (1976) measured it by money value of productivity per unit area. However, for the ensuring analysis, Jasbir

Singh's (1976) yield and concentration indices ranking co-efficient method is adopted, as it gives due weightage to per hectare yield, area occupied and ranking of various crops. As such to recon the microlevel disparities in levels of agricultural production, dominant crops in terms of land occupance are considered. And then results thus derived are grouped into three categories i.e. high, moderate and low productivity areas which are further mapped and correlated with irrigation facilities. Here the entire analysis is based on the empirical yield statistics collected for all the villages of study region.

Areal Variation in Crop Productivity

During the study period the productivity of sugarcane and soyabean seems to have increased. The area under high productivity of sugarcane has increased by 18.55 per cent of the gross cropped area. The high productivity of sugarcane is confined to the river valleys where soils are very fertile, and intensity of irrigation is high (58.28%) and use of chemical fertilizers are high. Moderate and low productivity are found away from the river sides where intensity of irrigation is low (32.5%). Besides the high rate of other inputs, areal extent of sugarcane is also equally important to increase the productivity of sugarcane (Table 14.2).

Table 14.2: Shirol Taluka: Area under Major Crops

Crops	*1976-77*		*1998-99*		*Volume of Change in %*
	Area in hectare	*% of G.C.A.*	*Area in hectare*	*% of G.C.A.*	
Sugarcane	9302	26.55	13783	39.38	+12.83
Soyabean	91	0.25	10097	28.85	+28.60
Groundnut	5571	15.90	3112	8.89	–7.01
Jowar	9116	26.02	1448	5.28	–20.74
Rice	3493	9.97	515	1.47	–8.50
Wheat	1191	3.4	193	0.55	–2.85
Gram	147	0.42	98	0.28	--0.14

Source: Compiled by the Authors through fieldwork.

The area under high productivity of soyabean has increased by 31 per cent. It is mainly because soyabean is coming up rapidly as a substitute crop for jowar, sugarcane, groundnut and wheat in the study region. The high productivity of soyabean is observed in the central Krishna Valley and in the village of Yadrav and Kawathesar where soils are very fertile and intensity of irrigation is high (52.63%). The moderate productivity of soyabean is observed in the villages of Chinchawad, Danoli, Ghosarawad, Nandani and Takali, where intensity of irrigation is moderate (46.34%). The low productivity is found where intensity of irrigation is also low.

During the study period the productivity of jowar, wheat, gram, groundnut and rice has decreased. Although the region is well endowed with facilities of irrigation, the tendency of the farmers is yet, to switch over to commercial crops like sugarcane and soyabean from traditional cereal crops like jowar, wheat and rice, as soon as the land is irrigated. Thus the reduction in areal extent of these crops caused the decline in productivity.

Areal Variation in Overall Agricultural Productivity

Areas of High Productivity

The high productivity is noted in the villages located along the river banks (Fig 14.2D). At present the area under high productivity is about 75.54 per cent of the gross cropped area which was 43.95 per cent during the year 1976-77. During the period under review area under high productivity has increased by 31.59 per cent of the gross cropped area. The high intensity of irrigation (47.82%), high consumption of fertilizer (above 900 kg./ha.), fertile soils and adoption of modern technology (Personal observation) are some of the important factors responsible for increasing agricultural productivity. The State level study regarding agricultural productivity carried out by Shinde *et al.* (1978), also reveals that Kolhapur district (in which Shirol taluka ranks top) stands supreme for, it is endowed with favourable physio-socio-economic factors leading to a developed agricultural economy.

Areas of Moderate Productivity

The moderate productivity is noted in the villages of Kothali, Umalwad, Nimshrgaon, Kondigre, Chipri, Haroli, Dharanguti, Ghosarwad, Akiwat, Rajapur and Bastawad. It occupies area of about 21.27 per cent of gross cropped area which was 28.46 per cent during the year 1976-77. The moderate intensity of irrigation (37.19%), moderate consumption of fertilizer (800 to 900 kg./ha.) medium deep black soils are found in this area. During the study period area under moderate productivity has

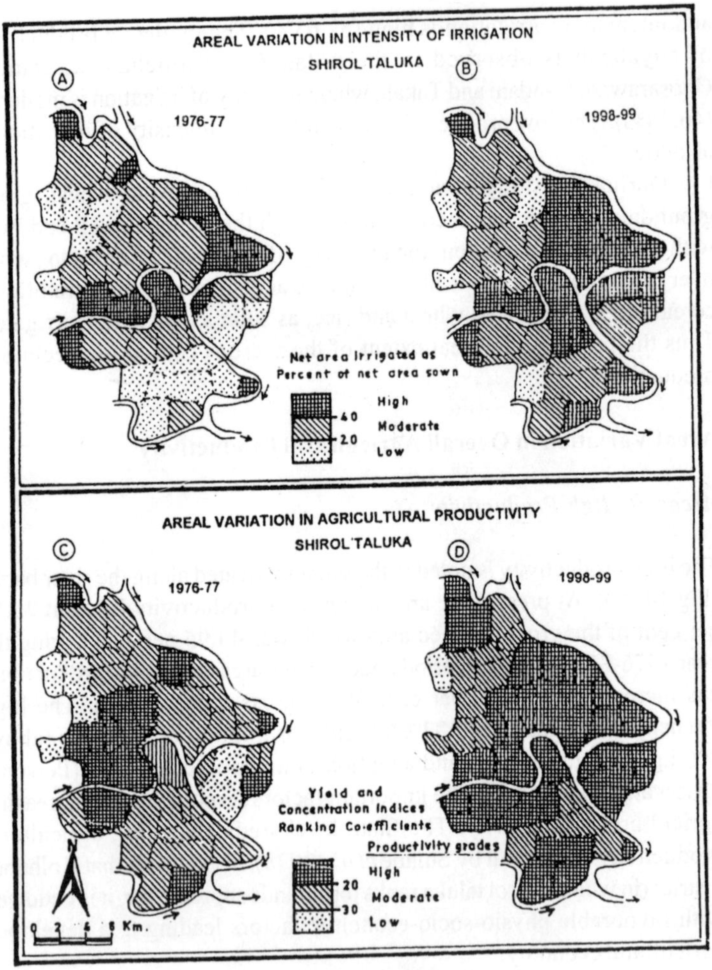

Fig. 14.2: Areal Variation in Intensity of Irrigation and Agricultural Productivity of Shirol Taluka

decreased by 7.19 per cent of the gross cropped area due to the shift of areas from moderate productivity category to high productivity category.

Areas of Low Productivity

At present low productivity is noted only in the Tamdalage village, which contributes an area of about 3.14 per cent of the gross cropped area. While in the base year the area under low productivity was about 27.56 per cent of the gross cropped area. During the study period area under low productivity has decreased by 24.42 per cent of the gross cropped area. The growth of lift irrigation which have enabled the farmers to use the other inputs is mainly responsible for transforming low productivity area into moderate productivity. The hilly area, poor soils, low intensity of irrigation (15.76%) and low consumption of fertilizer are some of the contributing factors for low status of productivity in this area.

Conclusions

The role of cooperative sector is noteworthy in regards to the development of irrigation. The important irrigation sources available in the region are lift and well. The preponderance of lift irrigation is observed all over the region which shares 80.61 per cent of irrigated area. The intensity of irrigation has increased from 30.64 to 43.76 per cent during the period under review. However, areal variation prevails very much at village level.

The productivity of cash crops like sugarcane, soyabean is high throughout the region which was moderate in the base year. However the productivity of cereal crops like rice, jowar and wheat has declined considerably.

The overall agricultural productivity has increased where there is a rise in the intensity of irrigation. As such the high productivity is observed in the areas adjacent to river banks where intensity of irrigation is also high. Whereas low productivity is observed in areas away from the river banks where intensity of irrigation is also low. During the study period area under high productivity has increased by 31.59 per cent of the gross cropped area. This can be well attributed to the conclusion drawn by Gharpure and Pawar (1991 and 1992) that, increased and improved irrigation facilities, development of cooperative sector and industrious farmers are responsible for changing pattern and steady development of agriculture in Panchanganga Basin.

The foregoing analysis reveals that in general the agricultural productivity is increasing steadily. The rate of increase in agricultural productivity is commensurate to the rate of growth of irrigation facilities in the region. However it is observed that due to the excessive use of irrigation water, chemical fertilizers and practice of non-rotation system of crops the problems such as soils becoming saline, alkaline and waterlogged are emerging very fastly which needs immediate attention of the experts to study the 'soil-water-crop management' to prevent the process of desertification in the study region.

References

Buck, T.L. (1937), *Land Utilization in China*, Vol. 1, University of Nanking.

Bhatia, S.S. (1967), A New Measures of Agricultural Efficiency in Uttar Pradesh, India, *Economic Geography*, Vol. 43, 3, pp. 244 to 260.

Dikshit K.R. (1986), Maharashtra in Maps. Maharashtra State Board for Literature and Culture, Bombay, p. 27.

Gharpure V.T. and Pawar C.T. (1991), Expected Perspective on Agro-Service Centres in Panchaganga Basin (Maharashtra), *Indian Journal of Regional Science*, Vol. XXIII, 2, pp. 17 to 23.

Hussain, M. (1976), A New Approach to Agricultural Productivity Regions of the Sutlej-Ganga Plains of India, *Geographical Review of India*, Vol. 38, 3, pp. 230 to 236.

Pawar, C.T. & Shinde S.D. (1979), Well Irrigation in Upland Districts of South Maharashtra Region: A Spatio-temporal Perspective; *Geographical Review of India*, Vol. 41, 4, pp. 314-320.

Pawar C.T. (1989), *Impact of Irrigation: A Regional Perspective*. Himalaya Publishing House, Bombay.

Pawar C.T. and Gharpure, V.T. (1992), Spatial perspective on Agro-Service centres in Panchaganga Basin, Published in *New Dimension in Agricultural Geography*, Editor Noor Mohammad, Concept Publishing Co., New Delhi, Vol. 8, pp. 335 to 372.

Singh, J. (1979), A new technique of delimiting agricultural production typology in food-crop dominated economy: Haryana case study, *Geographical Polonica*, Vol. 40, p. 21.

Singh, J. (1976), *Agricultural Geography of Haryana*, Vishal Publications, Kurukshetra, India.

Shafi, M. (1960), Measurement of Agricultural Efficiency in Uttar Pradesh, *Econ. Geog.* Vol. 36, pp. 296-305.

Shinde, S.D.; Jadhav, M.G.; & Pawar C.T. (1978), Agricultural Productivity in Maharashtra Plateau: A Geographical Analysis, *National Geographer*, Vol. XIII, 1, pp. 35 to 41.

Stamp, L.W. (1953), *Our Developing World*, Faber and Faber, London, p. 93.

15

CHANGING PATTERN OF CROP LAND- USE IN DADRI TAHSIL (HARYANA) 1966-93

A.K. CHHAUKAR & YOGESH KUMAR MITTAL

Study Area

The study area Dadri tahsil of Bhiwani District lies in the South-Western part of the Haryana. There are one town and 173 villages which are administratively grouped into three development Blocks viz. Dadri I, Dadri II and Badhra. The total area of the study region is 1378.85 sq. km. On the whole, this tahsil have nearly 88.69 per cent of the cultivated area as per cent to total area and only about 27.43 per cent of the net area sown is irrigated by means of canal. Indira Gandhi Canal and tubewells are the main source of irrigation. The topography of the study area is a mixture of sandy undulating plain, dunal plain and pocket of old alluvial plain with some Aravalli outcrops.

Cropping Patterns

Over a period of time, basically geographic patterns of agricultural land-use are the outcome of concurrent interaction between the variable combinations of natural conditions and human circumstances. Primarily, these are influenced by natural conditions and thereafter affected by human circumstances because of their colonising capability. Interestingly the human circumstances are mainly responsible for dynamism in agricultural land-use or changing cropland occupancy. Therefore, efficient cropland occupancy, say cropping pattern, implies the most successful use of agricultural land, consequent upon development of irrigation facilities and application of modern methods of farm technology.

No cropping pattern can be good for all the times to come. At the same time, there is a tendency for cropping pattern to change in the newly settled and irrigated areas and to stabilize in the old settled and irrigated areas. As such, it is essential to study cropland occupancy, so as to understand a spatial and inter-village differences in it during the year 1966-69 and 1990-93 triennials as tabulated in Table 15.1. Moreover, the analysis of volume of change in cropping structure is also essential to identify the areas of dynamism as well as stagnation in terms of swing in cropping patterns which was directed by the changes in socio-economic circumstances, particularly by the changes in the intensity of irrigation and intensive use of biochemical inputs.

Not surprisingly, there is a wide gap in the percentage share of cropland occupancy of five important groups of crops, namely, fine foodgrains, coarse foodgrains, industrial crops, pulses and fodder crops. The existing aspatial distribution for the triennials 1966-69 and 1990-93 as presented in Table 15.1 which provides an idea of the unbalanced and less diversified farm economy during 1993 in the study area, because about 39.62 per cent of cropland occupancy was shared by bulrush millet; (28.43%) by gram; (14.07%) by wheat and green fodder (7.87%) – indicating commercial character of intensively tubewell and extensively canal irrigated agriculture. Contrastingly, it was more diversified during 1966 as significant proportion of arable land was occupied by bulrush millet (42.87%), gram (31.48%), green fodder (8.81%) and wheat (4.72%) an expected cropland occupancy because of dominance of rainfall farming. Further, the shift was from subsistence and dry farming crops like bulrush millet and gram to commercial crops like wheat, sugarcane, oilseeds, gram and bulrush millet which involved about 13.60 per cent of the gross cropped area – a very high volume of change in cropping structure with a trend towards commercialisation and specialisation in agriculture. An emphasis was given on wheat in winter and bulrush millet in summer cropping season.

For the purpose of agricultural regionalization and planning, it is necessary to divide the study area into homogeneous cropping regions on some well defined basis. There can be a number of physical, climatological and agro-economic variants which influence cropping pattern of an area. With an assured supply of water and availability of modern inputs specially high yielding varieties of seeds, fertilizers and tractors – it becomes possible for the farmers to replace less profitable crops with more profitable ones. The most revolutionary changes in cropping structure are those brought about by the extension of irrigation

Table 15.1: Dadri Tahsil – Cropping Pattern – 1966-69 and 1990-93 Triennials

	Classification/Crop	*Percentage of Total Cropped Area*		*Changes in per cent Point in 1990-93 over 1966-69*
		1966-69	*1990-93*	
I	*Fine Foodgrains*	4.72	14.11	+9.39
	1. Wheat	4.72	14.07	+9.35
	2. Paddy (Rice)	0.00	0.04	+0.04
II	*Coarse Foodgrains*	47.53	42.77	–4.76
	3. Bulrush Millet	42.87	39.62	–3.25
	4. Sorghum (Jowar)	2.78	2.16	–0.62
	5. Barley	1.83	0.84	–0.99
	6. Maize	0.05	0.15	+0.10
III	*Industrial Crops*	2.72	6.45	+3.73
	7. Cotton	0.21	0.67	+0.46
	8. Oilseeds	1.96	5.61	+3.65
	9. Sugarcane	0.55	0.17	–0.38
IV	*Pulses including Gram*	33.96	28.73	–5.23
	10. Gram	31.48	28.43	–3.05
	11. Other Pulses	2.48	0.30	–2.18
V	*Fodder Crops*	8.81	7.87	–0.94
	12. Green Fodder	8.81	7.87	–0.94
VI	*Miscellaneous Crops*	2.26	0.07	–2.19
	13. Vegetables	0.12	0.07	–0.05
	14. Wheat-Gram/Barley Mixture	0.53	0.00	–0.53
	15. Others	1.61	0.00	–1.61
	Total	100.00	100.00	
	Volume of change			13.60

facilities and introduction of modern farm implements including tractors to farm.

An spatial analysis of cropping pattern as presented in Table 15.1 reveals that the cropland occupancy for the 1993 may be classified into six groups, viz.

Group I is fine foodgrains which occupied 14.11 per cent of the total cropped area (1993). The percentage cropland occupancy rose about 4.72 per cent from (1996). The dominant crop in this group was wheat (14.07%) followed by a very unimportant crop like rice (0.04%). These are the crops which are mostly irrigated, and demanding on soil and water with intensive use of bio-chemical inputs.

Group II comprises coarse foodgrains which are dryland crops occupying 42.77 per cent of the total cropped area (1990-93). The principal millet crop in this category was bulrush millet on pearl millet (bajra) occupying 39.62 per cent of the cropped area and it was followed by sorghum (jowar) as a secondary crop (2.16%). Other minor crops in this group were barley (0.84%) and maize (0.15%). The total cropland occupied by coarse foodgrain was about 47.53 per cent during 1966-69 which showed a falling-off trend over the period 1990-93, when 4.76 per cent of total cropped area went down the same set of crops. It owed to shift to cotton cultivation associated with improvement in irrigation infrastructure.

Group III includes industrial crops, such as oilseeds, cotton and sugarcane. These are the cash crops of the State which shared 5.61, 0.67 and 0.17 per cent of the gross cropped area respectively in Dadri tahsil during 1990-93. The overall area under these crops increased from 2.72 per cent (1966-69) to 6.45 per cent (1990-93) of the total cropped area, particularly under oilseeds having +3.65 per cent of cropping pattern. It was to be expected due to improvement in irrigation adequacy and efficiency during the 1990-93 over 1966-69, particularly during the summer cropping season.

Group IV relates with pulses including gram which are dry farming crop. Gram cropping pattern (28.43%) is dominated over other pulses, particularly arhar, moong, moth and masri whose cropland area have a insignificant proportion of 0.30 per cent in the total cropped area of the study area. The area under gram decreased significantly, as was likely to happen quite normally due to improvement in irrigation intensity accelerating area under wheat. The ratio of this group declined from about 33.96 per cent (1966-69) to 28.73 per cent (1990-93), a significant decrease of about –5.23 per cent (1990-93) points, of which –3.05 per cent points were shared by gram.

Group V constitutes green fodder crops which occupied about 7.87 per cent of the total cropland occupancy, and was considerably below the recommended norm of 20 per cent of the total area under crops for standard feeding of farm livestock: draught as well as milch livestock.

Group VI covers miscellaneous crops, such as vegetables, wheat-gram or gram-barley and some condiments and species covering only 0.87 per cent of the total cropped area.

It has been observed that an aspatial analysis of proportions under different crops masks the prevalent inequalities in regional patterns and dynamics of individual crops of spatio-temporal scale. Therefore, it is essential to examine the patterns and dynamics of individual crops, which has been attempted in the ensuing profile.

Group I: Fine Foodgrain Crops

Fine foodgrain crops, i.e., wheat and paddy, play an important role in the agricultural economy of Dadri tahsil due to their major contribution in providing food for human beings and dry fodder/straw for livestock. It would not be out of place to mention that only under fine foodgrains the agricultural land can produce enough to support a dense population base of the study area. If substantial share of the cropped area was devoted to green fodder crops to support better livestock as beef and milch stock which, in turn, would yield better protein and rich products, contributing to a better diet, but the total production in terms of meat and dairy products per capita and per hectare would be low. Looking at the problem of population explosion, India cannot afford a significant shift of cropland from foodgrains to green fodders. Therefore, any major dietary shift and improvement must wait for a reduction in the rate of natural growth of population and swing from agriculturalisation to industrialisation in rural environment.

On average, 14.11 per cent of gross cropped was under fine foodgrain crops, shared by wheat (14.07%) a dominant crop, and paddy (0.01%) – a secondary crop.

Wheat (Triticum Aestivum)

Wheat is the most distinctive and most important cereal crop of intensively irrigated commercial/semi-commercial farming areas of the study area. On average, area devoted to wheat was about 14.07 per cent of the gross cropped area, a considerably very high proportion was placed against about 0.04 per cent devoted to paddies. Interestingly, the inter-village variation in wheat cropland occupancy was considerably great, i.e., from under 5.00 per cent to over 20.00 per cent of the gross cropped area. Hence, it is a primary, secondary and predominant crop in the area under study.

Wheat was an extraordinarily important crop in the intensively irrigated areas of the eastern half of the Dadri tahsil. The interest in wheat cultivation declined with the increasing aridity and weak irrigation infrastructure towards the dunal and sandy undulating plains of the study area. Therefore, wheat production patterns are the familiar and expected ones in relation to intensity of irrigation patterns, textural characteristics of soils and climatic conditions.

On the peripheries of these areas were the belts of high degree of concentration of wheat cultivation (15.01 to 20.00%). Definitely, principal areas of actual productivity of wheat are confined to semi-arid climate area where the actuality is not to be controlled by the physical ecology but by the economics, particularly the groundwater and surface water resources, respectively intensively and extensively utilised by man. These have particularly offset arid climate conditions for wheat cultivation. The cropland occupancy of wheat increased by about 9.35 per cent points in 1990-93 over 1966-69 because of the necessity for increasing production of home-grown wheat for the increasing population at a faster rate ever before.

Paddy (Rice, Oryza Sativa)

Paddies share in the study area is absent or an unimportant crop over greater area on account of arid climate and light loamy soil with sandy associations and sandy soils. However, the area devoted to paddies was over 0.04 per cent of the total cropped area, significantly very lower when placed against wheat cropland occupancy of over 14.07. Too light, arid climate and lack of irrigation facilities are the causes for the negligible importance of paddies in the vast stretches of Dadri tahsil.

Village Mankawas and Palri of Dadri tahsil of Haryana recorded an increase of +0.04 per cent point in rice cropland occupancy in 1990-93 over 1966-69. On its peripheries, an increase of the rate of 2.00 to 4.57 per cent was experienced. On the whole, the shift to paddies was only observed in the alluvial plain – a consequence of reclamation of waterlogged low-lying area and intensive tubewell-*cum*-extensive canal irrigation. An average increase was only to the extent of 0.04 per cent points in the study area.

Group II: Coarse Foodgrain Crops

Among the foodgrain crops, coarse foodgrain crops (bulrush millet/pearl millet, sorghum, barley and maize) are in a position to rival fine foodgrain crops (wheat and rice) in terms of cropland occupancy but not in terms of production in Dadri tahsil. In aggregate, the important coarse foodgrain crops – bulrush millet/pearl millet, sorghum, barley and maize—occupied about 47.53 per cent of the total cropped area. The crop-wise cropland occupancy in 1990-93 was pearl millet (bajra) 39.62 per cent, sorghum (jowar) 2.16 per cent, barley 0.84 per cent and maize (0.15%) of the total cropped area. Obviously, pearl millet was a primary crop, sorghum, barley and maize were secondary crops. In the arid parts of the study area pearl millet constitutes staple food of the people, particularly in the dunal plain and sandy undulating plain of Dadri tahsil. Moreover, it has been observed that millets (pearl millet and sorghum) occupied an area slightly higher than fine foodgrains (wheat and rice). Unfortunately, millets contributed about 42.77 per cent of the total food production vis-à-vis fine foodgrains which constituted about 14.11 per cent. It implies that per hectare productivity of millets was much below the level for fine cereals. In other words, the Green Revolution technology has made an insignificant impact on the productivity level of millets.

Pearl Millet (Pennisetum Glacum)

Dryland farming is practised on light soils in the rain-starved areas where low levels of irrigation intensity and efficiency are encountered. In such areas, millets are habitually produced in the struggle for existence and subsistence by the locals. Pearl millet in some form is, by far, the most accessory coarse foodgrain and fodder crop in the dunal and sandy undulating plains of the study area. Usually it is rainfed crop, being marked by drought resistant, drought-escaping and quick-maturing and can be produced without irrigation in arid areas with an annual rainfall of even less than 450 mm.

Being a hard and narrow-leaves crop, pearl millet competes quite favourably with other *kharif* foodgrains, oilseeds and fibre crops, and can flourish well in areas of undulating terrain, low soil moisture, light well-drained sandy and loamy sandy soils and under-developed irrigation facilities.

On average, at the regional level pearl millet occupied about 39.62 per cent of the cropped area during the period of study. Inevitably, the geographic patterns of pearl millet, as shown gives an idea of the close relationship between agro-climatic conditions and pearl millet concentrations. Thus high (over 40.00%) and very high (40.01 to 50.00%) cropland occupancies were encountered. Contrastingly, in the alluvial plain of the eastern half of the study area its occupancies were nil/ negligible and insignificant under 20.00 per cent).

Overall decrease in pearl millet cropland occupancy was about –3.25 per cent point change and inter-village decrease was between under 5.00 per cent and over 20.00 per cent points. The decrease was proportionately high (over 15.00%) in the dunal plain where relative expansions in cropland occupancy of high-yielding and high-value foodgrains, fibre and oilseed crops have tended to displace the area under pearl millet due to improved irrigation facilities. In general, decreasing trend in pearl millet cultivation was more widespread due to improvements in irrigation dry farming technology.

Interestingly, area under pearl millet increased in the dunal plain of the study area wherein pearl millet ecology was not modified during the period 1990-93 over 1966-69, due to improved technology of dryland farming and favouring the expansion of area under pearl millet.

Sorghum (Sorghum Vulgare, Jowar)

Sorghum, a type of Chinese sugarcane, tends to be grown predominantly as a grain-millet in warm dry areas unfit for rice cultivation. It is cultivated in old alluvial plain and old aeolian undulating plain in the eastern half of the Dadri tahsil of Bhiwani district as a quick-ripening, drought-resistant and drought-escaping grain-millet crop. It ranked third in importance as a secondary crop among foodgrain crops and second among millets during 1990-93. Interestingly, during 1966-93 sorghum cropland occupancy was displaced by a very small proportion in the study area but increase was significant in the eastern parts of the alluvial plain, a situation created by the Green Revolution technology for the expansion of paddies.

On average, 2.16 per cent of the cropped area was under sorghum and inter-village sorghum cropland occupancy varied from 0.08 per cent in Santokh Pura village through 20.67 per cent in Bond Kalan village. It has been observed that primary share of sorghum in Dadri tahsil is used as a staple foodgrain and in some parts of the eastern half of the study area as a green fodder.

At the regional level sorghum cultivation recorded decrease to the extent of nearly – 0.62 per cent points. The prominent concentrations were observed in the eastern half of the tahsil where primary displacement was in the cultivation of wheat and due to the introduction of improved high yielding seeds, the adoption of dry-farming technology and the emphasis on high-yielding milch stall-fed livestock.

Barley (Hordeum Vulgare)

Barley can be produced as a grain crop at the drier limits of agriculture in the study area. It is an extremely restricted crop in Dadri tahsil because of emphasis on wheat and oilseeds cultivation. Barley is a nearly secondary crop at regional level and accounted for about 0.84 per cent of the total cropped area. Therefore, regional differences in barley concentration are obvious and ranked from negligible to over 2.00 per cent.

The chief pockets of barley cultivation were in the areas where its cropland occupancy was over 2.00 per cent and the same were surrounded by areas of secondary concentration, i.e. under 0.50 to over 2.00 per cent. At the regional level barley cropland occupancy decreased by about – 0.99 per cent points in 1990-93 over 1966-69.

Group III: Industrial Crops

Industrial crops are edible oilseeds, cotton and sugarcane. The area under study devotes edible oilseeds (5.61%), cotton (0.67%), and sugarcane (0.17%) of the total cropped area. The spatial patterns of industrial crops reveal regional differences in their concentrations and occupy an economic status at fourth level after coarse foodgrains, fine fodgrains and pulses including gram. At a regional level, the area under industrial crops was about 6.45 per cent of the total cropped area in 1990-93, and of which the major proportion was shared by oilseeds, i.e., nearly 5.61 per cent of cropland occupancy. Hectareage of industrial crops increased in 1990-93 over 1966-69 by nearly +3.73 per cent points and maximum of which was shared by oilseeds (+3.65%).

Edible Oilseeds

The edible oilseeds collectively form a very important group of industrial crops in the study area sharing 5.61 per cent of the total cropped area. The cropland occupancy of oilseeds increased by about +3.65 per cent point in 1990-93 over 1966-69 in the area under study.

The major oilseed in the study area is mustard. The oilseeds cropland occupancy varied from negligible to over 8.00 per cent of the total cropped area. This was apparent and expected due to the favourable crop ecological conditions for mustard cultivation. Secondary concentrations (4.01 to 6.00%) were found on the margins of primary concentrations (over 6.00%).

The high rate of increase were observed where shift was from gram cropped area to black mustard. These are the areas of south-western Haryana which are experiencing gold revolution and it is recommended that in the year to come it should be contained for improving farm economy, soil tilth and livestock wealth.

Cotton (Gossypium Species)

Among the vegetable fibres, in terms of cropland occupancy, cotton is only important in Dadri tahsil as it occupied 0.67 per cent of the total cropped area during 1990-93 and it is next to wheat, pearl millet, and gram. Although cotton was widely grown in the old alluvial plain and a pocket in the centre of the study area in old aeolian undulating plain but the principal area leading to cotton production was the reclaimed sand-dune areas of the north-eastern parts of the study area where it was a primary as well as secondary crop by status. The arid climatic conditions, coarse loamy soil and extensive canal irrigation, facilitated cultivation of the American type of long-staple cotton for the manufacturing of fine yarn are responsible for the high occupancy share of cotton. On average, cotton cropland occupancy increased by +0.46 per cent points in 1990-93 over 1966-69.

There is every possibility for further increase in the cotton cropland occupancy. Moreover, much of the land which at present is devoted to pearl millet, could be diverted to cotton.

Sugarcane (Saccharum Officinarum)

Though occupying a relatively very small share of the total cropped area (0.17%), the sugarcane farming is engaged in the old alluvial plain and a pocket of old aeolin undulating plain in the north-eastern parts. These areas devote under 0.50 to over 2.00 per cent of the cropland occupancy to sugarcane.

It is noteworthy that the area under sugarcane decreased by –0.38 per cent points in 1990-93 over 1966-69 and spatial patterning of change highlights that increase was more dominant.

Group IV: Pulses including Gram

Food pulses play an important role in the cropping pattern at an Indian farm fixing atmospheric nitrogen in soil and improving protein intake of ruralites and livestock.

Pulses require less moisture than companion crops and survive when others are wilting on poor soils. Therefore, these are insurance crops requiring little care and are useful cash crops in light soils in drought years. On average, the cropland occupancy of pulses are 28.73 per cent of the total cropped area of which 28.43 per cent is contributed by gram. At the same time, the other pulses are not important because they are grown collectively only in 0.30 per cent of the total cropped area.

Gram is the principle pulse crop grown for cash returns and is produced both as a food for human consumption and feed/fodder for draught and milch stock. On average, at the regional level, 28.43 per cent of the total cropped area was under gram in the Dadri tahsil. The geographic patterns reveal the great regional differences in interest in gram cultivation, which varied from 7.10 per cent in village Tiwala to over 52.61 per cent in village Mahrana of the total cropland occupancy.

The principal gram-growing area was the dunal plain where over 40.00 per cent of total cropped area was under gram. The belt of predominant cultivation of gram (over 40%) was bordered by areas of primary concentration (30.01 to 40.00%) in the dunal plain and a great stretch of primary concentration was also observed in the sandy undulating plain of Dadri tahsil. In these areas favourable gram ecological conditions, such as, sandy undulating terrain, coarse sandy soil, meagre rainfall and low level of irrigation intensity are responsible for its cultivation as an important crop. It attained a secondary status (20.01 to 30.00%) on the margins of areas where gram is a pre-dominant and primary crop. The intensively irrigated areas of old alluvial plain/eastern half of the study area recorded minor importance (under 20.00%) of gram as the agricultural land was devoted to wheat because of favourable conditions for the adoption of Green Revolution technology.

It is evident that gram cultivation has shrunk, and the decrease recorded was –3.05 per cent points in 1990-93 over 1966-69. It was more prominent (over 20.00 and 15.01 to 20.00% points) in the eastern half of the study area where wheat cultivation has displayed to this. The decrease was also prominent in the dunal plain and sandy undulating plain where black mustard cultivation has encroached on gram fields. On the margins of primaries were the secondary decreases (10.01 to 15.00%); and elsewhere, the decreases were minor under (10.00%) and nil/negligible.

Other Pulses

The other pulses grown in the study area are brown gram, green gram, black gram and red gram known as pigeon pea and lentil.

On average, at the regional level 0.30 per cent of the total cropped area was under other pulses during 1990-93. The primary (over 2.00%) and significantly secondary (1.51 to 2.00%) areas of production were found in the north-eastern part of the Dadri tahsil. On the peripheries of these areas of moderate cropland occupance of other pulses was noted (1.01 to 1.50%). Elsewhere, their proportion was small, i.e. under 1.00 per cent and they formed minor crops in the cropping structure.

Group V: Fodder Crops

Grazing lands are another source of forage for livestock. But grazings are a poor source due to over-grazing and areal shrinking of pasture lands as being put to other uses. Therefore, green fodder cropland occupancy remains the major source of forage for livestock.

Because of the rapid population growth in India more and more arable land is being devoted to foodgrains, pushing other crops to secondary/ minor position. Since the overall cropping pattern of the area was dominated by wheat-bulrush millet-gram oilseeds commercial farming, the cultivators devoted on average only about 7.87 per cent of the total cropped area of their holdings to green fodders which was shared by *kharif* and *rabi* fodders respectively about 7.41 and 0.46 per cent of total cropped area. At the same time, the regional average (7.87%) as much below the recommended green fodder cropland occupancy of 20 per cent which farmers should set aside for green fodder crops to meet the average requirement of green fodder for their livestock.

The area under wheat and oilseeds increased during 1990-93 over 1966-69 without a significant emphasis on green fodder crops under which an average 0.94 per cent point decreased was recorded during the same period. The popular *kharif* fodders small pearl millet (bajri), sorghum (chari), cluster bean (*Cyamopsis teragonoloba*, guar) and maize (*Zea maya*) which are grown in arid and semi-arid areas, possess certain hardy characteristics.

On average, very high (12.00%) and high (9.01 to 12%) proportions of the total cropped area under green fodder crops were recorded in dunal plain and old aeolian undulating plain of Dadri tahsil. At the same time in the major parts of the dunal and sandy undulating plains the fodder crops was under 3.00 per cent and even negligible.

During the period under study, the fodder cropland occupancy decreased at a very low rate, as is evident from an increase of about 0.94 per cent points at the regional level. The increase was more prominent in the eastern segment of the study area which was about over 9.00 per cent point, and it brought to limelight the great regional difference in the dynamics of fodder which varied from nil/negligible to over 12.00 per cent point.

Group VI: Unimportant Crops

Unimportant crops such as vegetables and miscellaneous crops of coriander and chillies covers an insignificant area of 0.07 per cent of the total cropped area in the old alluvial plain and north-eastern parts of old aeolian plain.

Volume of Change in Cropping Pattern

The overall and village-wise aggregate percentage of total cropped area involved a shift in cropping structure was calculated and highlights the fact that major shift was from coarse foodgrain crops like pearl millet (–3 25% points) and gram (–3.05% points) to wheat (+9.35% points) and oilseeds (+3.65% points). The other crops which gained cropped area were paddy (+0.04% points) and black mustard (+3.65% points). Therefore, the trend to agricultural development during 1990-93 over 1966-69 was towards commercialisation because of increase in cropland occupancy under fine foodgrains (+9.39% points) and industrial crops (+3.73% points). Unfortunately, green fodder cropped area recorded a decrease of –0.94 per cent points, the trend which may not be considered healthy in an agricultural economy dependent on livestock wealth.

The regional picture of volume of change in cropping pattern, highlights the situations of considerably very high rate of dynamism (over 48.00%), high rate of dynamism (36.01 to 48.00%) and where, by contrast, it was in a state of semi-dynamism (24.01 to 36.00%) and relatively stable (under 24.00%) during the period under study 1966-69 and 1990-93.

The relatively stability (over 36.00%) in cropland occupancy was recorded in a large number of villages in the dunal plain and sandy undulating plain of the study area constituting areas of either low intensity of irrigation or minimum agricultural potential of dunal plain having desert soil.

The areas of relatively dynamic (24.01 to 36.00%) swing in cropping pattern were encountered in the old aeolian undulating plain and elsewhere in many pockets. Alongwith these there were observed a few villages which noticed shift in cropping of highly dynamic (over 48.00%) order. At the same time, a very large number of villages were in a state of semi-dynamism (24.01 to 36.00%) which experienced a high rate of shift in cropland occupancy and might be considered the potential agricultural areas of Dadri tahsil of Bhiwani district of Haryana. The shift was impressive in terms of cropped area involved in shift to wheat and oilseeds and particularly to paddies in old aeolian undulating plain and dunal plain of the study area.

Dynamism in cropping structure at spatial scale was motivated during the period 1966-69 and 1990-93 due to improvements in irrigation intensity, adoption of dry farming technology; incentive-oriented support price; changes in farm-management practices and tendency of farmers to shift from subsistence farming to commercial farming. Although the swings in the cropland occupancies were in the right directions, the farmers should be given proper guidance by farm experts to propagate restructuring of cropland occupancy along planned lines without any further decrease in gram and green fodder cropland occupancies as these crops are essential for sustainable agriculture.

Primary solution to the problems of weaker areas and the geo-economic inequality of cropping pattern within the borders of study area, at least in the near future, lies in:—

(i) the intensification of the existing irrigation facilities and assurance of the availability of agricultural water,

(ii) the extension of lift irrigation in the *bagar* and sandy undulations of the study area,

(iii) an appreciable improvement in cropping patterns resulting improvement in agricultural productivity affecting economic development,

(iv) an aggressive extension and production drive in the fine foodgrains and industrial crop region which can certainly provide good returns to the farmers,

(v) the transformation of the traditional system of agriculture through technical innovations and suitable modifications of the policies relating to the supply of inputs and institutional arrangements,

(vi) an efficient use of fertilizers to the recommended doses, coupled with improving the credit and extension services.

(vii) strengthening the extension services for the development of Intensive Dairy Development Programmes in areas where a keen interest is taken by the farmers in the cultivation of forage crops, and

(viii) an appreciable progress in the cropping patterns, agricultural productivity which affect economic development and improving the standard of living of rural masses of the study area.

References

Bhatia, S.S. (1967), A New Measure of Agricultural Efficiency in Uttar Pradesh, India, *Economic Geography*, Volume 43.

Chauhan, T.S. (1987), *Agricultural Geography: A Study of Rajasthan State*, Jaipur. Academic Publishers.

Gregor, Howard F. (1970), *Geography of Agriculture: Themes in Research*, London, Prentice-Hall Inc.

Gupta, A. Das (1978), *Economic and Commercial Geography*, Calcutta, A. Mukerjee and Co. Pvt. Ltd.

Husain, M. (1979), *Agricultural Geography*, Delhi, Inter-India Publications.

Husain, M. (1998), *Agricultural Geography*, Jaipur, Rawat Publications.

Khusro, A.M. (1964), Returns to Scale in Indian Agriculture, *Indian Journal of Agricultural Economics*, Volume 19.

Klages, K.H.W. (1958), *Ecological Crop Geography*, New York, Macmillan.

Mohammad A. (ed.) (1978), *Dynamics of Agricultural Development in India*, New Delhi, Concept Publishing Company.

Mohammad N. (ed.) (1980), *Perspectives in Agricultural Geography*, New Delhi. Concept Publishing Company.

Morgan, W.B. and R.J.C. Munton (1971), *Agricultural Geography*, London, Methuen & Co.

Randhawa, M.S. (1974), *Green Revolution: A Case Study of Punjab*, Delhi, Vikas Publishing House.

Shafi, M. (1974), Perspective of the Measurement of Agricultural Productivity, *The Geographer*, Volume 21.

Singh, Jasbir (1976), An Agricultural Geography of Haryana, *Kurukshetra*, Vishal Publications.

Singh, Jasbir and Dhillon, S.S. (1994), *Agricultural Geography*, New Delhi, Tata McGraw Hill Publishing Company Limited.

16

SPATIO-TEMPORAL INEQUALITY IN MAN-LAND RATIO IN UTTAR PRADESH

NOOR MOHAMMAD & ANURADHA PATHANIA

Introduction

Land is one of the basic natural asset to man providing him food, fuel, raw materials and various other materials of his requirement but it is not uniformly available across the world as per its standard requirement (Baslowe, 1978 and Mohammad, 1981). Many of the developed countries have plenty of land resource per head of their population while a large number of developing countries specially the densely populated ones have its meagre availability. However, due to increasing pressure of population over the years the availability of this valuable resource per head of population has further declined (Burman, 1984; Dayal, 1984 and Karan and Iijima, 1985). Therefore, there are spatio-temporal variations in man-land ratio. And, it has become more influential source of economic, social and political powers. Moreover, it is not the absolute land resource which matters from agricultural point of view but it is the availability of net sown area (hereafter NSA) and gross cropped area (hereafter GCA) which is more important and significant. The main user (Man) of this land resource is neither uniformly distributed across the country nor has uniform occupational structure. The availability of this vital resource, should, therefore, not only be gauged in terms of total population but also in relation to rural population. This chapter is, therefore, a modest attempt to describe and explain the spatio-temporal inequalities in man-land ratio in one of the most densely populated and predominantly agricultural State of India viz. Uttar Pradesh with the following hypotheses:

(i) Per head availability of NSA is inversely related with fertility and productivity of land and high density of population.
(ii) Availability of GCA is positively associated with the level of agricultural modernization and mechanization.
(iii) The areas of surplus availability of land are, by and large, found in western central Uttar Pradesh, while the deficit areas are found in eastern, hilly and tarai regions of the State.
(iv) There is a positive relationship between per head availability of land and size of holding.

Data Source and Methodology

The study is entirely based on secondary data collected from different government and quasi-government publications specially from Directorate of Economics and Statistics and Census of India publications. The agricultural year 1990-91 has been taken because the latest data at national level was available only for this period for both land-use and population data while 1980-81 has been selected to represent the situation of the earlier decade so that a comparative assessment of man-land ratio could be made. The land resource data for the year 1980-81 has been obtained from Indian Agricultural Statistics – Vol. II (District level), while the same has been taken from the unpublished records of Ministry of Agriculture for the year 1990-91. District has been chosen as unit of analysis. Although the number of districts in 1990-91 has increased as compared to 1980-81, but the number of districts in the former period has been brought in conformity with number of districts in the latter period.

For the assessment of availability, NSA and GCA of each district has been divided by its total and rural population, individually and separately, which ultimately gives the availability of land at various level.

Net Sown Area and its Availability–1980-81

Spatial Distribution of Net Sown Area

Net sown area refers to the land which comes under cultivation in an agricultural year (Singh, 1974 and 1994). It does not include the land sown more than once (Mohammad, 1978). Although it covers roughly 58 per cent of the total area of the State, there is a lot of variation in it at district level ranging from 83 per cent in Deoria to 4 per cent in Uttar Kashi mainly due to differential level of physical, techno-economic and socio-institutional conditions. However, on the basis of percentage range of NSA, the districts have been divided into three categories (Table 16.1).

Table 16.1: Percentage Coverage of Net Sown Area: 1980-81

Category	*Percentage Range*	*No. of Districts*	*Percentage to Total*
High	More than 75	14	25.00
Medium	75-65	21	37.50
Low	Less than 65	21	37.50
Total		56	100.00

More than 75 per cent of the total area of one-fourth districts of the State is under cultivation. There are five almost compact regions in addition to the exception of Jalaun district of Bundelkhand region. The largest block consisting of 9 districts is located in western part of the State. The continuity of this zone is disturbed by Ghaziabad district where NSA occupied 73 per cent of the total area. The other compact block consisting of 4 districts, is found in north-eastern part of the State with the exception of Gorakhpur and Ballia districts. The homogeneous fertile plain coupled with high level of techno-economic input are the main causes in the former region, while fertile soil together with higher density of population are the basic cause in the later.

The areas with moderate percentage of NSA ranging from 75 to 65 per cent cover about 38 per cent of the total number of districts and in fact, it emanates from the core of its highest concentration forming almost a transitional belt between the two cores. However, its continuity is broken due to the interference of districts with lower percentage of NSA. The percentage of NSA in the low category ranges from 64 per cent in Mainpuri to 4 per cent in Uttar Kashi. There are two major blocks of concentration of these areas. The first block is found in all the 8 hilly districts and two tarai districts (Kheri and Pilibhit) of the State. The other block is found in the southern part of the district projecting towards north from Mirzapur and Jhansi districts. Rugged topography, infertile soil and poor infrastructural facilities are the main causes for low percentage of NSA in this region.

Net Sown Area per head of Total Population

For the assessment of land resources, it is not only the percentage strength of NSA which is to be considered but its availability to the inhabitants of the area is even more important. And in this respect, the spatial pattern of availability of NSA to total population is almost contrary to its percentage strength. It ranges from 0.07 ha. in Dehradun to 0.42 ha. in Hamirpur. On this basis the districts have been divided into three categories (Table 16.2). There are two compact blocks having more than 0.20 ha. land per head of total population. The largest block is found in Bundelkhand region including five districts, while the second block is located in Ruhelkhand region including four districts. The availability of NSA ranges from 0.21 ha. (Bahraich) to 0.42 ha. (Hamirpur) in this category which covers roughly 16 per cent of total number of districts. In the former region high availability may be attributed to lower density of population, while in the latter it is due to high density of population coupled with comparatively higher percentage of NSA.

Table 16.2: Net Sown Area per head of Total Population: 1980-81

Category	*Percentage Range*	*No. of Districts*	*Percentage to Total*
High	More than 0.20 ha.	9	16.07
Medium	0.20-0.15 ha.	25	44.64
Low	Less than 0.15 ha.	22	39.29
Total		56	100.00

About 84 per cent districts have less than the standard requirement of NSA. Out of this about 45 per cent districts fall in the second category and are widely distributed in the State. About two-fifths districts fall in the third category having per head NSA from 0.07 ha. in Dehradun to 0.14 ha. in Saharanpur. Leaving four hilly districts, all districts belong to fertile alluvial tract of Ganges plain with high percentage of NSA. Besides other, the main cause of lowest availability of NSA is the high density of population with higher dependency on agriculture. The largest belt consisting of 11 districts is found in eastern Uttar Pradesh where high density of population and lower availability of NSA due to lower level of agricultural technology are the basic causes. The other block covers 6 districts of western Uttar Pradesh and 2 hilly districts. In the former high density of population, while in the latter detrimental environmental conditions, specially relief, soil and climate leading to comparatively lower percentage strength of NSA are basic causes of such a situation. The situation can be improved by diversifying the occupational structure of a population and improvement in the level of agricultural technology.

Net Sown Area per head of Rural Population

In conformity with the common belief, the spatial pattern of per head availability of NSA ranging from 0.10 ha. (Jaunpur) to 0.58 ha. (Ghazipur) becomes simpler and widens in case of rural population. The areas with comparatively higher availability cover more than one-third of the total districts.

Table 16.3: Net Sown Area per Head of Rural Population: 1980-81

Category	*Percentage Range*	*No. of Districts*	*Percentage to Total*
High	More than 0.20 ha.	19	33.93
Medium	0.20-0.15 ha.	28	50.00
Low	Less than 0.15 ha.	9	16.07
Total		56	100.00

In fact the two major cores of higher per head availability to total population have extended in their peripheral areas. The Bundelkhand region has extended towards north including the district of Kanpur, while the Ruhelkhand region has extended towards north-west encompassing 6 more districts. Besides these, Mirzapur and Ghazipur have also shown higher availability. The main cause is, perhaps, the diversity in occupational structure which has released the burden on agricultural land resource. Besides this, the migration of male population to urban centres for better job, leaving female, children and old people behind is another important reason.

Exactly 50 per cent districts fall in the moderate category which has wider distribution in north and central Uttar Pradesh with the exception of only one hill district of Pithoragarh. This shows higher level of dependency on agricultural resources. About 16 per cent districts fall in the third category having 0.10 ha. to 0.14 ha. of NSA. Leaving the exception of only Chamoli district, all the districts are found in eastern Uttar Pradesh which is basically the result of very high density of population and lack of other means of livelihood. Hence, there is heavy dependency on agricultural land resources which could be reduced by developing various agro-based industries for which there are a lot of potentialities in the State.

Net Sown Area and its Availability – 1990-91

Spatial Distribution of Net Sown Area

Owing to induction of modern agricultural technology, the areal strength of NSA has increased over the decade. Although the State average is only 58 per cent but it goes as high as 82 per cent in case of many districts. On the basis of the percentage strength, the districts have been grouped into three categories (Table 16.4). About 29 per cent of the districts have recorded more than 75 per cent of their total area under NSA. The largest block consisting of 12 districts is in almost a semi-circular form in central and western part of the State.

Table 16.4: Percentage Coverage of Net Sown Area: 1990-91

Category	*Percentage Range*	*No. of Districts*	*Percentage to Total*
High	More than 75	16	28.58
Medium	75-65	21	37.50
Low	Less than 65	19	33.92
Total		56	100.00

In all these districts the level of modern agricultural technology is high which is the main cause of higher percentage of NSA. Besides this, there are three isolated pockets of one/two districts each in eastern Uttar Pradesh. The regions with moderate percentage have larger area including 21 districts (38%) which are found in 5 blocks of varying sizes. The largest block covering 13 districts (23%) is found in southern and eastern part of the State. The other block of sizeable area including 4 districts is found in western part of the State encircling the district of Mainpuri. Besides these, Ghaziabad, Saharanpur, Muzaffarnagar and Bijnor have also moderate percentage of NSA. In the remaining 34 per cent districts the percentage of NSA is less than 65 but it is as low as 4 per cent in Uttar Kashi. In all the hilly districts of Uttarakhand the percentage of NSA is less than 16. In the plateau district of Jhansi, Lalitpur and Mirzapur also the percentage of NSA is low. In these two belts detrimental physical conditions and low level of agricultural technology is the main cause of lower percentage of NSA.

Net Sown Area per head of Total Population

Due to increasing pressure of population on agricultural land resources, and inadequate expansion of NSA owing to lower level of agricultural technology and attainment of saturation point, its availability per head of total population at State level has declined to 0.12 ha. from 0.16 ha. over the decade. However, its availability ranges from 0.05 ha. in Dehradun to 0.36 ha. in Hamirpur district. On this basis these districts have been divided into three categories (Table 16.5).

Table 16.5: Net Sown Area per head of Total Population: 1990-91

Category	*Percentage Range*	*No. of Districts*	*Percentage to Total*
High	More than 0.20 ha.	5	8.94
Medium	0.20–0.15 ha.	8	14.28
Low	Less than 0.15 ha.	43	76.78
Total		56	100.00

The distributional pattern of per head availability of NSA to total population is very simple as compared to 1980s. There are only 5 districts of Bundelkhand region which have higher availability of NSA mainly due to lower density of population and its rural to urban movement. This region has retained its category of 1980-81 in this connection, although there is general decline here also. The region of moderate availability of NSA is also found in a compact block with the exception of two isolated pockets of one district each i.e. Mathura and Fatehpur. In this block, higher availability of NSA and rural to urban migration of population are the root causes of it. However, there is general deterioration in this region because per head availability of NSA has declined to 0.15 ha.

About 77 per cent districts fall in the lowest category and are distributed all over the State except two blocks of higher and moderate availability. It really shows very high density of population and saturation point in extension of NSA.

Thus the comparative study of availability of NSA at both the time periods proves our proposed hypotheses of inverse relationship between density of population and soil fertility on the one hand and availability of NSA on the other.

Net Sown Area per head of Rural Population

The distributional pattern of per head availability of NSA gets somewhat changed in case of rural population. There is an overall increase in its availability. The State figure has gone up to 0.16 ha. from 0.12 ha. and its per head availability ranges from 0.43 ha. in Hamirpur to 0.09 ha. in Varanasi. On the basis of this range the districts have been divided into three categories (Table 16.6).

Table 16.6 shows that less than one-fifth districts fall under higher category and these are found in two blocks of different sizes besides an isolated pocket of Mathura district. The largest block including 6 districts is found in Bundelkhand region and its adjoining northern area. Here low density of population coupled with rural to urban movement of population is the main cause of higher availability. The other blocks consisting of only 3 districts–Kheri, Pilibhit and Shahjahanpur found in almost tarai belt where a lot of people have migrated from rural to urban areas in search of better jobs and opportunities. The region of moderate availability covers the largest percentage of districts (43%) and with the exception of an isolated single district of Mirzapur, is found in a single contiguous block running from western to central part of the state. Its perfect continuity is interrupted by occurrence of a few districts of other categories.

Table 16.6: Net Sown Area per head of Rural Population: 1990-91

Category	*Percentage Range*	*No. of Districts*	*Percentage to Total*
High	More than 0.20 ha.	10	17.86
Medium	0.20–0.15 ha.	24	42.86
Low	Less than 0.15 ha.	22	39.28
Total		56	100.00

The regions of lowest availability are found in all major blocks with a single exception of an isolated pocket consisting of Meerut and Ghazipur districts. The largest block is found in eastern Uttar Pradesh where the density of population is extremely high while the other block is found in 5 northern hill districts of Uttarakhand. The basic cause in the former is the extremely high density of population, while in the latter it is due to less availability of NSA.

Availability of Gross Cropped Area – 1980-81

Gross cropped area covers the area cropped during one agricultural year including *kharif*, *rabi* and *zaid* seasons. Hence, it naturally increases areal strength of cropped area, and consequently its per head availability. But the total volume of increase depends on physical, techno-economic and socio-institutional factors. If all factors are acting positively, the volume of increase would be highest, and in contrary condition it would be lowest. However, with various permutations and combinations of all these factors, the areal strength fluctuates. Besides these, time is also very significant component to be considered. The availability of GCA has, therefore, been considered during 1980-81 and 1990-91 in terms of its percentage of NSA.

Spatial Distribution of Gross Cropped Area

Although the State level percentage of GCA is more than 143, there is a lot of variation among the various districts ranging from 175 in Pithoragarh to 104 per cent in Hamirpur. Based on these variations the districts have been grouped into three categories (Table 16.7).

Table 16.7: Percentage Coverage of Gross Cropped Area: 1980-81

Category	*Percentage Range*	*No. of Districts*	*Percentage to Total*
High	More than 150	20	35.71
Medium	150–140	17	30.36
Low	Less than 140	19	33.93
	Total	56	100.00

Table 16.7 shows that there is not much variation in number of districts in each category, but nevertheless the highest percentage of districts (36%) fall in the first category. Substantial number of these districts are found in the north and western part of the State in a form of inverted garland. All the districts of upper Ganga-Yamuna doab, districts of Uttarakhand except Garhwal, and Rampur and Pilibhit districts fall into this category. In the Upper Doab and Rampur districts agricultural modernization is the main cause of higher percentage of GCA, while in the Uttarakhand region intensive subsistence agriculture with very little scope of horizontal expansion due to rugged topography and harsh climate leading to utilization of same land almost during both the

seasons is the basic reason. Besides this, there are six more districts in this category found in almost three pairs i.e. Agra and Eta, Barabanki and Gonda, and Gorakhpur and Ballia. Comparatively higher agricultural technology coupled with high density of population with no alternate occupation leading to intensive agriculture may be accounted for it. The districts with moderate availability of GCA are found in almost a high compact block in north-eastern Uttar Pradesh. Such districts are also found in the east of Upper Doab region. In almost all these districts low level of agricultural mechanisation and modernization is the main cause of lower availability of GCA. A little more than one-third districts forming a compact block with the exception of Aligarh, Budaun and Bijnor have lower GCA. Undulating terrain and infertile soil are the basic cause in Bundelkhand and Baghelkhand regions, while in lower Doab and Tarai districts low level of agricultural modernization is the basic reason.

Gross Cropped Area per head of Total Population

The overall picture in this connection improves and its per head availability at State level comes out to be 0.22 ha. but the district level availability ranges from 0.44 ha. in Hamirpur to 0.10 ha. in Lucknow. On this basis the districts have been grouped into three categories (Table 16.8). About one-fourth districts have high availability of GCA and are found in three pockets besides the other isolated units of one district each.

Table 16.8: Gross Cropped Area per head of Total Population: 1980-81

Category	*Availability Range*	*No. of Districts*	*Percentage to Total*
High	More than 0.25 ha.	14	25.00
Medium	0.25–0.20 ha.	26	46.42
Low	Less than 0.20 ha.	16	28.58
Total		56	100.00

The largest block consists of 5 districts of Bundelkhand, where the lower density of population coupled with rural to urban migration of population are its main causes. The other belt including the similar number of districts is found in almost a circular form in central northern part of the State. Bahraich and Gonda districts form the third pocket from where large number of people have moved to urban centres of not only the district or State but outside the State also. About 45 per cent districts have moderate availability of GCA and are found almost all over the

State except its eastern portion with the exception of Mirzapur. In the hilly districts of Uttarakhand low density of population and in remaining districts rural to urban migration are the basic cause of it. The largest chunk consisting of 10 districts of low availability of GCA is found in eastern Uttar Pradesh where extremely high density of population is its root cause. Besides this, there are 5 isolated pockets consisting of one district each.

Gross Cropped Area per head of Rural Population

As a result of diversity in occupational structure and rural-urban migration, overall situation in this connection is satisfactory and average State level per head availability is 0.27 ha., although it ranges from 0.17 ha. in Varanasi to 0.53 ha. in Hamirpur. On the basis of this variation the districts have been grouped into three categories i.e. high, medium and low (Table 16.9).

Table 16.9: Gross Cropped Area per head of Rural Population: 1980-81

Category	*Availability Range*	*No. of Districts*	*Percentage to Total*
High	More than 0.25 ha.	37	66.07
Medium	0.25-0.20 ha.	15	26.79
Low	Less than 0.20 ha.	4	7.14
	Total	56	100.00

About two-third districts have more than 0.25 ha. of GCA per head and cover western, southern, northern and central parts of the state with few isolated exceptions. Low density of population coupled with rural to urban movement of population are the main causes of higher availability in Uttarakhand, Bundelkhand and part of Baghelkhand regions, while in western and central part agricultural mechanisation and modernisation together with varied occupational structure and higher level of urbanization are the main causes of higher availability of GCA. The districts with its moderate availability are found in almost continuous block in eastern part and core of the central part of the State. The continuity of this block is, in fact, interrupted by the occurrence of two patches of the districts with lowest availability of GCA. The bigger patch consists of Varanasi, Jaunpur and Pratapgarh, while the other one is the only district of Gorakhpur. In all these four districts high density of population is the main cause. Two isolated pockets of one district each–Dehradun and Chamoli of moderate availability are found in the Uttarakhand region.

The above analysis of availability of GCA clearly highlights the shortage of precious agricultural resource, heavy dependence on agricultural activities, paucity of alternate means of livelihood, high density of rural population and low level of urbanization which lead to acute poverty resulting into undernutrition and malnutrition. However, regional variations in its availability is very much explained by the proposed hypotheses of the study.

Availability of Gross Cropped Area – 1990-91

With the increasing level of technological advancement in agriculture, GCA has increased almost all over the State during the decade. Although the average increase at State level is only 4 per cent during the decade, there is considerable achievement among individual districts. However, on the basis of percentage strength of GCA over NSA, the districts have been grouped into three categories (Table 16.10).

About 54 per cent of districts fall under first category as against 36 per cent in the previous decade. These districts are mostly confined to north-eastern, western and Uttarakhand regions of the state. The largest block with a single interruption of Ghazipur district lies in north-eastern Uttar Pradesh extending from Bahraich in the west to Ballia in the east, Nepal border in the north to Varanasi in the south. Here high density of population and lack of alternate occupational provision have led to intensive utilization of scarce land resource. The entire Uttarakhand together with Pilibhit also falls under high category due to limited agricultural land resource owing to rugged topography and harsh climate which has led to its intensive utilization. In western Uttar Pradesh specially Upper and Middle Ganga, Yamuna Doab, the higher percentage of GCA could be attributed to mechanization and modernization of agriculture.

Table 16.10: Percentage Coverage of Gross Cropped Area: 1990-91

Category	*Percentage Range*	*No. of Districts*	*Percentage to Total*
High	More than 150	30	53.58
Medium	150–140	11	19.64
Low	Less than 140	15	26.78
Total		56	100.00

Slightly less than one-fifth of the districts have moderate availability of GCA. These districts are found almost in contiguous belt with the exception of Ghazipur district running from Bareilly in the north-west to Mirzapur in south-east. Here the availability of GCA is commensurate with level of agricultural technology and overall physical conditions. The regions of lower percentage of GCA account about 27 per cent of the total districts and are found in two block besides in three other small isolated pockets consisting of one or two districts each. The largest block including six districts is found in Bundelkhand region where surface terrain and lower level of agricultural technology are the root cause of lower percentage. In the next block consisting of Kheri, Sitapur, Hardoi and Lucknow the reasons for lower percentage are varied and complex including physical, techno-economic and socio-institutional.

Gross Cropped Area per head of Total Population

Although the percentage of GCA has increased during the decade its share per head of total population has declined which is a clear indicator of two facts: Firstly, the population has increased much faster than GCA which has not kept pace with it; Secondly, agriculture is still main source of livelihood and alternate occupations have not been developed. The State level availability of GCA has declined from 0.22 ha. to 0.18 ha. during the decade and the position of almost all the districts has degraded. However, on the basis of its availability the districts have been classified into three categories (Table 16.11).

Table 16.11: Gross Cropped Area per head of Total Population: 1990-91

Category	*Availability Range*	*No. of Districts*	*Percentage to Total*
High	More than 0.25 ha.	8	14.28
Medium	0.25–0.20 ha.	22	39.29
Low	Less than 0.20 ha.	26	46.43
Total		56	100.00

Table 16.11 shows that there are only 8 districts in the first category which are found in two blocks. The larger block including 5 districts covers the Bundelkhand region, while the other one includes three tarai districts—Bahraich, Kheri and Pilibhit. In this block, in spite of lowest percentage of GCA its higher availability points out towards lower density of population and lesser reliance on agriculture. About two-fifth districts fall in the moderate category which is mostly found in

central, western and Uttarakhand regions. The largest block running in north-south direction begins from Pithoragarh in the north and continues upto Fatehpur in the south. Its continuity, of course, is interrupted by occurrence of the districts of lowest availability of GCA such as Bareilly, Bijnor, Moradabad, Ghaziabad and Meerut. All these districts have a very high density of population. There are two isolated pockets of moderate availability. One is found in Mirzapur, while the other covers the districts of Gonda and Basti. The largest belt of lowest availability of GCA is found in eastern Uttar Pradesh in Ganga-Ghaghara belt. It also includes the trans-Ghaghara districts of Gorakhpur and Deoria, and Allahabad district of Doab region, perhaps, no other reason except very high density of population with lack of alternate means of livelihood could be accounted for lowest availability of GCA.

Gross Cropped Area per head of Rural Population

There is absolute deterioration over the decade in this case also and the State average of its availability has come down to 0.23 ha. from 0.27 ha. per head, although inter-district variation is 0.12 ha. in Dehradun to 0.46 ha. in Hamirpur. Keeping the range of its availability, the districts have been classified into three groups (Table 16.12).

As is evident from Tables 16.11 and 16.12 only 20 districts (37%) as against 37 districts (66%) fall in the higher category in 1990-91 and as such the areal coverage of this category of 1980-81 has got shrunk and is now found in three blocks of varying sizes. The largest block covering part of western, central and tarai region of the State covers 12 districts. Its continuity is disturbed by island appearance of Bareilly district. The second block consisting of six districts covers Bundelkhand region with its extension towards north-east. In the former urbanization and diversified occupational structure is the main cause, while lower density of population is the reason in the latter. Saharanpur and Muzaffarnagar form a separate block where diversified occupation and higher percentage may be accounted as its root cause.

Table 16.12: Gross Cropped Area per head of Rural Population: 1990-91

Category	*Availability Range*	*No. of Districts*	*Percentage to Total*
High	More than 0.25 ha.	20	35.71
Medium	0.25-0.20 ha.	23	41.07
Low	Less than 0.20 ha.	13	23.22
Total		56	100.00

The districts with its moderate availability are scattered all over the State except in eastern Uttar Pradesh. However, there are two truncated but continuous belts under this category. One is found in northern part of the State including few districts. Its continuity is interrupted by Dehradun and Chamoli which have lower availability. The other belt covering 12 districts runs from Basti in the east to Agra district in the west with the exception of two isolated pockets of one district each (Dehradun and Chamoli). The region of lowest availability is found in a compact block of 11 districts in eastern Uttar Pradesh. Here also high density of population, lack of alternate employment and low level of urbanization are the basic causes of lowest availability of this precious agricultural resources.

Determinants of Man-Land Ratio

While describing the availability of land resource (NSA and GCA) with reference to total and rural population at both the points of time qualitative analysis of various determining factors have been done, but here an attempt is made to assess the quantitative role of three selected factors on it. Some of these factors determine the distribution of land resources, while others affect their per head availability. These factors are soil rating index, density of population and size of holding.

There are several methods evolved by scholars for the quantitative assessment of the soil (Marbut, 1935; Bennett, 1939; Stamp, 1960; Shafi, 1969 and Storie, 1933), but soil rating index having been worked out by Raychaudhuri and Shome (1960) who have worked mainly on the principles of Storie, has been taken into consideration with the simple reason that it, by and large, represents overall physical condition of the area. District-wise soil rating index, shows the variation from 51.7 in Mirzapur to 68.67 in Bulandsahar but about two-fifth districts fall in the higher category, while only 11 per cent districts come under lower category. The correlation co-efficient between soil rating index and availability of land resource is in general negative i.e. there is inverse relationship between the two which is very much in accordance with our proposed hypotheses. However, when the relationship between availability of NSA and GCA with reference to total and rural population is worked out, it turns out to be positive in our case i.e. NSA to total population which could be either accidental or some error in data.

In the ultimate analysis, it is the density of population which affects the availability of land resources, and the region under study is one of the most densely populated area of the earth surface. But even in this region the density of population ranges from 30 persons (Uttar Kashi) to 1205 persons (Kanpur) per sq. kilometre. However, a little less than one-third districts have a density more than 650 persons per square kilometre, while a little more than one-fourth districts have a density of less than 350 persons per square kilometre. However, the results of correlation co-efficients indicate inverse relationship which is very much in conformity with our proposed hypotheses.

Size of holding also determines the availability of land. Generally larger the size of holding, more is the availability of land and vice-versa. In case of Uttar Pradesh, the average size of holding is 1.01 ha. but it ranges from 0.51 ha. in Jaunpur to 2.42 ha. in Lalitpur. There are only 3 districts (5.36%) where size of holding is more than 2.0 ha. while in about 50 per cent districts it is less than one hectare. However, the statistical test of correlation co-efficient indicates that on the whole there is a positive relationship between the two but when the co-relationship is considered individually between NSA and GCA with reference to total and rural population the result in one (NSA and total population) out of four cases comes out to be slightly negative. It is, perhaps, due to error in data or extremely high density of rural population. On the whole, therefore, it proves our proposed hypotheses which is in conformity with other earlier studies (Mohammad and Pathania, 1995).

Surplus and Deficiency of Land Resource

Although the standard land support unit per head is a very good indicator to assess the well-being and prosperity of predominantly agricultural population of a region, but to precisely ascertain, it is a very difficult and complex exercise because of the varied nature and character of the land resource due to differential physical, socio-institutional and techno-economic conditions. Hence, there are a lot of variations in it, ranging from 5 hectares to 0.4 ha. (Dayal, 1984; Mathur and Karan, 1978 and Ramanaih and Reddy, 1983). However, in the present study 0.20 ha. has been taken as standard land support unit because of very fertile and potential soil of the region (Shafi, 1960, Mohammad, 1978; and Chakravarty, 1970). On this basis the surplus and deficit regions have been identified for the years 1980-81 and 1990-91 with reference to total rural population of the districts.

Surplus and Deficit Regions 1980-81

Besides an isolated pocket of northern districts, there are two major blocks consisting of 5 districts each with surplus availability of NSA with reference to total population. The larger block in terms of areal strength is found in Bundelkhand region where lower density of population is, perhaps, the main cause of surplus availability. The other block consists of tarai districts and some districts of central Uttar Pradesh. Here, by and large, higher availability of NSA is the basic cause. However, only one-fifth districts have adequate NSA for its entire population. The remaining 80 per cent districts fall under deficit category having per head NSA ranging from 0.07 ha. to 0.19 ha. However, the picture becomes a little greener when we consider the carrying capacity of land with reference to only rural population which is almost entirely dependent on agricultural land resources. About 34 per cent districts have surplus availability and are found in two major blocks besides four isolated pockets of one district each—Mirzapur, Ghazipur, Mathura and Kanpur. The largest block covering 10 districts is found in central north-eastern part of the State. Here higher availability of NSA owing to soil fertility and mechanization of agriculture and comparatively lower density of population is the root cause of surplus availability. The other block consisting of six districts is found in Bundelkhand and its north-eastern projected portion. Lower density of population is the basic cause of emergence of this region.

Table 16.13: Surplus and Deficit Districts with Preference to NSA: 1980-81

T. Population \ *R. Population*	*No. of Districts*	
	Surplus	*Deficit*
Surplus	11 (19.64)	8 (14.29)
Deficit	—	37 (66.07)

Note: Figures in parenthesis indicate the percentage to total number of districts.

A cross tabulation of surplus and deficit availability of NSA with reference to total and rural population shows that there are 11 districts (20%) of surplus availability in both the cases, while 37 districts (66%) have recorded deficit condition in both the conditions, but 8 districts (14%) have surplus situation in case of rural population and deficit position in case of total population.

Surplus and Deficit Regions: 1990-91

As the preceding analysis indicates that the overall increase in NSA over the decade has been very low whereas population density has considerably increased. Hence, per capita availability of NSA has declined reducing on the whole the areal strength of the surplus regions. In case of total population the number of surplus availability of districts has declined to 5 from 11 (1980-81). In fact it has now concentrated to only Bundelkhand region. The remaining 51 districts (91%) fall in deficit category. Carrying capacity of land shows slightly improved picture with reference to rural population. Besides the earlier 5 districts, 6 more districts have emerged as having surplus land. Out of these 4 districts—Budaun, Shahjahanpur, Kheri and Pilibhit form a continuous belt while Mathura and Kanpur form the isolated pockets of each. The basic reasons for such a pattern are almost the same as accounted earlier.

The cross tabulation of these shows than only 5 districts (9%) fall in surplus category with reference to table and rural population, while 45 districts (80%) come under deficit category in reference to both. There are 6 districts (11%) which fall in deficit category with reference to total population and surplus category in case of rural population. However, on the whole the State does not have the adequate amount of land to feed its booming millions.

Table 16.14: Surplus and Deficit Districts with Preference to NSA: 1990-91

R. Population / *T. Population*	*No. of Districts*	
	Surplus	*Deficit*
Surplus	5 (8.93)	6 (10.71)
Deficit	—	45 (80.36)

Note: Figures in parenthesis indicate the percentage to total number of districts.

References

Barlowe, R. (1978), *Land Resource Economics*, Englewood Cliffs, N.J.

Bennett, H.H. (1939), *Soil Conservation*, New York.

Burman, S.G. (1984), 'Population, Settlements and Socio-Economic Patterns, Development of Himalayan Resources, in J.S. Lall *et al.* (eds.) *Mimeograph*, New Delhi, Indian Council of World Affairs.

Chakravarty, A.K. (1970), 'Foodgrain Sufficiency Patterns in India' *Geographical Review* (60), pp. 208-28.

Chopra, P.N. (ed.) (1975), *The Gazetteer of India*, New Delhi.

Dayal, E. (1989), "Agricultural Land and Man-Land Ratio in India: An Analysis of Change" in O.J. Bee (ed), *Natural Resources in Tropical Countries*, Singapore University Press, Singapore pp. 346-67.

FAO (1976), 'A Framework for Land Evaluation, *Soil Bulletin* (32) Rome.

Grigg, D.B. (1976), Agricultural Responses to Population Pressure: *Progress in Geography* (8), pp. 147-75.

Indian Agricultural, Statistics Vol.II, Directorate of Economics and Statistics, Department of Agriculture and Co-operation, Ministry of Agriculture.

Karan, P.P. and Iijima, S. (1985), 'Environmental Stress in the Himalayas'. *Geographical Review* (75) pp. 71-92.

Marbut, C. (1935) Soils of the United States, *Atlas of American Agriculture* U.S. Department of Agriculture.

Mathu, C. and Karan, P.P. (1978), Concept of Land Support Unit: Bhutan, *Geografiska Annaler*, GOB, pp. 28-35.

Mohammad, N. (1978), *Agricultural Landuse in India*, Concept Publishing Co., Delhi.

Mohammad, N. (1981), *Perspective in Agriculture Geography* (I to V), Concept Publishing Co., Delhi.

Nath, V. (1969), The Growth of Indian Agriculture, *Geographical Review* (59), pp. 348-77.

Ramanaih, Y.V. and Reddy, N.B.K. (1983), Carrying Capacity of Land in Andhra Pradesh, *Indian Geographical Journal*, pp. 107-118

Raychaudhuri, S.P. and Shome, K.B. (1960), Rating of Soils of India, *Proceedings of the National Institute of Science of India*, 25 (1).

Shafi, M. (1960), *Land Utilization in Eastern U.P.*, Aligarh.

Shafi, M. (1969), Land Use Planning, Land Classification and Land Capability–Methods and Techniques, *The Geographer*, Aligarh.

Spate, O.H.K. and Learmonth, A.T.A. (1965), *India and Pakistan: A General and Regional Geography*, London, Methuen.

Stamp, L.D. (1954), *The Under Developed Land of Britain*.

Stamp, L.D. (1969), *Our Developing World*, London.

Storie, T.E. (1933), *An Index for Rating the Agricultural Values of Soil*, California Experiment States Bulletin No. 556.

Tiwari, R.N. (1970), *Agricultural Development and Population Growth*, S. Chand and Co. Delhi.

17

POST-HARVEST MANAGEMENT OF HORTICULTURAL CROPS IN INDIA

J.L. MANGAL, J.K. SANDOOJA, SALEEM SIDDIQUI & S. LAL

India having varied agro-climatic conditions produces almost all types of horticultural crops in one or the other parts of the country. The area under horticultural crops has been estimated to be about 1 million ha. accounting for roughly 7 per cent of the total cropped area. Horticultural crops contribute about 170 million tonnes to the agricultural produce of the country which accounts for 18 to 20 per cent of the gross value of agricultural output.

Today India has emerged as the world leader in fruit and vegetable production being first in fruits production and second largest producer of vegetable after China. India produces 9 per cent of total world production in fruits and about 18 per cent of the total vegetable production. Unfortunately, unlike other horticulturally rich countries, Indians do not get the basic daily requirement of fruits and vegetables. High rate of population growth offset the higher production of fruits and vegetables. In addition, there is considerable gap between the gross production and net availability of fruits and vegetables. Furthermore, only less than 2 per cent of the produce is used for processing compared to 70 per cent in Brazil, 65 per cent in USA, 83 per cent in Malaysia and 50 per cent in Israel. Therefore, in order to achieve our target of feeding the population as well as meeting the requirement of processing industry and export trade, only increasing production and productivity of horticultural crops will not be enough. A lot more emphasis needs to be given to post-harvest management of fruits and vegetables. India produces 50 million tonnes of fruits and 72 million tonnes of vegetables every year. Taking the post-harvest loss of about 30 per cent, the net availability was about 35 million tonnes in case of fruits and 50 million tonnes of vegetables during that period. In our country, there is considerable gap between gross production and net availability of fruits and vegetables for consumption due to uncontrolled post-harvest losses. With the anticipated growth rate, if loss rate is not reduced, the total loss will also increase simultaneously with the increased production. Therefore, loss rate has to be gradually cut down in order to achieve the target of surplus produce for industry and export after meeting the nutritional requirement of the country. However, it is not possible to nullify the loss rate as some inevitable losses will always take place. These losses occurred in post-harvest chain of harvesting, grading, packing, transportation, storage and marketing. Hence, towards the post-harvest management of highly perishable fruits and vegetables. Government of India has already acted on this line. In the Ninth Plan budget allocation for horticulture research is more than 20 per cent for post-harvest management of horticultural crops.

Causes of Losses

The practices currently used in India for post-harvest handling, packing, transportation and storage are outdated and contribute directly to post-harvest losses. Most fruits and vegetables contain 80-95 per cent water. As little as 5 per cent loss in water causes to appear wilted or shrivelled and eventually unmarketable. Further large unit size, high respiration rate, soft texture, susceptible to bruising, rotting and senescence limit the shelf life of these commodities. These losses become more serious because of lack of elaborate harvesting equipments, collection centres in major producing areas, suitable containers, commercial storage plants, proper transportation facilities, ignorance of Indian producers about post-harvest technology and poor marketing facilities.

The post-harvest losses for important fruits and vegetables in India are listed in Table 17.1.

These losses vary according to variety, stage of harvesting, packing types, transportation and distribution/marketing system.

The important site where these post-harvest losses are noticed in India are as under

Site	*Losses (%)*
1. Farmers field	18-20
2. Packing house	15-20
3. Transportation	30-45
4. Marketing	40-45

The minimization of these losses have the following advantages:

(a) Supply of horticultural products can be significantly increased without bringing addition land into production.
(b) The problem of garbage disposal and consequent pollution will reduce.
(c) Scare and costly inputs will be more cost effective in economic terms.
(d) Consumer need will be satisfied and better nutrition will be insured with the same amount of non-renewable sources.

Table 17.1: Post-Harvest Losses in Fruits and Vegetables

Name of the crops	*Post-harvest losses (%)*
(a) Fruits	
Mango	17.1-36.7
Banana	12.0-14.0
Oranges	8.3-30.7
Guava	3.4-15.1
Apple	10.0-25.0
Pineapple	5.0-20.0
Grapes	23.0-30.0
(b) Vegetables	
Onion	14.7-3.0
Garlic	0.9-2.7
Tomato	13.5
Brinjal	8.04
Cabbage	11.48
Cauliflower	13.27
Beans	7.45
Okra	5-10
Chilli	10-15
Carrot	5.90
Radish	3-5
Potato	5-14

Control of Post-Harvest Losses

It is not possible to nullify the loss rate as some inevitable losses will always take place. In order to minimize the loss rate, it is essential to make efforts in the following two directions.

I. To strengthen the post-harvest facilities of the country.
II. To develop technological needs.

I. Strengthen the Post-Harvest Facilities

1. Packing stations
2. Primary processing
3. On farm storage
4. Palletisation
5. Containerisation and transport
6. Packaging and pre-cooling
7. Cool store
8. Establishment of cold/cool chain systems
9. Irradiation
10. Control atmosphere/modified atmosphere storage
11. Cooperatives system of marketing
12. Innovations in organised marketing
13. Rural, urban and major terminal markets
14. Price support operations and marketing information
15. Export promotion

Efforts are now on for the creation of suitable infrastructure for post-harvest management. For research and development, a pilot scale grading and post-harvest treatment plant for Nagpur oranges has been installed at the National Research Centre for Citrus, Nagpur. Similarly, a mechanical washing, waxing and grading unit has been installed at Bangalore for the use of the local traders in export.

In the public sector, three organizations, namely, the National Horticultural Board (NHB), the National Cooperative Development Corporation (NCDC) and Agricultural and Processed Food Products Export Development Authority (APEDA) have been entrusted with creating infrastructure for post-harvest management. The NHB under the "Integrated Project for Management of Post-Harvest Infrastructure of Horticultural Crops" has established 127 grading/packing sheds, 64 pre-cooling units/short duration cool stores, 39 cold storages, 76 specialised transport vehicles, retail outlets and 11 auction platforms and has provided subsidy for plastic crates.

During 1997-98, the NCDC sanctioned 386 projects involving financial assistance of Rs. 40.82 crores that would improve marketing and reduce post-harvest losses. The corporation approved 167 projects in Maharashtra for establishment of pre-cooling and cold storage units involving financial assistance of Rs. 24.90 crores. It also assisted a marketing project to be implemented by HIMFED, Shimla and Lahaul Potato Growers Cooperative Society, Manali at a cost of Rs. 3.59 crores.

The first phase of the project is nearing completion and the project has already handled fruits and vegetables worth Rs. 4.66 crores. Almost the entire cold storage capacity in cooperative sector has been creating with the technical and financial assistance of NCDC. The major facilities are listed as under and will be discussed separately.

Packing Stations

In India, there is absolute lack of concept of establishing packing stations. Most of the vegetables are packed right in the field. In case of fruits also some empty portion of farm building is used for the purpose or some natural protected places in the field itself are used as packing place. Most of the material is transported to the market without any treatment and some of them are even transported without packing. At some places, especially for super markets, the material is fully graded, packed and cooled in packing stations. Therefore, to establish packing stations with refrigeration facilities on important locations is the need of hour and Government of India is giving due consideration in this direction. NCDC has done very good work in this direction.

Primary Processing

Unlike durable crops, perishable horticultural produce in our country is marketed immediately after harvesting without primary processing as a result large amount of inedible parts are transported for marketing. These inedible parts generate a large amount of valuable wastes which end up a garbage. However, if they gainfully utilized at the proper time, they can become value added products such as cattle and poultry feed. Some vegetables like cauliflower, peas, leafy vegetables etc. can be primarily processed so that inedible parts are removed before the produce is sent to metropolitan city market. They should be unit packed at packing stations situated at proper place. Following are the advantages of primary processing:

(a) reduction of bulk,
(b) longer shelf life,
(c) less transportation cost,
(d) convenient food, and
(e) employment generation.

On Farm Storage

In a tropical country like India, tremendous amount of quality deterioration takes place immediately after harvest due to lack of on farm storage facilities. In order to overcome this problem, low cost environment friendly zero energy cool chambers have been developed. These chambers work on the principle of evaporative cooling using locally available materials like bricks, sand, bamboo, etc. and do not require any refrigeration. Recently, commercial size chambers have been developed and these chambers are getting great popularity in our country. The small cool chambers can be utilized in the farm home to store fresh fruits and vegetables. Small and marginal farmers in India uses to store a few days harvest. In big storage during rainy season, onion can be stored very safely. The temperature in these chambers is not expected to rise beyond 15°C even when the day field temperature may rise to 30°C resulting in softening of the horticultural products. These chambers are very useful to store citrus crops and guava, mango and ber.

These chambers have been developed by Indian Agricultural Research Institute, New Delhi. For a 100 kg. capacity chamber, the outer dimensions are kept 190 × 115 × 60 cm and inner cavity is kept 130 × 58 × 60 cm. The floor of the chamber is made of single layer of bricks. Side walls are made of double layer of bricks leaving approximately 7.5 cm space between the bricks. The cavity between the bricks is filled with river bed sand. The top of the storage space is covered khaskhas/gunny cloth in a bamboo frame structure. The cool chamber is constructed under a shed with lot of aeration. Before storage of fruits and vegetables, the sand in double wall cavity and the top cover is completely saturated with water. Once the cool chamber is completely wet, sprinkling of water daily in the morning and in the evening is enough to maintain the required temperature and humidity. According to studies conducted, the physiological loss in weight and shelf life of some important horticultural crops are given in Table 17.2 under zero energy chambers and room temperature conditions.

Efforts are also on to bring down further the temperature of the cool chambers by primary evaporative cooling and secondary cooling with the help of some non-conventional techniques so that the temperatures of cool chambers does not go beyond.

Table 17.2: Shelf Life and Physiological Losses in Weight (P.L.W.) of Vegetables

Vegetables	*Storage months*	*Outside*		*Cool Chamber*	
		P.L.W. (%)	*Shelf Life (days)*	*P.L.W. (%)*	*Shelf life (days)*
Mint	May-June	58.5 (73.1)	< 1	18.6	3
Coriander	May-June	30.0 (44.0)	< 1	13.0	3
Amaranthus	May-June	49.8 (63.8)	< 1	10.9	3
Spinach	Feb.-March	16.0 (31.5)	3	7.3	8
Methi	Feb.-March	18.0 (43.5)	3	10.8	10
Lettuce	Feb.-March	9.5 (29.6)	5	2.3	10
Okra	May-June	14.0 (32.5)	1	5.0	6
Bittergourd	May-June	18.2 (38.1)	2	5.6	6
Chilli	May-June	23.3 (32.2)	3	8.8	6
Tinda	May-June	17.8 (35.0)	2	5.4	6
Parwal	May-June	32.8 (89.5)	2	3.8	5
Cucumber	May-June	19.4 (35.6)	3	5.5	8
Kakri	May-June	31.4 (63.0)	1	5.2	3
Carrot	Feb.-March	29.0 (46.6)	5	9.0	12
Beet	Feb.-March	14.5 (29.2)	5	2.3	12
Radish	Feb.-March	24.7 (58.4)	5	4.1	10
Turnip	Feb.-March	16.0 (35.4)	5	3.4	10
Peas	Feb.-March	29.8 (51.7)	5	9.2	10
Cauliflower	Feb.-March	16.9 (27.3)	7	3.4	12

Note: Figures in parenthesis are P.L.W. at the end of storage in cool chamber.

Pelletization

Loading and unloading of fruits and vegetables are very important steps in the post-harvest handling of horticultural crops but are often neglected. One of the problems in our country is the non-introduction of pallets in the trading. The post-harvest losses can be considerably reduced by using pallets. All the subsequent handling become very easy once the boxes are placed on pallets. With the introduction of Corrugated Fibre Board (CFB) boxes, India is now seriously considering to introduce pallets and essentially thinking to introduce mechanical loading and unloading particularly with the use of fork-lift trucks while handling pallets.

Containerization and Transportation

Though containers have been introduced recently in our country in a big way especially for fruits crops. These are not at present used for carrying fresh horticultural produce for internal distribution. We are looking to develop low cost containers fabricated suitable to our requirement by introducing ventilation and evaporative cooling. Palletization and containerization will go a long way in establishing both internal and international trade on a firm footing.

Road and rail are two important transport in India for movement of goods. Railway can play a very significant role in the shipment of fruits and vegetables by improving the movement of trains carrying them and making provision of cooling and ventilation. All these operations are to be backed by sufficient research at every stage of post-harvest handling and transportation and efforts in this direction are on.

Packaging and Pre-cooling

Traditionally, vegetables and fruits are packed in gunny bags, wooden boxes and bamboo baskets. Ventilated Corrugated Fibre Board (CFB) boxes are also used mainly for fruits and export of vegetables. Wrapping of vegetables in HM film delay senescence and increase the shelf life during transportation. Similarly, film wrapping coupled with ethylene absorbent extend the shelf life, further packing followed by pre-cooling considerably enhances the shelf life and retain the quality of horticultural produce by reducing physiological and biochemical changes. The environment friendly low cost evaporative cool chambers can be gainfully used for partial pre-cooling of fruits and vegetables.

Vegetables can be protected from dry air by packing in various types of plastic films. Polyethylene packing provides modified atmosphere and consequently reduces decay, softening and loss of solids as observed in tomato, cauliflower, brinjal and okra. The thickness of film and its permeability to CO_2 and O_2 and water vapour are important parameters for each vegetable packing. In case of brinjal and cauliflower, thick films were found to develop off flavour, whereas thin and gas permeable films maintained cauliflower flavour for longer period and okra could last for nine days without deterioration. Bagging of carrot roots in perforated films significantly reduces their weight and water loss during transportation.

More recently plastic film bags, plastic nets, corrugated board boxes, moulded plastic trays, plastic hollow boards and woven sacks are in use for packing horticultural commodities. On smaller scale, whereas bamboo baskets, wooden boxes, old jute bags, etc. are used on commercial scale.

Cool Store/Cold Storage

The ideal condition for storage of fresh vegetables and fruits is the lowest temperature which does not cause chilling injury to the product. In India, the first cool store was established in Calcutta in 1892. The progress of cold storage industry was initially slow but the expansion of cool storage industry was noticed only after independence. In 1956, there were only 83 units with a total installed capacity of 42,956 tonnes. With the increase in the production of potato, there was phenomenal increase in the number of cold storage. At present, there are 2,970 cold storage with an installed capacity of 77,87,599 tonnes. The cool storage space available in India is mostly used for storage of potato, partly for apple with particularly no space is left for storage of other fruits and vegetables. About 89 per cent of the installed capacity is used for potato and remaining 11 per cent for apples, oranges and other horticultural crops. Electricity is the most important input for cool storage but unfortunately it is not available freely and abundantly in India.

Establishment of Cold/Cool Chain

One of the important reasons for advancement in the trade of horticultural commodities in developed countries is the adoption of cold chain in handling of fruits and vegetables. The maintenance of low temperature during transit and at different stages of handling process results in reduction of losses and retention of quality of vegetables, fruits and their products. APEDA, recently has initiated some efforts in this direction near big cities like Delhi and Bombay. In whole country, it may not be possible to introduce cold chain system in the pattern of developed countries immediately owing to several difficulties such as high cost, lack of abundant and uninterrupted power supply, etc. Therefore, in place of mechanical refrigeration, we can try some other alternating cooling system. In this respect, the advantage of evaporative cooling can be utilized and cool chain based on the principle of evaporative cooling can be established in our country. This system will at least reduce the post-harvest deterioration and retain the quality of fresh and processed fruits and vegetables in much better form than the existing conditions.

Irradiation

In India, irradiation is used not so much to kill the germs in meat but to reduce the post-harvest losses and increase shelf life of horticultural products. Scientists at the Bhabha Atomic Research Centre (BARC) have shown that small doses of irradiation can inhibit sprouting in onion, potato and garlic. The ripening of mango, banana and other fruits and vegetables can also be delayed. Insect and their eggs which infest grains, pulses, vegetables and fruits can be killed.

Although research on irradiations have been in operation at BARC for many years, it is only now that facilities are being established in India for commercial scale food irradiation. The first of these is for spices irradiation and is coming up at VASHI on the outskirts of Bombay. The production and trade in irradiated spices has risen rapidly from 5,000 tonnes in 1987 to 20,000 tonnes in 1992 and over 90,000 tonnes in 1995.

The Department of Atomic Energy is establishing an other food irradiator, which it has named POTON (for potato and onion) at Nasik in Maharashtra. Nasik was chosen because it is in the heart of a major onion growing region. With small dose of radiation, onions can be prevented from sprouting.

BARC scientists estimate that about 20 per cent of onion is lost due to simply sprouting. The POTON irradiator, which is expected to become operational in two years time will be able to irradiate potatoes and onions to prevent sprouting and rotting. Such facilities should be developed at more locations to make it more popular among farmers.

Controlled Atmosphere/Modified Atmosphere

The main purpose of Controlled Atmosphere (CA) or Modified Atmosphere (MA) is to adjust the atmospheric composition surrounding the commodity by removal (mainly) or addition (mainly CO_2) of gases that is different from the atmosphere. Modified Atmosphere does not differ in principle from Controlled Atmosphere storage except that the control of gas concentration is less precise. The first requirement of controlled atmosphere is a sufficiently gas tight chamber and the second is some means of maintaining the concentrations of CO_2 and O_2 at the desired level. This method in combination with refrigerating markedly enhances the storage life of vegetables. For example in case of pea stored under refrigerated condition at 0°C hold good for 7-10 days. In contrast, controlled atmosphere storage with 5-10 per cent O_2, and 5-7 per cent CO_2 at 0°C can extend the storage life of pea for upto 8 to 10 weeks.

It is worthwhile to mention that even over half a century of research and development, the large scale use of CA and MA is still restricted mainly to fruits like apples for long-term storage. In India, commercial application of CA and MA are yet to be introduced. However, there is a scope for using this technology for high value crops.

Cooperatives System of Marketing

Of late, cooperative organizations have started undertaking procurement, storage and marketing of fruits and vegetables. National Agricultural Cooperative Marketing Federation (NAFED), at the national level, in collaborating with affiliated State Federations and Primary Marketing Societies, has taken up procurement and marketing of commodities like potato, onion, ginger, apple, etc.

Besides, NAFED, there are 12 State/Central level societies and 275 primary marketing societies directly engaged in marketing of fruits and vegetables. Their total turnover is estimated at about Rs.150 crores, out of which 45 per cent is accounted by NAFED alone.

NAFED is also doing export work for onion and potato. Other cooperatives which are providing good services to its members in marketing of fruits and vegetables are:

(a) Bangalore Horticulture Produce Marketing and Processing Societies Ltd., Lal Bagh.
(b) Lahaul Potato Growers Cooperative Marketing Society Ltd., Manali
(c) Nilgiris Cooperative Marketing Societies, Udhagamardalam.

Almost all States have cooperative societies for marketing of different fruits and vegetables.

NAFED is also engaged in import of fresh fruit. The Government of India has canalised import through NAFED about 5,729 tonnes of fruits (value Rs. 3.46 crores), particularly grapes from Afghanistan.

One more organization i.e., National Cooperative Development Corporation (NCDC) is assisting in marketing of fruits and vegetables. It is extending financial assistance to cooperatives for practically all the aspects for post-harvest operations. The details of its activities are as under:

(a) Strengthening of share capital base of fruits and vegetables cooperatives.

(b) Construction of cold storage.
(c) Margin money assistance for raising working capital.
(d) Construction of packing and grading sheds and godowns.
(e) Assistance for purchase of transport vehicles.

To enable the growers to derive maximum benefits, the Corporation has started promoting integrated fruit and vegetable projects. One such project on request of Government of India was prepared by NCDC for Mizoram State which involving marketing and processing of oranges, pineapples, banana and ginger. The total cost of the project is about 3 crores of Indian rupees. This organization is setting chain of cold storages in the growing and consuming areas of potatoes, apples and oranges. The Corporation has also availed of World Bank assistance under NCDC-II-IDA Project for expanding the network of cooperative cold storage and marketing.

Though, there is a network of 3,789 primary societies in India, only 275 Cooperative Marketing Societies are handling fruits and vegetables with 12 State and district level societies. The value of fruits and vegetables marketed by cooperatives is of the order of Rs.100 crore of which NAFED account for Rs.60 crores. NAFED experience has shown that an integrated approach comprising a package of better technology of production, post-harvest operations including storage, combined with an improved network for domestic marketing and export can create a healthy climate in which we can have a steady growth of production, increased availability to consumers at reasonable prices and steady growth in the exports and foreign exchange earnings. NAFED has been able to demonstrate the benefit of such an integrated approach in case of onion.

Innovations in Organised Marketing

A variety of marketing innovations have been in operation in the country. One of the first in this direction was establishment of the Horticultural Produce Marketing and Processing Corporation Ltd. (HPMC) in Himachal Pradesh and J&K. HPMC becomes a landmark for apple industry in India and helps the fruit growers to improve their income substantially and ensured the availability of apples all over the country. Grading, packaging and post-harvest treatments help in a big way in the profitable disposal of the produce. Setting up an RTS (Ready to Serve) juice dispensing network all over the country has gathered the momentum as consumers get refreshing drinks at a reasonable price.

Other marketing innovations include the establishment of large number of outlets for the sale of fresh fruits and vegetables by National Dairy Development Board in Delhi, HOPCOM in Bangalore, FRESH in Hyderabad and VINITA for marketing of orchards in Kerala.

APNI MANDI, where producers are allowed to sell their produce to consumers on certain days of the week is also in practice in Punjab and Haryana.

The present 12 State/Central level societies and 275 primary marketing societies are handling about 4.5 per cent of the total production. Total turnover of these cooperatives in the marketing of horticultural produce during 1997-98 was Rs. 444.53 crores.

In another major initiative, of the 29 cooperatives of grape growers in Maharashtra, 20 have formed their own marketing organizations – "Mahagrape". This organization exported 279 tonnes of fresh fruits of grapes, pomegranate, tomato, straw berries and other vegetables to the U.K., Holland, Germany and other European countries making Rs.1.40 crores during 1997-98. "Mahamango" formed by mango growers of Konkan region is also doing good job in this direction.

Rural, Urban and Major Terminal Markets

We have about 6,000 wholesale markets for fruits and vegetables in India. The number for primary rural markets is about 12,200. These markets are congested with very limited facilities for cold storage and public conveniences. However, most of our major terminal markets all over the country are in commendable position and functioning very well. During last few years, considerable efforts have been made to provide lot of facilities to the market users. Unfortunately, their present status is a dishevelled look, unorganized, devoid of real benevolent patronage and full of questionable identities, elements and priorities.

The following suggestions should be followed to improve the present status of these markets:

1. Operational area must not be congested.
2. Well connected by roads/trains and effective communication system.
3. Adequate steps for future expansion should be taken into account in the beginning of setting of such terminal markets.

4. Facility of cold storage should be available in all major terminal markets.

Price Support Operations and Market Information Service

A special feature of trading operations of perishable commodity is that the market arrivals in the season are of a high order while the minimum constituent in the local market is much less which normally leads to deterioration of quality and sagging of prices. Thus the need for market intervention to stabilize the prices in the benefit of growers arises. For this purpose, Government of India, Ministry of Agriculture has declared Market Intervention Scheme for procurement of perishables in the producing areas, as and when called for giving better prices to the growers and avoiding distress sale.

NAFED is doing a wonderful job on commercial basis in implementing the scheme of Government of India for arranging procurement of perishables under market intervention scheme. In 1975-76 and 1978-79, severe slumps occurred and price of potato fell to the level of Rs. 15 to 20 per quintal. The bumper potato harvest during these years lead to a crisis. At this juncture, NAFED came to the rescue of potato growers and purchased substantial quantities of potato by giving voluntary support prices of Rs. 45 to 60 per quintal. It is worth mentioning that NAFED went to the extent of sharing its export earnings with the potato growers from whom potato stock was purchased. This is also done in case of apple, mango and onion crops.

Market information services scheme was started in the Eighth Plan period under the aegis of the National Horticultural Board to make available the latest price and market trends in respect of horticultural commodities being traded in different markets of the country. Started from scratch in 1987-88, there are now 33 centres covering all States and Union territories. The Board has proposed to cover more markets in future. Currently, 20 AIR stations, eight Doordarshan Kendras and 220 local and regional newspapers disseminate this information. Plan is at foot to tie up with NIC Net which will enable the information data to reach all district headquarters. The scheme, however, need to be extended to other crops.

Export Promotion

The export of horticultural produce in India is yet to make a dent in the international market, except in the case of cashew and spices. Strategies for increasing exports primarily concern enhancement of production of export quality material, improving post-harvest handling and strengthening other logistic and infrastructural support. For making export a sustained activity, substantial investments are essential to establish auction houses for flowers, separate terminals under controlled environment at airports and sea ports and cool chain facility, etc. Recently a "perishable cargo centre" was set up by APEDA at the International airport in New Delhi for handling and storage of export cargo of perishable agro-products, including fruits, vegetables and flowers. Similar such facilities are planned for Chennai, Hyderabad, Bangalore and Thiruvananthapuram, where work has already started. Transportation by sea being much cheaper than by air. Attempts are being made to transport by sea the mango variety Kesar from Gujarat, Alphonso from Maharashtra and Banganpalli from Andhra Pradesh. Through controlled atmosphere containers, litchi is being successfully transported under refrigerated conditions to Rotterdam and such bulk transport of perishables horticultural commodities by sea under segregated conditions will make the Indian produce competitive in the international market.

The absence of proper cool (cold) chain facility and non-adoption of appropriate technology for increasing shelf life to reduce post-harvest loss, restrict the export of fresh fruits and vegetables. The absence of appropriate marketing network and involvement of a number of intermediaries in the marketing of the produce are certain other impediments in export promotion. Of late, Government of India has taken certain steps to counter these handicaps and launched APEDA sponsored schemes as follows:

1. Export promotion and market development.
2. Packaging development.
3. Assistance to promote quality and quality control.
4. Development of infrastructure.

The National Horticulture Board (NHB) has already advanced soft loan to 100 per cent during the Eighth Plan and may continue the facility during the Ninth Plan as well.

Export will have to be focussed on selected commodities. Fresh fruits, vegetables, including onion and potato, floriculture products including cut flowers and planting material, processed fruits and vegetables including pickles, walnut, cashewnut, spices, chillies, medicinal and aromatic plants and their products are the priority items identified for export.

Value added chemicals, jasmine, tuberose concentrates, mint oils and dry flowers, etc. are some of the Indian products which are well received in international markets. Presently the benefits made available by government agencies for promoting export are mainly shared by exporters and not by growers. Involvement of growers and their training to improve production and post-harvest technology will go a long way to ensure the supply of export quality produce on a sustainable basis. Now, it is high time to provide desirable price support and on farm storage, packaging and transportation facilities to the farmers as incentives to produce export quality fruits and vegetables.

Table 17.3: Export of Horticultural Products during 1996-97 and 1997-98

Products	*1996-97 (Rs. in lakhs)*	*1997-98 (Rs. in lakhs)*	*Growth (value) in US dollars*
Fruits and vegetables	57877.83	56562.67	-4.9
Fresh fruit	24439.70	25929.15	3.15
Fresh vegetables	33438.13	30633.52	-10.93
Process fruits & juice	20944.25	28152.99	30.68
Processed vegetables	116788.68	10888.35	-9.36
Floriculture	6339.85	7750.56	18.86
Fruits/Vegetable seeds	4208.12	5606.76	29.54

The export statistics shown in Table 17.3 reveal the comparative performance of export of different horticultural commodities during 1996-97 and 1997-98. There is only a marginal improvement in the export of fresh fruits, while in case of fresh vegetables, a negative growth has been recorded during the period. A reasonable good growth has been recorded in the export of floriculture and processed fruits products, showing our strength. However, value-wise, our export is still quite low. Much remains to be done in R&D and export promotional areas to make India's presence felt in the international horticultural produce market.

Development of Technological Needs

The technology developed for some important vegetables is described in the following seven heads:

1. Suitable cultivars with longer shelf life.
2. Cultural practices.
3. Harvesting and curing.
4. Protective treatments.
5. Preparations for markets.
6. Packaging.
7. Storage.

1. Suitable Cultivars with Longer Shelf Life

In India, besides nutritive and processing qualities, certain post-harvest qualitative traits like slow ripening which leads to long shelf life, thick skin facilitating long distance transport are also equally important in quality improvement programme. In tomato, three single gene mutants, namely Rin (ripening inhibitor), Nor (non-ripening) and NR (never ripening) have been identified as to alter the fruit ripening process. The usefulness of these mutant for breeding tomato genotypes for better storage life has well been recognised. These appeared to be more than two alleles at the locus Nor (Nor and Nor) which differ in degree of slowing down the ripening process, Tomato cultivars PKM-1 developed at TNAU by induced mutagenesis is very popular among tomato growers of Tamil Nadu and Andhra Pradesh mainly for its slow ripening as well as strong skin with green shoulder. In onion, the main objective is breeding varieties or hybrids with better storage life exhibiting low physiological and pathological loss. Onion cultivars vary in their suitability for storage (Table 17.4).

Table 17.4: Percentage Loss in Weight in Storage

Cultivars	*Cultivars tested*	*Wt. loss (%) at days*			
		21	44	55	88
White cultivars	5	33	64	75	86
Yellow cultivars	5	16	58	72	87
Red cultivars	3	0	30	42	62
White cultivars	1	11	36	46	57

Genetically controlled factors that may influence storage performance include dry matter content, skin colour, number and quality, and length of natural dormancy of the cultivars.

Similarly in potato, tomato and garlic, efforts have been made to identify the cultivars with longer shelf life. Hybrid tomatoes have better keeping quality as compared to open pollinated cultivars. Pear shape tomatoes have longer shelf life than round cultivars. By evaluating 45 cultivars of onion for four traits related to losses in storage, it was found that thin neck and small bulb size are associated with long storage. In water melon, the hybrid between varieties Dixie Queen and Honey Cream was reported to possess a rind which is twice as thick as that of Dixie Queen, the better of two parents. One of the first transgenic products released for commercial cultivation in USA is "Flavr-Saur" tomato with increased shelf life. Ethylene production was inhibited by 93 per cent in ripening transgenic tomatoes expressing anti-sense gene.

Similarly in fruit crops varietal difference is there with respect to post-harvest losses. In a study conducted on mango reported that Totapari mango had 36 per cent post-harvest losses, whereas Neelum 22 per cent, Deshehri 17.1 per cent and Bangana Palli 20 per cent under uniform storage conditions.

Cultural Practices

Several reports have indicated that high doses of nitrogen application (above 60 kg./ha.) had an adverse effect on storability of onion bulbs due to rotting and sprouting. However, phosphorus and potash at the higher rates improved the keeping quality of the bulbs and also moderate the adverse effect of nitrogen. Regular irrigation and enough nutrition during development of bulb, tuber and fruit vegetables are of vital importance. In the case of onion, irrigation stopped 15 days before harvesting and one week after 50 per cent neck fall helps in reduction of post-harvest losses. Interrupted supply of water causes cracking of carrot and radish while splitting of outer scales for onions. Excessive watering leads to poor quality roots in carrots and more post-harvest losses. Stalking, training and trellising of vine crops such as cucurbits and beans avoid contacts with soil and reduce post-harvest losses. Thus apart from selection of right cultivars, timely irrigation and cultural operations, application of fertilizers and chemicals influence post-harvest quality and storage life of the produce.

Harvesting and Curing

Optimum maturity at harvest of material depends on the market or intended use (storage, fresh consumption and processing). The maturity that is considered optimum at harvest can vary because of the use to which the commodity is put. For many vegetables, the optimum eating quality is reached before full maturity e.g. leafy vegetables, cucumber, green beans and okra. Early harvesting of onion bulbs caused shrivelling, rotting and faster weight loss in storage. Harvesting method and time of harvesting also affect shelf life of vegetables.

Some of the vegetables like potato, sweet potato, yam, cassava, onion and garlic are stored better and for long duration when they are cured before storage. Curing is most simple and effective way of reducing water loss and decay during post-harvest storage. Incurring bruised and injured surface are allowed to heal and form periderm. During the process of curing, wounds are healed by producing a new cork cambium, thus preventing infection by pathogenic organism. The optimum condition for curing for root, tuber, and bulb vegetables are given in Table 17.5.

Table 17.5: Optimum Conditions for Curing

Commodity	*Temperature (degree)*		*Relative Humidity (%)*	*Duration (days)*
	Celsius	*Fahrenheit*		
Potato	15-20	59-68	85-90	5-10
Sweet Potato	30-32	85-90	85-90	4-7
Yam	32-40	90-104	90-100	1-4
Cassava	30-40	86-104	90-95	2-5
Onion & Garlic	35-45	95-113	60-75	05

In case of onion, immature, soft, thick necked bulbs are not good for storage for long and should be disposed of immediately after harvest. Method of curing the commodity also affected the storage (Table 17.6).

Table 17.6: Effect of Curing on Storage Losses of Onion

Method of curing	*31 days*		*63 days*		*87 days*	
	Wt. loss (%)	*Rot (%)*	*Wt. loss (%)*	*Rot (%)*	*Wt. loss (%)*	*Rot (%)*
No curing	11.8	76.7	a	a	a	a
Artificial curing	6.3	12.3	10.8	16.3	13.2	24.8
Field curing	6.1	20.0	11.2	23.3	14.5	36.5

a = All rotted after first month.

The above discussions make it very clear that harvesting at optimum maturity and curing can play a big role in minimising the post-harvest losses in horticultural commodity.

In fruit crops like banana harvesting at 112-125 days after fruit set with less angularity in fruits or at stage known as "three quarters full" was found to be advantageous for long distance transport. Pineapple for longer shelf life should be harvested after 145 days of emergency of inflorescence – Guava is harvested for best shelf life when specific gravity is less than one. Harvest of many fruits in cooling parts of days is practiced when latex flow is minimal for better quality and storage. Harvested material should always have small pedicel attached to it.

Protective Treatments

The incidence of post-harvest diseases, wastage due to rotting, sprouting and weight loss in certain horticultural commodities can be controlled by the use of certain senescence retardants, ethylene absorbents, growth regulators, fungicides, fungicidal wax emulsion and other anti-transpirants as pre-harvest treatment or alongwith pre-cooling in post- harvest protective treatments depending on the produce concerned.

The following recommendations have been made and are in practice for the following crops:

1. In case of potato, complete inhibition of tuber sprouting was obtained by post-harvest spraying of tubers with CIPC @ 5 ml./kg. of potato. CIPC full form is 3-chloroisoproyl-14-phenyl carbamate.
2. In case of onion, pre-harvest spray (2-3 weeks before harvesting) of Maleic Hydrazide (MH), sprout inhibitor, with a concentration of 1500-2000 ppm improved storage life and reduced sprouting.
3. Dipping of okra fruits in cycocel solution (1000 ppm) for 10 minutes enhanced the shelf life for 12 days at room temperature.
4. Tomato fruits treated with fungicide sodium *O*-phynyl phenate 50 ppm and than dipped in 6 per cent and 9 per cent wax emulsion lasted longer at room temperature than untreated one. In case of fruit crops, Thaophanatemethyl (0.05%) effectively controlled the post-harvest losses in Dashehari mango. It was also worked out that 10-15 ppm GA_3 as pre-harvest spray control the maturity in case of mango. Application of Topsim-M (0.05%) fungicide at an interval of 15 days before harvest control post-harvest decay of mandarin. Pre-harvest spray of 0.6 per cent calcium chloride about 10-12 days prior to harvest improved shelf life by reducing spoilage in grapes.

Preparation of Produce for the Market

The step includes washing, sorting, grading, protective treatments and then packaging. Root and tuber crops are often washed to remove adhering soil. Besides, cleanliness, water used for washing improves vegetable appearance, reduces field heat and prevents wilting. It also reduces the load of organisms on them. Thus, commodities should be free from mud, dust, dirt and foreign matter. It should be free from insect damage/ infestation. Commodities should be free from shrinkage, blemishes, warts, scabs, cuts, damages, cracks and other visible faults likely to cause rejection by customers while selecting the items. Off grade, injured and diseased products should be eliminated as soon as possible, and insect damage and discoloured leaves of several vegetables such as cabbage, cauliflower, spinach are trimmed off.

The grading of vegetables is done depending upon the requirement of buyers. If we do not consider the best quality vegetables for export, for domestic consumption, vegetables are graded in India into two grades: (i) good quality or general grade, and (ii) Janta (People) quality or commercial grade. The various standards followed for grading various vegetables in these two grades are given in Table 17.7.

Table 17.7: Standards for Grading the Vegetables for Marketing

Vegetables	*General Grade*	*Commercial Grade*
Arvi (*Colocasia antiquorum*)	Dia 25 mm and above, length minimum 50 mm	Dia 25 mm and above, length 30-45 mm
Brinjal (long) (*Solanum melongena*)	No shrivelling, free from brown patches, green stalk	Shrivelling and brown spots, <20% surface area, dull appearance
Brinjal (round)	No shrivelling, proper shaped, no mechanical damage, lustrous, with green stalk, 65-150 mm dia and more than 5-10% packing/pressure damage, greenish brown area <10% (Jan.-March) and <25% (Sept.-Oct.)	Upto 20% shrivelling, misshape dull look dry or without stalk, upto 20% packing/pressure damage, greenish brown area <25% (Jan.-March) and <50% (Sept.-Oct.)
Coriander leaves	Should not be yellowish, tender stems	Slight yellow colour

Table 17.7: *Contd.*

Vegetables	*General Grade*	*Commercial Grade*
Capsicum (bell-pepper)	Dia 46-85 mm, length minimum 70 mm	Dia 30-45 mm (from stem end) length minimum 50 mm
Capsicum	Firm dia. 50 mm and above, length 50 mm and above	Slightly soft, dia. 30-49 mm, no length range
Cabbage (*Brassica oleracea* var. Capitata)	Puffiness not allowed, compact, light green colour, wt. 250-800 gm. without cuts	Slight puffy with light weight, whitish colour, open head, no weight specification, with clean cuts upto 50 mm long, 20 mm wide and deep
Cauliflower (*Brassica oleracea* var. Botrytis)	Ricines <10% surface area, snow white cream in colour, compact curd with no curd injury or injury <1 sq. cm., with no insect damage, with weight 200-1000 gm.	Ricines >10% surface area, loose curd with dull look, upto 2 sq. m injury, with insect damage < 2 sq. cm but insect not visible, with weight upto 1500 gm.
Carrot (*Daucus carota*)	Fresh red colour, well tapered, maximum 3 nodes on the surface with no cuts upto 10 mm long green top with dia. 25-40 mm and length 150 mm	Pale look, mis-shaped, not properly tapered, upto 5 nodes on the surface, with cuts <70 mm long and 3-5 mm wide and deep, 11-30 mm long green top, with dia. 11-25 mm or above 41-55, with no length range
Cucumber (*Cucumis sativus*)	Green or slightly brown colour, firm, straight, unshrivelled, dia. 35-50 mm and length 125-180 mm	Yellowish, curved, slightly shrivelled at ends dia. 30-34 mm, length minimum 75 mm
Ginger (*Gingibiralis officianalis*)	Thick, shiny, firm, dry pieces weighing >50 gm	Slightly dry with small pieces but weighing not less than 20 gm. each
Garlic (*Allium sativum*)	White or with violet exterior, compact, dia 30-35 mm	Bulbs of sizes smaller than general grade but less than 25 mm dia. or single cloves with minimum dia. 8 mm and length 15 mm
Bittergourd (*Memordica charantia*)	Green or upto 10% colour, tender and firm should not have bruising, dia. 25-55 mm, length 60-200 mm	Slightly yellow colour (upto 20% surface area) slightly poor look with slight bruising, size specification same as general grade
Kakri (*Cucumis melo* var. Utilissimus)	Green colour, tender should not be matured, dia. 10-30 mm	Slightly yellow (upto 10%), dia. 31-40 mm

Table 17.7: *Contd.*

Vegetables	*General Grade*	*Commercial Grade*
Okra (*Abelmoschus esculantus*)	Green/light green in colour, tender and turgid, with no visible seeds, lustrous, with no black edges, dia. <18 mm (at stalk end), length 50-130 mm (excluding stem)	With visible seeds but finger not mature less lustrous, with slight black edges, with no length limitation and dia. <20 mm
Bottle gourd (*Lagenaria zicerasia*)	Green/light green, tender uniform profile, without cut or maximum two cuts of <50 mm length, brown colour/scaling <10% of surface area, with no ruptured skin and black tip, with packing/pressure damage not more than 10% surface area, weight 300-800 gm.	Slightly puffy, with any number of cuts upto 50 mm length or maximum three cuts 50 mm long, brown colour, scaling 11-75%, with ruptured skin upto 75% surface area, black tip <30 mm, shrivelled tip, packing/pressure damage upto 25%, no weight restriction but without any defect
Methi (*Trigonella foenugraceum*) and Spinach (*Spinacia oleracea*)	Green, preferably small leaves and should be clean	Slightly, yellow/turning yellow leaves, slightly drooping leaves
Onion (*Allium cepa*)	Colour characteristics to the variety, well cured, cut not more than one layer deep and 10 mm long, with skin atleast at 25% of the surface area, no sprouting, with no sun burning, black powdery spots <25%, with no double/split, neck <15 mm dia. with no mechanical injury, with no discolouration, dia. 40-60 mm	With cuts not more than 3 layers deep and length 50% of bulb diameter, sprouted, without skin and sun burning 50% area of the bulb, black powdery spots <50% with double/split neck >15 mm dia. mechanical injury not covering >1 sq. cm area, discolouration upto 90% of surface, dia. 25-80 mm
Potatoes (*Solanum tuberosum*)	Colour characteristics according to the variety, should be without mud, with no green spot, with no cut or maximum cut not more than 2 mm deep and length maximum 25% of tuber diameter, with no natural cracks and properly shaped. Brown colour without surface skin not exceeding 15%, with no mechanical injury and blemishes, dia. 40-60 mm	With green spots, with maximum of 3 cuts but cuts not more than 2 mm deep and length maximum 50% of tuber diameter, upto maximum of three natural cracks, mis-shaped and twins allowed, brown colour without surface skin upto 75% of area, with slight (upto 20 mm dia.) injury, blemished tuber of any size

Table 17.7: *Contd.*

Vegetables	*General Grade*	*Commercial Grade*
Peas (*Pisum sativum*)	Green, lustrous, dry skin not exceeding 10% surface area, with no split skin, with no brown/black spots on pod, no black tip	Dry skin >10% surface area. With split skin, brown/black spots not exceeding 20% surface area and with black tips
Sweet potato (*Ipomea batatas*)	Colour according to variety but free from cuts and damage, having proper shape, dia. 40-80 mm, length upto 60 mm	Pieces broken from both ends but free from fungal infection, slight cuts allowed, dia. 25-90 mm, length 60 mm and above
Radish (*Raphanus sativus*)	White/snow white colour, clean turgid and proper shape, secondary roots trimmed, with brown/black spots <5 to surface area, with green leaves but not more than 50% of the total weight, dia. 25-50 mm and length minimum 150 mm	Mis-shaped/twisted/twins allowed, with brown/ black spots <10% surface area, leaves yellow/wilted which are to be removed, dia. 20-60 mm and length minimum 150 mm.
Tinda (*Citrulus vulgaris*)	Green colour, tender should be from dia. 25-60 mm	Without excessive black spots, dia. 60-70 mm
Tomato (*Lycopersicon esculentum*)	Colour typical of variety (Partly Red coloured) with no dry cracks and insect damage, with no white/yellow hard sun burn patches, properly shaped, with packing/pressure damage <10% surface area, with green/yellow colour <25% of surface area, with no black/brown spot, dia. 45-59 mm (desi) and 30-45 mm (oval) and length minimum 55 mm	With maximum of 4 dry cracks, with insect damage not more than diameter of pin head, sun burn patches not exceeding 210 mm diameter, mis-shaped, with pressure damage <50% surface area, with green/yellow colour upto 75%, with black brown spots covering <1 sq. cm surface area, if 30-44 mm (desi), 25-29 mm (oral) and length 30-54 mm or 35-45 mm round variety
Turnip (*Brassica compestris* var. Rapa)	Dia. 45-80 mm (round variety)	Dia. 35-45 mm (round variety)

Absence of careful handling, grading and preparation will lead to poor quality which can fetch less price to the grower, besides increasing transportational loss and increasing the transport and storage cost and finally marketing cost. Packaging and protective treatments are dealt separately.

Packaging of apple fruits in Corrugated Fibre Board (CFB) is much better than wooden boxes and reduce the post harvest losses by 40 per cent. Apple during transit get maximum damage in wooden boxes followed by CFB and minimum in plastic crates. To minimise the post-harvest losses in grapes, to 15-20 per cent, it should be packed in card board boxes and bamboo basket as compared to wooden boxes.

Packaging

Though packaging is certainly not the only cure for the problem of post-harvest loss, use of modern packaging materials, such as plastic, film bags, paperboard boxes lined with polythene, plastic nets can help upgrade the value, contribute towards cost effective distribution, in minimising product losses and to enhance product quality. It presents the produce better to the buyer and generate confidence. Use of polyethylene packaging provide modified atmosphere and consequently reduces decay, softening and loss of solids and weight and enhance shelf life of tomato. Inexpensive plastic nets made from polyethylene is a very good packing materials for onion, garlic and potatoes. Carrot roots go to the transparent film bags. Packaging films should be perforated to prevent the off flavour post-harvest losses in tomato were reduced from 15 per cent to 3 per cent by using "up right cone" basket together with dry grass as packaging material between layers of fruit in place of "invested cone" baskets. Peas and beans are packed for shipment in baskets, jute bags and boxes in India.

Storage

Storage of horticultural commodities is of great importance since it tends to stabilize the supplies by carrying over the commodities from a period of high production to period of low production. This would avoid market glut, maintain regular supply of produce to the consumer and help the producer to get optimum price for the product.

In India, among vegetables onion and potato are the important vegetables, which are stored for long periods in a large quantity. Hence, for onion and potato, storage structures have been designed to bring down their post-harvest losses. With other vegetables, the produce is either not stored at all but sent to the market for sale, or the main need of storage is mostly for short periods of few days or weeks only. In fruits crops, apples and oranges are stored for quite a longer duration as compared to other fruit crops. The various methods used for storage are discussed as under:

Refrigerated Storage

Low temperature storage must effectively shelf life of fruits and vegetables and reduce post-harvest losses by arresting metabolic breakdown and fungal deterioration of the commodity. However, many fruits and vegetables are of low unit value to bear the cost. High cost to erect and run the cold storage limits its use in India. Among vegetables, cold stores are almost exclusively used for storage of potatoes. Recommended storage temperatures, lower limit of temperature to avoid chilling injury, average storage life of different vegetables is given in Table 17.8.

Table 17.8: Recommended Storage Temperature and Relative Humidity of Vegetables

Vegetables	*Optimum Temp (°C)*	*RH (%)*	*Storage Life (weeks)*	*Temp. Limit*	*Chilling Injury Symptoms*
Brinjal	10.0-11.0	95	3-4	7	Surface scald
Green beans	7.5	85-90	2-3	7	Pitting, russeting
Cucumber	10.0-11.7	92	2	7	Water soaked spots
Okra	8.9	90	2	7	Discolouration, water soaked areas
Potato	4.4-5.0	85	34	4	Internal discolouration sweetening
Pumpkins	11.0-11.6	70-75	24	10	Decay
Tomato (mature green)	14	85-90	4-5	13	Decay, poor colour development
Tomato (ripe)	11	90	1-2	7-10	Decay
Onion bulbs	0.0	70-75	20-24		
Ginger	7.2-10.0	75	16-24		
Turnip	0.0	90-95	8-16		

If in refrigerated storage, Controlled Atmosphere (CA) is also maintained i.e. low oxygen and high CO_2 concentrations are maintained, it would still enhance the storage life of vegetables.

Evaporative Cool Chambers

Although best storage environment is provided by mechanical refrigerated cold stores, an average farmer does not have access to it because of various reasons. Hence evaporative cool chambers are of vital importance in Indian conditions. This has been discussed in detail under on farm storage facilities.

References

Arora, S.K., Siddiqui, S. and Jitender Kumar (1988), Packaging of tomato. In packaging of fruits and vegetables in India. Agri. Horticultural Society, Hyderabad, India.

Ghosh, S.P. (1999), Eyeing the export market. The Hindu Survey of Indian Agriculture. Deccan Exhibition Pvt. Ltd., Pune, p. 141.

Madan, M.S., Ullasa, B.A. and Gopalakrishna, Rao K.P. (1993), Post-harvest losses in vegetables. In Advances in Horticulture, Vol. 6, *Vegetables Crops:* Part 2. Eds. K.L. Chadha and G. Kallo. Malhotra Publishing House, New Delhi.

Pandey, U.B. and Yadav, R.K. (1989), On and off farm storage of fresh vegetables – emerging trend. In : Proc. of National Symposium on production and post-harvest management of vegetables. Nutritional Horticultural Board, Ministry of Agriculture, Government of India, Gurgaon, pp. 63-74.

Rao, S.K. (1989), Post-harvest technology of vegetable crops in India. *Indian Hort.* 33, 34 (4 and 1). 76-78.

Rao, S.K. (1998), Post-harvest management of vegetables crops. Souvenir, National Symposium on Emerging Scenario in Vegetable Research and Development, held at Varanasi (12-14 December, 1998).

Salunkhe, D.K. and Kadam, S.S. (1998), Handbook of vegetable science and technology: Production, composition, storage and processing. Marcel Dekker, Inc., New York, p. 736.

Shanta Krishnamurthy (1994), Analysis of factors contributing to post-harvest diseases in Indian conditions. In *Post-harvest Management of Horticultural Produce*. NHB technical communications (Eds. R.K. Sharma and D.K. Uppal), National Horticulture Board, Gurgaon, India.

Uppal, D.K.; Sharma, S.K. and Sharma, R.K. (1994). Post-harvest management of horticultural produce – Challenges before India. In *Post-harvest Management of Horticulture Produce*. NHB technical communications (Eds. R.K. Sharma and D.K. Uppal), National Horticultural Board, Gurgaon, India, pp. 195-203.

18

ADOPTION OF AGRICULTURAL INNOVATIONS AND THEIR IMPACT ON AGRICULTURAL PRODUCTIVITY IN MADHYA PRADESH

S.K. SHARMA

Adoption of modern agricultural innovations is supposed to be panacea for raising production and productivity. They include new and improved inputs, improved cultural practices and improved methods and practices of farm management and marketing (Dasgupta 1989,12). These agricultural innovations have been brought to rural areas but their adoption did not prove neutral to the social structure and is influenced by the personal, social and economic characteristics of farmers as well as by the physical environment (Sharma, 1992). Though the use of these modern inputs presents direct and positive correlation with the productivity, size of the holding and caste structure, with other things have created disparity in the level of adoption. Consequently, level of adoption varies in different communities and in different size classes of holdings. People of different communities and landowners of different size of holdings are found intermingled throughout the State. Therefore, spatial pattern of adoption is bound to be blurred. However, in areas dominated by certain community or certain class of holding these communities or holdings predominantly determine level of adoption. Thus adoption of innovations and consequent productivity have created inter- and intra-societal disparity. These two relations are discussed in this chapter. Spatial variation in use of inputs and productivity is analysed using secondary data while micro level analysis of adoption and productivity is based on data generated from 1161 questionnaires used for sample survey of agricultural households of different size classes and communities living in the Chhatisgarh basin (263 households), Betul-Chhindwara plateau (475) and the Tons basin (423). Sample households have been classified into five standard size classes and four broad community classes.

Spatial Pattern of Adoption of Innovations

Though fourteen innovations were considered at the time of sample survey on microlevel, only three of them, viz., irrigation, high yielding variety of seeds and fertilizers have been widely accepted by the farmers in this State. Therefore, spatial pattern of these variables is analysed here.

High Yielding Variety of Seeds

High yielding variety of seeds (HYVs) was at the core of the "Green Revolution" package programme. They are capable of giving higher yield than the local varieties. Other components of the package are irrigation and fertilizers. Usually they are employed simultaneously. It is evident from the significantly high positive correlation of the extent of area under HYVs with irrigation ($r = 0.759$) and use of fertilizers ($r = 0.771$). These high coefficients indicate that HYVs have been used in areas having irrigation facilities and with the fertilizers.

In the last two years of the Third Five Year Plan, several improved varieties of wheat and later of rice were introduced in the country. Ecologically and socially suitable areas of the State also started their use (Sharma, 1992). By the end of 1966-67, area under HYVs reached to 57.8 thousand hectares as against the target of 93 thousand hectares. It was only 0.48 per cent of the total area under cereals. It increased to 2325 thousand hectares in 1984-85 and 4431.9 thousand hectares in 1995-96, recording growth of more than 77 times during 1966-67 and 1995-96, but only 90.6 per cent in last decade. At present, only one-third (35.7%) of cereal cropped area is sown with these seeds. Wheat and rice are two principal cereals grown in the State. Total area under them is 4019.8 thousand hectares and 5344.4 thousand hectares respectively in 1995-96. Out of the total rice cropped area less than one-fourth (1247.7 thousand ha. 23.4%) is sown with HYVs, while more than two-third (2706.8 thousand ha. 67.3%) of wheat cropped area is sown with HYVs. Improved seeds of maize, jowar and bajra are also used. Still the use of HYVs is very limited in this State in comparison to the national average of 64.8 per cent (1992-93). The comparative position of the State with respect to the national averages of area under HYVs is presented in Table 18.1.

Table 18.1: M.P.: Comparison of Area Under HYVs of Cereals with India, 1995-96

Crops	*Area under the Crop 1995-96*	*Area under HYVs*		*% Area of the Crop under HYVs*		*India % Area 1992-93*
		1984-85	*1995-96*	*1984-85*	*1995-96*	
Wheat	4020	1486	2704	41.3	67.3	88.2
Rice	5344	528	1253	10.6	23.4	65.9
Jowar	994	198	286	10.4	28.9	53.1
Maize	857	83	132	9.8	15.4	43.6
Bajra	134	169	57	22.0	42.7	52.8
All Cereals	12404	2325	4432	17.9	35.7	64.8

Source: Commissioner of Land Records & Settlements, M.P.: *Tables of Agricultural Statistics of M.P., 1995-96 and Government of India: Economic Survey, 1994-95.*

Thus the State's average of the area under HYVs is half of the national average.

Pertinent point to note is that the rice is the first ranking crop in terms of area in the State but only one-fourth of it is under HYVs while national average is nearly two-thirds of the rice cropped area. As in the case of the country, wheat, the second crop of the State, comes first in the use of HYVs in this State also but is far behind the national average. As a result, productivity of these crops is lower in the State than in the country. Further, yield of rice (1151 kg/ha) is much lower than that of wheat (1730 kg/ha) in 1995-96 in this State. Another point is of the seasonality in adoption of HYVs. Out of the five crops mentioned in Table 18.1, all but wheat is *kharif* crops grown in the rainy season. Wheat alone contributes two-third (61.0%) of the total area under HYVs of these crops. Thus *rabi* (winter) season seems to be more conducive for the use of HYVs.

Proportion of cereal cropped area under HYVs varies from only 4.8 per cent in Rajnandgaon and 5.4 per cent in Bastar district, 87.2 per cent in Dewas and 88.8 per cent in Hoshangabad district. Coefficient of variation (55.7) is very high (Table 18.2). Out of 45 districts 25 have higher proportion than the State average (35.7%). They are concentrated over (i) the Malwa plateau (Mansaur, Ratlam, Ujjain, Indore, Dewas, Dhar, Shajapur, Sehore, Bhopal and Raisen districts), (ii) the Narmada valley (Narsinghpur, Hoshangabad, Khargone and Khandwa districts), (iii) Chambal sub-humid area (Morena, Bhind, Gwalior, Datia and Shivpuri districts), (iv) Bundelkhand region (Tikamgarh and Chhatarpur districts), and (v) the Central Satpura region (Chhindwara district). Raipur, Balaghat and Rewa are out of these belts (Fig. 18.1B). Contrary to it, most of the districts of southern, eastern and central parts of the State have low and very low proportion of area under HYVs. Ten of them have below 50 per cent and other four between 50 per cent and 75 per cent of the State's average. Most often these districts have low productivity per unit.

Table 18.2: M.P.: Characteristics of Use of Certain Agricultural Inputs, 1995-96

Characteristics	*HYVs*	*Irrigation*	*Fertilizers*
Area ('000 hectares)	4432	5828	—
Percent of area	35.7	30.0	33.4*
Mean of district percentages	43.3	23.0	33.8*
Standard deviation	24.9	11.3	18.8
Coefficient of variation	57.5	49.1	55.6
Lowest % value	04.8	02.8	04.24*
Highest % value	88.8	74.6	82.52

* Kilogram per hectare of cropped area.

Irrigation

Among the inputs essential for agricultural development one is water. Its use for irrigation is conditioned by several variables, however, low rainfall and its variable.

Nature necessitate the development of irrigation and the increasing employment of fertilizers and, to some extent, high yielding variety of seeds make timely water supply as a pre-requisite. Co-existence of these inputs is evident from high correlation between irrigated area and use of fertilisers ($r = 0.732$), and between irrigation and area under HYVs ($r = 0.759$). On the other side, availability of water resource, nature of terrain and characteristics of farmers affect the supply side.

Location of the State in the sub-tropical region and concentration of rainfall in few summer months necessitate the creation of irrigation facilities. In the major part of the State irrigation is the creation of the plan periods (Sharma and Jain, 1992). In the beginning of the First Five Year Plan, 1950-51, net irrigated area was 890 thousand hectares which rose to 5928 thousand hectares in 1995-96, recording an increase of 566 per cent. The gross irrigated area increased from 905 thousand hectares to 6178 thousand hectares during the same period. At present, 30.0 per cent of the net cropped area is irrigated in the State while country's average was 40.8 per cent in 1992-93. Out of the total irrigated area only one-third (30.3%) was irrigated from governmental sources. Limited irrigation facilities have affected the adoption of other innovations adversely. It is felt that the basic among the agricultural development measures necessary for transformation of the face of agriculture in the State is irrigation and others are very closely associated with it.

Irrigation is a localised phenomenon in the State resulting in high coefficient of variation (49.1). On district level, net irrigated area ranges from 2.8 per cent in Bastar to 74.6 per cent in Hoshangabad district (Fig. 18.1C). Districts with higher proportion of net irrigated area than the State average are confined in five major tracts. These are: (i) the Malwa plateau, (ii) the Chambal basin, (iii) Bundelkhand uplands, (iv) middle Narmada valley, and (v) the Chhatisgarh basin. The Wainganga basin (Balaghat district) is out these belts. Eleven districts of the Malwa form an emerging highly irrigated area in the State. Net irrigated area ranges from 30.5 per cent in Rajgarh district to 52.5 per cent in Indore district. Second highly irrigated area extends over the Chambal basin of Gwalior, Morena, Bhind, Shivpuri and Datia districts, which happens to be the region of lowest rainfall and highest rainfall variability in the State. Irrigated area is also high over the Bundelkhand uplands, comprising Tikamgarh and Chhatarpur districts. Middle Narmada valley, comprising Hoshangabad and Narsinghpur districts, has emerged as a major irrigated tract. At present, 74.6 per cent of net cropped area is irrigated in Hoshangabad district which is highest proportion in the State. The core of the Chhatisgarh basin, comprising Raipur, Durg and part of Bilaspur district, is only major irrigated tract in the east. This 'rice bowl', located in the high rainfall zone, requires regular and ensured water supply. Conversely, vast area of the State is still lagging far behind in this basic facility. Southern and eastern half of the State, except the core of the Chhatisgarh basin, constitute the least irrigated part. In Bastar (2.8%), Mandla (3.5%), Surguja (4.8%), Shahdol (6.7%) and Raigarh (8.0%) irrigation has not started in the real sense. None is so poor in the western part. Because of this, adoption of yield-raising technology and consequently yield rates of crops and productivity is low to very low in these regions. All these areas are hilly and dissected, covered with thin low fertile soils and are occupied by the tribal people. Their socio-economic conditions have not yet accepted such inputs (Sharma, 1989, 71-89).

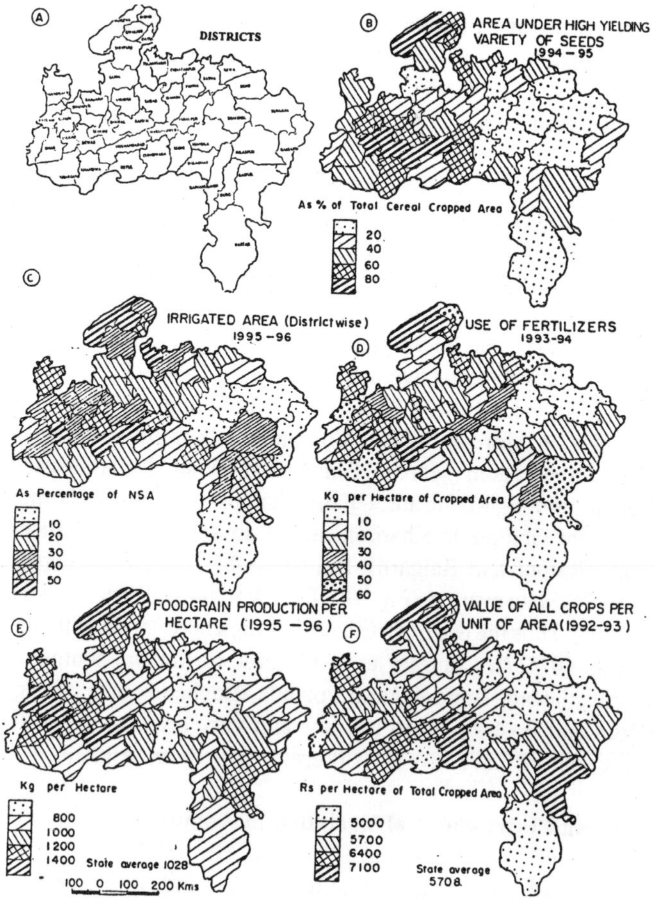

Fig. 18.1: Madhya Pradesh

Out of the total irrigated area (6177.9 thousand hectares) nearly two-third are under only two crops, viz. wheat (44.2%) and rice (20.3%). At present, more than 67.9 per cent of wheat cropped area receives irrigation water. Wheat irrigated area increased to 23 times during 1950-51 and 1995-96. Consequently, its yield per hectare increased from 512 kg. in 1950-51 to 1730 kg. in 1995-96. Yield of wheat under irrigation is 2092 kg. per hectare. On the other hand, only 23.5 per cent of rice cropped area receive irrigation water and its growth has been very sluggish (2.3 times) during 1950-51 and 1995-96. Despite this, yield increased from 357 kg/ha in 1950-51 to 151 kg/ha in 1995-96. Other beneficiaries of irrigation are gram, horticultural crops, rape-mustard and sugarcane.

Use of Fertilizers

Under the scientific management of farming, traditional methods of replenishing soil fertility have been replaced by the application of fertilizers. With the advent of Green Revolution, use of chemical fertilizers has been increasing very vastly. Application of fertilizers per hectare of cropped area increased from only 0.17 kg. in 1956-57 to 3.89 kg. in 1970-71 and 33.38 kg. in 1993-94 in the State. Still the State is far behind the national average of 75 kg. in 1994-95. Per hectare use of fertilizers varies from 4.24 kg. in Mandla and 5.40 kg. in Bastar to 82.52 kg. in Morena district. Comparatively more fertilizer is used in the Chambal region (Morena, Bhind, Gwalior and Datia), western Malwa (Ratlam, Indore, Mandsaur, Ujjain, Shajapur and Dhar), Narmada valley right from Jabalpur to Khargone and in south-eastern Chhatisgarh basin (Durg, Raipur and Rajgarh). Bhopal and Tikamgarh districts are also above the State average (Fig. 18.1D). All of these districts have irrigation facilities. Thus the use of fertilizers has high correlation with the irrigated area ($r = 0.737$). Contrary to it, the eastern Malwa, southern Madhya Bharat plateau, Bundelkhand uplands, Baghelkhand plateau, Satpura region and Bastar plateau use low and very low amount of fertilizers. These regions have low agricultural productivity also.

Inter- and Intra-Societal Variation in Adoption

Adoption of modern methods, techniques and inputs varies spatially and temporally. These are only two dimensions of the reality. There is third dimension also. Adoption also varies from community to community and from person to person with the capacity and capability of farmers. This capacity hinges upon the size of holding of the farmer and his social status donated by caste. Even these two characteristics of adopters have resulted in unequal accessibility of farmers to the new scientific knowledge and technology. Surveys conducted in this connection on household level in the Chhatisgarh basin, Betul-Chhindwara plateau and Tons basin of this State reveal this fact. Situation of adoption of certain innovations in these regions is presented in Table 18.3 in which adopters of each variable are converted as percentage of total households to the size, class or the community.

Table 18.3: Adoption of Innovations

Innovations	*Chhindwara-Betul*				*Chhatisgarh basin*				*Tons Basin*			
	Ma	*Me*	*L*	*All*	*Ma*	*Me*	*L*	*All*	*Ma*	*Me*	*L*	*All*
Irrigation	38.7	82.5	100.0	63.0	44.5	64.6	99.7	53.3	59.3	88.5	100.0	81.8
HYVs	80.6	80.0	81.3	79.8	11.5	37.5	50.0	25.2	56.0	77.0	78.1	66.2
Fertilizers	57.4	63.6	63.3	61.6	88.5	98.0	100.0	93.9	62.6	98.4	100.0	85.1
Treatment												
Land	16.1	17.5	25.0	15.0	—	6.3	33.4	4.2	—	1.6	14.1	3.8
Seeds	14.5	27.5	25.0	18.7	—	10.4	41.7	5.7	—	11.5	28.1	8.1
Pesticides	14.5	30.0	37.5	23.8	19.2	72.9	100.00	48.5	—	6.6	20.3	5.4
Thresher	38.7	46.3	56.3	43.2	—	1.6	—	0.4	—	—	—	—

Ma = marginal
Me = medium
L = large landholdings

Source: Sharma, 1998, p. 168.

Farmers have perceived the significance of irrigation and are trying their best to irrigate their fields. It is evident from Table 18.3 that more than half of the households of the Chhatisgarh basin, two-thirds of the Betul-Chhindwara plateau and more than three-fourths of the Tons basin practice irrigation. This proportion varies with the size of holdings. As a rule, proportion of irrigating households is lower in case of marginal and small holdings than their averages and much lower than the proportion of medium and large holdings. This proportion also varies with the community. Scheduled Castes (SC) are at bottom while backward communities are at top in this respect.

19

MICRO MARKETING OF VEGETABLES
An Empirical Study

M.I. SIDDIQUI

Introduction

Agricultural marketing in general and vegetable marketing in particular has been neglected in India and elsewhere. This is more so in case of marketing from rural production centre to distant consumption centres. Vegetable marketing, a minuscule of agricultural marketing, originating in the village or town on the fringe area of a city is still invisible in the prolific literature on agricultural economics.

Micro marketing may be ascribed to the distributive channels of an individualised nature. Marginal and small farmers generally develop, on their own, multi-tiered channels for the sale of their produce. How these are developed? Do these conform the notion of market integration in a traditional manner? How and why individual growers manage the sale of their produce in distant consumption centres? This set of questions provides the basic contours of the present study. Analogously, the following hypotheses form the core of this chapter.

— Micro marketing by the growers is efficient, and,
— Unidirectional yet divergent price movements in the city and distant markets cause diversion from one market to the other.

The first hypothesis needs a little elab7oration. Marketing by vegetable growers is generally price efficient. Less is supplied to the local markets at lower price. Conversely, more supply is made to these markets if the prices go up. Since there is no question of holding back the stock due to perishability, the rest finds the way to distant markets. However, the elasticity of supply for local markets is not as strong as it is in the case of distant markets.

The other hypothesis is reflected by the following figure:

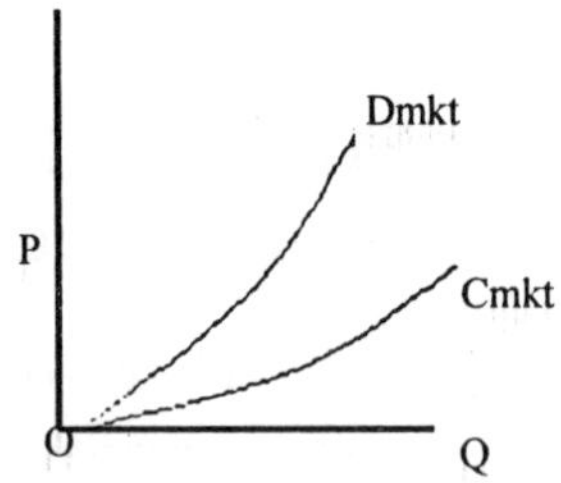

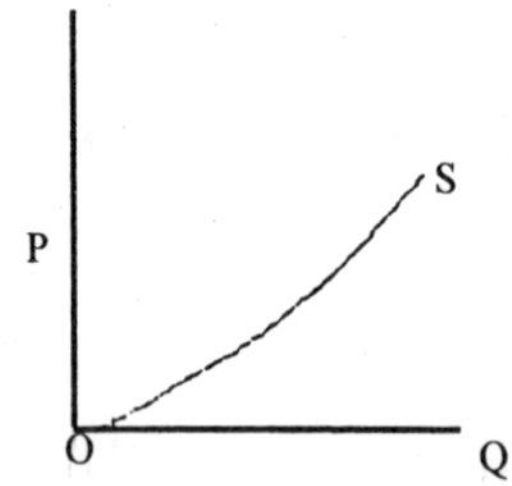

Divergent unidirectional price movements in distant and local city markets are given by Dmkt and Cmkt respectively. The gap between PDmkt and PCmkt makes supply responsive. Hence

$$QDmkt = fP\,(Dmkt - Cmkt).$$

where QDmkt, PDmkt and PCmkt are quantity supplied to distant market, price in distant market and price in local city market respectively. However, *ceteris paribus* assumption is implicit in both the hypotheses.

Data Base

The collection of data for the empirical analysis in the present study pertains to both the categories viz. primary and secondary Census data is not of much use as the Report lacks information on the area selected for the study. Official village records of the civic body and land records popularly known as Khasara and Khatauni have provided secondary data. Moreover quantitative as well qualitative information about the produce of various crops, sale quantum at local and other markets, area leased-in, transportation and its cost, periodicity of produce transportation etc. are the fruit of numerous visits to the production centre. While conducting the survey, questionnaire method has been pursued to record the responses of vegetables growers-*cum*-sellers, at different locales used for marketing purposes. Simple equations and functions have been applied in an attempt to draw specific inferences.

Brief Profile of Production Centre

Since the area of study namely, Thiriya has some distinctive characteristics, its locale and description shall go a long way in driving home the points inferred from the analysis.

The village is barely 8 kms. from the city and, therefore, is a fringe area. The land used for agricultural purpose may be categorised into three categories—land situated in the village itself, holdings leased-in from non-cultivating owners near the highway—a link road connects it with the village and, land owned and leased out by the cantonment allottees to the farmers of Thiriya.

Another distinctive feature is the crops grown on these lands. Since owner cultivators are either marginal or small farmers, they grow vegetables on more than 4/5 area and only 1/5 land is under foodgrains. Village land simply cannot sustain large population. The farmers, therefore, lease-in land from other cultivators and cantonment lease. These rented holdings vary between medium and large ones.

Thirdly, land falling under all the three categories is irrigated by own means. In the village and surrounding area, pump sets are generally used for irrigation while the cantonment area land has the facility of energised tubewells. In a sense, assured irrigation facility is a common feature. Uneconomic holdings from the view point of foodgrain production on the one hand and assured means of irrigation on the other have been catalytic in motivating farmers for vegetable cultivation.

Land-use pattern shows a shift from foodgrains to vegetable cultivation.

Again this is because of uneconomic size of land holdings in the village. Farmers generally grow bittergourd, bottlegourd, potato, tomato, cauliflower, brinjal and beans. Seeds are usually obtained from crop retention method or purchased from the local markets. High yielding variety of seeds is less affordable.

Fourthly, vegetable prices are more remunerative and therefore foodgrain cultivation is relegated to an insignificant position.

Another interesting aspect is related to the use of fertilizers. Most of the farmers sparingly use chemical fertilizers and compost. They have replaced both these by municipal solid waste which they get from various dumping grounds in the city. All vegetable growers use solid waste as the base fertilizer and chemical ones are applied for top dressing purpose. Few growers also use "*Khaddi*" (slaughter waste) for fertilization, which is purchased at nominal price from the nearby buffalo slaughter house. Surprisingly their yield is not affected in the absence of chemical fertilizers.

Lastly, village lacks the required labour force and thus hires from the *Adda* (labour market) situated across the highway which is only 2 kms. from the village. Wage rate in the village is high as compared to that of prevailing in the other labour markets. Most of the labour, on these two counts, is hired from other than the village.

Analysis

Distributive Channels of Marketing

Marketing system develops as per the level of development in a region. It is generally categorised into three levels—markets having low cost distribution of staple food to low income consumers, transitory phase from subsistence to commercialization, and marketing pattern influenced by consumption pattern.

There are, however, three distinctive streams of marketing which originate from the production centre. First is the local bulk sale centres near the village; second is the supply to the nearby city vegetable market and third related with grower-*cum*-trader marketing to the distant markets such as markets in Punjab. The flow chart showing these distributive channels of marketing is presented below:

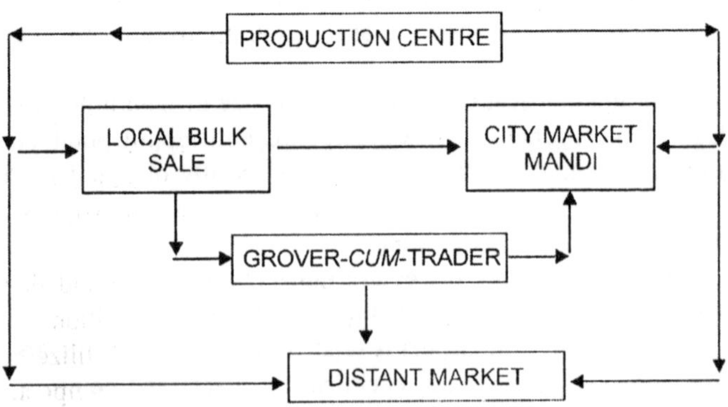

Vegetables grown in the village find the way to local bulk sale points in the vicinity of the village. They generally sell either at the road side approaching the village or near the highway. At these two places mostly bulk buyers purchase the lot. Second channel to sell the produce is the city market, just 10 kms. from the village. The growers sell the lot through the commission agents (*Aarhtis*) at their *aarhat*. Most of the vegetables like tomato, beans, brinjals, etc. are sold in the lots known as "*Dhadis*", that is, five kgs. Only potato or onion are sold in the lots of *Boris*—a weight of 80 kgs. This is an important channel. Third channel has two streams—one is that where the cultivator himself loads his large produce in the trucks and takes to distant markets. It is sold in the vegetable *mandis* through local commission agents, the other stream is the one where small growers pool their produce and also buy the lots of other small farmers to transport the total quantity to some distant market. This last mentioned channel is explored and ventured into only when they came to know about the price in distant market which is substantially higher than the price prevailing in the local city market. The more wide the gap between two prices, the more quantity is shipped to distant market. But this trading activity is occasional and does not conform a regular periodicity. Thus supply to local *mandis* is not a specific function of the price while it is a singular function of price in the case of a distant market. The last as well the least outlet of marketing is that of retailing their produce, by the grower himself, in a nearby market. A small quantity finds its way through this channel. Mostly marginal farmers prefer it. However, this option is exercised by small and medium farmers only when they require a small amount in cash immediately.

Why a distant market like that of Punjab is more lucrative for vegetable growers? Certainly because of the higher prices and also due to the fact that in these markets the percentage of consumer income devoted to food expenditure is high. Therefore the era of the establishment of separate markets for fruits and vegetables must be associated with linking the rural production and distant consumption centre.

Market channels outlined for vegetables are slightly different from the one's for foodgrains and cash crops existing even in backward regions. The usual retainer or payment-in-kind and contractual system commonly pervasive in case of paddy and wheat cannot be extended to vegetable crops. Institutional factors usually shift the tilt of farmers' attitude in favour of cash crops because "in response to a favourable relative price or yield rate, the surplus may take the form of a cash crop, with a higher proportion of cultivated land being devoted to such crops".

The form of market organization for commercial crops is conditioned by a number of forces, such as, those pertaining to conditions and relations of primary production and those related to manners in which crops reach out. However, commonality in the set of forces shaping market organization be ruled out. The nature and type of commercial crops lead to differentiation. Some of the prevailing system like that of contractual or auction on the farm do not confirm in case of market organization for vegetables. Moreover, institutional arrangements are generally missing in the vegetable cultivation activities.

The question which may be posed at this juncture is: what should be the market organization? It is generally agreed upon that it should encompass structure-conduct-performance. However micro marketing of vegetables is primarily influenced by the economic results flowing from "the system in terms of temporal and spatial pricing efficiency" and affects the nature of competition. It is basically oriented towards taking advantage of market margins including price spread for various levels of out station markets. This, in turn, depends upon the cost factor for a producer.

Inter-Relationships

Following are the relationships formulated from observed patterns in the area of study. These are divided into two categories, namely, equations and functions. Let us first consider the equations.

Supply Equations

$$Q_t = Q_{lbs} + Q_{cm} + Q_{dm} \quad \ldots(1)$$

Assuming retail outlet is negligible

Hence

$$Q_{lbs} = Q_t - (Q_{cm} + Q_{dm}) \quad \ldots(2)$$
$$Q_{cm} = Q_t - (Q_{lbs} + Q_{dm}) \quad \ldots(3)$$
$$Q_{dm} = Q_t - (Q_{lbs} + Q_{cm}) \quad \ldots(4)$$

where Q_t, Q_{lbs} Q_{cm} and Q_{dm} are total Quantity, Quantity marketed through local bulk sale points, Quantity marketed through city market or *mandi* and Quantity channelled to Distant markets respectively. Equation (1) presents aggregative figure while equations 2-4 are obtained by simple algebraic manipulations.

Now is the turn for the functions

Functions

$$Q_{dm} = f P\,(DM\text{–}CM) \ldots..1 \quad \Rightarrow \quad \text{Assuming } P_{dm} > P_{cm}$$

$Q_{cm} = f\,P\,(CM)\ldots\ldots.2$ ⇒ On *ceteris paribus* assumption
$Q_{lbs} = f\,P_{cm} - (T+C)\ldots\ldots 3$ ⇒ *f* shows inverse relation

where Q_{lbs}, P_{dm}, P_{cm}, T and C are Price in distant market, Price in city market, Transport and Commission rate at *Aarhat*. The functional relationship between dependent and independent variables i.e. quantities and prices are of a direct nature except in equation (3). It means there shall be unidirectional movement in the variables.

Conclusions

Quantitative flow of vegetables is peculiar. During the winter and summer seasons, ninety per cent of total quantity is supplied locally. These are crops of rainy seasons which are generally supplied to the distant markets. Hence the supply pattern vis-à-vis markets is totally reversed during the rainy seasons. Few vegetables like potato, chilly are sold in the local market while other like bittergourd and brinjal are supplied to distant markets.

Divergent price movements in the local and distant markets is the leading factor in the supply of vegetables to distant markets in Punjab and Jammu.

Another factor responsible for supply to distant markets is the absorption capacity of the local markets. Specific vegetables grown in the area like bittergourd and brinjals etc. have a larger supply than the demand for these in the local markets. Winter and summer crops are generally sold either at the bulk sale points, which are situated on both sides of the village, or at the wholesale market. However crops grown in the rainy season are totally sold in the distant markets where these fetch a higher price.

Growers-*cum*-traders keep themselves posted about the prices prevailing in the markets of Jammu, Ludhiana and Amritsar in Punjab, Banaras in U.P. They arrange trucks on their own and take the produce to these markets. The usual quantum is four to five trucks every day. Last year they pocketed a differential sum of atleast Rupees four thousand after deducting transport cost on every truck load of brinjals.

References

Bhaduri, A, "Class Relations and Commercialisation in Indian Agriculture. A Study in the Post-Independence Agrarian Reforms of U.P." in Raj *et al.* (eds.) *op. cit*

Duvvury, N. "Tobacco Trading and Forms of Market Organisation: A case study of Guntur District, in Raj *et al.* (eds.) *op. cit.*, p. 273.

Lele, Uma (1973), *Foodgrain Marketing in India*, Popular, Bombay, pp. 11-12.

Nagaraj, K.(1985), "Marketing Structure for Paddy and Arecanut in South Kanara: A Comparison of Markets in a Backward Agricultural District" in K.R. Raj *et al.* (eds). *Essays on the Commercialisation of Indian Agriculture*, O.U.P., Delhi, pp. 247-272.

Ravi, P.C., P.K. Mandanna and P.G. Chengappa, "New Agricultural Policy and Emerging issues in Agricultural Marketing", in Gowda and Subrahmanya (eds.) *op cit.* p. 229.

Shrivastava, O.P. (1996), *Agricultural Economics*, Rawat Publications, Jaipur, p. 234.

Subha Rao, K. (1986), "Agricultural Marketing" in *ISAE*, Indian Agricultural Development Since Independence, Oxford & IBH, New Delhi, p. 324.

Urs, D.S. Devaraj (1996), "Agricultural Market Development Strategies: Experiences and Future Directions" in M.V. Srinivasa Gowda & Susheela Subrahmanya (eds.), *Studies in Agricultural Development*, Deep & Deep, New Delhi, p. 198.

20

INTEGRATED PEST MANAGEMENT FOR THE SUSTAINABLE DEVELOPMENT OF AGRICULTURE AND THE ENVIRONMENT

ABDURAHEEM K. & ANISUR REHMAN

Introduction

The overwhelming preoccupation of agricultural development is mostly with the questions of *growth, equity* and *sustainity*. The issues of long-term ecological and agricultural concern such as conservation of biodiversity, preservation of agroecosystem, control of environmental pollution, public-health hazards, etc. were neglected for long time. Due to intensive attempt to enhance food production for feeding rapidly increasing population, high pressure was put on land in various means. The growing human and animal populations are making increasing demand on natural resources resulting in the exploitation of resources in an unsustainable manner (Swaminathan, 1991). Indiscriminate use of synthetic pesticides, critical modern input, has become an established global practice. Both the chemical fertilizers and pesticides increasingly polluting agricultural products and infertile the agroecosystem. Since the wide introduction of organochlorines in the early 50's farmers have heavily relied on the chemical pesticides for pest control. The veritable explosion in the wide use of these harmful chemical has led to many problems like development of resistance to the pesticide in the target species, pest resurgence, secondary pest outbreak and above all the environmental pollution.

Harmful Effects of Residual Pesticides

The extensive use of residual pesticides is the most serious one and needs to be tackled on a war footing level. The number of persistent chemicals that are sold in the country and the indiscriminate use of pesticides for crop protection are matter of grave concern to the public and the policy makers. The pesticide pollution in different parts of the country has been documented and even the pesticide residue in food chain, in vegetables, grains, eggs, fish, meat, milk, edible oil and in breast milk have been detected. The most productive agricultural and aquaculture regions in the country have been showing severe pesticide pollution. Kuttanad, the rice bowl of Kerala is facing serious fish diseases which had been caused by pesticide poisoning, and several useful organisms and the natural enemies of crop pests have also vanished with the excessive use of the pesticides. There are several cases of insects developing resistance to insecticides and farmers resorting to excessive use of the chemicals in vain. The over reliance on synthetic pesticide to agriculture without a proper understanding of the various consequences of the changes introduced into the conventional agricultural system may lead to an era of *agricultural disaster* in the long run rather than to an era of *agricultural prosperity*. The enormous success of chemical pesticides has tended to mask the significance of biological and cultural control despite early warning that over reliance on chemical control could have disastrous side effects. The undegradable residues of the pesticides persist in food stuffs and in the environment will be a potential threat to life supporting system.

The data in Table 20.1 reveal an enormous increase in the chemicals in agriculture overtime as the consumption of fertilizer jumped from 130.8 thousand tonnes in 1955-56 to 12,546.2 thousand tonnes in 1990-91 (96 times) and the consumption of pesticides boosted from 24,320 tonnes in 1970-71 to 69,789 tonnes in 1990-91 (2.9 times). Though in 1989-90 the consumption of pesticides was 91,507 tonnes. A considerable portion of these chemicals, alongwith agricultural and agro-based industrial wastes, has found its way to the rivers and underground aquifers and has created alarming situation of water pollution causing threat to human and animal lives. Consequently the government had to take huge capital consuming projects like Ganga Purification Project to project the environment and maintain ecology (Srivastava, 1995).

Table 20.1: Increasing Consumption of Fertilizers and Pesticides in India – 1955-1991

Year	*Consumption of Fertilizers ('000 tonnes)*				*Consumption of Pesticides (Tonnes)*
	N	*P*	*K*	*Total*	
1955-56	107.5	13.0	10.3	130.8	—
1960-61	201.7	53.1	29.0	283.8	—
1965-66	574.8	132.5	77.3	784.6	—
1970-71	1479.0	541.3	236.3	2256.3	24320
1975-76	2148.6	466.8	278.3	2893.7	42327
1980-81	3678.1	1213.6	623.9	5515.6	62000
1985-86	5660.8	2005.2	808.1	8474.1	—
1990-91	7997.2	3221.0	1328.0	12546.2	69789

Source: 1. Fertiliser Statistics (1992-93).
2. Pesticides Information (1992).

Observations and Findings

Certain experiments conducted by the present author on the persistence of residual toxicity of some chemical pesticides like fenitrothion, malathion, milphos and sevin on an insect pest named *Gastrallus indicus* reveals that residual toxicity of the pesticides like malathion and fenitrothion persists and remain potent year after year. The relative toxicities of the residual films of these insecticides on the pest can be deduced as fenitrothion > malathion > milphos in the following decreasing order, 1.77 > 1.07 > 1> 0.56 respectively.

Table 20.2: Relative Toxicity of Different Insecticides against Larvae of *G. indicus*

Insecticides	*Leathal Dose (LD-90)*	*Relative Toxicity*
Fenitrothion	0.110%	1.770
Malathion	0.183%	1.077
Milphos	0.195%	1.000
Sevin	0.346%	0.564

Several evils are associated with the widespread use of synthetic pesticides in agriculture. Social awareness of these harmful effects has begun to develop among scientists, manufacturers and policy makers but farmers and consumers are by and large unconcerned and unaware. In so far as agricultural scientists are concerned this awareness is abundantly reflected in the latest shift of emphasis from prophylactic use of pesticides to their *need based* application and integrated pest management. But the awareness among farmers and consumers required *war footing level.* Farmers are now being asked to restrict the use of chemical pesticides sparingly, strictly according to recommendations and only when the pest population has reached the critical size.

Increasing use of pesticides has caused contamination of soil, air and surface and groundwaters besides affecting the crop plants and their products. The widely used *BHC, DDT, Aldrin and Chlordan* are resistant to degradation. They are thus able to thrive for long period in the environment and accumulate in animals. This persistence alongwith their animal carcinogenicity has caused concerned that exposed human to cancer risk. In plants effects like phyto toxicity, pollen sterility, tainting, growth retardation and accumulation of poisonous residues are noticed by the use of certain agrochemicals. Several positive steps have been taken towards this direction to tackle this problem. Integrated pest management and nutrient recycling systems have been advocated widely for the same.

Integrated Pest Management (IPM)

As there is no single method known to the science of pest control which could give an everlasting solution to the challenges posed by the insect pests. Therefore, it becomes imperative to design an integrated pest management in which all suitable control measures such as, biological, mechanical, chemical, cultural methods are blended to minimize the crop damage and for the sustainable development of agriculture and the environment. Judicious use of chemical pesticides as a component of IPM is the safest means of pest control. It is realised that there is an urgent need to evolve a coherent pest management programme that is environmental friendly and yet able to curtail loss. From out of this concern has emerged a new strategy called the IPM. Keeping this in view IPM is to manipulate the pest population and their natural enemies in a compatible manner so that it remains below threshold levels in economically and ecologically sound manner. The various component of the IPM practices comprises cultural, mechanical, physical, varietal, pest surveillance, quarantine, forecasting of outbreak, suppression programmes, chemical and other control methods like development of resistant varieties of crops etc.

Conclusions

What is need, in the present context is a sustainable agricultural development strategy that should not eat into natural assets. It is a process in which the exploitation of available resources by endogenous choice, in a compatible manner in which the economics equity and social justice, to meet development and environmental needs of present and future generation. The ultimate goal of sustainable agricultural and environmental development should be the improvement of the food and nutritional security of the country alongwith the environmental and health security of the nation. Therefore, there is an urgent need to promote sustainable and environmentally sound development effort to preserve our agroecosystem. Sustainability may be defined as successful management of all the resources refers to maintaining a fragile balance between productivity functions and conservation practice through identification and monitoring of problem areas and call for application of alternative techniques. Timely and reliable *Geoinformation* on natural resources is a prerequisite for planning the strategy for sustainable development.

Aside from all projections of the future contemporary issues like, rapid population growth and the necessity to live within the *carrying capacity* of the biosphere, to make the global economics more efficient in the use of natural resources and to reduce biotic pressures. Population stabilization, efficient and wise use of resources, prevention of pollution, integrated environmental system management, social and cultural changes, environmental awareness among the farmers and consumers etc. are some of the important elements of the sustainable development.

Prospects of our planet in the twenty-first century will be inextricably bound with these challenges. The industrialised countries in the vanguard of technological civilization have been both the leading beneficiaries and the principal contributors to the global risk and imbalances progress has produced. And their responses to the challenges which pose to the future of man will be critical if not decisive. But the developed countries however wealthy and powerful to deal with the challenges in some extent. The developing countries make up the majority of the world population share the *global risk* and their cooperation is essential to mitigate or avert these risks.

References

Fertilizer Statistics, 1992-93.

Srivastava Pankaj (1995), Environmental Aspects of Agricultural Development in India. *Agricultural Situation in India*, Vol. II, No. 4, pp. 195-198.

Pesticide Information, 1992.

Swaminathan M.S., Maladies and Remedies. *The Hindu*, Survey of the Environment, 1991.

21

WATER RESOURCE AND IRRIGATION DEVELOPMENT IN NORTH BIHAR PLAIN

SHAMSUL HAQUE SIDDIQUI

Irrigation plays an important role in the form of input in the process of agricultural production. The successful growth of crops is generally governed by a regulated supply of soil moisture. Irrigation also supports technological factors like fertilizers and improved seeds. The farmers having better irrigation facilities like tubewells, canals and other sources are not unduly depend on the vagaries of monsoon. North Bihar Plain has abundant water and groundwater resources. There are many perennial rivers supplying water for irrigation. The author has tried his best to exploit this potentiality through various means like canals, tubewells and other sources. An attempt is also made to assess the extent of irrigation and its progress in the study area during the period 1965-66 to 1990-91.

In 1965-66 irrigated area accounted for 5.05 lakh hectares which increased to 14.37 lakh hectares in 1990-91 and recorded a progressive increase of the net area irrigated by different sources in the region, in which tubewells hold the highest percentage (51.02) of the total irrigated area whereas canal irrigation by 23.00 per cent and other sources 22 per cent of the total irrigated area of the region. The data regarding the area irrigated by canals, tubewells and other sources have been collected from various issues of Annual Season and Crop Reports, Bihar through figures and from official records of the Directorate of Statistics and Evaluation, Government of Bihar, Patna.

The alluvial tract of North Bihar Plain forms a part of the central Ganga basin. The tract is composed of sand, silt and clay materials. The sediments attain a thickness of as much as 2,500 metres in Saran,

Vaishali and Muzaffarpur districts. These alluvial formations are prolific water bearing horizons under groundwater occur under confined conditions in the deeper reaches.

In central parts, around Begusarai the confined aquifers exhibit considerable salinity. The sediments show a marked increase in percentage of granular zones northwards. The Central Ground Water Board which monitors the water levels of shallow aquifers through 100 observation wells spread over entire North Bihar Plain has pointed out that the water levels are comparatively shallower (less than 5 metres) in all alluvial tract.

In Ghaghara, Gandak, Burhi Gandak and Kosi sub-basins of North Bihar Plain the underground water level fluctuations are as follows:

In the Ghaghara basin underground water level fluctuation ranges between 0.31 to 5.10 metres depth. In the Gandak basin it ranges between 0.79 to 7.00 metres whereas in Burhi Gandak basin ranges from 0.73 to 8.11 metres. The entire command area of Kosi is suitable for high yielding tubewells as well as shallow tubewells. Kosi command area is one of the richest groundwater zone. The river Kosi was flowing through Araria and Purnia about 125 years ago. The river has shifted about 112 kilometres westward direction during this period to its present coarse. Most of irrigation tubewells have been completed within 60 to 80 metres depth. State tubewells have gone to a depth of 104 metres in Purnia. At Barari and Manihari (near the river Ganga) depth of groundwater is more than 6 metres below ground level after monsoon. In command area of Kosi canal, groundwater level is ranging between 1 to 3 metres below ground level after monsoon but during the summer it is 2 to 4 metres below the ground level.

Districts of Saharsa, West Champaran, Gopalganj, Purnia and Saran have substantial areas with groundwater level being below 2 metres during November. These areas can pose problems for *rabi* crop in future due to progressive rise of watertable as a consequence of surface irrigation. The watertable is normally 2 to 6 metres below ground level in winter and 2 to 8 metres in summer. The use of underground water for agricultural purposes is much higher in the north than in the south Bihar.

Irrigation Development

Irrigation in the North Bihar Plain is provided through two different sources: firstly it is practiced by tapping subsoil water through tubewells and pump sets and secondly, by channelising surface water from rivers, canals and other sources. The main source of irrigation in the region is from the canals, tubewells and other sources like wells and tanks. The gradual increase of the net area irrigated by different sources in the study area is given in Table 21.1. It may be seen from Table 21.1 that more than 96.00 per cent of the net irrigated area of North Bihar Plain in 1990-91 was irrigated by canals, tubewells and other sources. It has also seen that tubewells alone irrigate 51.02 per cent of the net irrigated area whereas canals irrigate 23 per cent and other sources 22 per cent of the net irrigation area of the region.

It is quite clear from Table 21.1 that an appreciable increase in tubewells and canals irrigated area during the five points of time. It may be seen from Table 21.1 that 7.21 lakh hectares of irrigated land was added between 1965-66 to 1975-76 and 2.09 lakh hectares from 1975-76 to 1990-91. It is also seen that there was a significant increase in the net irrigated area of 9.31 lakh hectares between the periods 1965-66 to 1990-91. There has been a gradual decline in irrigation from tanks and other sources in the region.

Table 21.2 shows that district-wise distribution of irrigated area under three major sources i.e. proportion of area irrigated by canals, tubewells and other sources. The Table also shows intensity of irrigation with respect to the net irrigated area in each of the nineteen districts of North Bihar Plain for the year 1990-91 which is depicted in Fig. 21.1. The overall

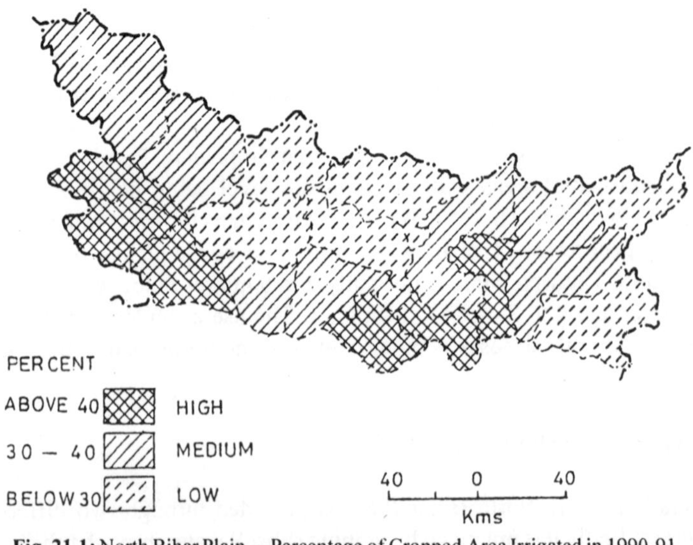

Fig. 21.1: North Bihar Plain —Percentage of Cropped Area Irrigated in 1990-91

Table 21.1: Source-wise Irrigated Area in the North Bihar Plain

(Per cent to the total)

Years	*1965-66*		*1970-71*		*1975-76*		*1980-81*		*1990-91*	
Sources	*Net Area Irrigated (in hectares)*	*Percent*	*Net Area Irrigated (in hectares)*	*Percent*	*Net Area Irrigated (in hectares)*	*Percent*	*Net Area Irrigated (in hectares)*	*Percent*	*Net Area Irrigated (in hectares)*	*Percent*
Canals	156,926	31.03	294,194	41.08	300,199	24.46	476,200	37.31	330,469	23.00
Tubewells	14,776	2.92	97,755	13.65	526,798	42.93	486,466	38.11	733,103	51.02
Tanks	49,715	9.83	46,142	6.44	47,076	3.84	29,316	2.30	57,149	3.98
Other sources	284,248	56.22	278,024	38.83	353,109	28.77	284,344	22.28	316,100	22.00
Total	**505,665**	**100.00**	**716,115**	**100.00**	**1,227,102**	**100.00**	**1,276,326**	**100.00**	**1,436,821**	**100.00**

Source: (i) Official Records of Directorate of Statistics and Evaluation, Government of Bihar, Patna.
(ii) Annual Season and Crop Reports, Directorate of Statistics and Evaluation, Government of Bihar, Patna.

Table 21.2: District-wise Distribution of Irrigated Area by Various Sources in North Bihar Plain, 1990-91

(Figures in Per cent)

Name of District	*Canal*	*Tubewells*	*Other Sources*	*Total Irrigated Area to the Total Cropped Area*
Saran	11.68	74.34	13.98	43.7
Siwan	24.02	66.01	9.97	44.7
Gopalganj	12.86	68.91	18.23	50.5
East Champaran	44.68	39.98	15.34	39.1
West Champaran	68.20	6.67	25.13	39.0
Sitamarhi	0.23	84.06	15.51	28.1
Muzaffarpur	4.36	78.56	16.28	27.9
Vaishali	3.19	67.01	30.80	36.2
Samastipur	—	94.62	5.38	38.5
Khagaria	—	75.70	24.30	53.0
Begusarai	—	80.65	19.35	47.7
Darbhanga	37.95	30.05	61.95	24.8
Madhubani	8.34	29.93	61.73	19.5
Saharsa	43.58	34.00	22.42	39.4
Katihar	21.80	66.71	11.49	25.0
Madhepura	49.10	33.55	17.35	44.5
Araria	40.50	6.50	53.00	30.0
Kishanganj	22.22	9.09	68.69	22.1
Purnia	54.70	33.04	26.05	30.0
Total	**23.00**	**51.02**	**25.98**	**32.6**

intensity of irrigation on the basis of percentage share of the net irrigated area to the district-wise total cropped area can be judged from Table 21.2 in which the share of all the nineteen districts with respect to different sources of irrigation is presented. The districts have more than 40 per cent of the total cropped area under irrigation fall under high grade of irrigation availability. The districts having an irrigated area between 30 to 40 per cent of the total cropped area are under medium grade while the area with less than 30 per cent of the total cropped area under irrigation are placed under low grade in terms of irrigation.

There are six districts, namely, Khagaria, Gopalganj, Begusarai, Siwan, Madhepura and Saran which have high extent of irrigated area. The irrigated area in these districts varies from 40 to 53 per cent of the total cropped area. The high spread area is seen lying in the extreme western part of the region and southern margin along the north bank of river Ganga. The area with medium extent of irrigation is seen in the north central part and north eastern part of the region and is covered by the districts West Champaran,

East Champaran, Vaishali and Samastipur. The districts lie in the eastern part is Saharsa, Araria and Purnia. Low irrigation spread is found in the north central part and eastern margin of the region where Muzaffarpur, Sitamarhi, Madhubani and Darbhanga make a compact block. There are two districts namely, Kishangaj and Katihar fall under low irrigation found in extreme eastern part of the region.

Canals

There are many canals in the North Bihar Plain but the important ones are Tribeni canal and Western Kosi canal. Tribeni canal takes its water from the left bank of the river Gandak at Tribeni (Bhainsa Lotan). Canal is the most effective means of the utilization of the surface water flow in the region. It irrigated 23 per cent, 3.30 lakh hectares of land in the region. In this region West Champaran ranks first for canal irrigation. The Western Kosi canal lies in the western part of the Kosi river and provides irrigation to 2.74 lakh hectares in the Saharsa, Madhepura, Araria, Purnia, Katihar and Kishanganj. It has been seen from Table 21.1 that canal irrigation is absent in Samastipur, Khagaria and Begusarai. There is vast scope for the utilization of surface water resource through canal system in these districts. There are four districts, namely, Sitamarhi, Muzaffarpur, Vaishali and Madhubani have a lower share with less than 10 per cent of their cultivated area under canal irrigation.

Tubewells

Tubewells irrigation is of recent origin in India and the rate of its diffusion to every corner of the country has been very fast. It has changed the cropping pattern of many parts of the country which were earlier beyond the spread of irrigation water. Tubewells irrigation holds the highest position in this area. It comes under the category of minor irrigation scheme based on the utilization of underground water. This region is suitable for the utilization of underground water through tubewells and wells.

The net area irrigated by tubewells in the North Bihar Plain was 4.86 lakh hectares or 38.11 per cent of the total irrigated area in 1980-81 which rose to 7.33 or 51.02 per cent in 1990-91. This indicates a sharp increase in tubewells irrigation in this region. The district-wise variation of tubewells irrigation is very large as shown in Table 21.2. Five districts of the region namely, Samastipur, Sitamarhi, Begusarai, Muzaffarpur and Khagaria receive more than 75 per cent of their irrigation water from tubewells. Samastipur district has received the highest percentage of irrigation from tubewell (94.62%) in this region. Irrigation from tubewells is extensive in the district of Saran, Gopalganj, Vaishali, Katihar and Siwan where they provide irrigation more than 65 per cent of the net irrigated area. Irrigation from tubewells is very poor in district of West Champaran, Araria, Kishanganj and Purnia where they provide irrigation less than 10 per cent of the net irrigated area. In the remaining five districts – East Champaran, Darbhanga, Madhubani, Saharsa and Madhepura, tubewells command 30 to 40 per cent of the net irrigated area. It may be seen that tubewells irrigation is gaining ground in every district of the region.

Other Sources

Whenever irrigation from canal and tubewells is inadequate, irrigation from other sources acts as a good supplement. The other sources including tanks, wells and ponds irrigated 3.73 lakh hectares or 25.98 per cent of the net irrigated in 1990-91 in the region. There are four districts namely, Kishanganj, Araria, Madhubani and Darbhanga which depend heavily on irrigation from other sources. The other important are the districts of Vaishali, Purnia and West Champaran where irrigation from other sources ranges from 25 to 30 per cent of the net irrigated area. In the remaining districts less than one-fourth of the total cultivated area is irrigated by other sources.

Major Cereals Area Under Irrigation

With the expansion of irrigation facilities the area under major cereals that received irrigation has also increased in the North Bihar Plain. It may be seen from Table 21.3 that rice and wheat have registered regular increase in the irrigated area from 1980-81 to 1990-91. The irrigated area under rice was 23.26 per cent in 1980-81 which increased to 44.0 per cent in 1990-91. It may be seen from Table 21.3 that there has been a sharp increase in irrigated area under rice in the region. The percentage of total irrigated area under wheat was 71.46 per cent in 1980-81 and rising to 78.2 per cent in 1990-91. The irrigated area under rice and wheat have increased much faster than any other crop in the region. The percentage of total irrigated area under maize and barley have declined in the region. The increase in the irrigated area under rice and wheat may be seen as a sign of farmers awakening and the beginning of cereals revolution which is taking place in the agricultural development of the North Bihar Plain.

Table 21.3: Irrigated Area Under Cereals in North Bihar Plain

(*Figure in per cent*)

Crops	*1980-81 Percentage to Total Cropped Area*	*1990-91 Percentage to Total Cropped Area*
Rice	23.26	44.00
Wheat	71.46	78.20
Maize	12.06	9.20
Barley	15.56	2.20

The results drawn from this study indicate that there has been a gradual increase in the total irrigated area in the North Bihar Plain due to new construction of canals and also increase in the number of tubewells and pump sets. Before the onset of Green Revolution irrigation from other sources shared a handsome percentage of net irrigated area accounting for 56.22 per cent in the region followed by canal at the second position accounting to 31.03 per cent. A sharp increase has since then been recorded in tubewells irrigation. Tubewells hold first position with 51.02 per cent to total irrigated area in the region. Rice and wheat are the only crops which recorded manifold increase in its area under irrigation. It is heavily irrigated by different sources and witnessed an increase of 23.26 per cent to 44.0 per cent rice and increase of 71.6 per cent to 78.2 per cent wheat from the period 1980-81 to 1990-91 in the region. More than 74 per cent of the net irrigated area of North Bihar Plain in 1990-91 was irrigated by canals and tubewells. The supply of diesel oil at reasonable rate will further help the farmers to operate the pump sets at the time of irrigation. Canals do not have adequate supply of water during the dry season owing to which crops suffer. If the facility of canal water is provided to the farmers throughout the year it is bound to yield beneficial results.

References

Ahmed, E. (1965), *Water Resources of Bihar*, Ranchi University, Ranchi.

Jha, U.M. (1984), *Irrigation and Agricultural Development*, New Delhi.

Mohammad, A. (ed.) (1979), *Dynamics of Agricultural Development in India*, Delhi.

Siddiqui, S.H. (1989), The Pattern of Irrigation in the North Bihar Plain, *Geographical Review of India*, Calcutta, Vol. 52, No. 4.

Waterlogged Areas in India, Unpublished Report of Central Ground Water Board, New Delhi, May, 1974.

22

LAND-USE CHANGES AND FOOD CROP PRODUCTIVITY IN INDIA
A Spatio-Temporal Analysis

H.N. MISRA & RAJANISH KUMAR

Land as basic resource base has very heavily influenced the economic fabric of India. The economy of India is predominantly agrarian as agriculture alone contributes nearly 31.0 per cent of the net domestic product of India. More than 65.0 per cent of its population depends upon agriculture for its survival. Land-use/land cover and agriculture have undergone vast changes during last millennium. Environmental constraints, social structure, economic compulsions and political decisions have played significant role in bringing about these changes. The purpose of this chapter is to capture the glimpse of changing land-use/land cover type during last four decades (1950-51 to 1990-91), and to evaluate the food crop productivity in the country in historical perspective. This chapter is, thus, divided into four sections. Section one deals with the land-use changes, Section two discusses the historical background of agriculture, and in Section three an analytical and explanatory note on food crop productivity at State level has been presented. Finally in Section four, conclusions and policy implications for sustainable development have been suggested.

Land-use Changes: A Temporal Analysis

Land has been put to a variety of uses. However, there are nine broad categories (see Table 22.1) under which land cover type has been arranged. A perusal of Table 22.1 clearly indicates that major area of land (46.6%) has been devoted to agriculture. It appears that it has almost reached the saturation point because it has increased only by 0.3 per cent during the last two decades. About 33 per cent of the total land should be devoted to the forests. However, forest cover in the past declined with such a staggering proportion that achieving this goal has become a remote possibility. During the last forty years the area under forest cover has moved forward from 14.2 per cent in 1950-51 to 22.3 per cent in 1990-91. Importantly, the area put to non-agricultural uses such as settlements, infrastructure, water bodies, etc. has been increasing continuously as it has gone up from 3.3 per cent in 1950-51 to 7.0 per cent in 1990-91. There has been a continuous decrease in the extent of barren and uncultivable land because of too much pressure due to increasing population. It has declined from 13.4 per cent in 1950-51 to 6.4 per cent in 1990-91.

This indicates the greed of human being to encroach more and more land for various uses, mainly industrial estates and settlements etc. The cultivable wasteland is being reclaimed for agricultural purposes as it has declined from 8.1 per cent to 4.9 per cent during 1950-51 to 1990-91. The traditional practice of farmers of keeping the fallow land to protect the efficiency of soil has also shown a declining trend as land put to this category has come down from 9.9 per cent in 1950-51 to 7.9 per cent in 1990-91.

The permanent pastures and grazing lands, which is common property, has also tapered off as it was 4.7 per cent in 1960-61 but in 1990-91 it was reduced to 3.9 per cent. Even though Government of India have launched massive efforts to promote social forestry, and agro-forestry schemes, etc., the area under miscellaneous trees and groves has not registered any significant increase. Instead, it has further truncated from 7.0 per cent in 1950-51 to 1.2 per cent in 1990-91.

Land-use and Agriculture: A Historical Perspective

Land has continued shaping the economy of India from times immemorial. However, records highlighting land-use/land cover type changes through time are not available in a systematic manner. But there are well documented references which reveal the status of farmers, agricultural practices and irrigation system that have been persisting since the beginning of the tenth century AD (Randhawa, 1980). Ibn-Khurdadba and Ibn-Haukal discussed about people and crops of Sindh and Multan in their books *Kitab-l-Masalik wa-l-Mamalik* and *Kita'bu-l-Masalik Wa-l-Mamalik* which were written in 912AD and 943-968AD

Table 22.1: Land-use Pattern in India – 1950-51 to 1990-91

(*Area in million hectares*)

Sl. No.	*Classification*	*1950-51*	*1960-61*	*1970-71*	*1980-81*	*1990-91*
1.	Forests	40.8 (14.2)	54.05 (18.1)	63.91 (21.0)	67.47 (22.2)	67.99 (22.3)
2.	Area put to Non-Agricultural Uses	9.36 (3.3)	14.84 (5.0)	16.46 (5.4)	19.66 (6.4)	21.22 (7.0)
3.	Barren and Uncultivated Land	38.16 (13.4)	25.91 (12.02)	28.16 (9.3)	19.96 (6.6)	19.66 (6.4)
4.	Permanent Pastures and Other Grazing Lands	6.68 (2.3)	13.97 (4.7)	13.26 (4.4)	11.97 (3.9)	11.80 (3.9)
5.	Land Under Miscellaneous Trees and Grooves	19.83 (7.0)	4.46 (1.5)	4.30 (1.4)	3.60 (1.2)	3.70 (1.2)
6.	Cultivable Waste	22.94 (8.1)	19.21 (6.4)	17.50 (5.8)	16.74 (5.5)	15.01 (4.9)
7.	Old Fallow	17.44 (6.1)	11.18 (3.8)	8.76 (2.9)	9.92 (3.3)	9.59 (3.2)
8.	Current Fallow	10.68 (3.8)	11.64 (3.9)	11.12 (3.5)	14.83 (4.9)	13.81 (4.5)
9.	Net Sown Area	118.75 (41.8)	133.2 (44.6)	140.27 (46.3)	140.00 (46.0)	142.24 (46.6)
10.	Reporting Area	282.32 (100.00)	293.46 (100.00)	303.76 (100.00)	304.15 (100.00)	305.02 (100.00)
11.	Gross Cropped Area	131.89	152.77	165.79	172.63	185.48
12.	Area Sown More than Once	13.14	19.57	25.52	32.63	43.24
13.	Cropping Intensity	111.1	114.7	118.2	123.3	130.4
14.	Gross Irrigated Area	22.56	27.98	38.19	49.78	61.78
15.	Percent of Gross Irrigated Area to Gross Cropped Area	17.1	18.3	23.0	28.8	33.3
16.	Net Area Irrigated	20.85	24.66	31.10	38.72	47.43
17.	Percent Net Area Irrigated to Net Sown Area	17.6	18.5	22.2	27.7	33.3

Source: Directorate of Economics and Statistics, Government of India and Agriculture Statistics in India.

respectively. Nevertheless, Zia-ud-din Barni was presumably the first scholar who pointed out the revolt of *Raiyats* and deterioration of agriculture in India in his book *Tarikh-i-Firozshahi*, written during 1325-1351. He also discussed about the famine during Sultanate period, and efforts made by the Sultan to reclaim the wastelands and thereby improve the agriculture by establishing a department called *Diwan-i-*

Amir-i-Koh. In his travelogue, *Ibn-Batuta* in 1035 AD attempted to present a detailed account of the crops, and cropping period of North India during Sultanate period. The canal system of irrigation was introduced during this period and the opening of Western Yamuna Canal to harness the floodwaters of the Yamuna and the Sutlej rivers in 1355AD is attributed to the initiative of Firoz Shah Tughlak. The system of taxation or irrigation was also introduced by him. The Anantraja Sagar Dam and Porumamilla Tank in Southern India were constructed in 1367 AD. A very graphic account of agriculture during Hindu Kingdom of Vijayanagar and Calicut has been presented by Abdul Razzak in his book *Matla'u-s-Sa'dain*. The dryland irrigation was introduced during the reign of Raja Krishnadevraya (1509-1529) by digging the Koragal and the Basavanna canals. The condition of peasantry was reasonably good during Bahmani Kingdom. The importance of land evaluation was realised by Sultan Jain-ul-Abidin who was also responsible for ordering the reduction of land taxes between 1/4th to 1/7th. This provided a great incentive to peasantry to extend the land under cultivation. Several canals came into existence during this period.

In 16th century wheat was mainly produced in the provinces of Lahore, Multan, Delhi, Agra, Oudh, Allahabad, Malwa and Ajmer; barley was a common crop almost in all the parts of the country except Bengal and Orissa; and rice was mainly produced in Bengal, Orissa, Oudh, Allahabad, Lahore, Khandesh and Kashmir. The book entitled *Ain-i-Akbari* clearly mentions about the three crops of rice which were being produced in a year in Bengal. Few other crops such as millets and pulses were also being grown during this period. Francois Bernier in his book *Travels in the Mughal Empire* described about the crops being grown and also threw light on the land-use/ land cover types in Bengal and Kashmir. The book also discusses the revolt led by Jats and Satnami peasants against unreasonable hike in taxation. The permanent land settlement system introduced by Lord Cornwallis in Bihar, Bengal and Orissa during 1786-1793 brought a very significant change in land tenure system and thereby the crops and productivity. The *Raiyatwari System* introduced by Sir Thomas Munro in 1813 provided great security as well as dignity to the cultivators of Madras and Punjab. Opening of the East Yamuna Canal in 1830 brought significant structural changes in agriculture in North-west India. The Cauvery and the Krishna Delta Schemes, which were introduced during 1836-1838 and 1846-1855 respectively, helped to combat the drought situation in southern India. Likewise, the opening of the Great Ganga Canal and the Lower Ganga Canal constructed in 1854 and in 1878 respectively also helped in ameliorating the famine situation which used to visit frequently in northern India. All these irrigation schemes promoted the production of foodgrains and provided special incentive for larger land area to be brought under cultivation.

The occupancy rights confirmed on cultivators during the tenure of Lord Dalhousie provided great incentive to the tillers of land. The Tenant Act of 1868 helped the farmers of Punjab while settling the claims of the landlords. The East India Irrigation and Canal Company launched a series of schemes for construction of canals during 1869-1894. All these canals were intended to protect the farmers against the recurrent famines. The *Imperial Agricultural Research Institute*, which came into existence in Pusa in 1905, promoted the agriculture in India in a big way. Gradually technology in agriculture also improved and tractor and tubewell irrigation were also introduced to farmlands. The scheme of consolidation of land holdings introduced by *Hubert Calbert* also provided incentive for increased productivity. The Consolidation of Holdings and Prevention of Fragmentation Act was passed in 1948 at the initiative of Gyani Kartar Singh, the then Revenue Minister. It may, however, be mentioned that Green Revolution Technology introduced during 1960's revolutionalized the Indian agriculture as the cropping pattern, crop productivity and efficiency of land changed significantly thereafter.

India has registered very significant increase in crop production, area under crops as well as per hectare yield during the last three decades. A country which was marked by famine and hunger due to poor fertility and low yield has been able to overcome the situation very successfully, and new agricultural technology introduced in the form of Green Revolution has, indeed, played vital role in heralding new era of transformation in agricultural arena. Tables 22.3, 22.4 and 22.5 present the state of the art of area, production and yield of various food crops during 1970-71 and 1995-96. The area under food crops has risen from 111 million hectares in 1970-71 to 114 million hectares in 1990-91 registering an increase of 3 million hectares over 20 years.

Table 22.2: Production Area and Yield of Foodgrains in India (1970-96)

Category \ *Decades*	*1970-71*	*1980-81*	*1990-91*	*1995-96*
Area ('000 hect.)	111016	113998 (2.69)	114179 (0.16)	110789 (-2.96)
Production ('000 tonnes)	96200	119513 (24.23)	166322 (39.16)	181155 (8.92)
Yield (kg/hect)	790.00	885.00 (12.03)	1150.0 (29.94)	1230.00 (6.9)

Source: Food and Agricultural Organisation, Directorate of Economics and Statistics, Government of India.

Note: Figures in parenthesis show growth percentages.

Table 22.3: Decadal Variation in Food Crop Production in India (1970-96)

Sl. No.	*Crops*	*Production in '000 Tonnes*			
		1970-71	*1980-81*	*1990-91*	*1995-96*
1.	Rice	40805	49911	72784	80577
2.	Wheat	20859	34551	53032	62743
3.	Jowar	9210	11172	11583	9976
4.	Bajra	5719	4953	7108	5842
5.	Maize	6287	6253	8947	9309
6.	Ragi	1973	2780	2506	2567
7.	Barley	2641	2020	1613	1417
8.	Small Millet	1841	1631	1221	846
9.	Gram	5018	4475	4901	5479
10.	Arhar	1847	1767	2627	2399
	India	**96200**	**119513**	**166322**	**181155**

Source: Food and Agricultural Organisation, Directorate of Economics and Statistics, Government of India.

There has been a marginal downfall in the total area under food crops during 1995-96 as it was 110.8 million hectares during this period. Importantly, the area under crops has not increased so much as the total production and yield per hectare. The total production has gone up from 96.2 million tonnes in 1970-71 to 181.2 million tonnes in 1995-96. This is an improvement over last 25 years by about 88.31 per cent. The production has been continuously rising and according to current estimates, the total foodgrains production has gone upto 200 million tonnes. This is explained by the increasing yield per hectare. In 1970-71 per hectare yield was 790 kg., whereas, in 1980-81 it was 885 kg. per hectare. In the next ten years (1990-91) country's yield per hectare went up to 1115 kg. per hectare. It has been rising continuously and in 1995-96 it was 1230 kg. per hectare. This is very well reflected at State level as well. Table 22.3 presents the trend of production of different crops during the last 26 years (1970-1996).

A perusal of Table 22.4 reveals that rice and wheat have become the dominant staple food crops as they together occupied 68 million hectares of agricultural land in 1995-96 which was nearly 6 per cent of the total. It is also noticeable that the area under wheat is increasing more rapidly than that of rice. It occupied 15 per cent of the area under food crops in 1970-71 but in 1995-96 it expanded over 22.8 per cent of the total land under foodgrains. Likewise, the area under rice increased from 33.7 per cent to 38.6 per cent during 1970-71 and 1995-96. The dominance of coarse crops has been declining since 1970-71. The coarse grain like millets, maize, small millet etc. engaged 41.7 per cent of the area in 1970-71, whereas the area under these crops reduced to 29.2 per cent in 1995-96. Obviously the irrigation technology has basically been responsible for this kind of change. Diffusion of innovation in the field of irrigation technology, changing social status and thereby the food habits, economic well-being and regional policies have been responsible for this kind of structural changes. Among the pulses, tuar (*arhar*) and gram are normally quite important. However, the area under gram has been declining except during 1995-96. But in case of tuar, it has increased

Table 22.4: Decadal Variation in the Area under Different Food Crops in India (1970-96)

Area in, '000 hectares

Sl.No.	*Crops*	*1970-71*	*1980-81*	*1990-91*	*1995-96*
1.	Rice	37413	40016	42196	42754
2.	Wheat	16942	22364	23926	25323
3.	Jowar	18237	16210	14598	11890
4.	Bajra	12486	11210	11140	9717
5.	Maize	5810	5828	5905	6048
6.	Ragi	2498	2615	2277	1853
7.	Barley	2693	1802	1011	856
8.	Small Millet	4754	4125	2631	1844
9.	Gram	7565	7092	6934	7033
10.	Arhar	2618	2736	3561	3471
	India	**111016**	**113998**	**114179**	**110789**

Source: Food and Agricultural Organisation, Directorate of Economics and Statistics, Government of India

except in 1995-96. The impact of Green Revolution is directly visible on rice and wheat crops. In both the cases the production has gone up.

A perusal of yield/hectare (Table 22.5) during 1970-71 to 1995-96 demonstrates that almost all crops have registered increase. India ranks third only after USA and China in the production of wheat/hectare. At the State level Punjab with yield of 3990 kg./hectare ranks first followed by Haryana where it is 3660 kg./hectare. This is in fact much higher than that of the average yield of China (3389 kg./hectare) and USA (2577 kg./hectare). Rice which is the most important staple food in India, has also witnessed improvement in average yield. In 1970-71 it was 1090 kg./hectare in 1995-96 the average yield of rice has gone upto 1880 kg./hectare. The crops like jowar, bajra, maize and gram have also recorded significant improvement in the average yield/hectare. However, *Arhar* shows exception because its yield has declined from 710 kg./hectare in 1970-71 to 692 kg./hectare in 1995-96. But it appears only a temporary phenomenon because in 1990-91 the average yield of *Arhar* was 740 kg./hectare which, was an improvement over the previous decades. The above analysis, however, does not present the comprehensive picture of the level of productivity of different food crops in the country. The ecological setting, socio-economic structure, changing infrastructural facilities and agricultural policies and programmes have had varying impacts in different parts of India.

Table 22.5: Trends of Food Crops Yield in India (1970-96)

Yield in kg./hectare and Growth in percentage

Sl. No.	*Crops*	*1970-71*	*1980-81*	*1990-91*	*1995-96*
1.	Rice	1090	1250	1720	1880
2.	Wheat	1230	1540	2220	2480
3.	Jowar	510	690	790	840
4.	Bajra	460	440	640	600
5.	Maize	1080	1070	1520	1540
6.	Ragi	790	1060	1100	1380
7.	Barley	980	1120	1600	1650
8.	Small Millet	390	400	460	460
9.	Gram	660	630	710	780
10.	Arhar	710	650	740	690
	India	**790.0**	**885.0**	**1150.0**	**1230.0**

Source: Food and Agricultural Organisation, Directorate of Economics and Statistics, Government of India.

Food Crops Productivity: Spatio-Temporal Patterns

The exercise of measuring the levels of productivity has engaged the attention of several geographers. Several efforts have been made to measure the variation of food crop productivity in India. The mention may be made of Bhatia (1967), Bandhudas & Sen (1967), Nair (1977) and Reddy (1993) etc. In the present analysis Bhatia's method has been used to compute the composite productivity index which may be written as under.

The formula can be expressed as:

$$\text{(i)}\quad CPI = \frac{Lya \times Ca + Lyb \times Cb + Lyc \times Cc + \ldots\ldots.. Lyn \times Cn}{Ca + Cb + Cc + \ldots\ldots\ldots + Cn} \times 100$$

where CPI is the Composite Productivity Index

Lya, Lyb, Lyc..., Lyn are the yield indices of various food crops in different States;

Ca, Cb, Cc,....... Cn per cent area under various food crops in different States.

$$\text{(ii)}\quad Lya = \frac{Yc}{Yr} \times 100$$

where Lya is the Yield Index of Crop 'A'

Yc = Average Yield of Crop 'A' in the respective State

Yr = Acreage Yield of Crop 'A' in India,

The results are used to explain the food crops productivity in India. The productivity indices for different States have been presented in Table 22.6. The composite scores of all the crops (CPI) are divided into five groups viz. Very High Productivity States (140 and above), High Productivity States (121 to 140), Medium Productivity States (101 to 120), Low Productivity States (81 to 100), Very Low Productivity States (80 and below) for 1970-71, 1980-81, 1990-91 and 1995-96. During 1970-71,Punjab (168.6) was one of the highest productivity states followed by Tamil Nadu (147.5). There were 4 States under the category of high productivity States viz., Haryana (132.6), Manipur (131.4), Kerala (124.9) and J&K (122.5) whereas, Himachal Pradesh (114.9), Karnataka (109.9), West Bengal (109.39), Goa (108.4),Gujarat (107.5), and Andhra Pradesh (100.3) were in the category of medium productivity States. The States of U.P., Maharashtra, Assam, Meghalaya, Mizoram, Orissa and Arunachal Pradesh were in the category of low productivity States. Least productivity States were Rajasthan, Bihar, Tripura, M.P., and Nagaland.

Table 22.6: Composite Productivity Index (1970-96)

States	*CPI 1970-71*	*CPI 1980-81*	*CPI 1990-91*	*CPI 1995-96*
Jammu & Kashmir	124.98	126.87	91.71	91.79
Punjab	164.97	182.79	168.63	166.01
Himachal Pradesh	114.93	106.58	90.28	89.51
Rajasthan	76.28	68.07	79.87	68.58
Bihar	78.17	78.10	76.88	79.56
West Bengal	109.40	108.01	107.48	109.24
Assam	81.98	78.93	67.94	71.09
Meghalaya	88.36	99.61	68.22	65.22
Manipur	131.35	122.12	94.96	136.78
Mizoram	81.51	43.16	70.56	85.70
Tripura	73.11	132.02	102.27	97.15
Madhya Pradesh	67.69	55.16	62.02	58.94
Karnataka	109.93	108.85	94.06	98.54
Kerala	122.52	127.61	107.63	104.15
Orissa	86.73	76.12	77.91	76.38
Andhra Pradesh	100.38	122.99	121.49	123.91
Gujarat	107.55	142.46	105.59	105.54
Nagaland	73.11	64.60	72.11	79.64
Arunachal Pradesh	97.48	113.72	85.26	89.97
Goa	108.40	147.53	141.12	127.75
Maharashtra	82.06	98.89	97.68	98.21
Delhi	0.00	152.51	125.08	134.06
Uttar Pradesh	84.98	85.66	98.79	98.78
Tamil Nadu	147.53	158.14	160.25	161.22
Haryana	132.61	132.05	140.37	139.60

Source: Based on computations.

During 1980-81 productivity in India increased in a big way, Punjab (182.8) ranked first with highest productivity followed by Tamil Nadu (158.1), Delhi (152.5), Goa (147.5) and Gujarat (142.4). The high productivity States were Haryana (132.0), Tripura (132.0), Kerala (127.6), J&K (126.9), Andhra Pradesh (122.9) and Manipur (122.1). The medium productivity States were Arunachal Pradesh, West Bengal, Karnataka and Himachal Pradesh with the CPI values of 113.3, 108.8, 108.1 and 106.6 respectively. Low productivity was registered in the States like Meghalaya (99.48), Maharashtra (98.9) and U.P. (85.6). Least productivity was observed in the States of Assam, Bihar, Orissa, Rajasthan, Nagaland, Madhya Pradesh and Mizoram, with the CPI values of 78.9, 78.0, 76.1, 68.6, 64.5, 55.1 and 43.1 respectively.

Table 22.7: Levels of Food Crops Productivity in India (1970-96)

Levels of Productivity	*States in 1970-71*	*States in 1980-81*	*States in 1990-91*	*States in 1995-96*
Very High	Punjab and Tamil Nadu	Punjab, Gujarat, Goa, Delhi and Tamil Nadu	Punjab, Goa, Haryana and Tamil Nadu	Punjab and Tamil Nadu
High	Haryana, Manipur, Kerala and J&K	J&K, Tripura, Kerala, Haryana, Manipur and Andhra Pradesh	Andhra Pradesh, Delhi	Andhra Pradesh, Haryana, Goa, Manipur and Delhi
Medium	West Bengal, Karnataka, Andhra Pradesh, Gujarat, Goa and Himachal Pradesh	West Bengal, Karnataka, Arunachal Pradesh and Himachal Pradesh	West Bengal, Kerala, Gujarat and Tripura	Kerala, West Bengal and Gujarat
Low	U.P., Maharashtra, Assam, Meghalaya, Mizoram, Orissa and Arunachal Pradesh	U.P., Maharashtra and Meghalaya	U.P., Maharashtra, J&K, Himachal Pradesh, Manipur, Karnataka and Arunachal Pradesh	J&K, Tripura, Mizoram, Himachal Pradesh, Maharashtra, Karnataka, U.P. & Arunachal Pradesh
Very Low	Rajasthan, Bihar, Tripura, M.P., Nagaland and Delhi	Rajasthan, Bihar, Assam, M.P., Orissa, Nagaland and Mizoram	Rajasthan, Bihar, M.P., Nagaland, Assam, Meghalaya, Mizoram and Orissa	Rajasthan, Bihar, M.P., Assam, Meghalaya, Nagaland and Orissa

Source: Based on Table 22.6.

In 1990-91 similar trend was observed in the levels of productivity. Although the productivity level of Punjab decreased by 14.2 points, yet it maintained its place among very high productivity States in India with composite productivity index of 168.6. The other States in this category were Tamil Nadu (160), Haryana (141.2) and Goa (141.1). The high productivity States were Delhi (125.0) and Andhra Pradesh (121.5). The productivity of J&K, Kerala and Manipur decreased and these States joined medium and low productivity categories. Under medium productivity category there were only four States, namely Kerala,

West Bengal, Gujarat and Tripura with the composite productivity index values of 107.6, 107.4, 105.6, 102.2 respectively. U.P. (98.78), Maharashtra (97.6), J&K (91.7), Himachal Pradesh (90.2), Manipur (94.9), Karnataka (94.0) and Arunachal Pradesh (85.26) joined the low productivity class. Rajasthan, Bihar, Madhya Pradesh, Nagaland, Assam, Meghalaya, Mizoram and Orissa were the States lying in the category of very low productivity States with CPI values ranging below 80.

It may be pointed out that Punjab and Tamil Nadu continued occupying highest productivity during all the four periods. Nevertheless, the productivity value of Punjab declined in 1990-91 as well as in 1995-96. The productivity of Tamil Nadu has, however, increased. The States of Haryana (139.6), Manipur (136.7), Delhi (134.5), Goa (127.7) and Andhra Pradesh (123.9) fall in the high productivity category as their CPI values vary between 121-140. The medium productivity States remained West Bengal (109.14), Gujarat (105.54) and Kerala (104.15). The States of Uttar Pradesh (98.78), Karnataka (98.54), Maharashtra (98.21), Tripura (97.15), Jammu & Kashmir (91.79), Arunachal Pradesh (89.97) and Mizoram (85.70) were in low productivity class. The least productivity was represented by the States of Nagaland (79.64), Bihar (79.56), Orissa (76.38), Assam (71.09), Rajasthan (68.58), Meghalaya (65.22) and Madhya Pradesh (58.94). These States registered CPI values less than 80. The varying levels of productivity at State level for four periods has been portrayed in maps (see Figures 22.1, 22.2, 22.3 and 22.4). Based on these maps yet another map showing overlay through GIS technique has also been prepared (see Figure 22.5). This map shows the varying mosaics of productivity during 1970-71 to 1995-96 in various States. This map presents an interesting scenario of agriculture. The situation appears slightly grim in case of Rajasthan, Jammu & Kashmir, Madhya Pradesh, Orissa, Bihar and West Bengal. So is the case with Gujarat, Andhra Pradesh, Assam and Meghalaya.

Conclusions and Policy Implications

A perusal of land-use changes in the country reveals that major portion of land is devoted to agriculture and the area under agriculture has reached to saturation limit and there is hardly any chance for further expansion. The wasteland, uncultivable land, pastures and groves have already declined. The area under forest represents ecologically most sensitive land cover type. However, in spite of several programmes and policies launched by the Government in the field of forestry, the national target is yet to be achieved.

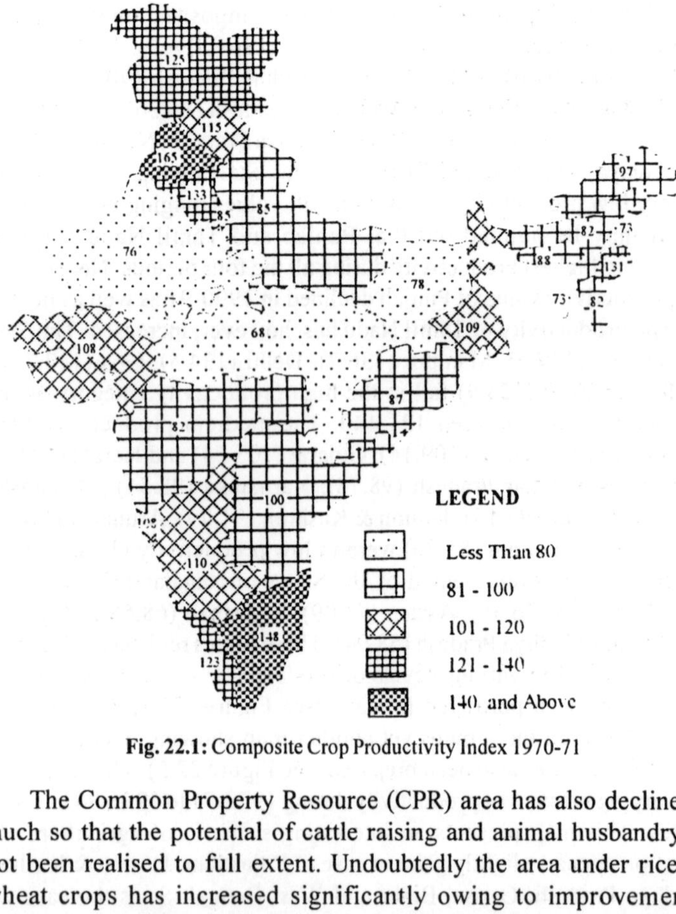

Fig. 22.1: Composite Crop Productivity Index 1970-71

The Common Property Resource (CPR) area has also declined so much so that the potential of cattle raising and animal husbandry has not been realised to full extent. Undoubtedly the area under rice and wheat crops has increased significantly owing to improvement in irrigation technology. Nevertheless, the diversification of crops has not gained momentum. The States, where once upon a time the productivity was very high, have witnessed declining trend. The States of Punjab, Haryana, Karnataka, Kerala and Gujarat are glaring examples of declining productivity. The sustainability of agriculture has, therefore, come to be questioned. There are several policy measures, which need to be taken up to plug the entry points, which remain quite vulnerable, and these are as under:

1. To re-emphasise the importance of Agro-Climatic Regions because this is the best way to promote the sustainable agriculture in the country keeping in view the ecological setting

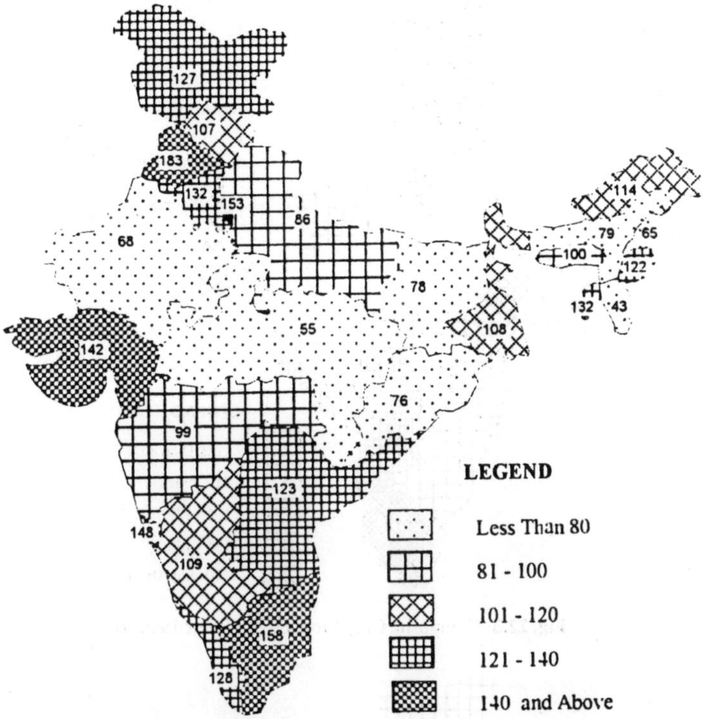

Fig. 22.2: Composite Crop Productivity Index 1980-81

of different regions. Basically there are four categories of regions in the country;

(a) Water surplus areas such as eastern States where special water management schemes need to be launched in order to harness the full potentials of water for increased productivity of land under agriculture.

(b) Water deficient areas such as Rajasthan and plateau region where watershed management programme is to be launched on priority basis in order to link the land with water and promote sustainable agriculture.

(c) Ecologically fragile areas such as Himachal Pradesh, Jammu & Kashmir and hill districts of Uttar Pradesh where cultivation can be practised keeping in view the slopes. Horticulture, beekeeping, apiculture, sericulture, vegetable crops, etc. need to be promoted in such areas.

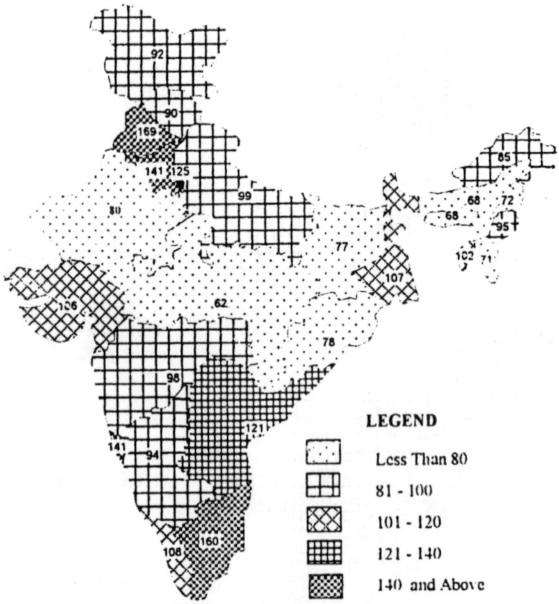

Fig. 22.3: Composite Crop Productivity Index 1990-91

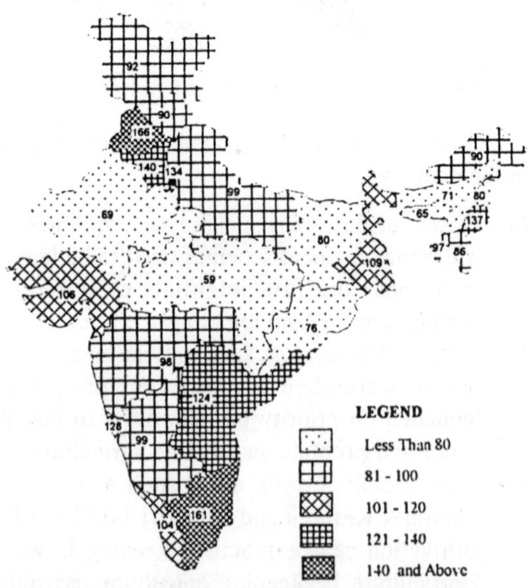

Fig. 22.4: Composite Crop Productivity Index 1995-96

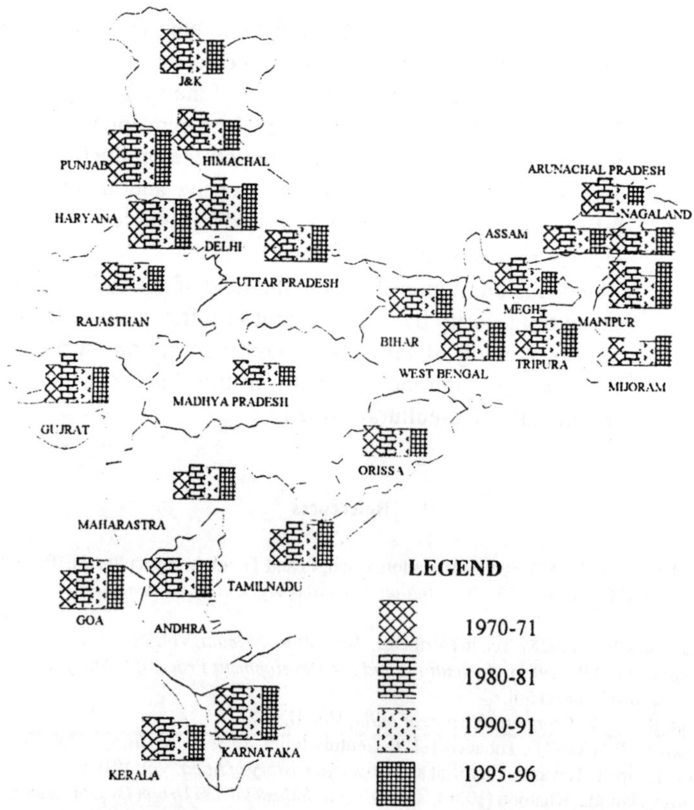

Fig. 22.5: Composite Productivity Index 1970-71, 1980-81, 1990-91, 1995-96

(d) North-western region, which, once upon a time was marked for high productivity, has now witnessed a declining trend. These areas specialised mainly in the production of wheat and rice, but in order to make agriculture sustainable, there is a need to diversify agriculture by introducing commercialization.

2. To diversify cropping pattern, which can be done by investment both from private and public sectors and this needs to be encouraged by the government through appropriate policy measures.
3. While, use of chemical fertilizers may be promoted in areas marked by low use such as Uttar Pradesh, Madhya Pradesh,

Orissa, Rajasthan, Bihar, West Bengal, etc., the organic bio-fertilizers and green manuring need to be encouraged for sustained and enhanced productivity of the soil.

4. The size of holdings and agricultural land per capita are getting truncated and this has great bearing on the productive power and, therefore, there is a need for extensive and intensive land reforms such as consolidation of holdings and testing of soils etc. are required on priority basis.
5. The diffusion of innovations in the field of agriculture may be given top priority by improvement in infrastructural facilities and awakening of farmers through appropriate agricultural extension programme especially in those areas, which have traditional socio-cultural milieu.

References

Bhatia, Shyam (1967), Spatial Variation, Changes and Trends in Agricultural Efficiency in Uttar Pradesh. 1953-1963, *Indian Journal of Agricultural Economics*, Vol. 22 (1), pp. 633-648.

Carpenter, P.H. (1928), Tea in Northeast, *Agriculture F. India*, Vol. 23.

Chaudhary D.P. (1985), *Agriculture and the Development Process: A Study of Punjab*, Land Croom Helm.

Dutt, R.C., *The Economic History of India*, Vol. II, p. 22.

Gokhale, B.G. (1971), Tobacco in 17th Century India, *Agriculture History,* Vol. 48.

Mukhtasiru-t- Tawarikh, in Elliot and Dowson, *History of India*, Vol. VIII, p. 4.

Naqvi, Hamida, Khatoon (1986), *Agricultural, Industrial and Urban Dynamics under the Sultans of Delhi*. 1206-1555, New Delhi. Munsi Ram Manohar Lal Publications.

Narayan, Dharam (1977), Growth of Productivity in Indian Agriculture. *Indian Journal of Agricultural Economics*, Issue I, Volume 32. p. 1.

Reddy, V. Ratna (1993), New Technology in Agriculture and Changing Size Productivity: An Evaluation Study. *Indian Journal of Agricultural Economics*, Volume 48(4), pp. 633-648.

Randhawa, M.S. (1980), *A History of Agriculture in India*, Vol. II, National Printing Works, New Delhi, pp. 1-189.

Rana, R.K. (1990), Land Productivity Differentials in India: An Empirical Study. *Indian Journal of Agricultural Economics*, Issue I, Volume 45, p. 51.

Sen, Bandhudas (1967), Farm Productivity and Soil Fertility in Indian Agriculture. *Indian Journal of Agricultural Economics*, Volume 22(2), pp. 70-78.

23

TECHNO-INSTITUTIONAL AND SOCIO-ECONOMIC DETERMINANTS AND THEIR CORRELATION WITH THE ADOPTION OF AGRICULTURAL INNOVATIONS

A Case Study

ATEEQUE AHMAD & FAZLUR RAHMAN

With the inception of Green Revolution, different forms of agricultural innovations have been introduced in India, which has radically transformed the methods and techniques used in agricultural practices. The response of the farmers to agricultural innovations subject to vary depending upon cognitive behaviour of the environment and the farmers themselves. This variation is mainly due to existing diverse physico-cultural and socio-economic conditions in ecological setting of the region. Besides, the varied response to innovations is also found among farmers and within different communities. These variations are attributed to the size of land holding, literacy rate, socio-economic status, caste, exposure to mass-media and the location of their villages near or far away from the respective headquarters, as well as their accessibility to the means of transportation and communication; because the headquarters are considered as the centres of the diffusion of innovations. With this view an attempt has been made to examine the impact of techno-institutional and socio-economic factors on diffusion of agricultural innovations in Upper Ganga-Yamuna Doab.

Study Area

The Upper Ganga-Yamuna Doab covers an area of about 20,624 sq. km. and consists of five districts namely, Saharanpur, Muzaffarnagar, Meerut, Ghaziabad and Bulandsahar. The region lies in between 28°4' to 30°24' north latitude and 77°2' to 78°29' east longitudes (Fig. 23.1). According to 1991 census, it accounts of 14,243,132 population with a density of

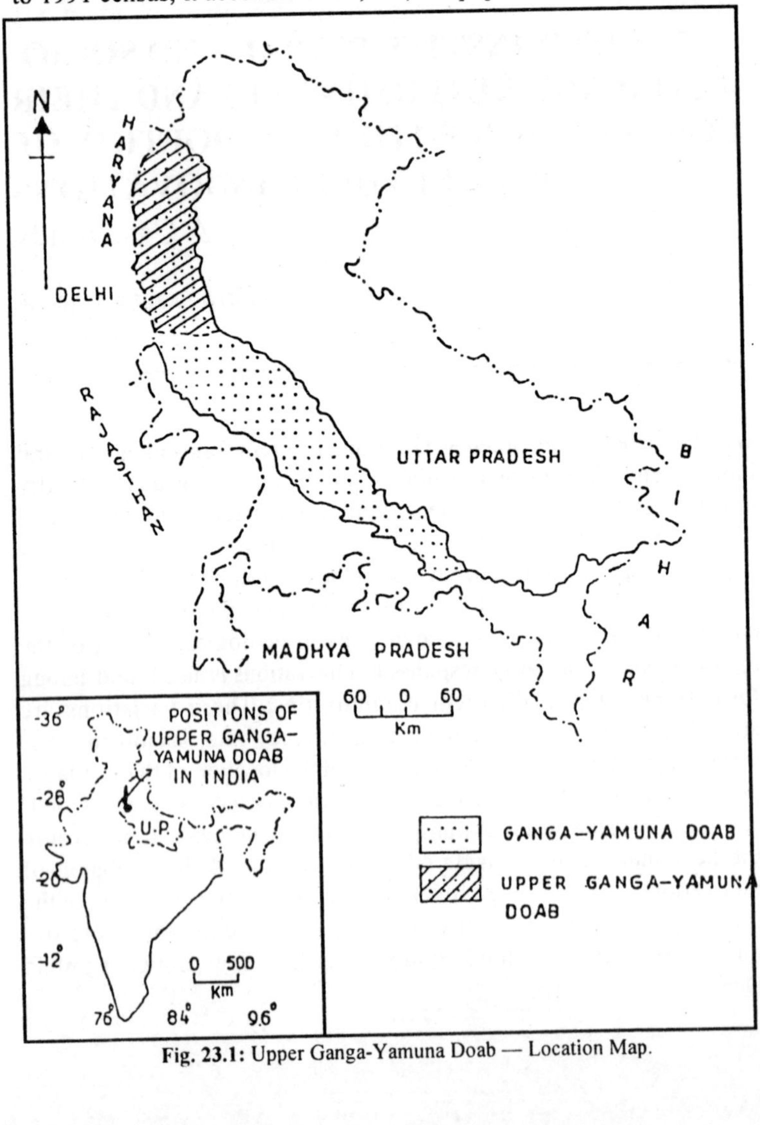

Fig. 23.1: Upper Ganga-Yamuna Doab — Location Map.

690 persons per square km. It is a monotonous and fairly productive plain. Cultivation of crops has been the main occupation of the people in the region.

Methodology

For the present analysis the region has been divided into five homogeneous stratas on the basis of relief, climate, drainage, soil, land-use, cropping pattern together with crop combinations. The total number of twenty villages (Fig. 23.2) have been identified for the analysis in different proportion from different stratas out of 3,125 households of twenty villages only twenty per cent households (625) have been taken into consideration for the analysis. The selection of villages is based on stratified purposive sampling technique keeping in mind to their communication index which has been examined on the basis of its means of transport, location with their respective headquarters (district, tehsil and block), markets, educational institutions, cooperative banks, rural banks and cinema hall. It is a well known fact that several agricultural innovations have been introduced in the region since 1966-67 to 1997-98, but only important and major innovations have been taken into consideration to test the hypothesis. Broadly three important factors, they are institutional, technological and socio-economic together comprises of sub-factors such as size of land holding, tenurial status, irrigation, electric power and diesel, credit, subsidy, input, yield, fair prices, level of exposure to mass media, level of education and social position have been taken into consideration. The field work was done in 1996-97 in both the agricultural seasons to obtain primary data through personally interviewed to farmers and secondary data has been collected from district and tehsil headquarters. With the help of the scoring scheme the individual scores of all the respondents with respect to adoption of selected innovations were worked out. The standing score of each respondent was also calculated with respect to economic variables so as to group him or her in various categories. Finally in order to know the rate of adoption individual group of the entire variable, the average adoption is worked out. With the help of individual adoption score of the respondents of each group, various hypotheses have been formulated regarding the impact of different factors on diffusion of agricultural innovations. They have been tested through average adoption index.

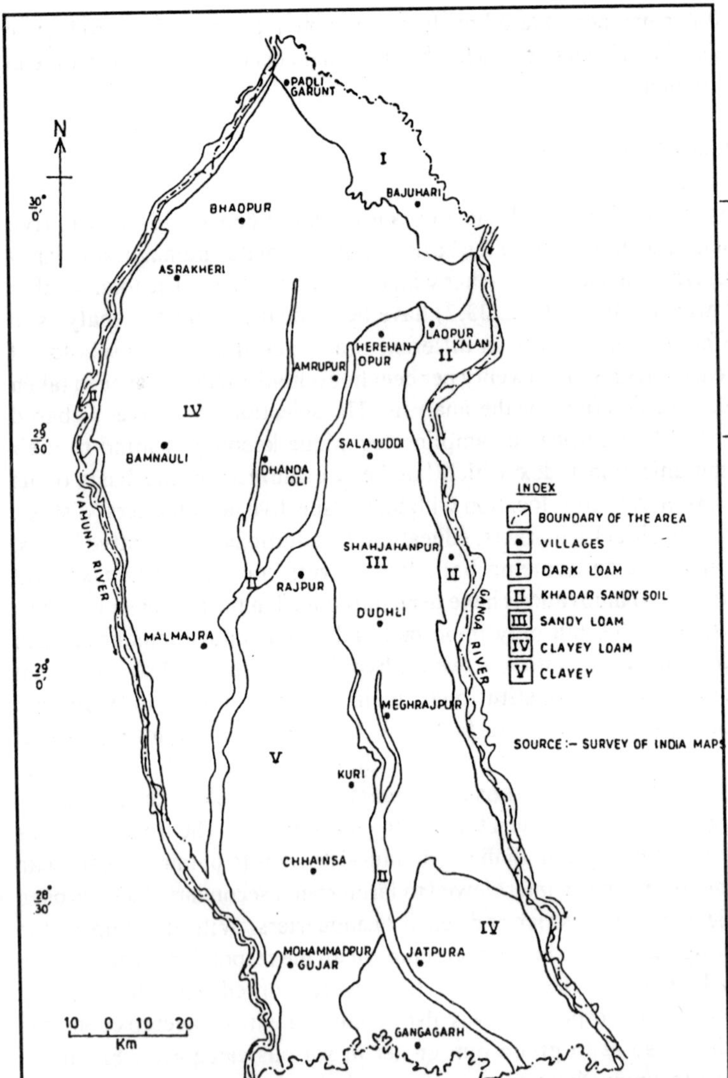

Fig. 23.2: Upper Ganga-Yamuna Doab—Location of Selected Villages

Size of Land Holding *vs.* Adoption of Agricultural Innovations

In order to test the relationship between the size of holdings and adoption of agricultural innovations following hypothesis has been put forth.

The farmers of large size of holdings tend to adopt improved agricultural practices more than the farmers of other size of land holdings.

For the assessment of size of land holding, operational holdings have been taken into account for which data were obtained during fieldwork and were cross checked with the records of the village accountant. The operational size of holding varies from 0.2 hectares to 20 hectares but the average size of holding is 1.4 hectares. On the basis of size of holding the sample farmers were classified into five groups as given below:

Group	A	Large size farmers	> 10 hectares
Group	B	Medium size farmers	> 10-4 hectares
Group	C	Semi-medium size farmers	> 4-2 hectares
Group	D	Small size farmers	> 2-1 hectares
Group	E	Marginal farmers	< 1 hectare

On the basis of total individual scores of the respondent, the average adoption index of each group of farmers is worked out. Table 23.1 shows that there are only 27 farmers (4.32%) whose size of holding is more than 10 hectares but their average adoption index is highest (4.8561). The marginal farmers (302) accounting 48.32 per cent of the sample farmers have lowest average adoption index (0.5382).

Table 23.1: Size of Holding *vs.* Average Adoption Index

Sl. No.	*Group*	*No. of Farmers*	*Average Adoption Index*
1.	Group A	27	4.8561
2.	Group B	58	4.3293
3.	Group C	93	2.1987
4.	Group D	145	0.9796
5.	Group E	302	0.5382

The semi-medium and medium farmers together account 24.16 per cent of the sample farmers have an average adoption index of 2.1987 and 4.3293 respectively. The small farmers constituting 23.20 per cent of sample farmers have an average adoption index of 0.9796. Table 23.1 and Fig. 23.3 clearly shows that there is a positive correlationship between the size of holding and average adoption index viz., with the increase in size of holding, adoption index also increases.

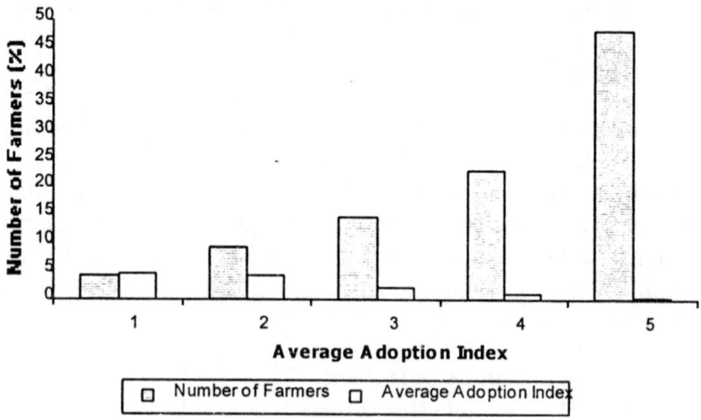

Fig. 23.3: Size of Holding *vs.* Average Adoption Index

Tenurial Status *vs.* Adoption of Agricultural Innovations

In an agricultural economy like ours, the value of land hardly needs any emphasis and in fact it is one of the most important indicator to measure one's socio-economic status. In order to test the relationship between tenurial status and adoption of agricultural innovations the following hypothesis is put forth.

The rate of adoption among owner farmers is high as compared to owner-share-cropper or share-croppers.

Table 23.2: Tenurial Status vs. Average Adoption Index

Sl. No.	*Group*	*No. of Farmers*	*Average Adoption Index*
1.	Owner	209	3.9072
2.	Owner-share-cropper	314	3.1392
3.	Owner-cropper	102	1.3465

It is quite obvious from Table 23.2 and Fig. 23.4 that owner farmers who account roughly one-third of the total respondents have highest average adoption index (3.9072), whereas the share-croppers have an average index of 1.3465. There are only 102 (16.32%) exclusively share-croppers. The owner-share-croppers account roughly half of the total respondents have also high adoption index (3.1392) and, therefore, the

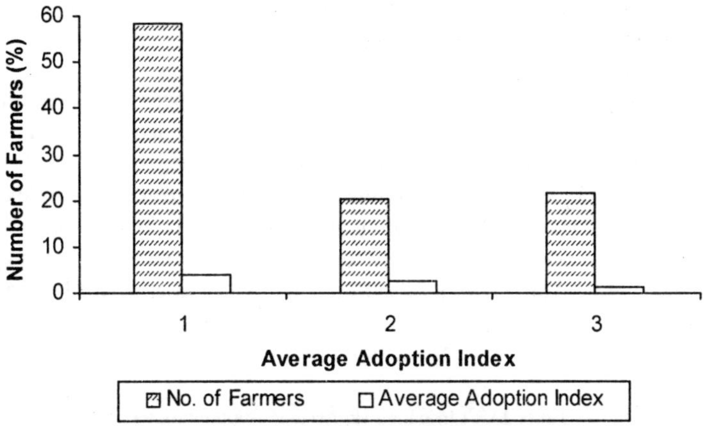

Fig. 23.4: Tenurial Status *vs.* Adoption of Agricultural Innovation

analysis proves the first proposition i.e., the tenurial status and adoption of agricultural innovation are positively related.

Irrigation *vs.* Adoption of Agricultural Innovations

Irrigation is indeed the life-breath of agriculture. Its importance in the development of agriculture in general and monsoonal countries in particular hardly needs any emphasis. An attempt has been made to test the relationship between irrigation and adoption of agricultural innovations.

The farmers having adequate and assured irrigation facilities are more adoptive of agricultural innovations as compared to others.

For the assessment of the individual standing of the farmers with respect to irrigation facilities, a scoring scheme is evolved. For each crop the farmer having adequate, average, poor and very poor irrigation facilities is given the score of 4, 3, 2 and 1 respectively. His total score is worked out by adding his scores in respect of all the crops grown by him and this figure is divided by number of crops cultivated by him in order to get his average scores. The average adoption score varies from 0 to 4. Finally on the basis of their average scores the farmers are classified into following four groups:

Group A	Adequate irrigation facilities	> 3.0 scores
Group B	Average irrigation facilities	30.20 scores

Group C	Poor irrigation facilities	21.10 scores
Group D	Very poor irrigation facilities	< 1.0 score

Table 23.3 and Fig. 23.5 shows that only 10.4 per cent of the total farmers have adequate irrigation facilities and their average adoption index is highest (4.6872). The farmers having average irrigation facilities account 29.92 per cent of the sample and their average adoption index is 2.9235. The farmers having poor and very poor irrigation facilities account about 59.68 per cent of the respondents and their average adoption indices are poor i.e., 1.6482 and 0.8763 respectively. The above analysis is very much in conformity with the earlier studies and it proves that there is positive correlation between these two variables.

Table 23.3 : Irrigation *vs.* Average Adoption Index

Sl. No.	*Group*	*No. of Farmers*	*Average Adoption Index*
1.	Adequate	65	4.6872
2.	Average	187	2.9235
3.	Poor	256	1.6482
4.	Very poor	117	0.8763

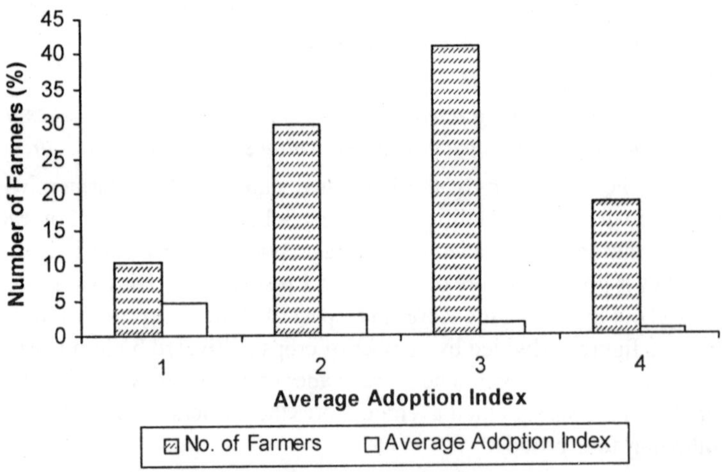

Fig. 23.5: Irrigation *vs.* Average Adoption Index

Electric Power and Diesel *vs.* Adoption of Agricultural Innovations

The electric power and diesel (hereafter written as power) play very significant role in the development of agriculture especially in the mechanisation and rationalisation of farm operations. Therefore, the hypothesis is,

> *Adequate and timely availability of power tends to promote speedy adoption of agricultural innovations among farmers.*

On the basis of mode of consumption of power, farmers are classified into four groups. Group A consists of those farmers who use power for both irrigation and other agricultural operations; Group B includes the farmers using power for irrigation only; Group C consists of farmers using power for agricultural operations; and Group D is the group of farmers who do not use power at all.

The average adoption index of each group is calculated with the help of individual adoption score. From Table 23.4 and Fig. 23.6, it is obvious that there are 220 farmers (35.2%) who do not use power and consequently their average adoption index is lowest. The farmers of Group C have highest average adoption index (3.6573) and they account roughly 22.88 per cent of the sample farmers. The farmers of Group A and Group B together account 41.92 per cent of the sample farmers and their average adoption indices are 3.4975 and 1.8961 respectively.

Table 23.4: Power *vs.* Average Adoption Index

Sl. No.	*Group*	*No. of Farmers*	*Average Adoption Index*
1.	Group A	58	3.4975
2.	Group B	204	1.8961
3.	Group C	143	3.6573
4.	Group D	220	1.0387

Credit *vs.* Adoption of Agricultural Innovations

Finance is one of the most important economic determinant and lifeblood of any enterprise, and agriculture is no exception to it. The following hypothesis has been formed in this regard,

> *Availability of adequate and timely credit facilities promote quick adoption of agricultural innovations.*

There are 390 farmers (62.4%) who had applied for credit and remaining 37.6 per cent did not do so. Out of this, a small percentage do

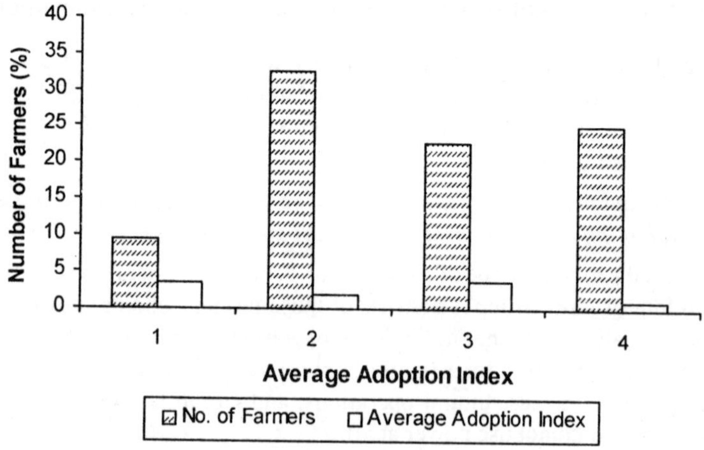

Fig. 23.6: Power vs. Average Adoption Index

not need credit at all but the large percentage of farmers did not apply for credit to a number of reasons viz., fear of high compound interest, wrong higher entries inability to return in time resulting to social insult and harassment and doubt of getting it sanctioned within time. Hence, only 390 farmers have been included in the study. In order to assess the standing of farmers in case of credit facilities a scoring scheme in which 4, 3, 2 and 1 scores were given to adequate-timely, inadequate-timely, adequate-untimely and inadequate-untimely availability of credit respectively. Zero score was given for non-availability of credit. According to the scoring scheme the total score of the individual farmers was worked out and was divided by number of items for which he had applied for credit in cash or kind. This gives his average score, which varies from 0 to 4. According to average score the farmers were classified into five groups as given below:

Group A	Got credit adequate-timely	> 3.0 scores
Group B	Got credit inadequate-timely	3.0 – 2.0 scores
Group C	Got credit adequate-untimely	2.1 – 1.0 scores
Group D	Got credit inadequate-untimely	< 1.0 score
Group E	Did not get credit	0 score

Table 23.5 and Fig. 23.7 shows that there is a close relationship between the adequate and timely availability of credit and adoption of agricultural innovations.

Table 23.5: Credit *vs.* Average Adoption Index

Sl. No.	*Group*	*No. of Farmers*	*Average Adoption Index*
1.	Group A	39	3.9127
2.	Group B	110	3.4932
3.	Group C	53	2.3553
4.	Group D	81	1.6102
5.	Group E	107	0.8120

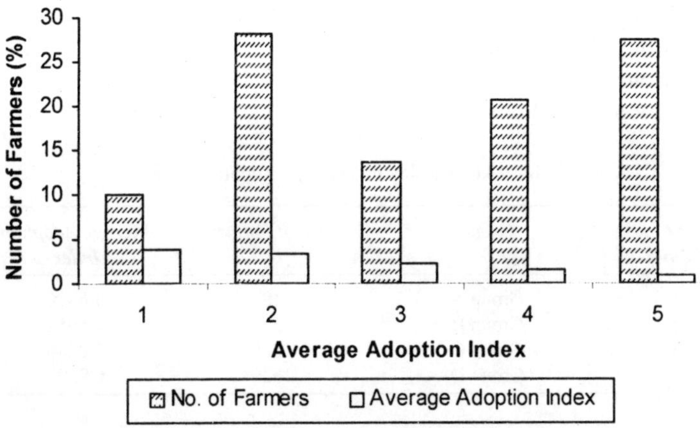

Fig. 23.7: Credit *vs.* Average Adoption Index

The farmers who got adequate and timely credit have highest average adoption index (3.9127) while the adoption index of those farmers is lowest who were in need of credit and applied for that but did not get it. There are 107 such respondents. The farmers of Group B account for the highest percentage (28.2) and their average adoption index is reasonable. The farmers of Group C and D who together account for 34.35 per cent has average adoption indices 2.3553 and 1.6102 respectively. The above analysis proves that adequate and timely availability of credit facilities for needed potential adopters promotes adoption of agricultural innovations.

Subsidy *vs.* Adoption of Agricultural Innovations

The provision of incentives in some form or the other immensely contributes to increase production and efficiency. The hypothesis put forth in this connection is as follows,

Availability of incentives in the form of subsidies tends to promote speedy adoption of improved agricultural practices.

In order to test hypothesis only those sample farmers (369) have been taken who applied for various kinds of subsidies. The average score of each farmer is worked out by dividing his total score with by number of items he had applied for subsidy. Finally the respondents were classified into following groups on the basis of their response and feeling towards subsidies

Group A Very good
Group B Good
Group C Satisfactory
Group D Poor

Table 23.6: Subsidy *vs.* Average Adoption Index

Sl. No.	*Group*	*No. of Farmers*	*Average Adoption Index*
1.	Group A	48	3.6398
2.	Group B	57	2.5952
3.	Group C	102	1.8786
4.	Group D	162	0.9893

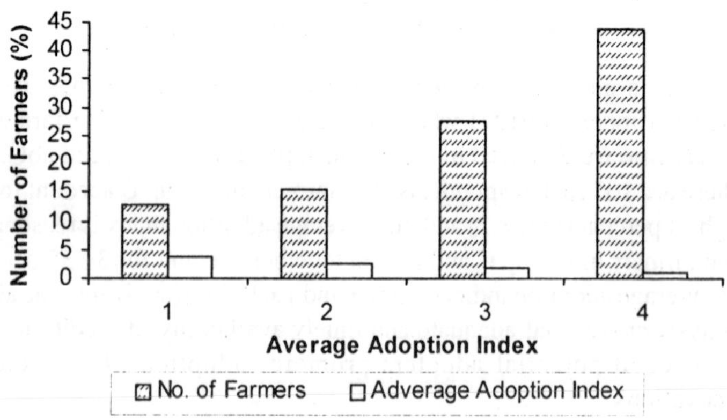

Fig. 23.8: Subsidy *vs.* Average Adoption Index

It is evident from Table 23.6 and Fig. 23.8 that the number of respondents is in ascending order while average adoption index in descending order. This is a clear proof of the fact that the farmers who got very good amount of subsidies in time have highest adoption index whereas reverse in the case for last group. About 13 per cent of respondents of the study fall in Group A and 43.9 per cent in Group D. The respondents of Group B who accounts for 15.4 per cent have reasonable adoption index of 2.5952. The average adoption index of the respondents of Group C accounts for 27.6 per cent is also poor.

Input *vs.* Adoption of Agricultural Innovations

The process of adoption of new farm practices is a complex one and it involves in many stages such as awareness interest, evaluation, trial and finally adoption. The hypothesis formulated in this connection is as follows:

> *Timely and Adequate Availability of Inputs Promotes Adoption of Agricultural Innovations*

In order to assess the standing of farmers in case of availability of inputs a scoring scheme is evolved in which adequate-timely, inadequate-timely, adequate-untimely and inadequate-untimely, availability of inputs are given in 3.5, 2.5, 2.0 and 1.0 scores respectively. Zero score was given for non-availability of inputs. On the basis of this scoring scheme the farmers' total score is worked out and is divided by the number of item he had applied for in order to get his average score. The average score of farmers varies from 0 to 3. Finally on the basis of the average score, the farmers were classified into 5 groups as given below:

Group A	Adequate-timely	>2.0 scores
Group B	Inadequate-timely	2.0 – 1.5 scores
Group C	Adequate-untimely	1.4 – 1.0 scores
Group D	Inadequate-untimely	0.9 – 0.5 score
Group E	Did not get at all	< 0.5 score

The average adoption index is worked out on the basis of the adoption score of the individuals. Table 23.7 and Fig. 23.9 show that the adoption index of Group A is much higher (4.5694) than the rest of the groups, but there are only 69 farmers (11.04%) who have got inputs adequate and timely to a large extent. About one-fifth of the farmers did not get the required inputs and, perhaps, as a result their adoption index is lowest (0.7358). The adoption index of farmers of Group D who account more than one-fifth of the total farmers is also low (1.3821). The farmers of Group C constitute slightly less than one-third of total respondents is 1.6857 while the adoption score of the remaining 15 per cent respondents falling in Group B is 3.3987 which is almost satisfactory. This analysis clearly establishes the fact that adequate and timely availability of input affects the adoption of agricultural innovations to a considerable extent.

Table 23.7: Input *vs.* Average Adoption Index

Sl. No.	*Group*	*No. of Farmers*	*Average Adoption Index*
1.	Group A	69	4.5694
2.	Group B	94	3.3987
3.	Group C	197	1.6857
4.	Group D	136	1.3821
5.	Group E	129	0.7358

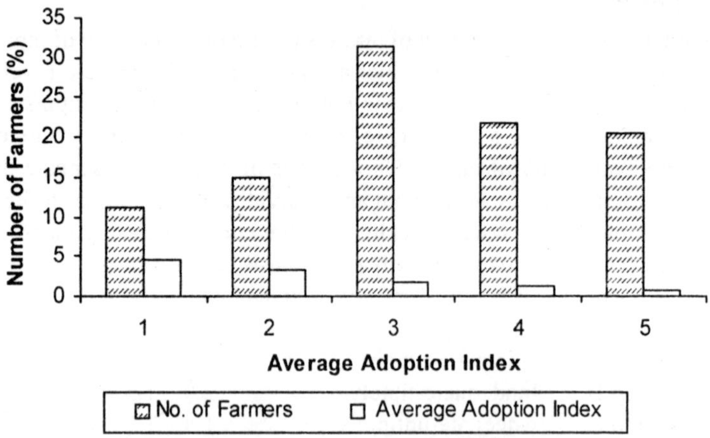

Fig. 23.9: Input *vs.* Average Adoption Index

Yield *vs.* Adoption of Agricultural Innovations

Yield is another economic variable, which affects the adoption of agricultural innovations. It is altogether different variable as it is a practice centred characteristics whereas other variables are all predominantly farm centred. The hypothesis in this connection is as follows:

> *The rate of adoption of an innovation is positively related to its ultimate returns.*

In order to assess the standing of farmers with respect to yield position, a scoring scheme is evolved in which a comparison could be made between per hectare yield obtained by applying purely traditional method and that obtained by using modern techniques. With the help of this, the standing score of each farmer is worked out and they are divided into the following groups:

Group A	Respondents getting greater yield	< 1.5 scores
Group B	Respondents getting equal yield	1.5 – 0.5 scores
Group C	Respondents getting lesser yield	< 0.5 score

Table 23.8 and Fig. 23.10 show that about 58.14 per cent of the sample respondents (485) got good and more yield and their average adoption index is high 3.9672. There are 104 respondents (21.4%) whose average adoption index is 1.4376, whereas average adoption index of remaining 20 per cent respondents is 2.6243. This analysis clearly proves the fact that the respondents who have got greater yield are more adoptive as compared to others.

Table 23.8: Yield *vs.* Average Adoption Index

Sl. No.	*Group*	*No. of Farmers*	*Average Adoption Index*
1.	Group A	282	3.9672
2.	Group B	99	2.6243
3.	Group C	104	1.4376

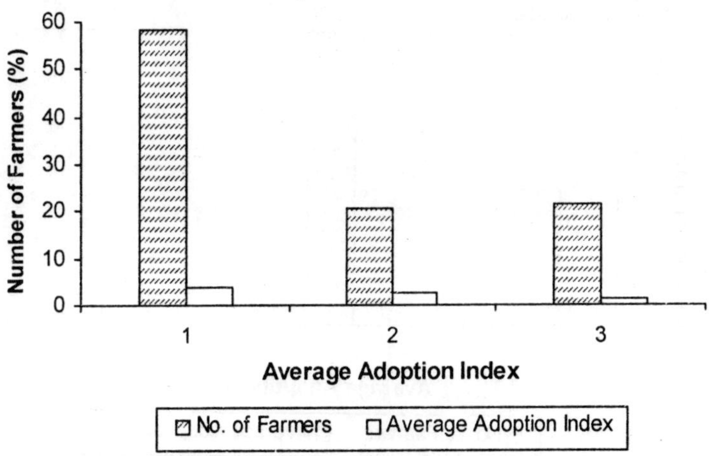

Fig. 23.10: Yield *vs.* Average Adoption Index

Fair Prices *vs.* Adoption of Agricultural Innovations

The availability of fair prices for the agricultural produce is another important economic indicator, which stimulates the farmers to adopt agricultural innovations. In this regard the following hypothesis is formed.

Availability of incentives in the form of assured fair prices for agricultural produce tends to promote speedy adoption of agricultural innovations.

For the assessment of the standing of the farmers with respect to availability of fair prices, a scoring scheme is introduced for all the farmers who sold their farm produce at fair prices or otherwise. There are 538 such respondents. Their adoption score is worked out by dividing their total score with number of produce taken into consideration. On the basis of this, respondents were classified into three groups viz., Group A consists of those who got good prices, Group B for satisfactory prices, and Group C unsatisfactory prices. The average adoption index of each group is calculated with the help of the individual score of respondents. Then the pattern of adoption of different group of farmers was studied.

Table 23.9: Fair Prices *vs.* Average Adoption Index

Sl. No.	*Group*	*No. of Farmers*	*Average Adoption Index*
1.	Good	172	3.6425
2.	Satisfactory	313	3.1743
3.	Unsatisfactory	53	2.4987

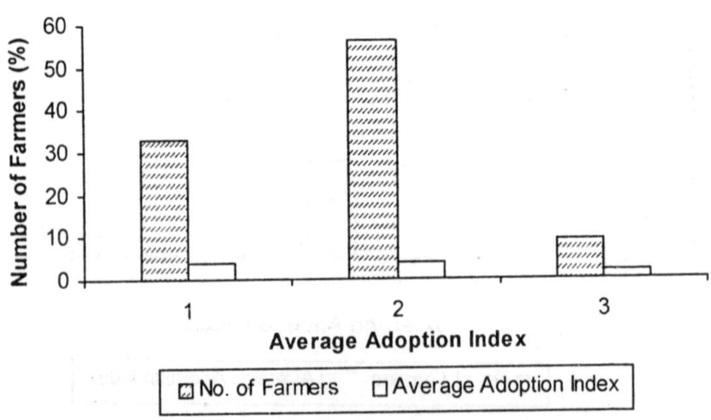

Fig. 23.11: Fair Prices *vs.* Average Adoption Index

Table 23.9 and Fig. 23.11 shows that the largest percentage of (538) respondents (58.17%) are satisfied with the price they have got for their agricultural produce and their average adoption index is also high. There are 343 respondents who have got good prices whose average adoption index is highest (3.6425). Only 9.8 per cent of the respondents were not satisfied with the prices they have got and their average adoption index is low. The above analysis proves that the availability of fair prices for agricultural product does promote the speedy adoption of agricultural innovations.

Level of Exposure to Mass Media and Innovativeness

Farmers in the study of selected villages are, exposed to variety of mass media, such as television, radio/transistor, newspaper, cinema and so on. In spite of several limitations, mass media plays an effective role in diffusion of agricultural innovations. It has generally been observed that level of exposure to mass media is positively correlated with the agricultural innovations. For the assessment of level of exposure of mass media of individual respondents, communications, six form of mass media such as television, radio/transistor, cinema, newspaper, magazine and agricultural fair, and exhibitions has been taken. On the basis of the individual response, the total score of each respondent has been worked out with the help of a scoring method and they have been classified in 5 categories. On the basis of total individual scores of the respondents, the average adoption index of each group of farmer is worked out.

Table 23.10: Exposure to Mass Media *vs.* Average Adoption Index

Sl. No.	*Category*	*Score Range*	*No. of Farmers*	*%age of the Farmers*
1.	A—Very highly exposed	>8.50	26	4.16%
2.	B—Highly exposed	6.0–8.50	101	16.16%
3.	C—Moderately exposed	3.51– 6.00	135	21.6%
4.	D—Less exposed	1.50–3.50	169	27.04%
5.	E—Least exposed	<1.50	194	31.04%

Table 23.10 and Fig. 23.12 substantiates the belief of positive relationship between exposure to mass media and level of adoptions of innovation. The respondents of least exposed category have an average innovative adoptions index. The largest number of respondent is in the least exposed to mass media and their adoptions index of innovativeness

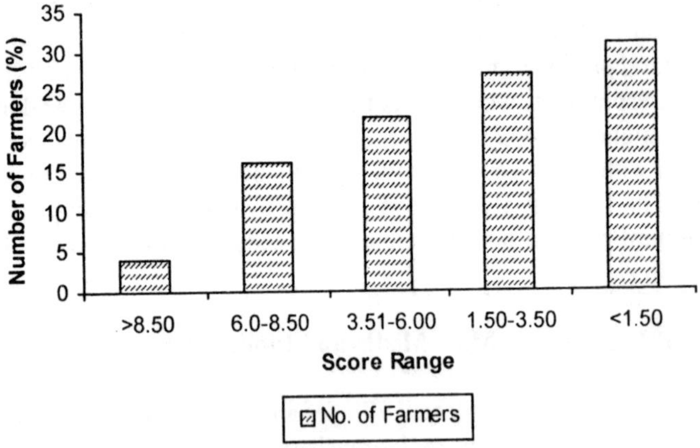

Fig. 23.12: Exposure to Mass Media *vs.* Average Adoption Index

is less than 1-50 score range. Only 4.16 per cent of respondents (26) are very highly exposed to mass media with the average adoptions index is more than 8.50. The above analysis proves the hypothesis of positive relationship between level of exposure to mass media and adoptions diffusion of innovation. The basic reason for such an association is that the highly exposed respondents also belong to high caste with high socio-economic status and high literacy index. They have large size of holding with better agricultural infrastructure. All these factors are very helpful to the adoption of agricultural innovations, which subsequently increases agricultural productivity.

Level of Education *vs.* Agricultural Innovations

The role of education in the process of development of a region is quite obvious. It is one of the chief instruments through which society socialises its members and brings desirable changes in the social life of the people.

Table 23.11 and Fig. 23.13 reveal level of education *vs.* adoption of innovativeness of 625 respondents. The highly educated respondents and very high educated respondents account 8 per cent of the total respondents have very high adoption of innovative index whereas more than 50 per cent of the respondents have very low adoption index that is below 2.50. It proves the hypothesis that high literacy index has high adoptions index of innovativeness. It further clarify that there is positive correlation between level of education and adoptions of innovations.

The reasons for positive correlation between educational status and adoptions of agricultural innovations are quite obvious. The educated farmers are well informed about agricultural innovations, more mobile, more liberal, and more receptive to agricultural innovations, and are capable of working out precisely the benefits and loss in agriculture by adopting innovations in it. Thus the above analysis shows the positive relationship between level of education and adoptions of agricultural innovations.

Table 23.11: Education Level vs. Average Adoption Index of Innovativeness

Sl. No.	*Category*	*Score Range*	*No. of Farmers*	*%age of the Farmers*
1.	A—Very highly educated	>4.50	16	2.56%
2.	B—Highly educated	3.51–4.50	34	5.44%
3.	C—Moderately educated	2.51–3.50	51	8.16%
4.	D—Less educated	Below 2.50	318	50.88%
5.	E—Illiterate	0.00	206	32.95%

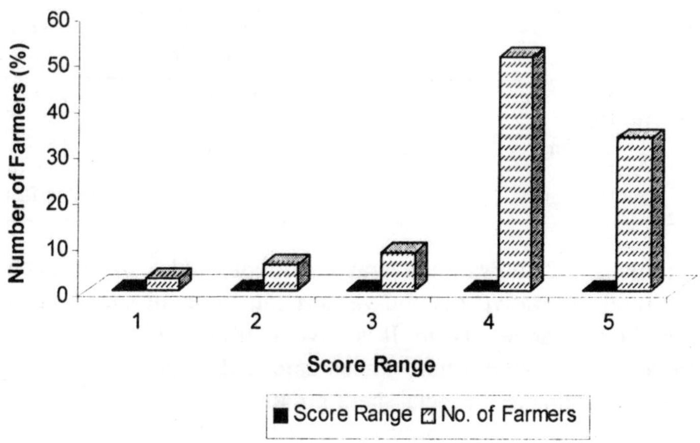

Fig. 23.13: Education Level *vs.* Average Adoption Index of Innovativeness

Social Position *vs.* Adoption of Agricultural Innovations

India is basically a social country where the religious and social norms, values, traditions and customs play an important role in all walks of life. The social status of the people is, by and large, ascertained by his caste, occupation, educational level, standard of living, family income, administrative position, political involvement, level of involvement in various socio-religious and political activities. It has been generally observed that the respondents of high social status and more liberal, open minded and receptive to agricultural innovations. Therefore, in the present study it has been hypothesised that there is a positive correlationship between the social status of the respondents and adoptions of agricultural innovations. Hence, the social status of all the respondents have been ascertained on the basis of the above indicators. Since the questions for ascertaining social status, included in the questionnaire, were of varied nature, and the answers given by the respondents were even more complex and heterogeneous, it was difficult to compare the respondents with one another. Therefore, a judicious scoring scheme was evolved, and all the respondents were given scores as per their response to questions. The score of individual respondents were added up, and they were arranged in ascending order. Finally, the respondents were classified into social status categories.

Table 23.12: Social Position vs. Average Adoption Index of Innovativeness

Sl. No	*Category*	*No. of Farmers*	*Percentage of Farmers*	*Score Range*
1.	A—Very High	25	4.00%	>5.50
2.	B—High	167	26.72%	3.50 – 5.50
3.	C—Medium	292	46.72%	2.50 – 1.00
4.	D—Low	122	19.52%	1.0 – 0.50
5.	E—Very Low	19	3.04%	Below 0.50

Table 23.12 shows the average adoptions index of diffusion of agricultural innovativeness and various categories of social status in Upper Ganga-Yamuna Doab. It is obvious from Table 23.12 that the adoption of agricultural innovations among the respondents is quite uneven, according to the social status group. Table 23.12 and Fig. 23.14 further show that there is a positive correlation between the social status of the respondents and their average adoption index of agricultural innovations. The analysis of Table 23.12 further reveals that under very high social status group has the highest adoption index of agricultural innovations, but it constitute only 4 per cent of the total respondents. This average adoption index is slightly higher than the high social status groups. They are generally Rajput, Brahmin, Jat and some Muslims respondents with large size of holding. Their overall socio-cultural conditions are similar to the respondents belonging to high social status

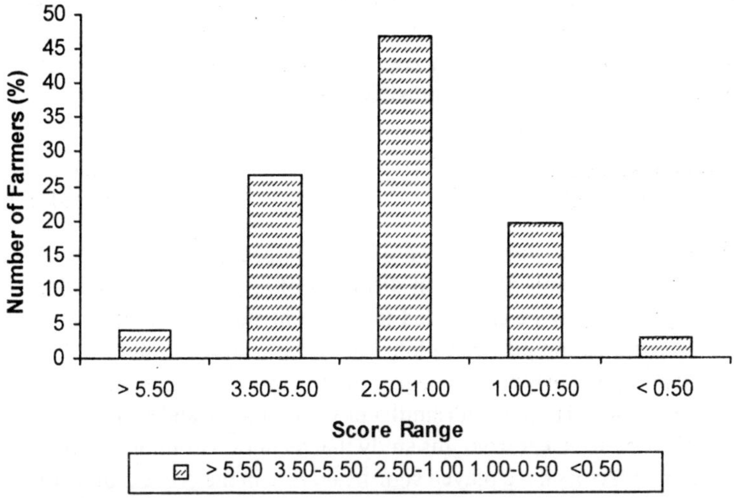

Fig. 23.14: Social Position *vs.* Average Adoption Index of Innovativeness

category. About 27 per cent respondents have high social status with adoption index ranging between 3.50 to 5.50. In this group, by and large, the respondents of high castes are found. They are more educated and play major role in the socio-cultural affairs of the village. They are active members of various social, religious and political organizations. By virtue of being associated with various organizations, they come in contact with various government and quasi-government officials who come to the village for implementing various governmental programmes and policies for agricultural development. By virtue of being active and versatile members of the villages they are more receptive involved and respective to agricultural innovations, which results in higher agricultural productivity.

About 47 per cent of cultivating respondents have medium social status. These respondents are found in the north-western and south-eastern and some places of central part of Upper Ganga-Yamuna Doab. Generally the medium social status comprises of Kurmi, Jat, Ahir, Shaikh and some Rajputs are predominant caste. About 22.55 per cent of the respondents belong to low and very low social status group and out of them only 3.04 per cent belongs to very low social status group. They are mostly scheduled castes and backward castes with a very low literacy index. Majority of them are illiterates and few of them are less educated. Hence, the level of reception of agricultural innovations is very low. This analysis proves that the social status of respondents, which is the reflection of overall socio-economic and cultural conditions, is very much positively associated with adoption of agricultural innovations.

Conclusion

After foregoing discussion regarding the impact of techno-institutional and socio-economic factors on diffusion of agricultural innovations in the region, it may be concluded that present study is too brief to make any generalization either at global or at national level, but predictions could be made fairly at high degree of certainty in this connection for all the geographical region with similar physico-cultural and socio-economic conditions. It is clear from this study that techno-institutional and socio-economic factors have played significant role in the process of diffusion of agricultural innovations. All the 12 factors considered in the present study have proved statistically significant and all have positive correlation with diffusion of agricultural innovations. The Upper Ganga-Yamuna Doab is covered under the settlement scheme of consolidation of land, and in most of the sample villages this programme is almost over. But the size of land is still, by and large, is very small. The size of plots can be judged by the fact that about 63.63 per cent of the holdings are less than one hectare. It is due to several socio-economic reasons.

Suggestions

In the light of the above conclusions the following suggestions are made with regard to the impact of techno-institutional and socio-economic factors on diffusion of agricultural innovations in the study area.

1. It is suggested that rational programme of consolidation should be implemented and legal restrictions should be imposed on fragmentation of holding. Besides this, attempt should also be made to consolidate the small holdings through co-operative and joint farming.
2. The land should belong to its real cultivators and, if it is not possible and practicable, share-croppers should be given large size of holdings on contract for longer period of time.

3. The government should give top priority to develop irrigation facilities in its plan and policies in order to revitalise Indian agricultural technology.
4. Various kinds of subsidies should be given to the farmers in various forms to develop medium and minor irrigation schemes. Besides this, farmers should also be educated about the proper and profitable use of water as most of them do not know ideal frequency of irrigation and optimum water requirements of the crop.
5. The government should also encourage research on these lines so that farmers could apply irrigation water economically and cultivate their fields with the optimum use of water.
6. Power generation should be accelerated to cope up with the increasing demand of power supply for both irrigation and other agricultural purposes. Similarly the supply of diesel for all agricultural purposes should be rationalised and the farmers should be assured of getting it when they need it.
7. In order to make the same available in time and in adequate quantity, various distribution centres should be opened by the government and private agencies and proper arrangements must be made to give adequate and timely credit to the farmers whenever they require for it.
8. Attempt should be made to introduce and propagate such improved practices and inputs such as new varieties of seed.
9. All kinds of incentives should be given to the farmers in the form of subsidies in cash or kind through various government and quasi-government agencies.
10. Every attempt should be made to give higher prices to agricultural products through regulating markets.
11. However, it is finally suggested that policy makers and social researchers should give much emphasis to economic variables.

References

Chaudhary, K.M. and Maharaja, M. (1966), Acceptance of Improved Practices and their Diffusion among Wheat Growers in Pali District of Rajasthan, *Indian Journal of Agricultural Economics*, Vol. XXI.

Dasgupta, S. (1963), Innovation and Innovator in Indian Villages, *Man in India*, Vol. 43.

Mohammad, N. (1978), Technological Change and Diffusion of Agricultural Innovations, *The Geographer*, Vol. XXIII, No. 1, Aligarh.

Mohammad, N. (1978), *Agricultural Land Use in India*, New Delhi.

Roy, P., *et al.* (1968), *Agricultural Innovations among Indian Farmers*, Hyderabad.

Savale, R.S. (1966), Technological Change in Agriculture: Study of the Sources of Its Diffusion, Efficiently of the Sources and the Economic Factors affecting the Adoption of Improved Practices, *Indian Journal of Agricultural Economics*, Vol. XXI.

24

IMPACT OF W.T.O. ON INDIA'S AGRICULTURAL TRADE

MOHD. IZHAR AHMAD

SECTION I

Introduction

India is now a part of the global economic system. Every section of the Indian economy is now linked with the world outside, either through its direct involvement in international trade or through its indirect linkage with the export or import transactions of other sectors in the economy. All trade is now subjected to strict and self-abiding multilateral trade obligations, most ostensibly to the overarching principles of most favoured nation and national treatment clauses. International scrutiny, and transparency. The WTO obligations, however, do not seem to work equally between the developed and the developing world. The whole developing world is worried about its economic future. So is India, especially because disturbing signals, most distressingly about the basic life sustaining parameters of employment, growth and poverty, have started surfacing on a wide scale.

Agriculture contributes a small share of the national income in the developed industrialized countries. This has made it possible to heavily subsidies agriculture in these countries. The extent to which tariff and non-tariff barriers can be bought down with respect to agricultural products was the centre of acrimonious debate among developed countries.

The World Trade Organization, formed in 1994, has 135 member countries including India. The WTO was formed in lieu of GATT and it deals with the tariffs and quotas between the member countries so as to remove any anomalies. Agriculture was also included in the WTO (Agreement on Agriculture). India, being one of its signatory and furthermore after losing its appeal in the WTO, was forced to liberalize trade on agro-commodities as per the WTO norms. The whole exercise, started in budget 2000-01.

Objectives

The objective of the Agreement of Agriculture is to reform trade in the sector and to make policies more market oriented. This would improve predictability and security for importing and exporting countries like India. The WTO wishes to liberalize trade barriers within member countries by reducing the tariff and non-tariff barriers (e.g. quota restrictions).

Features of WTO

- The WTO agreement requires the conversion of all non-tariff barriers on agro-commodities trade into equivalent tariffs. These tariff rates equivalent are to be combined with existing tariffs and the resulting composite tariffs are to be bound at that rate.
- Each country is given the flexibility in distributing the average tariff cut over different commodities, as long as each individual tariff is reduced by at least 15 per cent (10% for the developing countries) over the relevant period.
- Where the resulting tariff is prohibitive, a minimum level of imports, equal to 3 per cent of domestic consumption is to be guaranteed. These "minimum access" quotas will rise to 5 per cent of domestic consumption after six years.
- The minimum allocation quotas for developing countries constitute 2 per cent of domestic consumption moving upto 4 per cent after 10 years.
- The agreement also provides for a cut in the subsidies from the 1986-90 levels by 36 per cent (24% for the developing countries) over six years (ten years for the developing countries) in equal annual instalments.
- Developed countries are also required to reduce the volume of

exports of each subsidized commodity by 21 percent over six years with average exports levels of 1986-90. A corresponding reduction by 14 percent is required for the developing countries.

SECTION II

Agriculture and WTO

India is an agricultural country, two-third population depends on agriculture sector directly or indirectly. Agriculture continues to be the mainstray of the India economy. Indian agriculture contributes to the National Gross Domestic Product is about 25 per cent. With food being the crowing need of the mankind, much emphasis has been on commercializing agricultural production. Hence, adequate production and even distribution of food has lately become a high priority global concern. With the changing agricultural scenario and global competition, there is a need of exploiting the available resources at maximum level.

In Indian agriculture the factors like high soil productivity, supply of balanced crop nutrients, efficient water management, improved crops, better plant protection, post-production management for value-addition and marketing, are responsible for higher yield as compared to most of the other countries. Achievements of Indian agriculture like development of HYVs, new hybrids of different crops, research in the area of vaccine production, varietal development through somoclonal variations, developing better quality products and transgenic in crops such as brinjal, cauliflower and cabbage have strengthened the field. In 21st century agriculture, application of modern biotechnologies like DNA finger printing, tissue culture, terminator gene technology and genetic cloning will hold the key in raising the productivity.

In the new millennium, the challenges in Indian agricultural sector are quite different from those met in the previous decades. The enormous pressure to produce more food from less and with shrinking natural resources is a tough task for the farmers. To keep up the momentum of growth a careful economic evaluation of inputs like seeds, fertilizers, irrigation sources etc. are of considerable importance.

Diffusion of fertilizer consumption in Indian agriculture has been quite widespread. The imbalance in the use of N, P and K have become highly conspicuous. The intensity of fertilizer use has gradually gone up from about 3 kg/ha. In early sixties to about 88 kg/ha in 1997-98.

Therefore, wider distribution of fertilizer needs to be promoted by covering regions with low use of fertilizers such as central and eastern regions of Uttar Pradesh (in the case of wheat and rice) through creation of an extensive network of rural infrastructure (including roads and credit) for establishing an appropriate interface of input markets and output markets in these regions.

In Indian agriculture, multiplication, distribution and availability of good quality seed is crucial to accelerated food production. With entry of MNCs in seed production and distribution and consequent effects of patenting under the WTO regime, providing quality seeds to farmer at an affordable cost will be a measure challenge in future. To meet the growing competition companies should adopt modern processing technologies and seed growers have to be trained in cost reducing methods of growing quality seed material.

Indian agriculture has to become most cost-effective to meet the growing challenges and opportunities arising out of WTO agreements and the consequent globalization impacts. For this, future growth of agriculture has to be yield based. Development of infrastructure is essential to support this growth. The farm credit system in Indian agriculture, evolved over decades has been instrumental in enhancing production and marketing of farm produce and stimulating capital formation in agriculture. Credit for Indian agriculture has to expand at a faster rate than before because of the need to step-up agricultural growth to generate surplus for exports, and also because to change in the product mix towards animal husbandry, agriculture, fish farming, horticulture and floriculture, medicinal plants, which will necessitate larger investments.

Indian agriculture has potential and prospects in the following areas of agri-business. India is the third largest producer of fruits and the 2nd largest grower of vegetables. The total production is about 27.83 MT in fruits and 54 MT in vegetables. The farmers can grow any type of vegetable and fruits throughout the year.

India has attained self-sufficing in food. It is now exporting rice and wheat to some countries including China. There is a vast scope of exporting the cereals to various countries. Though India's irrigated area is about one-third of the world, the area under drip and sprinkler irrigation is very meagre compared to total drip and sprinkler area in the world. The area under drip is 1,60,000 ha and under sprinkler, it is about 0.60 Mha. It is essential that in the next 7 years, the area under drip and sprinkler will be about 1 Mha and 5 Mha respectively.

SECTION III

India's Agricultural Trade

India's share in the world market has risen to 0.7 per cent. If the trend continues it is expected that the trade may go upto 1.5 per cent. This is because of rising exports and the opening up the domestic market rapidly. India will make its presence felt on the world trade scene.

In Indian agriculture, rural women play a vital role and participate in all stages of crop production, as they constitute 50 per cent rural labour force. They contribute in agricultural operations like, transplanting, manuring and fertilizing, harvesting, threshing, winnowing, drying and carrying the product. To better exploit the emerging opportunities, there is need for changing property rights in favour of women, evolving technologies to suit women farmers, increasing the number of women extension workers, educating and training women farmers.

According to Dr. C. Rangaranjan the purpose of the various rounds of discussions on world trade has been to expand world trade. The world trade environment holds out many interesting opportunities for Indian agriculture. It must be noted that there are many countries, which are knocking at the doors of WTO to enter it.

Calculations show that if the economy is to grow at 7 per cent per annum and also if the base is to expand, the value of agricultural output must increase at an annual rate of 4.5 per cent between 1997 and 2002. If export growth is excluded and domestic requirements alone are taken, the required growth rate comes down to 3.52 per cent. Looking at agricultural crops alone, the required growth rate of 1997-2002 is 3.82 per cent as compared with the actual annual compound growth rate of 2.77 percent during 1980-1994. While the targeted growth rate of food-grains is 3.05 percent per annum as against the actual growth rate of 2.67 per cent in the period 1980-1994, a substantial increase in growth rate is required in the case of pulses, oilseeds and fruits and vegetables.

The challenges before Indian agriculture are immense. This sector needs to grow at a faster rate than in the past to allow for higher per capita consumption. A slowdown in the growth rate of production and productivity has been seen in the recent period. We need to reserve this trend. It is true that genetic yields or maximum attainable yields have hit a kind of barrier of late. While scientific research must continue to improve the maximum attainable yield, we need to bridge as a first step the considerable gap that still exists between attainable yields and actual productivity levels in the fields.

Trade in agriculture continues to be outside the mainstream of liberalization of international trade. A feature of the policies of many industrialized countries is that in the agricultural sector their actions affect not only access to their domestic markets but also influence the conditions of access in third country markets. Competitive subsidization of agricultural products has assumed unprecedented dimensions. The competition appears to be becoming one of the subsidies rather than of efficiency of production.

Development countries are required to reduce tariff by 24 per cent. In addition, countries are required to provide 3 to 5 per cent markets access for agricultural goods.

The market access rule was introduced because it was felt that even if individual countries reduce the tariff by 36 per cent in six years, there still would not be any market access opportunities. Hence, the provision of 3 to 5 per cent minimum market access opportunity was introduced. The rule does not apply to India at the present moment because quantitative restriction is in place for BOP reasons. Even when this constraint does not operate, the impact of the rule may not be much as the tariff rates to when India is binding itself are high. The minimum market access opportunities established by other countries will on the other hand create a wider market for Indian exports. Reduction in tariffs by the developed countries should work to the advantage of India rather than its disadvantage.

SECTION IV

Indian Farmers Gain from W.T.O. Agreement

Five years after the World Trade Organisation (WTO) came into existence, the anticipated gains for India from the trade liberalization process in agriculture are practically zero. And yet, undaunted by the negative fallout from the implementation of the WTO's Agreement on Agriculture, the Ministry of Agriculture is aggressively pushing for the second phase of reforms.

The WTO's Agreement on Agriculture had incorporated three board areas of commitments from member states, namely in market access, domestic support and export subsidies. The underlying objective was to correct and prevent restrictions and distortions in world agricultural markets.

India was forced to either phase out or eliminate the quantitative restrictions (QRs) on agricultural commodities and products latest by 1 April 2000. India has, therefore, opened its market and in turn made the farming community vulnerable to the imports of highly subsidies products. Already, cheaper imports of skimmed milk powder, edible oils, sugar, tea, areca nut, apples, coconut etc. have flooded the market.

Export Subsidies

The kind of export subsidies that need to be pruned is not provided in India. Whereas the WTO enables only 25 countries to provide export subsidies for their agricultural products and commodities, India is keen to support the Cairns Group (food-exporting countries), which demands the elimination of export subsidies, not realizing that joining such a group will invite problems on various other fronts.

It was expected that with the removal of trade-distorting measures, agricultural exports from the developing countries will increase. In fact, India has seen a massive increase in the imports of agricultural commodities and products — from about Rs. 50,000 million in 1995 to over Rs. 2,00,000 million in 1999-2000 — a four-fold increase. Nor has the so called fair trading system helped efficient producers in realizing a higher price for their products. On the contrary, prices of most agricultural commodities are declining in the world markets.

Market Access

A recent FAO study concludes there has been hardly any change in the volume of exports. Tariff peaks continue to block exports from the developing countries. Tariffs still remain very high, especially for cereals, sugar and dairy products. Sanitary and phytosanitary measures continue to be a major barrier in diversifying exports in horticulture and meat products. Selective reduction in tariffs by the developed countries have also blocked the exports from developing countries. And on top of it, only 36 countries (all developed) have the right to impose special safeguard provisions if agriculture imports distort their domestic market.

India was forced to either phase out or eliminate the quantitative restriction (QRs) on agricultural commodities and products latest by April 1, 2000. India has therefore, opened its market and in turn made the farming community vulnerable to the imports of highly subsidized problems. Already, cheap imports of skimmed milk powder, edible oils, sugar, tea, areca nut, apples and coconut have flooded the market.

Domestic Support

In India, we are being told that our Aggregate Measure of Support (AMS) being negative, we can still raise our subsidies to farmers. In reality, India is committed to do away with agricultural subsidies under the Structural Adjustment Programme of the World Bank and the IMF. In any case, India provides only $ 1 billion worth of indirect subsidies to 550 million farmers. It was anticipated that due to reduction in domestic support in developed countries, cereal production would shift from developed countries to developing countries. Empirical evidence, however, shows that such a trend is not visible. Moreover, with such massive subsidies intact, and with the QRs being lifted, India is sure to be inundated with food imports.

Export Subsidies

India has seen a massive increase in the imports of agricultural commodities and products from about Rs. 5,000 crore in 1995 to over Rs. 20,000 crore in 1999-2000—a four-fold increase. Nor has the so-called fair trading system helped efficient producers realize a higher price for their products. On the contrary, prices of most agricultural commodities are declining in the world markets.

According to Dr. Prakash, "To assess the impacts of WTO on Karnataka agriculture, all the related issues are grouped in to three categories: the core issues, the issues concerned to basic premises of WTO and the vital issues associate with WTO. The core issues are the main components of WTO, which include trade liberalization, market access; export subsidy and Intellectual Property Rights. The WTO is carrying through these core issues with three basic premises; protected agriculture, perfect market condition and uniformity in agricultural economies across the World. In addition the issues related to three vital subjects; food security, economic concentration and the environmental sustainability are kept "auxiliary'.

SECTION IV

Conclusion

The liberalization of the world trade in agriculture, under the present circumstance, is going to benefit more to develop countries rather than the developing countries. The expected gain to the members of Third World 23 per cent of the projected benefit. Under this circumstance of a very high rate of tariffs in the developed world and a low or nil tariffs in the developing countries, the removal of quantitative restrictions on agricultural commodities will tilt the balance in the global trade in favour of former with a detrimental effects on the producers in the Third World.

In the emerging post-WTO world economic order, one thing is certain that the direct competition from imported goods can't be prevented. While one can argue on the merits and demerits of exposure of the Indian agriculture to foreign invasion, the relevant question is whether we can really stop the imported agricultural products from getting into the Indian market? The answer is a clear 'no' with the eventual dismantling of the quantitative restrictions and reductions of industrial tariffs our choice of warding off foreign competition is nothing more than wishful thing. So we must focus on how India can use the changed than wishful thinking. So we must focus on how India can use the changed conditions to earn benefits. For this, first and foremost the economy has to identify and develop a modern infrastructure to facilitate the agricultural exports. The post-harvest technology and the storage facilities need to be upgraded.

There is a need to commercialize the farm operations by improving the management and marketing techniques. This can be achieved by establishing mutually beneficial linkages with the industry. Thus this is plenty of scope for Indian to change from a mere producer to an exporter of value-added and processed farm products and high quality seeds.

Our food and farming system are in deep crisis. Food scares are spreading. Farmers are committing suicide in thousands or selling their kidneys to pay back debts for high cost agricultural inputs such as seeds and pesticides, which were supposed to have brought them prosperity by increasing their productivity. The prosperity that globalisation was supposed to spread elusive.

Prices of agricultural commodities are collapsing as import restrictions are removed and subsidies products flood domestic markets. Even while domestic producers are denied price support and procurement subsidies.

Yet, low prices from farmers do not mean low prices for third world consumes, the majority of whom are desperately poor and already malnourished. Food prices are rising in the Third World, even as prices of agricultural produce collapse as food subsidies are removed, and the polarization between prices farmers receive and prices consumers pay increases.

Prices of food are also measuring as vertical integration increases corporate profits, and as pseudo hygienic laws are used to legally ban low cost, culturally and economically appropriate food processing systems such as the "*ghanis*" (tiny cold pressed oil mills), the "*chakkis*" (the small family run floor mills), the "*halwai*" shops (sweet and savoury snack markets).

The livelihood and food rights of million are eroding as Indian agriculture is being reduced to a market for global corporation—for their seeds and agrochemicals, for their processed foods, for dumping their subsidized grain and commodities.

The corporate takeover of Indian agriculture has been facilitated by the globalisation of agriculture, through the imposition of structural adjustment by the World Bank and IMF, and the trade rules of WTO as embodied in its Agriculture Agreement and TRIPs (Trade in Intellectual Property Rights) Agreement. This corporation is now part of India's National Agriculture Policy (NAP).

Trade Liberalisation rules have camouflaged the corporation of agriculture by creating a jargon about competitiveness, market access, aggregate measure of support which hides the emergence of corporate monopolies, the dumping of subsidized products, and the growth of corporate subsidized.

Trade liberalization as deregulation of commerce privileges traders over producers, profits over needs.

Both peasants and poor consumers are paying the price for globalisation in terms of their very lives—either through malnutrition and hunger, or through suicides.

India is faced with the paradox of falling farm prices, rising food prices. Even as farm prices are falling, retail prices of food and essential commodities are rising.

The normal explanation for falling prices is over production, and the normal explanation for rising prices is scarcity.

However, we do not have over production of food, nor do we have a new scarcity. The paradoxical and double crisis of falling prices at the farm and rising food prices for consumers is the direct result of the World Bank and WTO driven economic reforms and trade liberalization policies which have removed price controls.

These policies have pushed farm prices downwards and cost of production, upwards.

Withdrawal of subsidies in the input sector and the deregulation of the seed and input sector have worked together to raise costs of production and push farmers into a debt trap. The withdrawal pf price support and procurement guarantee has taken the floor out of farm prices. With inventory and price controls removed, traders and the processing industry are also exploiting the farmer, by refusing to buy agricultural produce except at prices much below the cost of production.

In meantime, the withdrawal of food subsidies and amendments of the Essential Commodities Act have taken the ceiling out of food prices. Subsidies are being withdrawn from farmers and are being given to trading corporations.

The sudden withdrawl of the government subsidies from procurement and the crisis farmers are facing in terms of collapse of markets is also in preparation of handing over India's domestic markets to seed giants like Cargill, which is no saviout of farmers.

The second cause of the collapse of farm prices is the removal of the Quantitative Restriction (QR) on imports. Growers of coconut, mustard, coffee, tea, spices are all facing threats to their survival as highly subsidized artificially cheap products are dumped on the Indian market. Even small quantities of artificially cheap imports can used spices into a downward spin, wiping out domestic markets and consequently domestic production. In a season or two, with domestic production destroyed, import dependence can become absolute.

In any case, no trade sanction could do more economic damage than the destruction being caused to India's economy by the removal of QRs.

Farmers' suicides, and the growing number hunger among the poor, show that the removal of import restrictions and economic reformer have started to threaten the very survival of Indian farmers and poor consumers. The Government has an obligation under the Indian Constitution and a right under the WTO to act in defence of the protection of the right to life and livelihood of Indian peasants and the Indian people.

The real security threat to the country is not a war—it is the dismantling of our food security and the potential displacement of three quarters of India.

A farm leader recently said: "As long as farmers have their sickle, they will be peaceful. But if their sickle is snached from their hands, it will be replaced by a gun".

The largest democracy, home to the majority of farmers in the world, must its democratic rights and duties in the defence of its food security and the survival of its people.

The increased market concentration and enhanced control by the MNCs will result in the charging of higher 'monopoly margin' on inputs and technologies and increases the cost of production for farmers. This is also going to affect the consumers in the long run.

Preventing the destruction of our agriculture and our framers will be the most severe test for our functioning as a democracy and as a free economy. If we fail this test, we will be wiped out as a society, as a civilization.

References

Bhagwati, J (1993), *India in Transition*, Oxford: Clarendon Press *Economist*, November 1-7, 1997.

Gulati, A. and Rao, H. (1992), "Indian Agriculture: Emerging Perspectives and Policy Issues". *Economic and Political Weekly*. December.

Gulati, A. and Sharma, A. (1997), "Freeing Trade in Agriculture", *Economic and Political Weekly*, 27 December.

Hashim, S.R. (1998), "Economic Growth and Income Distribution", *Economic and Political Weekly*, 21 March 1998.

IMF (1995), *India: Economic Reform and Growth*. Occasional paper 134. Washington: International Monetary Fund.

Keshari, K. *et al.* (1995), "Implications of GATT-94 on exports of Indian agro-processing firms". *World Trade Research and Information Report*. Vol. 1, No. 3.

Patnaik, P. (1997), "The context and consequences of economic liberalization in India", *Journal of International Trade and Development*, Vol. 6, No. 2, July 1997.

Purcel, G. (1996), "Some aspects of the liberalization of South Asian agricultural policies: How can the WTO help?" Draft paper for the Food and Agricultural Organization.

Rao, K.V. (1995), "GATT and the trade in services". *State Bank of India Monthly Review*. March.

Sharma, A. (1996), "*Indian Agricultural Trade Liberalization and the Uruguay Round Agreement*". Paper for the World Bank Conference on the Implications for South Asian Agriculture. Nepal, April.

Storm, S. (1997), "The unfinished agenda: Indian agriculture under the structural reforms". *Journal of International Trade and Development*, Vol. 6, No. 2, July 1997.

Thomas, P. *et al.* (1994), "Dunkel Text: Implications for Rural Sector". *Economic and Political Weekly*. March.

UNCTAD (1996), *Strengthening the participation of developing countries in world trade and the multilateral trading system*. Geneva: United Nations Conference on Trade and Development.

World Bank (1996), *India: Recent Economic Developments and Prospects.* Washington: World Bank.

World Bank (1997), *India: Five years of stabilization and reform and the challenges ahead.* Washington: World Bank.

WTO (1998), *Trade policy review on India*, Geneva: World Trade Organization.

Yap, C.L. (1996), "The impact of the Uruguay Round Agreement on Agriculture on the World Rice Economy" Paper for the World Bank Conference on the Implications for South Asian Agriculture. Nepal, April.

25

PRICE ARRIVAL RELATIONSHIP AND NET RETURN ANALYSIS OF HORITICULTURAL PRODUCE

A Case Study

RAIS AHMED & ALI GHUFRAN

Introduction

Theoretically, under orderly marketing conditions, prices move according to the changes in arrivals. From this point of view, changes in prices may be considerably influenced by the fluctuations in arrivals. Under ideal conditions, other things remaining the same, the increase in arrivals may lead to pro rata fall in prices and *vice-versa*. To ascertain to what extent the changes in vegetable arrivals are influencing the changes in prices, an attempt has been made to examine the relationship between the prices and arrivals of selected vegetables in Allahabad, Agricultural Produce Marketing Committee. In order to analyze the impact of market arrivals cn the prices of three vegetables i.e. Potato, Tomato and Onion, the data has been collected on monthly arrivals and prices for the period January-June, 1999 of Agricultural Produce Marketing Committee, Allahabad. Degree of heterogeneity/homogeneity in arrivals and prices is expressed in arrivals and prices are expressed in terms of Standard Deviation and Coefficient of Variation, and, for the purpose of quantifying the response of Price to a given change in market arrivals, Least Square Technique is used for the available data.

Agricultural Produce Marketing Committee of Allahabad is situated at Mundera, the sub-urban area of the city. Producers of Fruits & Vegetables bring their produce from their fields to the market and place them on platforms prescribed for them, produce-wise. The Market Committee provides Weighing Scales to sellers and charges a certain fixed amount from both the buyer and seller as *Mandi* fee, as fixed by the Market Committee.

As some vegetables are most perishable in nature, arrivals in the market affect their prices. Monthly market arrivals and weighted average prices of randomly selected vegetables Potato, Tomato and Onion for the year January-June, 1999 is presented in Table 25.1.

Table 25.1: Monthly Market Arrivals and Prices of Vegetables

Month	*Potato*		*Tomato*		*Onion*	
	Qty. (Q)	*Price (P)*	*Qty. (O)*	*Price (P)*	*Qty. (O)*	*Price (P)*
January	3500	250	2000	250	2445	650
February	3545	225	1650	260	2655	665
March	3865	233	1600	260	3025	650
April	3700	230	1500	275	3543	645
May	2895	250	1200	310	3600	625
June	2700	265	900	315	3400	660

Quantity (Q) = Quintals, Price (P) = Rs. /Quintal.

Source: Agricultural Produce Marketing Committee, Allahabad.

Calculation

In order to calculate the SD, CV and Price-Quantity relationship, the formulas used are:[(1)]

Mean $(X) = 1/n\ \Sigma X_i$

Standard Deviation $(\sigma) = \sqrt{1/n}\ \Sigma\left(X_i - X\right)^2$

Coefficient of Variation = $S/X \times 100$

Linear equation of Straight Line is:

$$Y = a + b\,X$$

where n = number of observations i = 1, 2,............6

a & b = arbitrary constant

$\Sigma Y_i = na + b\Sigma X_i$

$\Sigma X_i Y_i = a\Sigma X_i + b\Sigma X_i^2$

On the basis of Table 25.1 we have calculated Mean, Standard Deviation, Coefficient of Variation and Linear equation of Straight Line (with respect to price and quantity) for Potato, Tomato and Onion separately, which have been shown in Table 25.2.

For Potato

Mean (Quantity) = 20205/6 = 3367.50

Mean (Price) = 1453/6 = 242.17

$$\text{SD (Quantity)} = \sqrt{\frac{1075937.50}{6}} = \sqrt{179322.92} = 423.47$$

$$\text{SD (Price)} = \sqrt{\frac{1170.84}{6}} = \sqrt{195.14} = 13.97$$

$$\text{CV (Quantity)} = \frac{423.47 \times 100}{3367.50} = 12.58$$

$$\text{CV (Price)} = \frac{13.97 \times 100}{242.17} = 5.77$$

Linear Equation of Straight Line:

$$1453 = 6a + 20205\,b \qquad \ldots(1)$$

$$4863420 = 20205\,a + 69116275\,b \qquad \ldots(2)$$

From Equations (1) & (2), we get:

$$a = 343.20, \text{ and } b = -0.03$$

Therefore, Linear Equation of Straight Line for price and quantity is:

P = 343.20 – 0.03 Q

For Tomato

$$\text{Mean (Quantity)} = \frac{8850}{6} = 1475.00$$

$$\text{Mean (Price)} = \frac{1670}{6} = 278.33$$

$$\text{SD (Quantity)} = \sqrt{\frac{728750}{6}} = \sqrt{121458.33} = 348.51$$

Table 25.2: Statistical Calculation for Selected Agricultural Produce

				Potato				
Month	Q	P	$(Q–Q)$	$(Q–Q)^2$	$(P–P)$	$(P–P)^2$	$P \times Q$	Q^2
January	3500	250	132.50	17556.25	7.83	61.31	875000	12250000
February	3545	225	177.50	31506.25	–17.17	294.81	797625	12567025
March	3865	233	497.50	247506.25	–9.17	87.09	900545	17938225
April	3700	230	332.50	110556.25	–12.17	148.11	851000	13690000
May	2895	250	–472.50	223256.25	7.83	61.31	723750	8381025
June	2700	265	–667.50	445556.25	22.83	521.21	715500	7290000
Total	**20205**	**1453**		**1075937.50**		**1170.84**	**4863420**	**69116275**

Table 25.2: *Contd.*

				Tomato				
Month	*Q*	*P*	*(Q–Q)*	$(Q-Q)^2$	*(P–P)*	$(P-P)^2$	$P \times Q$	Q^2
January	2000	250	525	275625	–28.33	502.59	500000	4000000
February	1650	260	175	30625	–18.33	335.99	429000	2722500
March	1600	260	125	15625	–18.33	335.99	416000	2560000
April	1500	275	25	625	–3.33	11.09	412500	2250000
May	1200	310	–275	75625	31.67	1002.99	372000	1440000
June	900	315	575	330625	36.37	1344.69	283500	810000
Total	**8850**	**1670**		**728750**		**3833.34**	**2413000**	**13782500**

Table 25.2: *Contd.*

					Onion			
Month	*Q*	*P*	*(Q–Q)*	$(Q-Q)^2$	*(P–P)*	$(P-P)^2$	$P \times Q$	Q^2
January	2445	650	–666.33	443995.67	0.83	0.69	1589250	5978025
February	2655	665	–456.33	208237.07	15.83	250.59	1765575	7049025
March	3025	650	–86.33	7452.87	0.83	0.69	1966250	9150625
April	3543	645	431.67	186338.99	–4.17	17.39	2285235	12552849
May	3600	625	488.67	238798.37	–24.17	584.19	2250000	12960000
June	3400	660	288.67	83330.37	10.83	117.29	2244000	11560000
Total	**18668**	**3895**		**1168153.34**		**970.84**	**12100310**	**59250524**

$$\text{SD (Price)} = \sqrt{\frac{3833.34}{6}} = \sqrt{638.89} = 25.28$$

$$\text{CV (Quantity)} = \frac{348.51 \times 100}{1475.00} = 23.63$$

$$\text{CV (Price)} = \frac{25.28 \times 100}{278.33} = 9.08$$

Linear Equation of Straight Line:

$$1670 = 6\,a + 8850\,b \qquad \text{...(1)}$$

$$2413000 = 8850\,a + 13782500\,b \qquad \text{...(2)}$$

From Equations (1) & (2), we get:

$$a = 381.58 \text{ and } b = -0.07$$

Therefore, Linear Equation of Straight Line for price and quantity is:

$$\mathbf{P = 381.58 - 0.07\,Q}$$

For Onion

$$\text{Mean (Quantity)} = \frac{18668}{6} = 3111.33$$

$$\text{Mean (Price)} = \frac{3895}{6} = 649.17$$

$$\text{SD (Quantity)} = \sqrt{\frac{1168153.34}{6}} = \sqrt{194692.22} = 441.24$$

$$\text{SD (Price)} = \sqrt{\frac{970.84}{6}} = \sqrt{161.81} = 12.72$$

$$\text{CV (Quantity)} = \frac{441.24 \times 100}{3111.33} = 14.18$$

$$\text{CV (Price)} = \frac{12.72 \times 100}{649.17} = 1.96$$

Linear Equation of Straight Line:

$$3895 = 6\,a + 18668\,b \qquad \text{...(1)}$$

$$12100310 = 18668\,a + 59250524\,b \qquad \text{...(2)}$$

From Equations (1) & (2), we get:

$$a = 655.39 \text{ and } b = -0.002$$

Therefore, Linear equation of straight line for price and quantity is:

$$\mathbf{P = 655.39 - 0.002Q}$$

From Table 25.3 one can easily see the variation in prices and quantity of selected agricultural produce. As far as quantity is concerned, Tomato shows a high degree of heterogeneity followed by Onion and Potato. But when the prices are compared, it is found that Onion has the highest homogeneity followed by Potato and Tomato.

But as far as the relationship of the price and quantity of produce is concerned, it is found that an increase of one quintal of Potato, Tomato and Onion respectively, the price reduces by only Rs. 0.03, Rs. 0.07 and Rs. 0.002 respectively, which is just negligible. It means that the increase in market arrival brings no change in the price of the selected produce. But this result will not hold true for all the markets.

Table 25.3: Mean, SD, CV and Linear Equation for Selected Vegetables

Vegetable	*Mean*	*SD*	*CV(%)*	*Linear Equation*
Potato				
Quantity	3367.50	423.47	12.58	**P = 343.20 – 0.03Q**
Price	242.17	13.97	5.77	
Tomato				
Quantity	1475.00	348.51	23.63	**P = 381.58–0.07Q**
Price	278.33	25.28	9.08	
Onion				
Quantity	3111.33	441.24	14.18	**P = 655.39 – 0.002Q**
Price	649.17	12.72	1.96	

Thus the analysis on the whole reveals that the arrivals in the markets do not completely explain the variations in the prices of vegetables or *vice versa.* It can thus be concluded that arrival is not the significant factor, influencing the price of vegetables. Other factors like changes in the consumption pattern, traders etc. may play significant role in price changes.

Now after discussing the price-arrival relationships, it is considered necessary to find the net share of producer and market intermediaries in the final price paid by the consumer. For this we have taken the help of price-spread analysis.

Price-Spread Analysis

It is well known that the marketing channels for fruits and vegetables vary from commodity to commodity and from producer to producer. In rural areas and small towns, many producers perform the functions of retail sellers. Large producers directly sell their produce to the processing firms. Fruits and Vegetables market is one where there is exploitation both at producer's as well as the consumer's level. The middlemen take the major share of the amount left after the producer being paid. Some of the common marketing channels for Fruits and Vegetables are depicted in Fig. 25.1

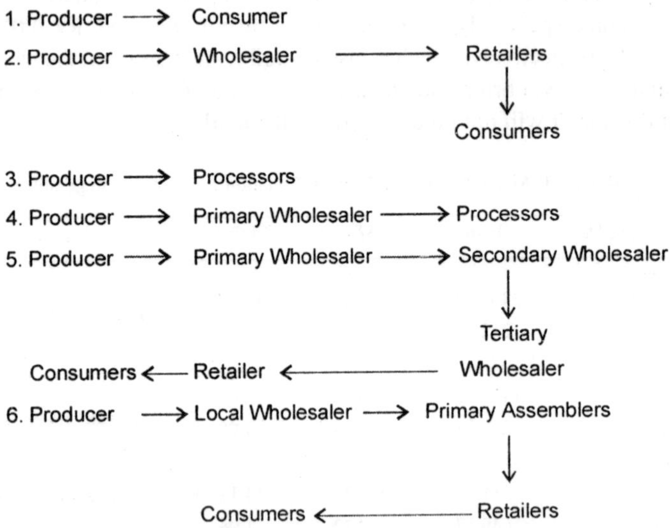

Fig. 25.1: Marketing Channels for Fruits and Vegetables

In all the above marketing channels (except 1 and 3), it is seen that a number of middlemen are in action, due to which the producer did not get the right price of his produce.

Thus, in this context the main thing is to make movement of goods from producer to consumer at the lowest possible cost, so that both the producer and consumer may achieve higher level of satisfaction. In this regard a survey has been conducted (through questionnaire) in order to know the marketing efficiency as well as the price-spread from consumer to producer, which is essentially the degree of market performance.

As we know that fruits and vegetables after leaving the farm, pass through some stages before they reach the consumer. Every one of the intermediaries, through whom the fruits and vegetables pass charge for the services performed by him.

It is therefore, worthwhile to examine as to what share of rupee paid by the consumer reaches the producer. For this purpose respondents were selected from producers, wholesalers, retailers and consumers to study the price-spread of the selected fruits and vegetables under study. The producer's share in consumer's rupee can be calculated by taking into account the following charges:

1. The gross wholesale price of the produce paid by the consumer;
2. Expenses incurred by the retailer;
3. Margin of the retailer and price paid by the retailer to the wholesaler;
4. Expenses incurred by the wholesaler;
5. Margin of the wholesaler and price paid by the wholesaler to the producer;
6. Expenses incurred by the producer such as; packaging, loading and unloading, transportation and commission paid to the middleman;
7. The gross wholesale price of the produce received by the producer; and
8. Expressing the whole transaction on percentage basis. Thus it gives the producers share in consumer's rupee.

In order to calculate the price-spread and marketing efficiency, we have taken into account few fruits and vegetables like: Potato, Onion, Tomato, Green Peas, Guava and Mango.

As we know that the prices of horticultural produce (especially vegetables) vary from place to place, day-to-day and even from morning to evening. So for this purpose we have taken up the account in the market price of fruits and vegetables of Allahabad district of 15th February, 1999 excluding market price of mango (which is of 20th June, 1999), in order to calculate the price-spread and marketing efficiency of the produce.

At present the prevailing marketing channel for the disposal of produce in the market is:

Producer → Wholesaler → Retailers

↓

Consumers

So for the purpose of calculating price-spread as well as marketing efficiency the above channel of marketing horticultural produce has been taken into account.

First of all we have calculated the price-spread and then marketing efficiency (Tables 25.4 to 25.9).

Table 25.4: Price-spread between Producer and Consumer for Potato

	Items	*Price/80 kg. (in Rs.)*	*%age of Consumers Pric*
1.	Price paid by the consumer (to retailer)	**240.00**	**100.00**
2.	Expenses of the retailer	12.00	5.00
3.	Margin of the retailer	28.00	11.67
4.	Price paid by the retailer (to wholesaler)	**200.00**	
5.	Expenses of the wholesaler	9.60	4.00
6.	Margin of the wholesaler	16.90	7.04
7.	Price paid by the wholesaler (to producer)	**173.50**	
8.	Expenses of the producer	33.50	13.96
9.	Price received by the producer	**140.00**	**58.33**

Table 1.4 shows that out of Rs. 240.00 paid by the consumer for 80 kg. of Potato, the producer gets only Rs. 140.00 i.e. 58.33 per cent of the consumer's price. 13.96 per cent of the consumer's price i.e. Rs. 33.50 is the amount of expenditures incurred by the producer for bringing and selling his produce to the market. While Rs. 28.00 and Rs. 16.90 representing 11.67 per cent and 7.04 per cent of the consumer's price is the retailer's and wholesaler's margins respectively.

Table 25.5: Price-spread between Producer and Consumer for Onion

	Items	*Price/80 kg. (in Rs.)*	*%age of Consumers Price*
1.	Price paid by the consumer (to retailer)	**560.00**	**100.00**
2.	Expenses of the retailer	28.00	5.00
3.	Margin of the retailer	84.00	15.00
4.	Price paid by the retailer (to wholesaler)	**448.00**	
5.	Expenses of the wholesaler	22.40	4.00
6.	Margin of the wholesaler	44.80	8.00
7.	Price paid by the wholesaler (to producer)	**380.80**	
8.	Expenses of the producer	70.00	12.50
9.	Price received by the producer	**310.80**	**55.50**

Table 25.5 reveals that out of Rs. 560.00 paid by the consumer for 80 kg. of Onion, the producer gets only Rs. 310.80 i.e. 55.50 per cent of

the consumer's price. 12.50 per cent of the consumer's price i.e. Rs. 70.00 is the expenditure incurred by the producer for bringing and selling his produce in the market. While Rs. 84.00 and Rs. 44.80 representing 15.00 per cent and 8.00 per cent of the consumer's price are the retailers and wholesalers margins.

Table 25.6: Price-spread between Producer and Consumer for Tomato

Items	*Price/20 kg. (in Rs.)*	*%age of Consumers Price*
1. Price paid by the consumer (to retailer)	**60.00**	**100.00**
2. Expenses of the retailer	3.00	5.00
3. Margin of the retailer	8.10	13.50
4. Price paid by the retailer (to wholesaler)	**48.90**	
5. Expenses of the wholesaler	2.40	4.00
6. Margin of the wholesaler	5.40	9.00
7. Price paid by the wholesaler (to producer)	**41.10**	
8. Expenses of the producer	9.00	15.00
9. Price received by the producer	**32.10**	**53.50**

Table 25.6 depicts that out of Rs. 60.00 paid by the consumer for 20 kg. of Onion, the producer's share only Rs. 32.10 i.e. 53.50 per cent of the consumer's price. 15.00 per cent of the consumer's price i.e. Rs. 9.00 is the expenditure incurred by the producer for bringing and selling his produce in the market. While Rs. 8.10 goes to the retailer's pockets which amount to 13.50 per cent and Rs. 5.40 which is 9.00 per cent wholesaler's margin respectively.

Table 25.7: Price-spread between Producer and Consumer for Green Pea

Items	*Price/80 kg. (in Rs.)*	*%age of Consumers Price*
1. Price paid by the consumer (to retailer)	**450.00**	**100.00**
2. Expenses of the retailer	22.50	5.00
3. Margin of the retailer	67.50	15.00
4. Price paid by the retailer (to wholesaler)	**360.00**	
5. Expenses of the wholesaler	18.00	4.00
6. Margin of the wholesaler	42.75	9.50
7. Price paid by the wholesaler (to producer)	**299.25**	
8. Expenses of the producer	51.75	11.50
9. Price received by the producer	**247.50**	**55.00**

A simple look at Table 25.7 shows that out of Rs. 450.00 paid by the consumer for 80 kg. of green pea, the producer receives only Rs. 247.50 i.e. 55.00 per cent of the consumer's price. The producers spent Rs 51.75 i.e. 11.50 per cent on bringing his produce to market and selling it there. Rs. 67.50 i.e. 15.00 per cent went to retailer and the wholesaler pocketed Rs. 42.75 i.e. 9.50 per cent.

Table 25.8: Price-spread between Producer and Consumer for Guava

	Items	*Price/40 kg. (in Rs.)*	*%age of Consumers Price*
1.	Price paid by the consumer (to retailer)	**180.00**	**100.00**
2.	Expenses of the retailer	9.00	5.00
3.	Margin of the retailer	24.75	13.75
4.	Price paid by the retailer (to wholesaler)	**146.25**	
5.	Expenses of the wholesaler	7.20	4.00
6.	Margin of the wholesaler	15.30	8.50
7.	Price paid by the wholesaler (to producer)	**123.75**	
8.	Expenses of the producer	24.30	13.50
9.	Price received by the producer	**99.45**	**55.25**

Table 25.8 shows that out the consumer paid Rs. 180.00 for 40 kg. of Guava and the producer receives nearly half at Rs. 99.45 i.e. 55.25 per cent of the consumer's rupee. The producer incurred the expenditure of Rs. 24.30 i.e. 13.50 per cent on consumer's price. The retailer got Rs. 24.75 i.e. 13.75 per cent while the wholesaler grabbed Rs. 15.30 i.e. 8.50 per cent of the consumer's price.

Table 25.9: Price-spread between Producer and Consumer for Mango

	Items	*Price/40 kg. (in Rs.)*	*%age of Consumers Price*
1.	Price paid by the consumer (to retailer)	**400.00**	**100.00**
2.	Expenses of the retailer	20.00	5.00
3.	Margin of the retailer	64.00	16.00
4.	Price paid by the retailer (to wholesaler)	**316.00**	
5.	Expenses of the wholesaler	16.00	4.00
6.	Margin of the wholesaler	44.00	11.00
7.	Price paid by the wholesaler (to producer)	**256.00**	
8.	Expenses of the producer	48.00	12.00
9.	Price received by the producer	**208.00**	**52.00**

Table 25.9 reveals that out of Rs. 400.00 paid by the consumer for 40 kg. of Mango, the producer gets only Rs. 208.00 i.e. 52.00 per cent of the consumer's price. 12.00 per cent of the consumer's price i.e. Rs. 48.00 is the amount spent by the producer for transporting and selling his produce in the market. While Rs. 64.00 and Rs. 44.00 representing 16.004 and 11.00 per cent of the consumer's price is the retailer's and wholesaler's margins respectively.

An analysis of Tables 25.4 to 25.9 shows that, the producer's margin (in respect of consumer's price) lies between 52 to 58 per cent approximately, while his percentage of expenditure which includes loading-unloading, packaging, transportation as well as commission to the commission agent, lies between 11 to 15 per cent In this channel of marketing, the retailers and wholesalers capture a good percentage of amounts i.e. around 22 to 27 per cent, which vary from produce to produce due to its perishable nature. Therefore, it can be noted that the producer's share in the consumer's rupee is still low and un-remunerative. It seems to be mainly on account of high margins shared by retailers and wholesalers.

In case of green vegetables (like; Spinach, Cauliflower, Cabbage, Pumpkin, Chilly, Green Pea etc;) the producers are bound to sell their produce to wholesalers on low price, due to perishable nature of these items.

On the other hand, in order to calculate the marketing efficiency, which is the degree of market performance, different participants of the market have different expectations from the market, like:

- The consumers need good quality products at low possible prices within a short span of time;
- The farmers/producers need quick clearance of their produce with high prices; and
- The middlemen like, retailers, wholesalers and other functionaries expect a good amount of increase in income.

So in this regard, the movement of goods from producer to consumer at the lowest possible cost, consistent with the provision of the services desired by the consumer is termed as efficient marketing, without reducing consumer satisfaction.

In this context, various measures can be taken in order to assess the efficiency of the marketing system. For this purpose G. S. Shephard, has suggested that the ratio of the total value of goods marketed to the marketing cost may be used as a measure of efficiency. The higher is the ratio, the higher the efficiency and *vice versa.*

Shephard's idea can be expressed in a slightly modified form as follows:

$$ME = V/I - 1$$

where

ME = index of Marketing Efficiency.

V = value of the goods sold or price paid by the consumer.

I = input of marketing or total marketing cost.

The above formula has been applied on the data given in Tables 25.4 to 25.9 to calculate the Marketing Efficiency of selected produce for the prevalent marketing channel.

From Table 25.4:

V = Rs. 240.00

I = Rs. (12 + 28 + 9.60 + 16.90 + 33.50)

= Rs. 100.00

Therefore, $ME = V/I–1$

= 240/100–1

= 2.4–1

= 1.4

From Table 25.5:

V = Rs. 560.00

I = Rs. (28 + 84 + 22.40 + 44.80 + 70.00)

= Rs. 249.20

Therefore, $ME = V/I–1$

= 560/249.20 – 1

= 2.24–1

= 1.24

From Table 25.6

V = Rs. 60.00

I = Rs. (3 + 8.10 + 2.40 + 5.40 + 9.00)

= Rs. 27.90

Therefore, $ME = V/I–1$

= 60/27.90–1

= 2.15–1

= 1.15

From Table 25.7:

V = Rs. 450.00

I = Rs. (22.50 + 67.50 + 18 + 42.75 + 51.75)

= Rs. 202.50

Therefore, $ME = V/I–1$

= 450/202.50–1

= 2.22–1

= 1.22

From Table 25.8

V = Rs. 180.00

I = Rs. (9 + 24.75 + 7.20 + 15.30 + 24.30)
= Rs. 80.55

Therefore, $ME = V/I–1$
= 180/80.55–1
= 2.24–1
= 1.24

From Table 25.9

V = Rs. 200.00
I = Rs. (10 + 32 + 8 + 22 + 24)
= Rs. 96.00

Therefore, $ME = V/I–1$
= 200/96–1
= 2.08–1
= 1.08

In all the above cases one can find that the value of ME lies between 1.08 and 1.40. If we want to increase this, we have two options:

1. Either increase the price paid by the consumer; or
2. Decrease the share of intermediaries in all the above processes of delivering produce from producer to consumer.

The first option is not possible, because of this, the price of the produce will go up and consumer will suffer. So for this, the best option is to decrease the share of intermediaries in the overall process of delivering produce to consumer.

Now we know that the price-spread refers to the difference between consumer's price and the net price received by the producers. This difference consists of the charges borne by producers and other market functionaries against marketing cost and the margins of intermediaries involved in the system. Greater is the number of intermediaries, higher is the value of gross margins. Higher is the value of gross margins, higher the value of price-spread, lower is the marketing efficiency of producers, lower is their share in consumer's price.

References

Acharya & Agarwal (1994), *Agricultural Marketing in India*, Oxford & IBH Publishing Co. Pvt. Ltd., New Delhi, p.308.

Gupta & Kapoor (1989), *Fundamental of Mathematical Statistics*, Sultan Chand & Sons, New Deihi. pp.13, 46, 630-31.

Shephard. G.S. (1965), *Marketing Farm Products—Economic Analysis*, Iowa State University Press, Iowa, USA, p. 254.

26

CHANGING PATTERN OF NUTRITIONAL AVAILABILITY IN INDIA

A Post Independence Scenario

SYED WASEEM A. ASHRAF

Nutrition and human health is one of the most cherished aims of developing countries to be solved on priority basis. Land is the main and the most traditional source, which provide nutrition directly or indirectly to the people. Therefore, if land-use pattern is not in a proper direction (based on the requirement of the people) the imbalanced land-use will lead to the production, which will cause mal, and under-nutrition and will eventually affect health. The correlation between population growth and food production may help in planning a balanced land-use as well as balanced food that give enough nutrition to bring sustainability among the people. So that instead of being sick and inefficient may contribute efficiently in the resource utilization.

In chapter an attempt has been made to analyze the pattern of food production and population growth in India over the period of fifty years (1951-2001), to assess the nutritional availability of food grains and the changes thereon since 1951. As population kept on increasing at a higher rate than the growth in foodgrain production with the result there was an acute shortage of food during the sixties, Malthus (1798) in his classic thesis pointed out that the growth rate of food production will always lag behind the growth rate of population as former increases arithmetically white latter increases geometrically. Malthus was concerned about human capability to increase food production to a level needed to meet the needs of the growing population. He was right to some extent as the country had to import wheat at large scale to feed the teeming millions and this crisis had forced the country to adopt a new strategy to combat the problem on priority. India adopted a new strategy in early seventies, which gave a positive result. The achievement is known as Green Revolution, which however has not covered the entire country. Therefore at regional level it created disparities in food availability. Hence situation is not the same everywhere, but overall results were enough to turn the country from a chronic importer of foodgrain to an exporter of wheat. Moreover the impact of Green Revolution has not been seen in all the crops, some of the foodgrains have suffered badly over the period particularly pulses.

Fortunately, science and technology, coupled with appropriate public policies so far have helped to keep the Malthusian fear of widespread famines at bay. New Malthusian Lester Brown in his book "*Full House*" says that India may have to import over 45 million tonnes, quantity four times more than over a peak import of 10 million tonnes of foodgrain in 1966 under PL480 programme. FAO has also predicted that huge import in about 20 years, based on the assessment that the world agriculture production is going down under the conditions where trade is free but not fair, the prices of foodgrain will go up steeply at global market. If countries like India and China go for a large import as feared by Brown, even the developed countries may not be able to provide that much India and China may need by 2030.

Objectives

1. To study the trend of foodgrain production in India from 1951 to 2001 to assess the per capita availability of foodgrains to study the nutritional availability per capita (calories, carbohydrate and protein).
2. To analyze the ways and means to have the potential of meeting nutritional security means of the people, especially in pulses and brings sustainability to cereals to avoid fears and speculations of neo-Malthusians and FAO assessment/predictions of huge shortages.

Data and Methodology

The data of foodgrain production obtained from publications of Ministry of Agriculture while the population data have been taken from the decennial Census of India. The country on the whole is taken as a unit for detailed study and the states as unit. In case of states only 1951 and 2001 data are taken to find out the regional disparity/changes. Therefore, the population to get per capita availability of foodgrains divides the total production of food grains and the same has been converted into calories, carbohydrate and protein to assess the nutritional availability*. The present study is based on basic food items, namely, cereals (rice, wheat, maize, jowar, bajra) and pulses (gram, pees, arhar, moong, masoor). As nutritional requirement varies from age to age from time to time from the working people engaged in, therefore, an average has been worked out to assess the overall status. The present study provides only the assessment of food grains availability not the requirement of foodgrains that depends upon the purchasing power of an individual or people.

Trends of Foodgrain Production and Nutritional Availability

India has made a spectacular four-fold progress in foodgrain. Foodgrain production in the year 1951 was 50.8 million tonnes, which increased to 176.4 million tonnes in forty years and further increased to 208 million tonnes by 2001. Green Revolution has not only saved people from dying due to hunger but also succeeded in creating a huge buffer stock to meet any sudden eventuality; with the result the decadal growth rate in foodgrain production was higher than respective population figures, removing the fear of Malthus throughout the decades since 1961 to 2001. But the 1970 onward the productivity increased along with the area, with the result Government has a good buffer stock of wheat. Wheat, which was 6.46 million tonnes in 1951, it has touched record level of 75.6 million tonnes in 2000 while rice moved from 20 million tonnes to 89.5 tonnes during the period. But the trend of availability of foodgrains in terms of its nutritional value (Calories, Carbohydrate, Protein) reveals that the availability of these nutrients are not up to the mark. Although, there is much improvement over the 50 years. Calories, Carbohydrate and even Protein have shown a definite upward trend, while Calories increased by 28 per cent, Carbohydrates and Protein shared 32 per cent and 17 per cent respectively since independence. But still all the above nutrients are short of standard requirement (25.4%, –19%, –20%). Most alarming is that of pulses, as it is the main source of protein especially for vegetarians. The protein received from pulses even in the days of the Green Revolution is not even near to WHO recommended level of 80 grams. It is even less than 50 grams (Fig. 26.l). It is observed that

* The standard conversion table recommended by ICMR has been used for this purpose.

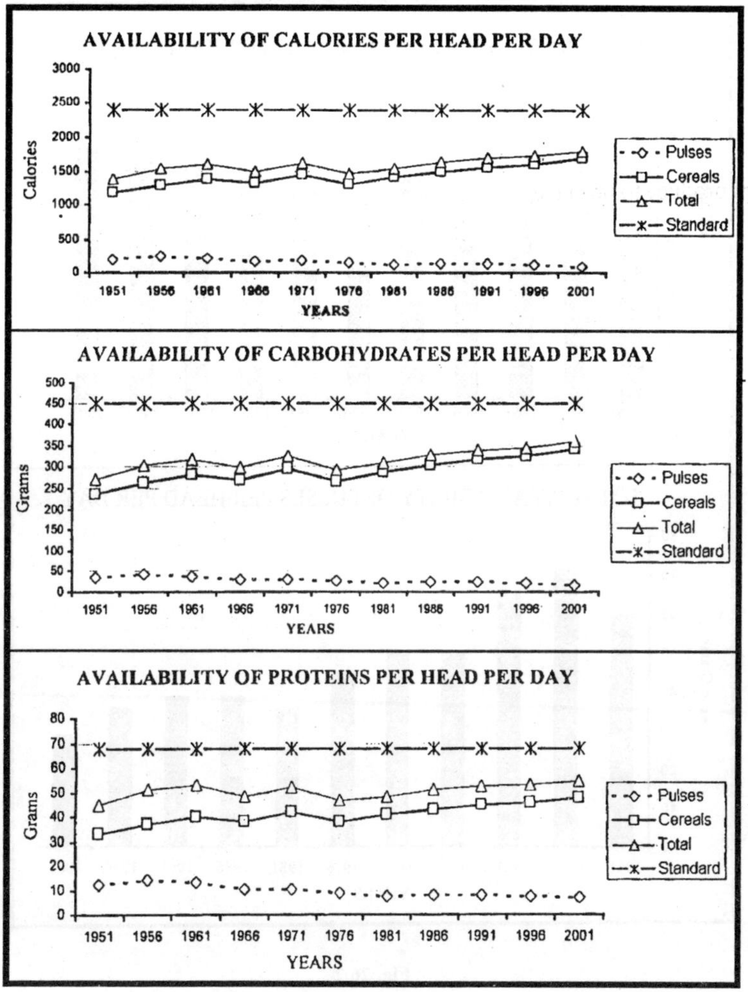

Fig. 26.1

whatever improvement taken place is because of cereals the share of pulses to these nutrients are continuously on decline since 1960 onward so much so to the level of 65 per cent (Down from 71 grams to 28 grams). The *Daal* (pulses) we take so much granted have attracted the attention of the scientist they are varied and wondering how to make a quantum jump in productivity to achieve self-sufficiency in this item. The target in minimum growth of 4 to 5 per cent in production with productivity

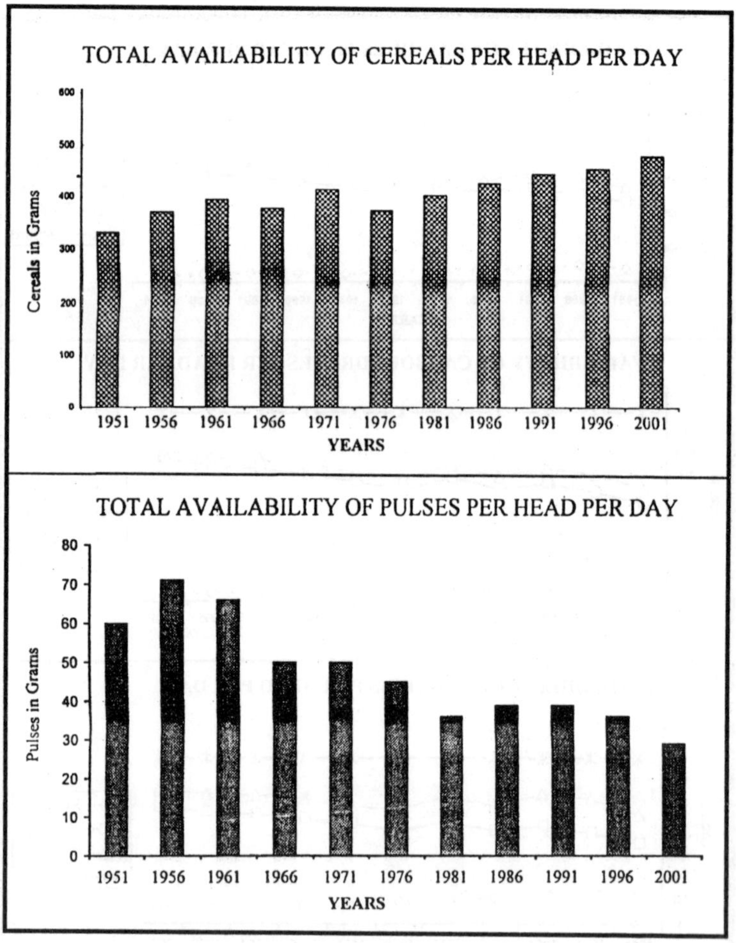

Fig. 26.2

level up from 660 kg/hectare to 800 kg/hectare is to be achieved by 2005. Pulses which have the potential of meeting nutrient security needs, essentially protein requirement and bringing sustainability to cereal cropping pattern by adding nitrogen to the soil have been restrained by problems over the past few decades. Perhaps it is pushed into what are described as *"Low endowed lands with more risk prone situation"*.

It is evident from Fig. 26.2, that since 1951 the availability of cereal kept on increasing (331 grams to 481 grams) except a slight decline in the year 1966 by 60 grams 1976 by 137 grams. But in case of protein declined is evident from 1961 onwards over the 1956 figures. But the drastic decline started from 1966 from 50 grams to 28 grams in 2001. It is because of the rapid increase in irrigation rate, which acquired even the marginal lands, which were under pulse crops.

National Scenario

At national level wide disparity exists between 1951 and 2001. Some of the states have done quite well while some are still in a poor state. In case of cereals the state where actually the Green Revolution reflected most in the state of Punjab, which has recorded +399 per cent change (571.2 grams to 2851.5 grams), followed by Himachal Pradesh +199 per cent (217 grams to 649.6 grams) and Gujarat + 99 per cent (94.5 grams to 188.9 grams). But the states, which have failed to improve or rather suffered, are Kerala –60 per cent (162.8 grams to 64.9 grams), followed by Madhya Pradesh –26 per cent (420.6 grams to 310.6 grams) and Maharashtra –24 per cent (316.3 grams to 239 grams). Other states, which are showing good per capita availability in 2001, are Haryana (1712.5 grams), Pondicherry (1755.5 grams), Uttar Pradesh (662.4 grams), and Karnataka (518.4 grams) respectively (Table 26.1). Since some of the states were not existing in 1951 at all.

But in case of pulses (Table 26.1) only few states have improved their pulses production, i.e. Orissa (+14.4 per cent) and Karnataka (+3 per cent). Other states have reduced their contribution, particularly states like Madhya Pradesh (186.8 to 94.5 grams) but still it is the leading state as it was in 1951. The most affected state which has shown out standing results in case of cereals, has performed badly is Punjab (down from 185.4 to merely 4.9 grams). In Punjab the highest negative change indicates the change in land-use. The area under pulses is shifted to cereals for more profit because rice and wheat in the state was treated as cash crop.

Conclusions

The relationship between population growth and food supply is an important aspect because situation even not the increase of foodgrains, which out placed the population explosion/increase. But the change in

Table 26.1: Statewise Availability of Cereals and Pulses (in grams per head per day) in India

States	*Cereals*		*Pulses*		*Percentage Change*	
	1951	*2001*	*1951*	*2001*	*Cereals*	*Pulses*
Arunachal Pradesh	–	496.6	–	31.1	–	–
Andhra Pradesh	388.9	494.7	52.6	15.1	+27	–71
Assam	487.3	422.1	6.5	6.38	–13	–2
Bihar	244.5	378	54.1	20.7	+54	–62
Chattisgarh	–	452	–	28.98	–	–
Delhi	–	7.9	–	–	–	–
Goa	–	299.6	–	14.3	–	–
Gujarat	94.5	188.9	13.5	10.3	+99	–24
Haryana	–	1712.5	–	9.6	–	–
Himachal Pradesh	217	649.6	10.3	6.3	+199	–39
Jammu & Kashmir	319.9	299.3	11.7	5.7	–6	–51
Jharkhand	–	194.9	–	9.8	–	–
Karnataka	340.6	518.4	48.5	50.4	+52	+3
Kerala	162.8	64.9	–	1.5	–60	–
Madhya Pradesh	420.6	310.6	186.8	94.5	–26	–49.4
Maharashtra	316.3	239	69.2	46.3	–24	–33
Manipur	–	433.6	–	–	–	–
Meghalaya	–	237.6	–	4.8	–	–
Mizoram	–	368.9	–	12.3	–	–
Nagaland	–	367.7	–	17.9	–	–
Orrisa	395.1	356.2	13.9	15.9	–10	+14.4
Punjab	571.2	2851.5	185.4	4.9	+399	–97.3
Rajasthan	297.4	451.6	82.1	35.3	+52	–57
Sikkim	–	496.7	–	25.3	–	–
Tamil Nadu	351.3	378.4	28.7	14.3	+8	–50
Tripura	578.7	443.8	–	5.2	–23	
Uttar Pradesh	278.7	662.4	148.5	35.8	+75	–76
Uttaranchal	–	550.9	–	7.1	–	–
West Bengal	418	464.3	75.5	8.2	+12	–89
Union Territories						
Andaman Nicobar	–	230.7	–	7.7	–	–
Dadar Nagar Haveli	–	260.9	–	49.7	–	–
Daman & Diu	–	52	–	17.33	–	–
Pondicherry	–	1755.5	–	–	–	

Note: Figures in respect of net per capita availability given above are not strictly representative of actual level of consumption as they do not include the stock in position and the food item other than food grains.

cropping pattern is the preference accorded to crops is not balanced one. Even it has regional imbalances. Hence it requires much more attention and detailed study, however, what is seen here is clear evidence that the importance of other than two cereal crops—wheat, rice but not given priority rather neglected especially of pulses. With the result the per capita availability has gone down since independence (from 71 grams to 28 grams) and their contribution to the food basket has reduced from 15 per cent to 6.6 per cent. Yet demand is raising, it is estimated that by 2010 demand is estimated to touch 23 million tonnes while production at present is just 14 million tonnes, therefore, a massive effort is required to develop technologies both in production and management. Since it is the richest source of protein particularly for vegetarians, its contribution to their diet is most important, which is at present amazingly low (28 grams). Also distribution patterns are not sound, Public Distribution System (PDS) is faulty due to which even in plenty there is scarcity for a certain sections of society. There is starvation at the time of plenty. It is said that rural India is eating grass to survive while FCI godowns are overflowing with grains. A sizeable percentage of the country is still unable to procure enough foodgrain to have two squire meals a day but food shortage is not the villain. As Amartya Sen said "serious famines do not occur in independent, democratic countries with free press. While famines kill millions of people but they never kill Prime Ministers, Ministers, Bureaucrats, Economists and Journalists". An estimated two million children die every year from diseases related to malnutrition in India. The case of Maharashtra in starvation death is recently a current example for this. Therefore, availability is certainly very important aspect which should be given more priority.

Right now there is nothing much to worry keeping in mind the yield which still has a good scope of going up. As at present it is significantly low as compared to developed countries even down in some cases to neighbouring countries. But if the population is not controlled, it will lead to increase demand and reduce per capita availability of arable land and irrigation water. Secondly, improved purchasing power with growing organization leads to higher per capita foodgrain requirement. Thirdly, increased pressure of land will cause damage to the ecological foundation of agriculture and no dramatic technological breakthrough are on the horizon which can help to halt the fatigue of the Green Revolution consequently the per person grain harvest would decline. But availability alone cannot guarantee the access to the down compressed people at the time of crisis. Therefore, it is recommended that along with measures to enhance production also there should be due consideration to extend the benefit to the most needy people in far-flung areas of the country.

References

Aykroyed, W.R. (1966), *The Nutritional Value of Indian Foods and Planning of Satisfactory Diet*, ICMR, New Delhi.

Ashraf, S.W. A. (1992), Distribution of Nutritional Deficiency Diseases in Relation to Environmental Factors in Central Ganga-Ghaghra Doab, Ph.D Thesis, A.M.U., Aligarh.

Census of India, 1951-2001, New Delhi.

Country Monograph, Series No. 10, U.N., New York.

Indian Agriculture Statistics, 1950-51, Vol. I, New Delhi, 1954.

Kurukshetra, August 1997.

Meantime November 15-28 (2002), Vol. IV, issue 15.

Mitra, A. (1982), *Population Growth and Food Supply in Population of India*.

Mohammed, A. (1976), *Food and Nutrition in India*, Rajesh Pub., New Delhi.

Statistical Abstract, India 2001, Ministry of Statistics and Programme Implementation, New Delhi.

Sukhatma, P.V. (1965), *Feeding India's Growing Millions*, Asia Publishing House, New Delhi.

Sud, Surinder (1966), Food Economy: Some Reflections., *Yojana*, Vol. 40. No. 5, October.

Times of India (2001), New Delhi, April 19.

INDEX